ATTACKS $^{ON}_{THE}$ PRESS $^{IN}_{2007}$

The publication of Attacks on the Press in 2007 *is underwritten by a grant from Bloomberg.*

THE COMMITTEE TO PROTECT JOURNALISTS
330 Seventh Avenue, 11th Fl., New York, NY 10001
t: (212) 465-1004   f: (212) 465-9568   info@cpj.org
visit us online for more information: **www.cpj.org**

Founded in 1981, the Committee to Protect Journalists responds to attacks on the press worldwide. CPJ documents hundreds of cases every year and takes action on behalf of journalists and news organizations without regard to political ideology. To maintain its independence, CPJ accepts no government funding. CPJ is funded entirely by private contributions from individuals, foundations, and corporations.

Bloomberg The publication of *Attacks on the Press in 2007* is underwritten by a grant from Bloomberg.

The Associated Press, Reuters, and Agence France-Presse provided news and photo services for *Attacks on the Press in 2007*.

Editorial Director: Bill Sweeney
Deputy Editor: Lauren Wolfe
Designer: Justin Goldberg
Copy Editors: Barbara Ross, Robin Lauzon
Proofreaders: Joe Sullivan, Sebastian Dettman
Maps: The Associated Press

Photo credits
Cover: Reuters/Patricio Valenzuela Hohmann – *Tear gas envelops a news photographer during May Day demonstrations in Santiago, Chile.*
Back cover: Reuters/Loay Abu Haykel – *Palestinian journalists place tape over their cameras to protest the abduction of BBC correspondent Alan Johnston.*

Attacks on the Press in 2007:
A Worldwide Survey by the Committee to Protect Journalists

ISSN: 1078-3334
ISBN: 978-0-944823-27-9

ATTACKS ON THE PRESS IN 2007

· · · · · · · · · · · · · · · **TABLE OF CONTENTS** · · · · · · · · · · · · · · · ·

PREFACE

• • • • • • • • • • • • • • • • • *by Christiane Amanpour* • • • • • • • • • • • • • • • • •

Murder is a terrifying reality for independent journalists around the world. A group or government embarrassed by a critical report hires a gunman rather than a lawyer to silence the messenger. More than 60 journalists were killed for their work in 2007, the second-deadliest year for the press that CPJ has ever documented.

In the Hollywood version, reporters and photographers die covering wars. They are caught in crossfire or are unlucky enough to be in the wrong place at the wrong time. To be sure, journalists are killed in combat—but those cases are the exception. In these pages you will see that murder is the main cause of work-related deaths among journalists. Seven out of 10 victims are targeted and hunted down, then shot, bludgeoned, or stabbed.

This fact is chilling enough. What is even more outrageous is that 85 percent of these murders are carried out with impunity. The killers and those who hire them walk away. To colleagues left behind, the message is clear: Stop reporting anything sensitive. In too many countries, that message is heeded. Journalists censor themselves and a whole society is the poorer, deprived of vital information and the ability to hold those in power to account.

On the face of it, the situation offers little hope. How, for example, can reporters in provincial Russia or rural Colombia protect themselves against powerful local officials or paramilitary groups? Faced with ineffective law enforcement, corrupt courts, and weak institutions, media owners and their staffs seem to stand alone.

They do not. Based on its 26 years of experience in fighting attacks on the press, CPJ believes passionately that advocacy can make a difference.

I have been to many countries—Russia and Iraq and others—where I have witnessed the violent and lawless climate that allows journalists to be silenced. When Russia's intrepid investigative journalist Anna Politkovskaya was shot at point-blank range on October 7, 2006, her murder was designed to send a message to all those who dared challenge the system. As her friend and family lawyer said, "When you kill, when you silence, the bravest journalist, it makes all the others think twice."

I have been very lucky myself, but many of my friends and colleagues in Iraq have been killed or injured by groups hostile to the notion of an independent press. Societies cannot thrive without journalists brave enough to put themselves on the line for important stories.

CPJ is now launching a comprehensive campaign to combat impunity. The strategy is simple. Garner human and financial resources to investigate journalist murders thoroughly and in a timely manner; publicize the killings and the findings of the official inquiries; pressure law-enforcement authorities and prosecutors through lobbying, public campaigns, and lawsuits; and finally, provide assistance to the families of victims to help them win justice.

It is high time for such a campaign. The support of international colleagues buoys local journalists and gives them courage to continue to tell their stories. The CPJ campaign, supported by a grant from the John S. and James L. Knight Foundation, has been launched with pilot projects in two of the world's most murderous nations for the press, the Philippines and Russia. Strategies are tailored to meet conditions that vary greatly between regions. For example, taking out advertisements to highlight journalist killings can be a successful technique in the Philippines, which boasts multiple, diverse, and independent media. In Russia, no broadcast or print outlet would dare run such ads. Meticulous research of journalist killings coupled with continuous international advocacy is a better approach toward the Kremlin, which has long dragged its feet on combating impunity.

Since 2000, when President Vladimir Putin came to power, 17 Russian journalists have been killed in direct relation to their work. Fourteen of them were murdered, and most of these were shot execution-style. In all that time, convictions have been secured in only one case. The Russian government has not been slow, however, to move against journalists themselves. It has progressively narrowed the boundaries of what is permissible to report. A series of measures adopted over the past two years effectively equates critical journalism with "extremism." Simply reporting on terrorist groups could in itself be construed as illegal. This dark shadow of censorship is now creeping across central Asia, as Russia's neighbors, all former Soviet states, take their cue from an increasingly authoritarian Kremlin.

Combating impunity is daunting. Yet after working extensively with local journalists' groups, CPJ has helped bring about success in the prosecution of journalist murder cases. In a breakthrough verdict in Russia, five people were convicted in 2007 in the murder of reporter Igor Domnikov seven years earlier. In the Philippines, gunmen were recently convicted in the murders of two journalists, including the 2005 slaying of investigative reporter Marlene Garcia-Esperat. Even so, Russia and the Philippines are among the worst in solving journalist murders, obtaining convictions in only about one in 10 cases.

Impunity is the single biggest threat facing journalists today. Murder, after all, is the ultimate form of censorship. That is why this book is so important. It reflects CPJ's work in documenting assaults on journalists and their right to gather and distribute information and opinion—the lifeblood of a healthy society.

. . . .

Christiane Amanpour is CNN's chief international correspondent and a CPJ board member. In her 24 years at CNN, she has reported extensively from the Middle East, the Balkans, and war zones across Africa.

PRESS FREEDOM ALMANAC

CPJ's TOP 10 BACKSLIDERS

Here are the nations where press freedom has deteriorated most in the last five years.

1 ETHIOPIA

Wholesale arrests decimate press. More than 30 journalists in exile. Three-quarters of newspapers that published in 2005 are now closed.

2 THE GAMBIA

At least 23 journalists in exile. Government detains journalist Ebrima Manneh incommunicado. Criminal penalties instituted for defamation.

3 RUSSIA

National television channels under state control. World's third-deadliest country for the press. Two journalists commit "suicide" in mysterious circumstances.

4 DEMOCRATIC REPUBLIC OF CONGO

Authorities ban 38 broadcasters. State-sponsored violence against the press is widespread. Four journalists slain since 2005.

5 CUBA

Twenty-four journalists imprisoned. Three foreign journalists denied visas, forced to leave in 2007. Island's sole critical publication stops running commentary.

6 PAKISTAN

Thirteen journalists killed, 15 abducted since 2002. Only one case investigated and prosecuted. All private television stations shut in November.

7 EGYPT

Government agents assault reporters covering demonstrations. Editor Reda Helal disappears in 2003. Four convicted of spreading "false" news.

8 AZERBAIJAN

Nine journalists imprisoned. The 2005 murder of journalist Elmar Huseynov is unsolved. Editor jailed after investigating Huseynov murder.

9 MOROCCO

Among Arab world's leading jailers. Authorities banish three top journalists through politicized lawsuits. Critical magazine ordered to pay record damages.

10 THAILAND

Junta nationalizes country's only private television station, orders radio stations to broadcast military-prepared news. Internet law among world's most restrictive.

Backsliders online: **www.cpj.org/backsliders**

IN THEIR OWN WORDS

"This law I compare to a surgical scalpel. It is only to be used against those who criticize—inconvenient individuals, inconvenient politicians, and, particularly, inconvenient journalists."

—Lawyer Karen Nersisian to CPJ, describing new Russian measures that equate dissent with extremism. *(page 155)*

"The fact that the killings remain unsolved heightens public distrust in our system of justice."

—Philippine Supreme Court Chief Justice Reynato S. Puno to CPJ, describing a failure of justice in more than 30 journalist slayings. *(page 139)*

"Journalists don't bother me. Mediocrity, incompetence, bad faith, and lies bother me—and there's a lot of that in the press."

—Ecuadoran President Rafael Correa during a radio program in May. *(page 88)*

"This time I am happy because I was summoned by police instead of being beaten up with iron bars."

—Rwandan editor Jean Bosco Gasasira to *The New Times* in September. Gasasira was assaulted earlier in the year because of his work. *(page 42)*

"You have to understand the equation that the regime is playing with the press in Morocco. On the one hand, they hate us; on the other hand, they need us."

—Aboubakr Jamaï, exiled publisher of the newsmagazine *Le Journal Hebdomadaire*, to CPJ. *(page 198)*

"Haitian politicians and investigators had not been interested in pursuing justice in cases of murdered journalists because some of them were implicated in these crimes. But now the situation has changed."

— Haitian President René Préval to CPJ. *(page 89)*

"The harassment and threats have never been worse. This is easily the darkest chapter in my 42-year career in journalism."

—Iqbal Athas, Sri Lankan journalist and former International Press Freedom Awardee, to CPJ. *(page 144)*

JOURNALISTS KILLED: 1992-2007

CPJ has analyzed records dating to 1992 to determine how, where, and why journalists are killed. Here are some of the main findings:

WHO*

Print reporters/writers: 31.6%
Broadcast reporters: 20.4%
Editors: 16.8%
Camera operators: 9.4%
Columnists/commentators: 9.1%
Photographers: 7.7%
Producers: 5.6%
Publishers/owners: 4.1%
Technicians: 2.1%

Male: 93%/Female: 7%
Local: 85.2%/Foreign: 14.8%
Freelance: 12%/Staff: 88%

HOW

Murder: 72.9%
Crossfire/combat related: 17.3%
During other dangerous assignment: 9.7%
Undetermined: 0.1%

WHY*
Beats covered by victims
War: 33.1%
Politics: 25%
Corruption: 20.7%
Human rights: 13.3%
Crime: 13%
Sports/culture: 4.4%
Business: 1.9%

* Total exceeds 100% because more than one category applies in some cases.

WHEN

2007: 65
2006: 56
2005: 48
2004: 59
2003: 41
2002: 21
2001: 37
2000: 24
1999: 36
1998: 24
1997: 26
1996: 26
1995: 51
1994: 66
1993: 57
1992: 42

WHERE

1.   Iraq: 125
2.   Algeria: 60
3.   Russia: 47
4.   Colombia: 40
5.   Philippines: 32
6.   India: 22
7.   Somalia: 21
8.   Bosnia: 19
     Turkey: 19
10. Pakistan: 17
11. Rwanda: 16
     Sierra Leone: 16
     Tajikistan: 16
     Afghanistan: 16
15. Brazil: 15
16. Sri Lanka: 14
17. Mexico: 13
18. Bangladesh: 12
19. Angola: 8
     Yugoslavia: 8

Deaths online:
www.cpj.org/deadly

SPOTLIGHT ON MURDER: 1992-2007

SUSPECTED PERPETRATORS
Political groups: 30.3%
Government officials: 18.5%
Criminal groups: 11.2%
Paramilitaries: 7.7%
Military: 6.2%
Local residents: 2.3%
Mob: 1%
Unknown: 22.8%

IMPUNITY
Complete impunity: 85.7%
Partial justice: 7.5%
Full justice: 6.8%

Threatened before murdered: 27.4%
Taken captive before murdered: 18.9%

JOURNALISTS IMPRISONED: 2007

TOP JAILERS OF JOURNALISTS AS OF DECEMBER 1, 2007
1. China: **29**   2. Cuba: **24**   3. Eritrea **14**   4. Iran **12**   5. Azerbaijan **9**

MOST COMMON CHARGES*
Antistate: 57%
No publicly disclosed charge: 17%
Retaliatory charges: 12%
Defamation: 7%
Religious, ethnic insult: 5%
Violating censorship laws: 2%
Spreading "false" news: 1%

BY MEDIUM*
Print: 51%
Internet: 39%
Television: 6%
Radio: 4%
Film/documentary: 2%

IMPRISONED BY YEAR
2007: 127
2006: 134
2005: 125
2004: 122
2003: 138
2002: 139
2001: 118
2000: 81
1999: 87
1998: 118
1997: 129

* *Total exceeds 100% because more than one category applies in some cases.*

LONGEST IMPRISONED
Chen Renjie and Lin Youping, who were jailed in China in July 1983 for publishing a pamphlet titled *Ziyou Bao* (Freedom Report). Codefendant Chen Biling was executed.

INTRODUCTION

• • • • • • • • • • • • • • • • • • • *by Joel Simon* •

In August 2008, when the Olympic torch is lit in Beijing, more than 20,000 journalists will be on hand to cover the competition between the world's greatest athletes. Behind the scenes, another competition will be taking place. If the Chinese government has its way, this one will remain hidden. It will be a battle over information, and it will have far greater implications for the world than the medal count.

Last August, a year before the Games were scheduled to begin, the Committee to Protect Journalists sent a delegation to Beijing to issue an in-depth report, "Falling Short," outlining China's appalling press freedom record. China is the word's leading jailer of journalists, with 29 editors and writers behind bars, but the government also relies on a sophisticated system of repression and rewards to control the media. Journalists, for example, receive bonuses if their articles are rated positively by local officials. They can be docked pay—or fired—if they earn a negative rating.

Some of the world's most repressive countries, including Cuba and Burma, simply block access to the Internet. But recognizing that modern communications are central to economic growth, China has welcomed the expansion of the Internet for the economic benefits, all while seeking to control and censor the content. Technology, some of it provided by U.S. companies, filters Web sites deemed subversive. Thousands of human monitors track postings and delete offensive content. If those strategies fail, the government wields an array of state security laws to imprison critics; 18 of the jailed Chinese journalists were working online.

Not long ago, Internet idealists argued that the Web was impossible to censor or control. Not anymore. China has proved them wrong. But the Chinese government's bolder gambit is that it can enter the world economy, enjoy international legitimacy, and even host the Olympic Games without loosening controls on the country's political life.

If the Olympic Games occur while China is still the word's leading jailer of journalists, still censoring and controlling access to the Internet, still restricting the global media, then it will have demonstrated that it's possible to join, even lead, the international community without honoring the basic right to express ideas and circulate information freely. That would be a terrible development for press freedom at a time when new models of authoritarianism are taking hold in so many areas of the world.

China's successful formula of economic liberalization and political control is being emulated in nations such as Vietnam. And as its international influence grows, China's no-questions-asked approach to foreign aid in Africa and Latin America is blunting efforts by international donors to link assistance to human rights.

China's evolving tactics pose one of many new challenges for press freedom advocates. Here are a few others from the pages of this book:

*   In Russia, where President Vladimir Putin has created a national security state ruled by spies, dissent has been redefined as "extremism." Under sweeping new laws, media criticism of public officials is now a criminal offense. The Kremlin's tactic of rewriting laws to criminalize journalism has been exported to countries such as Uzbekistan and Tajikistan.

*   In parts of Africa where democracy has supposedly taken root after years of strife, press conditions have actually worsened. While accepting accolades from Western donors, repressive leaders in Ethiopia, the Gambia, and the Democratic Republic of Congo have cracked down on critical media, shuttering newspapers and putting journalists in jail.

*   A similar strategy is unfolding in the Middle East, where a number of Arab governments are expressing public commitment to democratic reform while using less visible legal strategies to control the press. "Manipulating the media, they have found, is more politically palatable to the international community than outright domination," writes CPJ Senior Program Coordinator Joel Campagna.

*   In Venezuela, President Hugo Chávez Frías' government forced a critical television station off the air in May by failing to renew its broadcast concession. Venezuelan authorities said they were acting within the law, but a CPJ investigation found that the process was arbitrary and politically motivated.

In all these countries, powerful figures have developed a wide range of innovative approaches that cumulatively represent a soft authoritarianism that is spreading in many regions of the world.

Governments are now less likely to imprison a journalist explicitly for his or her work than to bring vague antistate charges such as subversion. Our research shows that imprisonments rose significantly after governments worldwide imposed sweeping national security laws in the wake of the 2001 terrorist attacks on the United States. Imprisonments stood at 81 in 2000 but have since averaged 129 in our annual surveys.

Journalists in many repressive societies suffer, if you will, from too much government: smothering, self-serving, and intrusive governments that seek to sharply restrict the boundaries of dissent.

The other threat to journalists is too little government. In Iraq, Somalia, Gaza, and the tribal areas of Pakistan, a state of pervasive lawlessness leaves journalists at the mercy of armed factions. Iraq has become a virtual killing field for the press, with more than 170 journalists and media support workers killed since the March 2003 U.S. invasion. In 2007, more than 40 journalists and media workers died on duty, the vast majority of them Iraqi reporters gunned down by local militants.

The Iraqi press grew rapidly in the period immediately after Saddam Hussein was overthrown. But without a functioning government to enforce the law, militants soon targeted these newly minted journalists for perceived partisanship or because of association with Western media outlets.

The same phenomenon has played out in strife-riven Somalia, the second-deadliest place for the press in 2007. A handful of independent radio stations emerged in Mogadishu during the periods of relative calm that have come amid 16 years of unrest. As the conflict intensified in 2007, journalists were in the crosshairs. At least three of the seven Somali journalists who died in 2007 were targeted by militants and murdered. With no effective central government, the violence occurs with impunity.

In other parts of the world where journalists are routinely killed or threatened, governments are unable to assert control or provide basic security. This is true in much of provincial Philippines, in the tribal areas of Pakistan, on the border between Mexico and the United States, and in rural Colombia, where the 40-year civil war continues to simmer.

Governments are often indifferent to violence against the press because they benefit from the pervasive self-censorship that the attacks engender. But all too often, CPJ research has confirmed, governments go further. While insurgent and opposition political groups are responsible for a good portion of the killings, government-allied forces, including paramilitaries, are behind many murders as well.

Journalists are whipsawed between periods when powerful governments suppress the media and periods when weak governments are unable to enforce the law. If journalists are to work freely, we must confront with equal force both categories of abusers: governments that do too much, and those that do too little.

• • • • • • • • • • • • • • • • • •

Joel Simon is CPJ's executive director. He led missions to Russia and the Philippines in 2007.

When Press Freedom
and Democracy Are Out of Step   18

The West praised Gambian, Congolese, and Ethiopian leaders for staging democratic elections. But when the balloting was all over, governments cracked down on the press.

by Tom Rhodes

PHOTOS

Section break: Reuters/Antony Njuguna – *Newspapers in Nairobi proclaim a standoff in Kenya's bitterly contested December presidential election.* Analysis (next): AFP/ Issouf Sanogo – *Congolese soldiers secure a Kinshasa neighborhood in the days before the country's historic elections.*

AFRICA

SUMMARIES

Angola, Benin, Burkina Faso, Burundi, Cameroon, Central African Republic, Chad, Comoros, Djibouti, Gabon, Ghana, Guinea-Bissau, Ivory Coast, Kenya, Lesotho, Liberia, Madagascar, Malawi, Mali, Mozambique, Senegal, Sierra Leone, South Africa, Togo, Uganda

WHEN PRESS FREEDOM AND DEMOCRACY ARE OUT OF STEP

by Tom Rhodes

• •

BALLOTS MAY HAVE REPLACED BULLETS IN MUCH OF AFRICA since the dawn of this new century, but one of the great political ironies for at least part of the continent has been a loss of press freedom following the voting. Leaders in a large swath of sub-Saharan Africa have drawn approving nods from Western politicians for holding sometimes unprecedented elections. Three such countries are the Gambia, the Democratic Republic of Congo (DRC), and Ethiopia. All have democratically elected presidents and Western support. Yet between them they hold the unenviable record of placing at or near the top of CPJ's 2007 list of the world's worst backsliders on press freedom.

Freedom of expression has not only failed to march in lockstep with democracy in these states, it has been severely curtailed. Elections may have pleased foreign governments, but autocratic leaders did not appreciate the consequences at home: an emboldened opposition, heightened public scrutiny and debate, and an independent press. Within months of the polling, leaders in the Gambia, Ethiopia, and the DRC began trying to put the democratic genie back into the bottle.

All three countries are signatories to international and regional human rights conventions, including the African Charter on Human and Peoples' Rights, and have national guarantees written in their constitutions to protect press freedom. Two of them, the Gambia and Ethiopia, even host offices of

the 53-member African Union (AU) in their capitals.

In 2006, the DRC overcame a decade of political strife and regional re-bellions to stage its first multiparty elections in 46 years. That feat earned President Joseph Kabila high praise from his U.S. counterpart, George W. Bush, during a visit to the White House in November. Bush was equally supportive of Ethiopia, which in 2005 staged only the second round of elec-tions in its long history. Prime Minister Meles Zenawi later garnered U.S. diplomatic backing after his country's military intervention in neighboring Somalia helped oust an Islamist gov-ernment from Mogadishu. Gambian President Yahya Jammeh, re-elected to a third term in 2006 in a vote con-sidered free and fair, is also seen in a

In Ethiopia, Gambia, and DRC, voting was followed by a crackdown on the press.

favorable light for his efforts to maintain economic stability, Britain's high commissioner in Banjul, Philip Sinkinson, told CPJ.

Yet in each case voting was followed by a crackdown on the press. Since 2005, the Ethiopian government has orchestrated the wholesale arrest and intimidation of media workers, compelling at least 37 journalists to live in exile—the second-highest number that CPJ has recorded worldwide. Ac-cording to the exiled head of the Ethiopian Free Press Journalists' Associa-tion, Kifle Mulat, 20 independent papers were in operation at the time of the 2005 elections. Now there are a quarter of that number, and "all are cen-sored, whether directly or indirectly," he said.

The DRC's press freedom defense organization, Journaliste en Danger (JED), estimated that more than 90 percent of the escalating number of at-tacks, threats, and harassment of DRC journalists were carried out with im-punity by government personnel. The Gambian media has suffered system-atic intimidation and harassment by government authorities over the past five years, culminating in a steady flow of professional Gambian journalists fleeing the country—at least 23 since 2002, according to CPJ research.

In unleashing this onslaught against the news media, the leaders of Ethiopia and the DRC were essentially reacting to the burgeoning popularity of political opposition parties. The last elections saw the opposition make strong inroads in both countries. In the DRC, Kabila's main opponent, Jean-Pierre Bemba, took 20 percent of the vote; Ethiopia's opposition parties, which once held a mere handful of seats, won about a third of parliament in the 2005 elections.

Berhanu Nega, vice chairman of the Ethiopian opposition party Coalition for Unity and Democracy, told CPJ that opposition forces had made progress in all major towns across the country—something neither Zenawi nor his party were expecting. When street protests erupted over vote-counting problems, an anxious government reacted swiftly by arresting Nega, dozens of political opponents, and 15 journalists.

The absence of independent judiciaries and civil society groups has hindered the press.

In Kinshasa, DRC authorities summarily pulled off the air for almost half a year Canal Congo TV, Canal Kin TV, and Radio Liberté Kinshasa—all broadcasters owned by opposition leader Bemba. President Kabila's clampdown on the press was partially sparked by media houses that produced biased, and often subsidized, election coverage, according to local journalists. JED Secretary-General Tshivis Tshivuadi told CPJ that some newspapers, radio stations, and television outlets were acting as a "propaganda press committed to defending the political interests of their own candidates." An estimated 80 percent of Congolese journalists do not have employment contracts, prompting many to write for hire, accepting payment from the very individuals they are supposed to be covering objectively.

None of the three countries' leaders have allowed the development of a truly independent civil society or judiciary, key components in protecting press freedom. "While the Gambian judiciary is weak, there hardly exist civil-society institutions worthy of the name," said former Gambian Press Union President Demba Jawo. "The few existing civil-society groups have all been neutralized, and none of them have the guts to challenge anything the government does—hence the frequent government suppression of the press." Similarly, veteran Ethiopian journalist Goshu Moges claimed only one Ethiopian civil society group is concerned with protecting press freedom and "most are too scared of government harassment to be effective."

In the DRC, as the judiciary calendar recommenced in November 2007, the country's top prosecutor, Tshimanga Mukeba, demonstrated his allegiance to the ruling party in his opening remarks by focusing on "outrages against the authorities and insults against the head of state." Mukeba threatened to severely punish anyone, whether parliamentarian or journalist, who criticized the government, Tshivuadi told CPJ.

External forces have shown limited willingness to push for the reform of repressive government practices. The Banjul-based special rapporteur on free expression in Africa, Faith Pansy Tlakula, is assigned to ensure African Union member states comply with Article 9 of the African Charter, which protects the right to free expression. "But the issue we are facing now is one of implementation," Tlakula told CPJ. Tlakula can only make recommendations; her office has no power to issue binding judgments. And recommendations are often poorly received—or ignored.

Despite increasing regional and international isolation, the Gambian government remains indifferent to regional pressures. Jammeh was noticeably absent from the AU January summit in Ethiopia's capital, Addis Ababa, and the July summit in Accra, Ghana. Similarly, Gambian government officials failed to show up for three hearings set by the Economic Community of West African States (ECOWAS). An Accra-based press freedom organization, Media Foundation for West Africa, filed a case with the court against the Gambian government regarding the disappearance of former *Daily Observer* journalist "Chief" Ebrima B. Manneh. Eyewitnesses said state security forces seized Manneh in July 2006 after he tried to publish a story critical of Jammeh. He was being held incommunicado in a secret location in late 2007.

Diplomatic threats to cut aid have held diminishing sway since the emergence of a powerful new donor nation willing to provide aid with fewer strings attached: China. In February, Chinese President Hu Jintao completed a 12-day tour of African countries during which he handed out unconditional support worth millions of dollars in investment, loans, and aid. Beijing has promised US$5 billion in soft loans and grants to African states in the coming years as China increases trade with the continent. Red lanterns were scattered across Addis Ababa in 2006 to welcome Hu to the China-Africa summit, attended by nearly 50 African heads of state.

> *Threats to cut aid hold less sway now that China has emerged as a donor nation.*

Strategic U.S. allies such as Ethiopia enjoy similar human rights record exemptions. President Bush opposed a 2007 bill introduced in the U.S. House of Representatives that linked some military aid in Ethiopia to support for human rights and democracy. The bill passed in the House but had yet to reach the full Senate for a vote. With the U.S. supporting Ethiopian troops in the ouster of the Islamic Courts Union in neighboring Somalia, U.S. Assistant Secretary of State for African Affairs Jendayi Frazer told the Bloomberg news

Staging an election is in itself no guarantee that press freedom will flourish. service that the House measure would "constrain" what Bush is able to do "to manage U.S. government interests."

Democracy is still young in the region, and for every two steps forward there is often one step back. Other African nations were successful in carrying off free elections and respecting a free press. Sierra Leone held what official observers considered a free and fair election in August, while 27 independent newspapers operated in the capital, Freetown, without government interference. Togo's first parliamentary elections, held in October, were also carried out with few attacks on press freedom, according to the newly appointed independent press union secretary-general, Augustin Koffi.

But the experience of the DRC, the Gambia, and Ethiopia should serve as a warning that staging an election is in itself no guarantee of democracy or the development of media freedom.

"Elections are useful for opening political space, but there is a lot more to democracy than just elections," said Dave Peterson, senior director of the Africa program for the U.S. government-funded National Endowment for Democracy. "Even democratically elected leaders are not always respectful of democracy." Without a functioning independent judiciary and strong civil society, the press cannot build on the democratic foundation laid down by a free election. In fact, the voting may prove to be simply a convenient cover for an autocrat. The polls in Ethiopia and the DRC encouraged international donors to turn a blind eye toward press violations that occurred in both countries. As a witness to the crackdown on the press after the Ethiopian ballot in 2005, exiled journalist Elias Wondimu believes the elections were designed more to please Westerners than Ethiopians. "Democracy must grow inside," said Wondimu. "It shouldn't be done just to please somebody. … It should be done to change the system."

JED's Tshivuadi agreed. "Although we recognized these elections as an important step toward democracy," he said, "they are still not synonymous with democracy restored. In fact, the elections were a way for the former belligerents to legitimize their power that was already taken by force of arms."

• • • • • • • • • •

Tom Rhodes is CPJ's Africa program coordinator. He monitored the Gambian government's 2007 court proceedings against journalist Fatou Jaw Manneh, who was charged with sedition for her critical reporting.

AFRICA

········ **DEMOCRATIC REPUBLIC OF CONGO** ········

The historic November 2006 presidential election—the first since the country's independence from Belgium in 1960—was followed by a yearlong nationwide wave of media abuses as the new administration struggled with rampant unrest, insecurity, and impunity in attacks against media workers. Interim President Joseph Kabila defeated former rebel leader Jean-Pierre Bemba in the divisive 2006 presidential runoff, ending a fragile power-sharing government and marking the start of a difficult transition to democracy.

"The policy of this government is that freedom of the press and freedom of opinion must be respected at all costs," Kabila declared in an official press conference in September. Yet CPJ research showed that national and regional officials and security forces were responsible for the overwhelming majority of media abuses in 2007. Broadcast outlets were the primary targets. In one notorious week in October, Information Minister Toussaint Tshilombo summarily banned 22 private television channels and 16 radio stations for alleged noncompliance with national media laws, while Higher Education Minister Sylvain Ngabu ordered police to beat two Horizon 33 TV journalists after a critical news program.

Numerous media outlets set up by candidates for the 2006 election were, in turn, targeted by their political rivals after the polls, according to journalist-turned-politician Modeste Mutinga. Mutinga headed the DRC's High Authority on Media, the official media regulatory agency under the former transitional government, until winning a Senate seat in January. Mutinga, also founder and board chairman of the leading independent daily *Le Potentiel*, said violence against the press was caused by intolerant politicians, unprofessional journalists, and the "total absence of justice."

In Kinshasa in March, authorities summarily pulled off the air Canal Congo TV (CCTV), Canal Kin TV, and Radio Liberté Kinshasa—all owned by Bemba—as the stations broadcast a taped interview with Bemba that was critical of the army. Soldiers subsequently ransacked and occupied the stations for a month following a deadly two-day street war with Bemba's armed guard. The fighting broke out after Bemba, who won a Senate seat after losing the presidential runoff, refused to disband his personal militia because of what he said were safety concerns. Bemba left the country on April 11 and was charged with high treason over his alleged role in the clashes. Authorities threatened to revoke his parliamentary immunity.

Bemba remained in exile in late year, and journalists working for his stations went into hiding for several months for fear of reprisal, according to CPJ research.
········

Country summaries in this chapter were reported and written by CPJ Africa Program Coordinator **Tom Rhodes**, Research Associate **Mohamed Hassim Keita**, and freelance writer **Alexis Arieff**.

The stations did not resume broadcasting until August. The airing of a 2006 interview of eastern Congolese rebel leader Gen. Laurent Nkunda the same month led intelligence agents to interrogate CCTV General Manager Stéphane Kitutu O'Leontwa for five hours. In response to a CPJ inquiry about the interrogation, Faustin Fwafa, chief of staff for Information Minister Toussaint Tshilombo Send, asserted that intelligence agents were entitled to question any citizen they deemed to be a national security threat.

On May 3, World Press Freedom Day, CPJ named the DRC one of the world's worst press freedom backsliders. The designation was based on dramatic spikes since 2002 in the numbers of imprisoned journalists, criminal libel prosecutions, and attacks. The report came in the midst of a nationwide surge of media abuses—including raids on the offices of eight broadcasters by government forces—after the DRC's new government took power on February 24. The local press freedom group Journaliste en Danger (JED) denounced "state violence" against the media, citing abuses committed by security forces in a climate of insecurity and impunity.

In a live discussion on U.N.-sponsored Radio Okapi in May, Information Minister Toussaint Tshilombo Send called CPJ's report "fictitious" and asserted that press freedom was "respected" in his country. He also accused JED—whose secretary-general, Tshivis Tshivuadi, participated in the debate—of "tarnishing the image of the country" to justify collecting funds from international donors. JED later received what it believed were credible death threats from government supporters, which prompted Tshivuadi and the organization's president, Donat M'baya Tshimanga, to go into temporary hiding.

Outside Kinshasa, particularly in the DRC's central and eastern provinces, local politicians sought to silence critical coverage, employing intelligence agents to police the airwaves, closing some stations on purported regulatory violations, and detaining and interrogating journalists about their sources. In one incident in June, agents of the Congolese National Intelligence Agency (known by its French acronym, ANR) forced private Radio Canal Satellite in the province of Western Kasaï off the air for "operating without ANR documents," and "broadcasting in bad French."

In the volatile eastern region of the country, despite the presence of the world's largest U.N. peacekeeping force, government security forces as well as rebels targeted the local media with impunity over critical coverage of insecurity, rights abuses, and control of the airwaves. In September, forces loyal to Nkunda looted community radio station Radio Colombe in Rutshuru, kidnapping two reporters and using the station's equipment to launch broadcasts calling for military support. Nkunda, a Tutsi backed by neighboring Rwanda, had reneged on a January peace agreement calling for the partial integration of his forces into the national army, after accusing the Congolese government of collaborating with the Hutu rebel group FDLR.

A Radio Okapi editor, Basile Bakumbane, fled to Kinshasa from his station in the Western Kasaï town of Kananga after receiving several threats linked to a June 7 story about the sacking of the local governor.

Violence in neighboring North Kivu province claimed the life of respected freelance photojournalist Patrick Kikuku Wilungula. Gunmen shot Wilungula and stole his digital camera as he returned home after covering a local conference on environmental protection. The gunmen, suspected to be soldiers, allegedly argued with the journalist before shooting him, sources close to Wilungula told CPJ. No arrests were reported.

At least two other journalists have been killed in unclear circumstances since 2005: political affairs journalist Franck Ngyke Kangundu and freelance journalist Bapuwa Mwamba. While authorities apprehended and convicted suspects in both cases, investigations fell short of exploring possible links between the killings and the journalists' work. As *Le Potentiel*'s Mutinga put it: "Despite the arrests, the truth was never known, the masterminds never identified. The end results have always been fuzzy."

The government came under fire in April after a Kinshasa military court convicted four people in the November 2005 murders of Kangundu and his wife at their home. JED and local journalists decried the trial's failure to establish a motive for the crime after the court sentenced two of the accused to death. In a separate case four months later, the same court convicted four people, sentencing three to die, in the fatal July 2006 shooting of Mwamba in his home.

In late year, lawmakers were drafting legislation to create a new media regulator, the Audiovisual and Communications Superior Council, as well as decriminalizing defamation. Three journalists were sentenced to prison in 2007 on criminal defamation charges following stories alleging official corruption: editor Rigobert Kwakala Kash of the twice-weekly *Le Moniteur*; editor Pold Kalombo of the private weekly *Le Soft International*; and Popol Ntula Vita, a correspondent for the private weekly *La Cité Africaine*. Kash served 35 days of an 11-month sentence before being released on bail. Kalombo and Vita, fearing arrest, went into hiding, according to CPJ research.

· **ERITREA** ·

Eritrea remained the leading jailer of journalists in Africa, with as many as 14 writers and editors held incommunicado in secret locations. At least one journalist died in state custody, sources told CPJ in February. The only country in sub-Saharan Africa without a single independent news outlet, Eritrea subjected its own state-media journalists to government surveillance and harassment. One state journalist died in June while trying to escape years of repression by fleeing into Sudan.

President Isaias Afewerki continued the brutally repressive policies that began a week after September 11, 2001, when the government effectively shuttered the nation's once-vigorous private press and arrested its most prominent journalists. The crackdown came shortly after the press covered a split in the ruling party, providing a forum for debate on Afewerki's rule.

The government, dominated by members of Afewerki's Popular Front for Democracy and Justice, refused to disclose the whereabouts, legal status, and health of the jailed journalists.

Fesshaye "Joshua" Yohannes, a publisher and editor of the now-defunct weekly *Setit* and 2002 recipient of CPJ's International Press Freedom Award, died in prison, according to several sources in the Eritrean diaspora. Yohannes, who was also a poet and playwright, had fought alongside Afewerki as a member of the rebel movement that sought Eritrean independence. Several sources said Yohannes died on January 11 after a long illness in an undisclosed prison outside Asmara, although one source said the journalist may have died much earlier in a prison in Embatkala, 21 miles (35 kilometers) northeast of Asmara. Information Minister Ali Abdu told CPJ in June that he had nothing to say about Yohannes. "I don't know," he said. "This is an Eritrean issue; leave it to us."

The government's monopoly on domestic media, the fear of reprisal among prisoners' families, and restrictions on the movements of foreigners have made it extremely difficult to verify unofficial information. An unbylined 2006 report that was circulated on several Web sites and considered credible by CPJ sources claimed that three other journalists also died in government custody. Abdu said he had no information on the fates of Said Abdelkader, Medhanie Haile, and Yusuf Mohamed Ali. CPJ continued to list them on its annual prison census as it investigated their cases.

The government did confirm the death of Paulos Kidane, a sports broadcaster for state-run Eri-TV and a journalist for other state media outlets. Tormented by ongoing intimidation from his own employer, Kidane joined a group of seven asylum seekers who set off on foot to cross the border into Sudan, several sources told CPJ for a special report released in October. His companions were forced to leave him in the care of villagers in northwest Eritrea after the journalist collapsed from seven days of walking in temperatures of more than 100 degrees, according to a woman who traveled with Kidane. The village was believed to be populated by government informants.

Kidane had been among nine state journalists detained for several weeks in late 2006. The detainees included five Eri-TV reporters, three journalists with state broadcaster Radio Dimtsi Hafash, and one reporter from the state-owned Eritrea News Agency.

The arrests, which followed the defection of several veteran state journalists, appeared to be sheer intimidation. Kidane and the others were held on suspicion of staying in contact with the defectors or planning to flee the country themselves.

At least 19 journalists have fled Eritrea since 2002 in response to threats, harassment, and imprisonment—among the highest totals worldwide, according to a CPJ special report issued in June. Fleeing the country is an extreme option, since the families of exiled journalists are targeted with government reprisals, according to local journalists.

The government continued to raise the specter of Ethiopian aggression to justify its absolute control over the media.

"The government had in fact no intention of preventing the free press from growing," presidential spokesman Yemane Ghebremeskel said in a July interview on the pro-government Web site *Shaebia*. But he also stated: "What is the normative practice in war times? I don't believe that there is free press without any curtailment, all the time, anywhere, in times of war and conflict."

Journalists told CPJ that professional life in Asmara is dominated by the country's tense stalemate over its border with Ethiopia. After the 1998-2000 conflict that claimed an estimated 80,000 lives, the nation remained on war footing, with about one in 20 Eritreans serving in its armed forces, according to U.N. figures.

An intensifying split with the West contributed to the poor press climate. Although U.S. President Bill Clinton once praised Afewerki as a "renaissance leader," U.S. Assistant Secretary of State Jendayi Frazer said in September that Eritrea was a potential rogue state. Afewerki, for his part, argued that U.S. foreign policy had fueled conflict in the Horn of Africa, pointing to Washington's support for Ethiopia's 2006 intervention in Somalia.

Only five international media outlets had Asmara-based correspondents in 2007: Agence France-Presse, Reuters, the BBC, Deutsche Welle, and the U.S. government-funded Voice of America. Afewerki's administration intermittently blocked foreign-based private radio stations that sought to send their signals into the country.

Anti-Western sentiments often accompanied acts of repression. Spokesman Ghebremeskel claimed Eritrea's once-thriving free press was largely funded by Western countries, and was easily manipulated "to serve ulterior purposes." Afewerki went even further in an October *Los Angeles Times* interview, calling jailed political opponents and journalists "crooks who have been bought. They provided themselves to serve something contrary to the national interest of this country. They are degenerates. I don't take [the jailings as] a serious matter."

······················· **ETHIOPIA** ·····················

Involved militarily in the conflict engulfing Somalia, engaged in a tense stalemate with arch foe Eritrea, assailed by allegations of human rights abuses in the eastern region of Ogaden, Ethiopia eased media repression slightly and released many journalists from prison. Yet the chilling effect of a brutal 2005 media crackdown that led to 15 arrests and numerous newspaper closings hung over Ethiopia's beleaguered private press in 2007. And continued government harassment drove many journalists out of the country.

On April 9, Ethiopia's High Court acquitted and set free eight editors and publishers of now-defunct Amharic-language newspapers charged with antistate crimes such as "outrages against the constitution." The court also tossed out "attempted genocide" charges filed against the journalists, although the government later sought to reinstate them. The acquitted journalists included award-winning publisher Serkalem Fassil, who gave birth to a child in prison.

The other journalists picked up in the 2005 crackdown were set free in July and August after signing incriminating statements, pleading guilty to antistate charges, and then receiving presidential pardons. Many observers saw the statements as being signed under pressure in order to receive a pardon, although government spokesman Zemedkun Tekle said the speculation was "absolutely false and baseless." A 2006 CPJ report, "Poison, Politics, and the Press," had concluded that the government's charges in the 2005 crackdown were baseless.

Prime Minister Meles Zenawi dismissed suggestions that the government issued the pardons in response to pressure from the United States, according to the private business weekly *Addis Fortune*. The weekly quoted Zenawi as saying the prisoners would be freed as long as they respected Ethiopia's rule of law, its constitution, and "constitutionally mandated institutions." He declared that the pardons showed the government had "no sense of revenge."

On May 3, World Press Freedom Day, CPJ named Ethiopia the world's worst backslider on press freedom over the previous five years. In addition to the 15 journalists arrested in 2005, the country has locked up numerous editors and writers for months at a time on defamation and other charges that sometimes date back several years. The list of problems goes on: At least eight newspapers were forcibly closed during the 2005 crackdown and others have since shut down; dozens of journalists have taken flight from the country to avoid prison; a critical foreign reporter was expelled in 2006; and Web sites were blocked on a recurring basis. In response, spokesman Tekle told the U.S. government-funded broadcaster Voice of America that "press freedom in Ethiopia is getting stronger and stronger," and that CPJ's report did not reflect the "reality."

For journalists, "reality" meant ongoing government intimidation. In January, authorities filed a contempt-of-court charge against *Addis Fortune* for its coverage of the 12-year trial of leaders of the Derg regime of ousted dictator Mengistu Haile Mariam. The government cited copy editor Olurotimi Akanbi in connection with a headline and an editorial focusing on delays in the case. The charge was later dropped, but the paper was issued a warning and ordered to publish an apology. In June, authorities summoned 17 journalists and staffers of the private English-Amharic weekly *African Best Business Index*, interrogating them in a police station for 11 hours about their backgrounds and knowledge of the paper. They were subsequently fingerprinted and released without charge.

Harassment and imprisonment have led many of Ethiopia's top journalists to go into exile. When CPJ issued a worldwide report in June, "Journalists in Exile," at least 34 Ethiopian journalists had left the country since 2001—a tally second only to Zimbabwe worldwide. (Their ranks continue to grow: Since CPJ issued its report, another three journalists fled.) Among those who took flight were editors such as Befekadu Moreda, a founder of the respected newsweekly *Tomar*, whose 2007 resettlement in the United States was documented in the October CPJ special report, "Flight from Ethiopia."

Several exiled journalists—including editor Abiy Gizaw of *Netsanet* and publisher Elias Kifle of the influential U.S.-based diaspora Web site *Ethiopian Review*—have been tried and convicted of crimes in absentia. Kifle, who founded *Ethiopian Review* as a college student, told CPJ he did not recognize the Ethiopian courts or consider legitimate the treason charge lodged against him in late 2005.

Popular Web sites like *Ethiopian Review* and others critical of the government were frequently inaccessible during 2007, according to several CPJ sources. In May, Internet monitor OpenNet Initiative cited Ethiopia for preventing its citizens from viewing independent Web sites and blogs discussing political reform and human rights. OpenNet pointed to "overwhelming evidence" based on diagnostic tests run by volunteers it had enlisted in Ethiopia, and said that more extensive censorship could ensue as Internet access expands across the country. In late 2006, security agents directed Internet cafés in Addis Ababa to register all users, but the initiative was abandoned shortly afterward without explanation, according to local journalists.

In an interview with CPJ in May, spokesman Tekle denied any government involvement in blocking Web sites, calling the assertions "baseless." He said that affected sites should inform the state-run Ethiopian Telecommunications Corporation or the Ministry of Transport and Telecommunications "if the problem really exists."

After the forced closing of Amharic-language newspapers during the 2005 crackdown, the remnants of the private press worked under pervasive self-censorship.

Newspapers publishing in Addis Ababa focused largely on sports, entertainment, and business news, with very little coverage of politics, according to CPJ research. *Addis Fortune*, the *Reporter*, *Capital*, and the *Daily Monitor* continued to publish well-regarded news and opinion pieces in English, but they had limited readership beyond the elite, according to local journalists.

Ethiopia's foreign press corps, shaken by the government's 2006 expulsion of Associated Press correspondent Anthony Mitchell, continued to operate under a strictly enforced regimen of renewable one-year residency and accreditation permits. In 2006, several reporters were required to submit for review all of the stories they had published since 2005 in order to renew their accreditations, according to CPJ sources.

The foreign press corps was often forced to practice self-censorship because officials were scrutinizing reports on sensitive topics such as the prosecution of opposition leaders, alleged human rights abuses, and the armed resistance in Ogaden, according to CPJ research. In May, three *New York Times* journalists reporting on the conflict in Ogaden were arrested by the military in the eastern town of Degeh Bur and held incommunicado for five days. The journalists, including Nairobi Bureau Chief Jeffrey Gettleman, endured threats, questioning at gunpoint, and confiscation of their equipment, according to the paper. *Times* photographer Vanessa Vick was kicked in the back, the paper reported.

The AP's Mitchell, 39, died in a plane crash in Cameroon in May, a month after breaking a story about rendition practices between Kenya, Somalia, and Ethiopia. The in-depth report had forced U.S. and Ethiopian officials to acknowledge a secret program of detaining terrorism suspects.

In April, CPJ learned through official statements and a videotape posted on the government Web site *Waltainfo* that those detainees included staff reporters Tesfalidet Kidane Tesfazghi and Saleh Idris Gama of Eritrean state broadcaster Eri-TV. The journalists were arrested by Kenyan authorities at the Somali border, held for three weeks, and handed over to the Ethiopian-backed Somali transitional government in January, according to the Eritrean Foreign Ministry. Wahid Belay, a spokesman for Ethiopia's Foreign Ministry, told CPJ in July that authorities had no information to provide about the journalists. Their whereabouts, legal status, and physical condition were still unknown in late year.

In May, parliament adopted new legislation restricting eligibility for broadcast licenses, granting the Ethiopian Broadcast Agency discretion over when to issue a decision and placing the regulator under the control of the government's Ministry of Information, according to press reports. In two notable steps in October, Ethiopia's first independent commercial radio station, Sheger Radio, and its first independent political publication since 2005, the private weekly *Addis Neger*, were launched.

In late year, lawmakers were drafting a new media bill. Press freedom advocates urged parliament to scrap defamation as a criminal offense and transform state-run news outlets into independent public media, according to news reports. Such liberalization would be at odds with the government's actions—though not its words. Zenawi continued to promote press freedom in his public comments. "I don't think people have any qualms about criticizing the government or rejecting its policies, or expressing dissenting views in any way," he declared in a July press conference, according to *Addis Fortune*.

Veteran journalists saw a complex picture. Goshu Moges—who was among those who received a pardon on antistate charges—told CPJ that Zenawi's government had indeed taken unprecedented steps in the past to promote a free press. But Moges, whose career began in 1975 under the brutal Derg regime, also noted that it was Zenawi's government that had crushed the independent media in recent years. "I went to prison five times," Moges said. "Many of my colleagues were forced to leave the country, and others are still suffering. This is the price the free press has paid."

· · · · · · · · · · · · · · · · · THE GAMBIA · · · · · · · · · · · · · · · · · ·

Fewer press-related detentions and attacks were reported in 2007, CPJ research showed, but local journalists said the decline reflected several years of intense government suppression. One prominent journalist was slain and others have been forced into exile since 2004, leaving a more compliant press that practices widespread self-censorship. A mere handful of publications provide critical coverage, television is state-controlled, and radio news is limited to state-run broadcasts.

The government of President Yahya Jammeh appeared to grow more isolated. Long resistant to international influence, Jammeh seemed to have fraying relations with regional leaders as well. The president failed to turn up for the African Union summit in Ghana in the face of mounting pressure to explain the fates of 40 Gha-

naians who disappeared after being picked up by Gambian security in 2005. His government ignored three dates before the Community Court of Justice of the Economic Community of West African States in Abuja, Nigeria. The court is seeking Gambia's explanation on the whereabouts of *Daily Observer* journalist "Chief" Ebrima B. Manneh, who was believed to be in government custody. The Ghana-based Media Foundation for West Africa (MFWA) had filed a suit with the court, claiming violations of the African Charter on Human and Peoples' Rights, seeking Manneh's release, and requesting damages for Manneh's family. Held incommunicado and without charge, Manneh has been seen publicly only twice since he was seized by government agents in 2006.

The administration also showed disdain for the international community. In February, Jammeh ordered U.N. representative Fadzai Gwaradzimba out of the country after she questioned the president's claim that he could cure HIV/AIDS. And fanned by Jammeh's rhetoric, state media were relentlessly critical of Western countries, especially former colonial power Britain.

For the press, years of government attacks and harassment have had a cumulative effect. The once-independent daily *The Point* has taken a more pro-government line since the 2004 murder of its editor, Deyda Hydara. The slaying remains unsolved. The news-heavy Sud FM closed under government pressure in 2005, leaving no private radio station covering news. Madi Ceesay, president of the Gambia Press Union (GPU) and a 2006 CPJ International Press Freedom Awardee, told CPJ that self-censorship had reached an unprecedented level. Despite repeated efforts over two years, the GPU was unable to secure even a meeting with the government's minister of information.

Local press groups put the number of exiled journalists at 23. Their ranks included *Daily Observer* reporter Momodou Lamin Jaiteh, who fled the country in June after receiving threatening phone calls and visits from security forces. Jaiteh said he was targeted for his work as a correspondent for MFWA. The threats came shortly after the foundation launched its lawsuit in the Manneh disappearance.

In October, Yahya Dampha, a journalist with the opposition newspaper *Foroyaa*, fled the country after security forces arrested him and two Amnesty International researchers on suspicion of espionage. The three were released without charge two days later, but security agents repeatedly visited Dampha's home after the arrest, his wife said. Dampha was helping the researchers gain access to prisons in the country's eastern region.

Jammeh's administration demonstrated a long memory in 2007. In March, National Intelligence Agency (NIA) officers arrested former Gambian journalist Fatou Jaw Manneh upon her arrival at Banjul International Airport from the United States, where she had been residing for about 10 years. She was charged with sedition for a 2004 interview, published in the now-shuttered *Independent* newspaper, in which she said Jammeh "is tearing our beloved country in shreds." Manneh, detained for a week at NIA headquarters in Banjul, was released on bail but barred from leaving the country. Two magistrates, reluctant to preside over the politically charged case, transferred the matter out of their courtrooms, leaving the case in limbo.

The NIA also picked up *Daily Express* Managing Editor Sam Obi, Sports Editor Abdulgafar Oladimeji, and reporter Modou Njie in March for four days of questioning. They had been accused of taking a printing plate from the government-owned *Daily Observer*, which had been printing the *Daily Express*. The accusation was considered spurious, local journalists said, and intended to further harass the year-old publication. The Nigerian-born Obi and Oladimeji had been detained in 2006, after they sought to print a press release from civil-society organizations in their inaugural edition.

In May, a *Foroyaa* reporter was threatened and harassed by police after covering police dispersal of a student celebration. Fabakary Ceesay said he was detained for four hours at the offices of the Kanifing Police Intervention Unit, where he was beaten, kicked, and forced to surrender his press credentials, tape recorder, and notebook. Ceesay was released the same day but received threatening phone calls in the following weeks. Ceesay said he believed the treatment stemmed in part from an April 2007 story concerning a former Guinea-Bissau refugee, Musa Bah, who died in police custody.

Domestic access to two U.S.-based, exile-run Web sites—*Freedom Newspaper* and *All Gambian*—was blocked for a month beginning in June, according to Internet site providers. Journalists for the Web sites, both of which are critical of the Jammeh administration, blamed the government. A government spokesman told CPJ that he was not aware that authorities had taken steps to block the sites.

In June, a court in the capital, Banjul, fined a reporter for the banned *Independent* in connection with a March 2006 story reporting the arrest of several suspects in the aftermath of a purported coup attempt, according to local journalists and news reports. Lamin Fatty of the private, biweekly *Independent* was fined 50,000 dalasi (US$2,500) on charges of publishing false information under Gambia's criminal code, defense lawyer Lamin Camara told CPJ. Fatty filed an appeal, Camara said.

The crackdown on journalists extended to those employed by the government. In September, Assistant State House Press Secretary Mam Sait Ceesay and state radio producer and presenter Malick Jones were arrested by the NIA and held at Mile Two Prison, Banjul, accused of communicating secret information to foreign journalists. The government did not specify the information or the alleged recipients, and a court eventually freed the two men after fining them 200,000 dalasi (US$8,970).

The culture of fear was prevalent within Gambian civil society as a whole. Under Jammeh's regime, civil servants faced high turnover rates and the ruling party's tight control over job security. A weak civil society and divided opposition ensured that self-censorship and repressive media laws remained intact. The 2004 amendments to the Criminal Act made "false statements" a criminal offense and established stiff penalties for libel, false publication, and sedition, including fines as high as 250,000 dalasi (US$12,500) and prison sentences of one year or longer. In addition, the 2004 amendment to the colonial-era Newspaper Act made it nearly impossible for a media house to start a new publication within the country, increasing the bond requirement to a prohibitive 500,000 dalasi (US$25,000).

Despite the tight repression, journalists continued to push for change. A new organization, the Network of Human Rights Journalists, held a public symposium in July calling on the secretary of state for the interior and the director general of the National Intelligence Agency to investigate the disappearance of Ebrima Manneh. Exiled freelance journalist Ebrima Sillah and former state radio director Amie Joof-Cole continued their efforts to launch a nationwide independent community radio station, Alternative Voice Radio, in 2008. The station would be based in neighboring Senegal.

•••••••••••••••••••• **GUINEA** ••••••••••••••••••••

During nationwide strikes and antigovernment demonstrations in January and February, state security forces attacked Guinea's newly launched private radio stations, blocked print publications, and threatened journalists. More than 130 people were killed, mostly by government security forces, during protests that were unprecedented in size and popular support. The unrest was quelled in late February when President Lansana Conté agreed to appoint as prime minister Lansana Kouyaté, a respected diplomat who was backed by local trade unions. Kouyaté's appointment marked a departure from Conté's brutal and often capricious rule, and local journal-

ists reported a decrease in harassment and censorship in its aftermath. Still, the president, who rarely appears in public and reportedly suffers from diabetes and other ailments, maintained de facto control over segments of Guinea's economy and political apparatus, and it remained unclear whether the transition would lead to long-term improvements for the Guinean press.

Conté, a military general and one of Africa's longest-serving leaders at 24 years in office, had long kept a tight rein on the media. Guinea's first private radio licenses were issued in August 2006, making it the last country in West Africa to allow private broadcasting. By 2007, four private stations were operating in the capital, Conakry, and they quickly found themselves at the forefront of the action when a general strike in January spiraled into mass civil disobedience. The government responded with force; then-Information Minister Boubacar Yacine Diallo issued an order on January 15 banning the broadcast of any news on the strike, asserting that "all the security forces are on the alert." Two days later, Diallo called the director of outspoken Liberté FM and instructed him to stop broadcasting an interview with a union leader on the government's repression of public demonstrations. Private newspapers, most of them based in Conakry, ceased publishing for several weeks after Diallo's announcement, according to the Ghana-based Media Foundation for

West Africa. Journalists' work was curtailed by violence as well. A reporter working for Radio France Internationale (RFI), Cyril Bensimon, had to be evacuated from the country for treatment of a severe eye injury after a protester threw a rock through the window of a car in which he and other journalists were traveling.

When the demonstrations intensified and spread in February, radio stations aired "dramatic firsthand accounts of violent street clashes between antigovernment protesters and security forces," Reuters reported. Mass rioting erupted across the country, as demonstrators attacked government installations, burned the homes of government and military officials, looted police stations, set up roadblocks, and battled security forces, according to a report issued by Human Rights Watch. The government declared martial law on February 12, leading to massive human rights abuses as soldiers went door to door, looting homes and attacking civilians. The martial law decree authorized the military "to take any suitable measures to ensure the control of the press and publications of any nature, as well as radio or television broadcasts." The same day, security forces, including members of the elite presidential guard, raided the headquarters of FM Liberté, destroyed valuable equipment, and forced the station off the air. A reporter and a technician were arrested in the raid and held for more than two days before being released without charge. FM Liberté had just broadcast a live phone-in program during which listeners called for Conté to step down. Another group of security forces shuttered Familia FM, which had featured live discussions and descriptions of looting in the capital. Soleil FM suspended its broadcasts after reporters were attacked by demonstrators and received threats.

In addition, Guinea's state-owned broadcaster was put under "the total control of seemingly pro-military forces," according to a BBC analysis. The report noted that Radiodiffusion-Télévision Guinéenne (RTG) "remained biased and downplayed the gravity of the crisis. ... A case in point was on 11 February, when the station failed to air its normal 1900 gmt news bulletin and instead broadcast a program about Christmas."

RFI's broadcasts on FM were interrupted for at least 24 hours during the crisis, but station managers cited technical problems stemming from power cuts in Conakry rather than political pressure. Nearly all of the capital's cybercafés and printing presses were shuttered, while newspapers that did try to publish were subjected to censorship by government authorities. A tightly enforced curfew further restricted journalists' ability to report on developments as they occurred. A commentator on *Aminata*, a diaspora news Web site, wrote that the crackdown "is an obvious attempt by Guinea's despotic regime to isolate the country from the rest of the world, and silence the media, whose role in such circumstances is to inform the people." The news Web site *Guineenews* lamented that "all freedoms that were not confiscated were given to soldiers."

On February 25, the unions agreed to suspend the strike following negotiations backed by the Economic Community of West African States, ending weeks of political uncertainty and economic paralysis. Kouyaté, Conté's newly appointed prime minister, promised to "take up the challenges for peace, reconciliation, and change." His early priorities centered on restoring ties to international lending institutions and improving basic services, such as water and electricity, to Guinea's beleaguered population.

In May, Kouyaté sent an encouraging message to the press by removing Diallo as information minister in favor of Justin Morel Junior, an experienced journalist and former communications officer at the United Nations Children's Fund. Radio stations reopened, although Soleil FM suffered technical difficulties that interrupted its broadcasts for months.

In May, the government announced in an official statement that it would grant broadcasting licenses to more than a dozen new private radio stations in order to "reinforce freedom of expression." Little media harassment was reported between March and year's end. Radio stations continued to air live call-in programs, though local journalists cited widespread self-censorship. In June, the BBC World Service announced it was establishing two FM relays in Guinea, one in Conakry and the other in the central city of Labe.

While Kouyaté's government appeared to refrain from the blatant censorship and intimidation employed by former members of the Conté administration, laws remained on the books that criminalize defamation and other press "offenses." As if to prove the point, a Conakry court handed down suspended prison sentences and a hefty fine in August to two local newspaper directors, Thiernodjo Diallo of *La Vérité* and Abdoul Aziz Camara of *Libération*, in connection with articles alleging corruption by a former government minister.

By late year, local journalists were welcoming what they hoped would be a new era of media freedom, one in which government officials would hesitate to apply defamation and other press laws. But the situation remained fragile, and Conté was clear about asserting his authority. On June 14, he granted a rare media interview to Agence France-Presse and France's TV5 in which he denied that he had acted under pressure for reform from unions and the international community, boasting that "there is no transition. I am in charge, and the others are my subordinates."

NIGER

President Mamadou Tandja pledged in January that his government would not obstruct the press, but journalists in Niger faced threats and restrictions as the military tried to repress a budding Tuareg insurgency in the north. In a country that has suffered devastating famines in recent years, food shortages remained another

sensitive topic for the press. Local journalists continued to face the threat of jail time for critical reporting under Niger's 1999 media law, despite a promise in January by then-Prime Minister Hama Amadou that a long-discussed bill to decriminalize press offenses would be introduced in parliament. Amadou resigned in June following a parliamentary no-confidence vote, and his successor, Seyni Oumarou, did not indicate whether he would follow up on the issue.

In February, an appeals court cleared senior journalists Maman Abou and Oumarou Keita, who run the Niamey-based weekly *Le Républicain*, of criminal charges brought in 2006. The two were arrested in August of that year and spent four months in jail in connection with an editorial suggesting the government may have tilted foreign policy toward Iran and Venezuela after Western donors alleged corruption involving foreign aid disbursement. Abou has been a frequent target of government ire due to *Le Républicain*'s reporting; during a phone interview from detention, Abou told CPJ he believed the government wanted to punish the newspaper for a series of articles alleging corruption in primary education financing. He continued to face criminal charges in connection with a defamation sentence handed down in November 2003, for which he had already served two months in prison.

Any optimism arising from Abou's court victory was quickly stemmed by a government crackdown on an insurgency launched in early 2007 by members of the nomadic Tuareg ethnic group in the northern region of Agadez. The Mouvement Nigérien pour la Justice (MNJ) released a list of demands in May, including the appointment of MNJ officials to key positions in the state security forces, government agencies, and mining operations, as well as greater revenue sharing from natural resources. (While Niger is one of the poorest countries on earth, its northern regions are rich in uranium, oil, gold, and other valuable commodities.) By midyear, more than 40 soldiers had been killed and dozens captured in confrontations with the rebels, according to international news reports, prompting Tandja to declare a "state of alert" in Agadez in August. Many MNJ members are believed to be military deserters, signaling the failure of a 1995 peace deal that ended a previous Tuareg insurgency and incorporated former rebels into the security forces.

The government refused to recognize the MNJ, claiming that its fighters were "bandits" and smugglers. As MNJ attacks grew more frequent and sophisticated, authorities moved to limit media coverage of the rebellion through a combination of intimidation and outright censorship. In June, the High Council on Communications (known by its French acronym, CSC) instructed local journalists not to report on the insurgency, while Communications Ministry officials told The Associated

Press in July that foreign journalists were barred from Agadez. Local journalists largely responded with self-censorship, though the international press continued to report regular statements released by the MNJ through its Web site and via satellite telephone interviews with journalists.

The CSC banned the Agadez-based bimonthly newspaper *Aïr Info* in June, accusing it of undermining troop morale. The newspaper's annual government subsidy of 1.4 million CFA francs (US$3,000) was also frozen. The ban was linked to articles on two rebel raids in the Agadez area in June; one story called for the resignation of army chief Gen. Moumouni Boureïma after an MNJ attack on a desert military outpost left 15 soldiers dead and 72 hostage. The council also issued warnings to four other local papers for their coverage of the MNJ. "The CSC decision is a grave threat to freedom of information because it aims simply to intimidate us, to stop us from covering the events in the north," Ahmed Raliou, director of the Agadez-based private radio station Sahara, told Reuters.

Among Niger's impoverished and largely illiterate population, radio broadcasts are far more influential than print media. Radio France Internationale (RFI), whose news reports are relied upon widely, quickly became another target of government intimidation. On July 19, the CSC suspended the station's FM broadcasts for a month, accusing the station of bias toward the Tuareg movement. CPJ sources linked the suspension to an interview aired on July 18 with army-officer-turned-rebel Kindo Zada. CSC President Daouda Diallo accused RFI of presenting Zada as "an army deserter," calling him instead a "runaway criminal." RFI stood by its reporting in a written statement protesting the council's decision.

On August 28, the CSC banned the broadcast of live debates on the northern crisis, after the nationwide network Radio Saraounya FM broadcast a live panel discussion in which some participants criticized the government's handling of the insurgency. Opposition leader Issoufou Bachar, who denounced Tandja's August decree granting security forces blanket powers to combat the rebels, was detained for 48 hours after speaking on Radio Saraounya, Director Moussa Kaka told CPJ. CSC chief Diallo told CPJ that broadcasters were free to air debates and opinions as long as they were not live.

On September 20, police arrested Kaka, a veteran reporter for RFI as well as head of Radio Saraounya, on accusations of "conniving" with rebels and "endangering state security," citing telephone conversations between the journalist and the rebel leadership. Kaka had done exclusive interviews with rebel leaders and taken photos that were reprinted in several newspapers in the capital, Niamey. He had previously been threatened by Gen. Boureïma in connection with his reporting, according to international news reports.

On October 9, *Aïr Info* Director Ibrahim Manzo Diallo was arrested by plainclothes police at Niamey's airport. A court in Agadez charged Diallo the next month with criminal conspiracy over his alleged involvement in an antigovernment demonstration, according to local journalists and Diallo's lawyer, Moussa Coulibaly. Local journalists believed the arrest was linked to a September 26 *Aïr Info* report listing 20 people suspected of rebel links, according to Agence France-Presse. Around 200 journalists and human rights activists marched in Niamey on October 20 to protest the detentions of Diallo and Kaka; both were still jailed when CPJ conducted its annual census of imprisoned journalists on December 1.

•••••••••••••••••••• **NIGERIA** ••••••••••••••••••••

Nigeria's diverse and freewheeling press weathered a tense political period in 2007, a year marked by fierce disputes surrounding April presidential and legislative elections and a surge of violence in the oil-rich Niger Delta region. Ruling party candidate Umaru Yar'Adua was declared winner of the April 21 presidential vote, the first transfer of power between two elected civilian leaders in Nigerian history. The elections were marred, however, by serious logistical flaws, widespread violence, and falsification of results. A report by the Brussels-based International Crisis Group concluded that the election was "poorly organized and massively rigged." The private press was harassed and intimidated by authorities in the run-up to the vote, starting in spring 2006 when the media took a leading role in opposing outgoing President Olusegun Obasanjo's unsuccessful attempt to amend the constitution so he could seek a third term. Yar'Adua, a former governor from northern Nigeria who was largely unknown at the national level before being nominated as the People's Democratic Party (PDP) candidate, sought to smooth tensions by inviting his erstwhile rivals to join a "government of national unity" and making peace in the Delta the cornerstone of domestic policy.

The unsolved December 2006 murder of veteran journalist Godwin Agbroko cast a pall over Nigeria's press corps. Agbroko, a well-known and respected editor who was jailed in the mid-1990s for challenging the repressive rule of then-military leader Gen. Sani Abacha, was most recently a columnist and editorial board chairman of the national daily *ThisDay*. He was found shot dead in his car, in what reporters initially termed a botched robbery. However, no further evidence of an attempted robbery was made public, and none of his belongings were stolen, prompting the police to announce on January 15 that he may have been killed by "unknown assassins." The investigation yielded no concrete results during the year, and CPJ continued to research whether Agbroko was killed in connection with his journalism. An editorial in *ThisDay* commemorated Agbroko as "a patriot who believed that journalism could be used to make Nigeria work for the good of her citizens."

In a separate incident shortly after Agbroko's death, fire gutted a compound housing *ThisDay's* management offices, its technology infrastructure, printing plants, and newsroom. There was no apparent investigation, Editor Simon Kolawole told CPJ in September, and it was unclear whether the January 6 fire was an accident or arson.

Local journalists generally reserved judgment on Yar'Adua's press freedom credentials, but they were dismayed to see the renewed use of the State Security Service (SSS)—an elite corps that answers directly to the presidency—to harass the press. In October, SSS agents arrested Jerome Imeime, publisher of the private weekly *Events* in southern Akwa Ibom state. Imeime was charged with sedition over a story critical of a local governor, making him the first Nigerian journalist to face such a charge since June 2006. Nigeria's colonial-era sedition law was abrogated in 1983, according to legal expert Femi Falana, but authorities have continued to invoke the charge to silence the press on sensitive subjects.

Deployment of the SSS against the news media had been a favorite tactic of the Obasanjo administration right up to the election. In January, SSS agents raided two privately owned newspapers in the capital, Abuja, in apparent reprisal for articles on political infighting. The newspaper *Leadership* was targeted on January 9 for a cover story contending that Obasanjo had forced would-be presidential candidate Peter Odili out of the PDP primaries. The following day, SSS agents raided the

Abuja Inquirer, holding the paper's editor and publisher for more than 24 hours of questioning over an article claiming that a military coup was possible because of a public row between Obasanjo and his former vice president, Atiku Abubakar, who was also a candidate for the presidency.

These incidents and Agbroko's murder prompted the British High Commissioner in Nigeria, Richard Gozney, to express concern over press freedom, while in February the anticensorship organization Article 19 pointed to an "environment of fear and intimidation that may serve to limit freedom of expression ahead of the 2007 election." Despite these and other protests, SSS agents raided the Abuja studios of African Independent Television (AIT), a leading private broadcaster, just four days before the presidential vote—pulling a paid political program off the air and seizing tapes of other paid programs scheduled to air that day. The SSS also shut down AIT's sister radio station, Ray Power FM, for an hour. The offending program, which had previously drawn a warning from the government's National Broadcasting Commission, was critical of Obasanjo's performance as president.

The raid on AIT came two days after a fire of undetermined origin damaged the building housing the radio and television transmitters of AIT and Ray Power

FM in the commercial city of Lagos, according to news reports. AIT's Abuja manager, Mac Amarere, said authorities had yet to determine the cause of the fire, but the station could not rule out the possibility that it was deliberate. On June 14, the Federal Capital Territory (a local government entity with jurisdiction over Abuja) demolished part of an office complex belonging to AIT's parent company, Daar Communications, over alleged land-use violations. Company Chairman Raymond Dokpesi said he believed the demolition was politically motivated and was intended to intimidate the station because of its critical coverage of the elections.

In many areas of Nigeria, local journalists operated amid violent conflict between ethnic, religious, and political factions. These challenges were especially stark in the southern Niger Delta, where militias, separatist insurgents, and armed criminal gangs battled the government for control of lucrative oil exports. Kidnappings of oil workers and shoot-outs between rival gangs were frequent; while journalists were not directly targeted, their ability to operate in the Delta was curtailed by general insecurity. For example, on June 5, two gunmen entered the bureau of the national newspaper *Punch* in the main Delta city of Port Harcourt and attempted to kidnap a staff member, who escaped by jumping out a window, according to the Lagos-based organization Media Rights Agenda. On July 25, gunmen stormed the Port Harcourt offices of the *National Point* newspaper, having apparently followed Michael Watts, a visiting professor from the University of California, Berkeley, from a nearby bank in the hopes of robbing or kidnapping him. The gunmen shot and wounded the professor and a security guard working for the paper. Watts' research concerned oil-related violence in the Delta region, Reuters reported.

Foreign journalists traveling to the Delta occasionally faced harassment from security forces. In September, two German independent filmmakers were arrested in the southern city of Warri and detained for two weeks. Freelance journalist Florian Alexander Opitz and cinematographer Andy Lehmann were held along with Nigeria-based American aid worker Judith Asuni and Nigerian national Danjuma Saidu. All four were charged with breaching Nigeria's Official Secrets Act by taking photographs and video footage of "protected places," including oil facilities in the Niger River Delta, defense lawyer Mohammed Bello Adoke told CPJ. Authorities also accused the Germans of making false statements on their entry visa applications but did not present any evidence substantiating the claims, Adoke said. By early October, the government dropped all charges against them. Opitz and Lehmann were the first members of the international media to be formally charged over coverage of the deadly unrest in southern Nigeria, according to CPJ research.

One Lagos-based journalist who reported on energy issues told CPJ that while many Nigerian media outlets maintained correspondents in the Delta region, reporters were constrained by the difficulty of accessing remote areas and by the often-conflicting accounts given by law enforcement agencies and militant groups.

Federal authorities were particularly sensitive to international media coverage of the Delta. The government lashed out at CNN in February after it broadcast a report on kidnappings, accusing the U.S.-based news channel of lacking balance and paying "criminals" to participate in interviews. CNN stood by its reporting.

Elsewhere, religious tensions threatened media freedom. In the northern majority-Muslim city of Kano, the headquarters of privately owned Freedom Radio were attacked after the station aired controversial views on the Eid al-Mawlid, a holiday marking the birthday of the Prophet Muhammad, according to Agence France-Presse.

Local journalists have long called for a freedom of information law to bolster reporting on Nigeria's endemic corruption. One bill, first introduced in 1999, was finally passed by the legislature in February, but local journalists and media activists were dismayed that Obasanjo declined to sign it into law. The bill was returned to the National Assembly, but its future was unclear.

• • • • • • • • • • • • • • • • • • • **RWANDA** • • • • • • • • • • • • • • • • • • •

Tension remained high between the independent news media and President Paul Kagame's government in the run-up to the 2008 parliamentary elections. Authorities summarily closed two private newspapers, stripped critical newspapers of vital advertising revenue, and jailed one journalist and harassed others in response to critical coverage. The bloody legacy of the 1994 genocide continued to affect press freedom as the government and its supporters invoked claims of hate speech to silence dissenting voices.

In February, three men armed with iron bars beat unconscious Editor Jean Bosco Gasasira of the private bimonthly *Umuvugizi* over stories alleging corruption and mismanagement by top officials, including army Gen. Jack Nziza and Finance Minister James Musoni. The men broke Gasasira's left hand and smashed his head, arms, and legs while shouting their intent to ensure he could not write again, according to news reports and local journalists. In July, Rwanda's High Court sentenced one man, an ex-soldier who once served as a bodyguard to top army officers, to life imprisonment in the attack, according to the same sources.

Gasasira resumed publishing several months later, following surgery and intensive rehabilitation, but was questioned by police for three hours in September over newly critical articles, according to local journalists and news reports. Gasasira ruefully commented that interrogation was an improvement. "This time I am happy because I was summoned by police instead of being beaten up with iron bars," Gasasira told the pro-government daily *The New Times* after his release without charge.

In response to headlines in the independent press trumpeting government corruption, nepotism, mismanagement, and infighting, the government suddenly terminated advertising contracts with Rwanda's leading private Kinyarwanda-language newspapers, including *Umuseso, Umuco, Umuvugizi,* and *Rushyashya,* according to local journalists. The papers, particularly dependent on advertising revenue, struggled to maintain normal circulation and staff, according to CPJ research. In March, *The New Times* quoted Kagame as confirming the move. "It is [a] waste of taxpayers'

money for the government to continue advertising in publications that relentlessly write only negative things about it, without recognizing the good things it is doing," he added.

Relations between the media and government have been "characterized by tension" and an "enormous trust deficit" since the landmark general elections of 2003, according to a 2007 report issued by the Rwanda-based League for Human Rights in the Great Lakes Region (LDGL). The league, whose report was commissioned by the European Union mission in Rwanda, noted that the problems had occurred despite a relatively progressive press law enacted in 2003 and the creation of a press union.

The government and its supporters frequently accused independent journalists of being biased and unprofessional. About 80 percent of Rwandan journalists lack professional experience, training, or formal education beyond high school, according to an LDGL study that surveyed 392 journalists from 34 public and private media outlets. Low revenue for media houses, low pay for reporters, and self-censorship also undermine working conditions, according to the report.

Top officials accused critical newspapers of serving antigovernment interests. On September 9, several top officials, including army spokesman Maj. Jill Rutaremara, accused critical media of collusion with "negative forces"—code for opponents of Rwanda's Tutsi-dominated government, including Hutu rebels in neighboring Democratic Republic of Congo and exiled dissidents. According to news reports and local journalists, Rutaremara's comments were aired during a four-hour state radio and television program on government and media relations. Rutaremara did not name specific media outlets, but his comments were widely interpreted to have been directed at the Rwanda Independent Media Group (RIMEG), publishers of *Umuseso,* the English-language *Newsline,* and the sports and entertainment tabloid *Rwanda Champion.*

RIMEG, already suffering from the loss of state advertising revenue, suspended publication for three weeks in response to the allegations. The company demanded that government officials substantiate their accusations, but there was no official response, according to local journalists.

During the same September 9 program, Interior Minister Sheikh Musa Fazil Harerimana also threatened to force journalists to reveal sources of leaked government documents. The law is unclear on the issue. Article 65 of Rwanda's press law contains an apparent contradiction, guaranteeing confidentiality of sources but requiring journalists to "collaborate" with courts upon request, according to CPJ research. Harerimana's threat drew a public rebuke from Kagame and the state regulatory agency, the High Council of the Press, but the minister did not retract the statement, according to CPJ research.

Throughout the year, journalists for RIMEG were harassed and detained by police and judicial authorities on unsubstantiated criminal charges, CPJ research found.

In June, police interrogated RIMEG Director Charles Kabonero and *Newsline* Editor Didas Gasana for three hours in connection with stories describing judicial probes into the activities of two public figures, including businessman Tribert Rujugiro, an influential member of the ruling Rwandan Patriotic Front, according to CPJ research. A court in Kigali later charged the journalists with criminal defamation in connection with the Rujugiro story.

Umuseso News Editor Gérard M. Manzi was detained in August on an unsubstantiated sexual assault accusation and held for a week. The case was pending in late year, although authorities could not locate the purported victim. Manzi was ordered to report to court every week.

Former *Umuseso* News Editor Emmanuel Niyonteze was held for four days in May on accusations of stealing a laptop during an international disability services conference in Kigali, according to *The New Times* and local journalists. The charges were later dropped, *Umuseso* Deputy Managing Editor Furaha Mugasha told CPJ. Mugasha himself was held for a week in August and released on bail on bogus charges of bouncing a check in February 2006, local journalists said. He also told CPJ that he was denied a passport renewal.

The government's crackdown on the independent press included the summary closure of two private newspapers. In June, Information Minister Laurent Nkusi revoked—without a hearing or court order as stipulated under Rwandan laws—the publishing license of *The Weekly Post* only a few days after its first edition was issued. The paper was founded by former journalists of the pro-government *New Times*. The High Council of the Press, exclusively mandated by Rwanda's 2002 press law to issue disciplinary recommendations against media outlets, was not informed of the ruling until several days after the fact, Executive Secretary Patrice Mulama told CPJ.

Nkusi later told CPJ the ruling was "perhaps" linked to "inaccuracies" in the paper's application for a publishing license, but he declined to comment further. Nkusi never substantiated the allegations, and the Rwandan Journalists Association did not find any evidence to back his claims upon review of the paper's application, President

Gaspard Safari told CPJ. *The Weekly Post* filed an appeal.

Nkusi also moved against the private French-language bimonthly *Afrique Libéra-tion*, suspending it indefinitely on April 5, according to CPJ research. In a letter to Director Bonaventure Bizumuremyi that was obtained by CPJ, Nkusi declared that the paper could not publish until a pending criminal defamation suit was settled.

The government continued to invoke vaguely worded laws against ethnic divi-sionism and genocidal ideology to quiet dissenting views on sensitive topics such as the 1994 genocide, interethnic relations, and the trial of genocide suspects in "gacaca" courts. The community-based courts were set up in 2001 to heal ethnic tensions and speed the trials of hundreds of thousands of genocide suspects.

During Genocide Remembrance Week, an April 15 radio interview of a Hutu Christian priest claiming to have saved the lives of 104 people led authorities to charge host John Williams Ntwali of private City Radio in Kigali with promoting "genocidal ideology," according to local journalists. Ntwali resigned from the station after Program Director Alex Rutareka suspended him over the interview, allegedly accusing the journalist of "promoting a second [Paul] Rusesabagina," Ntwali told CPJ. Rusesabagina, a Hutu hotel manager portrayed in the acclaimed 2004 film "Hotel Rwanda," is an outspoken critic of the Tutsi-dominated regime of Kagame.

The publication in January of an anonymous reader's open letter comparing eth-nic killings during Kagame's regime to those under the rule of the previous Hutu regime also led authorities to charge Agnès Nkusi-Uwimana of the small-circulation bimonthly *Umurabyo* with divisionism, sectarianism, and libel. Nkusi-Uwimana was sentenced in April to a year in prison and 400,000 Rwandan francs (US$750) in damages. Nkusi-Uwimana was still behind bars when CPJ conducted its annual census of imprisoned journalists on December 1.

In a statement released in March, the Rwandan League for the Promotion and Defense of Human Rights stated that "some independent newspapers like *Umuco* and *Rushyashya* were being accused of an ideology of genocide and separatism, with-out relevant evidence, in a scheme to muzzle them."

Rwanda's foreign press corps was at times targeted with threats and harassment. Some journalists who spoke on condition of anonymity told CPJ they were routinely denied access to official press conferences after identifying their affiliation.

In January and February, the pro-government press attacked U.S. government-funded broadcaster Voice of America (VOA), accusing the station of biased report-ing in interviews with government critics such as Rusesabagina and the Europe-based opposition leader Victoire Ingabire Umuhoza, according to CPJ research. A February editorial of the Kinyarwanda pro-government newspaper *Imvaho Nshya* called for the closure of the VOA, according to local journalists and news reports.

Sources in the VOA's Kinyarwanda service denied allegations of bias, add-ing that the station had always included the comments of officials in their reports.

VOA has operated under state scrutiny since the station signed an agreement with the government in August 2006 authorizing its FM broadcasts, according to Radio Rwanda.

By year's end, lawmakers were drafting legislation that could scrap prison sentences for defamation offenses, but challenges remained with removing libel from the country's penal code, local journalists said.

As supporters of press freedom and press control struggled to achieve an acceptable compromise, the role of Rwanda's hate media during the genocide hung over the debate. In November, the Tanzania-based International Criminal Tribunal for Rwanda reduced the lengthy prison sentences of three former state media journalists convicted of incitement to genocide, according to international news reports.

· · · · · · · · · · · · · · · · · · · **SOMALIA** · · · · · · · · · · · · · · · · · · ·

Attacks had become so pervasive in this conflict-riven state that the National Union of Somali Journalists described 2006 as "the most dangerous year for press freedom for more than a decade." Then came 2007—a year in which conditions grew dramatically worse.

With seven journalists killed in direct relation to their work, Somalia was the deadliest place for the press in Africa and second only to Iraq worldwide. The deaths came amid widespread violence in this Horn of Africa state, which has had no effective central government since 1991. The U.N. High Commissioner for Refugees reported that nearly 600,000 people had fled during the year, as the Transitional Federal Government (TFG), backed by Ethiopian troops, clashed repeatedly with the militias of the Islamic Courts Union (ICU), a coalition of fundamentalist law courts that had held power for six months in 2006.

Four Somali journalists—Mohammed Abdullahi Khalif of Voice of Peace, Abshir Ali Gabre and Ahmed Hassan Mahad of Radio Jowhar, and Abdulkadir Mahad Moallim Kaskey of Radio Banadir—died in crossfire during factional clashes, but three others were targeted for murder as the conflict turned more perilous in mid-year. On August 11, Mahad Ahmed Elmi, director of independent radio station Capital Voice, was shot four times at close range as he walked to work in central Mogadishu. That afternoon, Ali Iman Shamarke—head of the media network HornAfrik, Capital Voice's parent company—died when the Land Cruiser in which he was riding was destroyed by a remotely detonated bomb. Reuters correspondent Sahal Abdulle said Shamarke was returning from Elmi's funeral when he was killed. Two months later, the acting director of Radio Shabelle, Bashiir Noor Gedi, was shot and killed outside his home in Mogadishu after receiving a series of threats. Somalia police spokesman Abdel Wahid Mohamed said two ICU rebels had been detained in the killings of Shamarke and Elmi, but no immediate progress was reported in their prosecution.

Politically motivated attacks, arrests, harassment, and threats came from both sides in the conflict. In October, for example, insurgents targeted Mogadishu-based Radio Simba with threatening telephone calls and e-mails because of the station's anti-violence programming. That same month, government officials detained two Radio Simba journalists for broadcasting an interview with an ICU military leader. Many of the reprisals were triggered by the media's reporting on human rights abuses by both rebels and government forces. Nationwide, CPJ documented the arrests of at least 60 journalists in 22 separate cases, the vast majority of which were conducted without warrants or even formal charges.

In a public statement issued in October, Information Minister Madobe Nunow Mohamed accused private broadcasters of "creating insecurity, supporting terrorism, violating freedom of expression, misleading the public, and becoming antigovernment." He also released a letter ordering all media organizations to register with the ministry in order to operate in the country. The demand appeared to have been made without any legal basis, and it was widely ignored. Foreign governments and international organizations such as CPJ urged President Abdullahi Yusuf Ahmed to abandon the crackdown on the press. Following the lead of national leaders, Mogadishu Mayor Mohamed "Dheere" Omar Habeeb closed Radio Shabelle, Radio Banadir, and Radio Simba in November on charges of broadcasting "false" and "antigovernment" news. Facing local and international pressure, Habeeb relented three weeks later and allowed the stations to resume broadcasting.

Despite the adversity, Somalia's small corps of newspapers and radio stations— which emerged after the fall of dictator Siad Barre in 1991—continued to undertake critical, independent reporting. The clan warfare that emerged from the leadership struggle was a major focus for the press in 2007. Although Ethiopian-backed government troops forced the ICU out of Mogadishu in December 2006, elements of the Islamist coalition remained intact, waging a guerrilla war against government forces throughout the year.

The ICU draws its internal support predominantly from the Hawiye clan, the largest ethnic group in Somalia, while the government is widely seen as aligned with the Darod, the country's second-largest clan. The transitional government has reinforced this perception by pursuing policies that alienate the Hawiye, notably in its appeal for Ethiopian troops and its relocation of the central government from the traditional capital, Mogadishu, to the southwestern city of Baidoa. The age-old rivalry between the Hawiye, the dominant clan in Mogadishu, and the Darod, who populate Baidoa and the semiautonomous region of Puntland, have helped fuel the conflict.

The two leading independent radio broadcasters, HornAfrik and Radio Shabelle, have borne the brunt of attacks. CPJ documented at least 13 cases in which Radio Shabelle journalists were harassed, detained, censored, or assaulted, and another seven cases involving HornAfrik staffers. In mid-September, government security forces raided and shelled Radio Shabelle's Mogadishu compound, forcing the station off the air for 15 days. Security forces claimed they were responding to a grenade attack launched from within the compound, although station employees said they knew of no such attack. Government soldiers camped on the roads leading to the station, blocking any attempt to enter or exit, the BBC reported.

In April, government soldiers shelled the HornAfrik and Global Broadcasting Corporation (GBC) compounds during an attack on suspected insurgent strongholds in the Huruwaa district of Mogadishu. GBC closed four months later. "Every day government forces and unknown insurgent groups are opening fire and killing people in Mogadishu," GBC Director Dalmar Yusuf told CPJ. "We had to close down; we cannot operate in this environment."

The government closed the Somali operations of Qatar-based Al-Jazeera in March without providing a substantive explanation. "Al-Jazeera has conveyed the wrong messages to the world," Information Minister Nunow told The Associated Press. "We will shut down additional radio stations and channels if they distort facts." Authorities moved against another international news outlet in April, imprisoning three members of a camera crew from U.K.-based Universal Television in connection with questions they asked about peace talks during an interview with a presidential spokesman, according to local journalists. They were released six weeks later.

Both warring parties objected to the formation of professional journalism associations. Ali Moalim Isak, a correspondent for the independent Baidoa station Radio Warsan and organizing secretary of the National Union of Somali Journalists (NUSOJ), went into hiding in September after suspected Islamist insurgents went looking for him at his office in Mogadishu. Moalim told CPJ he had received several threatening phone calls ordering him to stop speaking out against attacks on journalists or he would be killed. The following month, Information Minister Nunow announced in an interview on Radio Shabelle that NUSOJ had no right to organize or represent journalists.

The conflict continued to have devastating effects on the economy, particularly in Mogadishu, where inflation drove up prices dramatically. According to *Chicago Tribune* correspondent Paul Salopek, the price of rice doubled during one five-day period in October. Beleaguered businesses were abandoning the city, leaving little advertising revenue for the media outlets that remained. "The city is getting emptier day by day," said Radio Shabelle Deputy Director Mohamed Amiin. "Soon none

AFRICA

of the independent media groups will be able to survive financially." Among the thousands who left Mogadishu in 2007, more than 30 were journalists, CPJ research showed.

While most of the attacks on the press were centered in Mogadishu, a number were reported in the less restive regions of Puntland and Somaliland. Puntland Minister of Information Abdirahman Mohammed Bankah imposed a ban on media activities that do not have prior permission from the ministry. Banned were such basic functions as seminars and professional associations. Radio Garowe was temporarily closed and three journalists detained by security forces in October after the station broadcast an interview with a former Somali National Security Agency employee who was critical of the country's security forces. The detainees were told not to report on the agency again, Radio Garowe journalists said. In March, the offices of the independent weekly *Shacab* were damaged in an arson attack, forcing the paper to suspend publication for more than a month, Editor Abdi Farah Nur told CPJ.

Authorities in the self-declared republic of Somaliland continued to harass journalists despite having a constitution that guarantees free expression. While Somaliland's 2004 press law prohibits prison sentences for press offenses such as defamation, three journalists with the privately owned daily *Haatuf* were tried under the region's 1962 penal code in January. The journalists were imprisoned for three months for "insulting the president of the republic of Somaliland and his wife," Police Commissioner Muhammad Sangade Dubad told Radio Hargeysa. "Any material that is critical of local authorities will get you in trouble," *Haatuf* correspondent Amin Jibril told CPJ. Jibril should know: He was detained three times after writing a series of reports that exposed abuses by security forces.

• • • • • • • • • • • • • • • • • ZIMBABWE • • • • • • • • • • • • • • • • •

It's the vacuum that illustrates the problem—all of the reporters who have fled, the news outlets that have closed, the stories that have gone unreported. Seven years of government intimidation and deteriorating economic conditions have

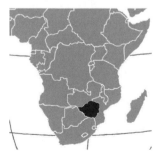

prompted a steady flow of Zimbabwean journalists to leave the country. CPJ has documented at least 48 journalists as having fled since 2001, although the number is twice that when data from exile organizations is considered. Those ranks include many of the nation's most prominent reporters, constituting the largest group of exiled journalists in the world, CPJ research shows.

Nyasha Nyakunu, a research officer for the Media

Institute of Southern Africa, said government harassment had decreased over the past several years simply because "there are fewer and fewer media workers in Zimbabwe." But, she said, "the pattern of intolerance remains unchanged." President Robert Mugabe and his ruling ZANU-PF party have used a battery of restrictive legislation—most notably the Access to Information and Protection of Privacy Act (AIPPA) and the Broadcasting Services Act—to suppress the few remaining independent media outlets. No independent dailies have published since the government forced the *Daily News* to shut down in 2003. Only four independent weeklies still circulate—*The Standard*, *The Zimbabwe Independent*, *The Zimbabwean*, and *The Financial Gazette*—and no independent domestic broadcasters have been licensed to operate.

With an official inflation rate of 7,600 percent (other estimates place it at nearly double that), four out of five Zimbabweans live below the poverty line, according to the International Crisis Group, an independent nonprofit that analyzes potential conflict areas. A military-led campaign to slash prices instead produced acute food and fuel shortages in 2007. Few journalists could survive without working for international news outlets or the Zimbabwean media-in-exile—but those who did became targets of government attacks.

AIPPA, considered one of the most repressive media laws in the region, requires all journalists and media outlets to register with the government-controlled Media and Information Commission (MIC). In December, parliament passed a series of largely cosmetic amendments to AIPPA and other media laws, a move that Zimbabwe Union of Journalists Vice President Njabulo Ncube likened to putting "lipstick on a frog." The changes eliminate criminal penalties for lack of accreditation but leave government controls firmly in place.

In practice, MIC grants accreditation selectively based on political considerations, while using AIPPA as a hammer to attack journalists linked to foreign or exile media outlets. In April, police arrested Gift Phiri of the London-based *Zimbabwean* on charges of practicing journalism without AIPPA accreditation after he was seen covering an opposition rally, Rangu Nyamurundira of the Zimbabwe Lawyers for Human Rights told CPJ. Phiri, who was beaten in police custody, was acquitted in September in a court in the capital, Harare, according to news reports.

The same law was used against foreign journalists. The correspondent for South Africa's private E.TV, Peter Moyo, was arrested in February and later fined for filming illegal diamond mining in the eastern region of Manicaland without AIPPA accreditation. Manicaland Bureau Chief Andrew Neshamba and cameraman William Gumbo of the state Zimbabwe Broadcasting Corporation (ZBC) were charged with "criminal abuse of duty" for assisting Moyo, defense lawyer Victor Mazengero told CPJ. Both ZBC journalists were suspended without pay and stripped of their media accreditation; Gumbo went into hiding in fear of further reprisal, according to local journalists.

Little more than a month later, Alexander Perry of the U.S. newsmagazine *Time* was detained for 48 hours and accused of lacking proper accreditation while covering a similar story about unregulated gold and diamond dealers.

The government had fired a broadside against foreign media in March when it released a statement threatening correspondents with unspecified reprisals because of supposed bias. The statement, issued by the Ministry of Information and Publicity, singled out prominent correspondents Jan Raath of *The Times* of London, Peta Thornycroft of Britain's *Daily Telegraph*, and the U.S. government-funded broadcaster Voice of America for reporting "fabricated stories." Thornycroft, a veteran Zimbabwe journalist and 2007 International Women's Media Foundation award winner, told CPJ that she had applied for AIPPA accreditation several times, but the government never responded. Foreign news outlets including the BBC and the South Africa-based E.TV have either been banned or refused AIPPA accreditation, according to CPJ research. Only four foreign media companies—Reuters, Agence France-Presse, Al-Jazeera, and The Associated Press—were based in Harare in 2007. "All of the correspondents are on a short leash," said exiled journalist Wilf Mbanga, editor of *The Zimbabwean*. "The correspondents are all nationals so that the government can control them easier than an international reporter."

One journalist believed to have leaked explosive footage to foreign media was killed in mysterious circumstances. Edward Chikomba, a former ZBC cameraman, was abducted on March 29 near his home in Harare by a group of armed men and found dead two days later near the industrial farming area of Darwendale, according to local journalists and news reports. Those reports and CPJ sources said Chikomba's death was likely linked to his alleged leaking of footage showing opposition leader Morgan Tsvangirai after he was beaten in police custody in February. The footage aired on several global media networks and sparked international condemnation of Mugabe; it was never shown on state television. The Chikomba murder instilled fear in the local press, especially in regard to collaborating with foreign media.

In September, journalists raised concerns about a purported government document that named 15 independent journalists who were to be "placed under strict surveillance and taken in." The authenticity of the list—first published by the South Africa-based news Web site *ZimOnline*—was denied by the government, although at least three of the journalists named had been targets of recent harassment. They included Bill Saidi, editor of *The Standard*, who received a bullet and a handwritten death threat in an envelope delivered to his office in February.

In a series of interviews with CPJ, Zimbabwean journalists noted that similar lists, all with shadowy origins, had circulated in the past. With presidential and parliamentary elections planned for 2008, some said, government operatives may be seeking to ratchet up tension in the press. Mugabe, in power since 1980, was expected to retain office in the March 2008 vote. "There is little hope for the elections to be free and fair without a free press," said Geoff Nyarota, former *Daily News* editor and 2001 CPJ International Press Freedom Award recipient.

The Associated Newspapers of Zimbabwe (ANZ), publishers of the *Daily News* and *Daily News on Sunday*, continued to pursue a Supreme Court case challenging AIPPA's constitutionality. Sikhanysio Ndlovu, head of the Ministry of Information and Publicity, announced in October that the MIC had named a board to address ANZ's application to resume publishing.

The country's private broadcasting industry remained virtually nonexistent. State-run ZBTV proclaimed itself the "station of first choice"—a laughable claim, since it was the only choice for many viewers. In March, state media reports said that the Kenya-based Gateway Communications planned to establish satellite television service in Harare. Those plans had not reached fruition by late year.

Three independent radio stations run by exiled journalists sent signals into Zimbabwe from bases across the globe. They included Studio 7, based in Washington; SW Radio Africa in London; and Voice of the People in Cape Town, South Africa. Forced to be innovative to get around media restrictions, SW Radio Africa began a text-messaging news service that reached 6,500 subscribers. Studio 7 said it expected to launch a similar service.

Applicants seeking domestic radio licenses were ignored or rejected. "Today there are numerous community radio initiatives that have lobbied unsuccessfully for the past three or more years for the liberalization of the airwaves," said Harare lawyer Chris Mhike in an interview with *The Zimbabwe Independent*. "Radio Dialogue in Bulawayo, for instance, could go on air tomorrow if the Broadcasting Authority of Zimbabwe ... could wake up from its slumber and issue broadcasting licenses." Government officials told a parliamentary hearing in September that their hands were tied by various Broadcasting Services Act regulations. In October, Information and Publicity Minister Ndlovu told the government daily *The Herald* that he would work to soften Broadcasting Services Act requirements, and that he would invite new applicants for broadcasting licenses.

In August, parliament enacted a sweeping communication surveillance law. The Interception of Communications Act allows authorities to intercept phone, Internet, e-mail, and postal communications. Despite the country's devastated economy, the government said it plans to establish a state monitoring center and require telecommunication providers to install systems "supporting lawful interceptions at all times," the Media Institute of Southern Africa reported. Ndlovu told CPJ the surveillance law will target "imperialist-sponsored journalists with hidden agendas" and "protect the president, a minister, or any citizen from harm."

SNAPSHOTS: **AFRICA**
Attacks & developments throughout the region

ANGOLA

- In September, the director of the private weekly *Semanário Angolense* was sent to prison after being sentenced to an eight-month term and an 18.7 million kwanza (US$250,000) fine in a criminal case filed by the former minister of justice, Paulo Chipilica, local journalists reported. Director Graça Campos was released in November pending the outcome of his appeal. Campos had been held in the San Paulo hospital prison outside of the capital, Luanda, according to his wife and local journalists.

BENIN

- Director Clément Adéchian and reporter Cécil Adjévi of the independent daily *L'Informateur* served two months of a six-month criminal libel sentence stemming from an August 2006 story accusing a court bailiff of rape. They were set free in February after retracting the story under pressure.

- In February, three journalists and an executive of the leading private media group Golfe received six-month prison terms and fines in connection with a 2005 story alleging corruption in the government of former President Mathieu Kérékou. All four were free pending an appeal.

BURKINA FASO

- In January, two journalists from the private bimonthly *L'Evénement* were fined 300,000 CFA francs (US$680) apiece and given two-month suspended prison terms over articles that raised questions about the role of President Blaise Compaoré's brother in the unsolved 1998 murder of editor Norbert Zongo. Director Germain Nama and Editor Ahmed Newton Barry appealed the conviction.

- In April, several e-mail death threats forced outspoken journalist and free speech activist Karim Sama into hiding. The e-mail messages pressed Sama to stop criticizing the policies of the government during his two popular reggae programs on Radio Ouaga FM. One message warned that Sama would be "gunned down" like Zongo.

- A month after resuming his program, Sama's BMW was set on fire outside the studios of Ouaga FM, according to the Media Foundation for West Africa and local journalists. The September 28 incident occurred while Sama was hosting his music program. A police investigation was launched, but no suspects were arrested.

BURUNDI

- In January, a panel of judges in the capital, Bujumbura, acquitted four independent radio journalists of charges of threatening public security in their coverage of a purported 2006 coup plot. Editor Serge Nibizi and journalist Domitile Kiramvu of independent Radio Publique Africaine and Director Matthias Manirakiza of private Radio Isanganiro were set free after more than a month in prison. Radio Bonesha Director Corneille Nibaruta was acquitted in absentia.

CAMEROON

- Prosecutors in the capital, Yaoundé, charged Georges Gilbert Baongla, managing editor of the weekly tabloid Le Démenti, with publication of obscene materials and contempt of morals and decency. The April charges stemmed from a March 27 story trumpeting an alleged "homosexual scandal" involving an unidentified government minister. Baongla was fined 500,000 CFA francs (US$1,200) and forced to serve a six-month prison term.

- In August, publisher Wirkwa Eric Tayu of the private weekly The Nso Voice, the sole media outlet based in the northwestern town of Kumbo, went into hiding shortly before he was sentenced to a year in prison and a fine of 850,000 CFA francs (US$1,800) on eight counts of alleged press offenses, including criminal defamation, according to defense counsel Blaise Berinyuy. The ruling was linked to the paper's publication of a government audit incriminating Kumbo's mayor in corruption schemes, Assistant Editor Alice Tomla told CPJ. An appeal was filed, but the paper stopped publishing for fear of official reprisals.

- Stories alleging mismanagement of public finances by Prime Minister Ephraïm Inoni and former Finance Minister Polycarpe Abah Abah led to libel convictions in September against directors Bernard Owona of La Vitrine and Robert Mintya of Le Devoir, according to news reports and local journalists. Owona and Mintya were fined 1 million CFA (US$2,100) apiece.

CENTRAL AFRICAN REPUBLIC

- In March, the official High Communication Council suspended for one month the private weekly Le Centrafriqu'Un in connection with an article critical of neighboring Chad, a close ally of the government in the deadly unrest spilling over from Darfur. The article outlined alleged human rights abuses by Chadian troops.

- Michel Alkhaly Ngady, president of the country's private publishers group (known by its French acronym, GEPPIC), was jailed for two months after issuing public statements challenging the High Communication Council's authority to suspend Le Centrafriqu'Un. Ngady was convicted in April of resisting public authorities and showing contempt for the law. In August, the Supreme Court dismissed a suit filed by GEPPIC alleging that two presidential appointees to the council lacked the professional experience required by the agency's own bylaws.

AFRICA

CHAD

- In May, authorities lifted censorship of local newspapers and blanket restrictions on radio news coverage as a six-month state of emergency expired. The state of emergency was imposed in late 2006 in response to unrest in eastern Chad. Censorship was initially adopted for a 12-day period in November 2006 but was later extended.

- In response to deadly interethnic clashes in northern Chad, authorities issued a 12-day state of emergency in three northeastern regions on October 16, reinstating blanket restrictions on nationwide media coverage, according to news reports. The measure was subsequently extended for another 45 days, according to local journalists.

- In October, authorities in the eastern town of Abéché detained two French journalists covering an aborted attempt by an organization named Zoe's Ark to fly 103 purported Darfuri orphans to France for adoption. Reporter Marc Garmirian of the news agency Capa and photographer Jean-Daniel Guillou of the photo agency Synchro-X were traveling with Zoe's Ark to report on the organization's activities when police intercepted a convoy of aid workers and children headed for the local airport, according to news reports. The journalists were held for 10 days on kidnapping complicity charges but were released on bail after intervention from French President Nicolas Sarkozy. The organization had portrayed the children as orphans from Darfur, but U.N. officials said most appeared to have living parents. Six organization workers were convicted on kidnap charges in December and returned to France for execution of their sentences.

COMOROS

- In May, an affiliate of the national broadcasting corporation Office de Radio et Télévision des Comores in the breakaway island of Anjouan was ransacked by troops loyal to Anjouan leader Col. Mohamed Bacar during violent clashes with the national army, according to news reports and local journalists. Police subsequently detained overnight Editor Sardou Moussa, presenter Idiamine Nathir, camera operator Ousseine Mahamoud, reporter Chamssidine Nassuha, and an unidentified driver after they attempted to salvage equipment not damaged in the attack.

- Following the clashes, authorities in the national capital, Moroni, summoned Director Aboubacar Mchangama of the private weekly L'Archipel for questioning over a front-page photograph showing soldiers of the national army held prisoner in Anjouan, according to media reports. All copies of the paper were ordered withdrawn from sale.

- In July, after returning from a reporting trip to Anjouan, Editor Ibrahim Ali Saïd Félix of the private station Djabal Télévision, based outside Moroni, was questioned for 10 hours at Moroni's airport over his alleged links to the Anjouan leadership.

DJIBOUTI

- *Le Renouveau*, the country's sole private newspaper, stopped publishing on May 18 after a series of attacks apparently stemming from the paper's affiliation with the opposition MRD party. Police in the capital, Djibouti City, raided the paper's offices in February and seized two computers and printing equipment. No warrant was issued or explanation given. On May 3, Djibouti City's special crime unit detained *Le Renouveau* Managing Editor Houssein Ahmed Farah for 10 days and newspaper distributor Hared Abdallah Barreh for three days. The arrests were related to an April article concerning an alleged sex scandal involving a prominent businessman. On May 13, police from the special crime unit ransacked the offices of *Le Renouveau*, seizing equipment that had replaced what the paper lost in the February raid. Days later, four of its vendors were beaten and detained by police for four days.

GABON

- In March, commentary critical of President Omar Bongo, Africa's longest-serving head of state, led the state-run National Communication Council to suspend for three months the private bimonthly *Edzombolo*. Authorities accused Director Jean de Dieu Ndoutoume of publishing "defamatory and insulting news directed at prominent state personalities" in connection with a February editorial headlined "Omar does not control anything anymore."

- In June, an editorial headlined "The last days of Bongo" led authorities to hand Director Guy-Christian Mavioga of the private periodical *L'Espoir* a one-month prison term, a five-month suspended term, and a fine on charges of offending the head of state. Mavioga was released after 38 days in prison, during which he was hospitalized for back pain and respiratory problems. The newspaper remained suspended by state media regulators on the grounds that Mavioga violated laws prohibiting a civil servant from controlling a newspaper.

- In October, the NCC blocked the Paris-based, satirical bimonthly *Le Gri-Gri* from printing and distributing in Gabon, according to news reports and local journalists. The council said the paper would be suspended until it officially registered with the government as a Gabonese publication. Prior to the ruling, a local firm had refused to print the September 27 issue because of an article critical of a government mining contract with a Chinese firm, *Le Gri-Gri* Managing Director

Michel Ongoundou Loundah told CPJ. Also in October, the council suspended local bimonthly *La Nation* for a month because of an article critical of Arts and Culture Minister Blandine Marundu, according to local journalists.

GHANA

- In January, investigative reporter Henry Addo and a driver for the private Metropolitan Television station were attacked by a dozen men guarding a disputed property in a suburb of the capital, Accra, according to the Media Foundation for West Africa (MFWA). The guards attacked Addo while he filmed a mechanic's shop, seizing his digital camera and vandalizing a station vehicle, according to the same source. Several arrests were made.

- On the evening of February 9, award-winning editor Samuel Kwabena Ennin of private radio station Ashh FM was gunned down by two unknown attackers in a bar near the station's offices in the central town of Kumasi. The assailants held patrons at gunpoint and collected mobile phones before escaping in an unmarked vehicle. In April, police announced the arrests of two suspects and said robbery had been the motive, according to Radio Ghana. CPJ inquiries did not find any evidence to suggest a link between the killing and Ennin's work as the host of a morning news talk show.

- Buertey Shadai, a photographer for the private biweekly *Hearts News*, suffered head injuries in March after angry soccer fans in the mining town of Obuasi pelted him with stones following a match, according to the MFWA. The fans, irate over a late goal by their opponents, seized and destroyed Shadai's camera, claiming he had photographed some "nasty incidents" in the crowd.

GUINEA-BISSAU

- In June, unidentified armed men burst into the home of journalist Allen Yero Embalo and stole his laptop, recorder, and camera. Yero received a death threat on the telephone the next morning concerning reports implicating the military in drug trafficking near the Bijagos archipelago. Yero and his family went into exile shortly after the incident.

- In late June, journalist Albert Dabo received several anonymous death threats via telephone and was ordered to face defamation charges by Navy Chief of Staff Jose Américo Bubo Na Tchuto. Dabo was accused of misquoting the naval officer in an article that cited military involvement in drug trafficking. For one week in July, Dabo went into hiding after repeated death threats were made.

IVORY COAST

- Police in Abidjan detained Claude Dassé, a reporter for the private daily *Soir Info*, for five days in January on a contempt charge after the journalist accused the state prosecutor of corruption in an interview published in the private daily *Le Rebond*. Dassé's allegation involved the government's investigation of a singer accused of trying to kill the reporter over a critical story. Police also questioned Editor Nando Dapa and reporter André N'Guessan of *Le Rebond* for two hours over their decision to publish the story.

- In February, police held Editor Denis Kah Zion and reporter André Silver Konan of the private daily *Le Nouveau Réveil* for 11 hours in connection with a story recounting alleged assassinations and scandals during President Laurent Gbagbo's rule.

- French and Ivorian investigations into the unsolved 2004 disappearance of Franco-Canadian journalist Guy-André Kieffer were boosted by the emergence of a purported witness and a political pledge by new French President Nicolas Sarkozy. On August 23, French television station France 3 interviewed Berté Seydou, who said he was the driver for an army commando unit that kidnapped Kieffer. Seydou said Michel Legré, the brother-in-law of President Gbagbo's wife, was in charge of the unit. Ivoirian prosecutor Raymond Tchimou said government involvement in the disappearance was a "false lead," according to news reports. Legré was questioned previously in the case but had denied involvement. In August, Sarkozy met with members of Kieffer's family and promised to pursue the investigation vigorously.

- In August, about 40 militants from the Student Federation of Côte d'Ivoire (known by its French acronym, FESCI) invaded the offices of private daily *L'Intelligent d'Abidjan*, sequestering journalists for two hours, seizing newsroom equipment, and knocking down the office door of Editor Laurent Okoué, according to news reports. The students demanded the staff publish a protest letter, but they dispersed after police intervened, Okoué told CPJ. The letter was in response to an August 14 story that said 100 student members of FESCI had defected to an opposition party.

- Separate stories trumpeting corruption scandals involving President Gbagbo led police in Abidjan to question five journalists for the pro-opposition dailies *Le Jour Plus* and *Le Rebond* in early September. Police interrogated journalists over three days for more than 10 hours at a time, according to news reports and local journalists. Four of the journalists were later charged with defaming the head of state and found liable for damages of 10 million CFA francs (US$22,600) each, *Le Jour Plus* Editor Frederick Koffi told CPJ. The rulings were appealed.

KENYA

- Mburu Muchoki, editor of the weekly tabloid *The Independent*, was sentenced in March to a year in prison on a criminal libel conviction. The case stemmed from a complaint filed by Justice Minister Martha Karua over a 2004 story detailing an alleged sex scandal involving the minister. Muchoki disputed the charge and in June was freed on a presidential pardon.

- In August, following local protests and an international outcry, President Mwai Kibaki rejected a bill that would have forced editors to name their sources if their stories led to court cases. Lawmakers also withdrew a bill containing provisions restricting media ownership and granting the government sweeping powers of search and seizure on national security grounds.

- The government imposed a ban on all live broadcasts on December 30, hours after the contested results of national elections were announced. President Mwai Kibaki was declared the winner of the December 27 vote over opposition candidate Raila Odinga, despite evidence of ballot rigging, according to international news reports. The announcement triggered widespread rioting, with the initial death toll reaching into the hundreds. The media ban allowed wild rumors to spread by text message and word of mouth, The Associated Press reported. The violence appeared to tap a deep vein of tribal tension; Kibaki is a Kikuyu, and Odinga a Luo.

LESOTHO

- Adam Lekhoaba, editor-in-chief of the private radio station Harvest FM, was deported to South Africa in February, after the government accused the station of inciting violence during that month's general elections. Prime Minister Pakalitha Mosisili later altered the charge to failure to renew a broadcast license. The station was closed for two days while final election results were announced.

- In June, Harvest FM reporter and presenter Thabo Thakalekoala was arrested and charged with treason after he read on the air a letter allegedly written by members of the Lesotho national army that was critical of the prime minister and several government officials. That same month, the government cancelled its advertising on Harvest FM and in the private weekly *Public Eye* after the minister of information accused the two outlets of being aligned with an opposition party.

LIBERIA

- Police in the capital, Monrovia, sealed the offices of the private biweekly tabloid *The Independent* in late February after the government revoked the paper's license

AFRICA

to publish. The action came after the newspaper published a sexually graphic photograph of Presidential Affairs Minister Willis Knuckles with two women, leading to the minister's resignation on February 26. Managing Editor Sam Dean briefly went into hiding as the scandal played out. In June, officials announced the lifting of the ban after the paper sued the government for constitutional and due process violations.

• An official with Liberia's soccer association, irate at a story in the private weekly *The News*, assaulted Sports Editor Julu Johnson in March, according to the Media Foundation for West Africa. The official, Napoleon Japloe, was suspended for a month by the association after slapping the journalist and pushing him to the ground.

• Reporters Daylue Gaoh of the *New Democrat* and Zeze Evans Ballah of *Public Agenda* were beaten by police and U.N. peacekeeping forces while covering a student demonstration at the University of Liberia in Monrovia in June, local journalists reported. U.N. troops took a digital photo memory disc from Ballah that had pictures of police and troops confronting the students, *Public Agenda* Editor-in-Chief J. Lyndon Ponnie said. The students were staging a demonstration urging the government to pay overdue wages to instructors.

• In September, presidential bodyguards harassed and beat three journalists trying to cover a meeting between President Ellen Johnson-Sirleaf and newly elected Sierra Leonian President Ernest Koroma at Monrovia's Roberts International Airport, the Media Foundation for West Africa reported. Journalists Jonathan Paylelay of the BBC, Dosso Zoom of Radio France International, and Alphonso Toweh of Reuters were beaten and bundled out of the interview area, according to local journalists. A few minutes after the incident, Sirleaf's press secretary, Cyrus Badio, met with the journalists and apologized.

MADAGASCAR

• During parliamentary elections on September 23, Editor-in-Chief Honoré Tsabotogay of the Roman Catholic Church-owned station Radio Rakama was struck with a stick by a ruling party supporter after filming a convoy of vehicles transporting voters to a polling station in the southeastern province of Vohipeno, according to media reports and local journalists. Tsabotogay and local journalists had questioned whether the people were residents of the polling district. Tsabotogay was charged with disrupting the election proceedings by filming the convoy, but the charges were later dropped, according to Madagascar Syndicate of Journalists President Harry Laurent Rahajason.

AFRICA

MALAWI

- In February, reporter Dickson Kashoti of the private *Daily Times* was injured after being punched in the face three times by Member of Parliament Joseph Njobvuyalema. The politician, later sacked by parliament and sentenced to three months in prison on assault charges, had stormed the newsroom over a story about his actions following the arrest of his brother on murder charges.

- In April, the Malawi Communications Regulatory Authority (MCRA) barred private radio stations from airing live broadcasts of political rallies without government permission. The directive effectively targeted leading private broadcasters Capital Radio, Joy Radio, and Zodiak Broadcasting over coverage of former President Bakili Muluzi, considered the most likely opposition challenger in the 2009 presidential elections. Malawi's High Court struck down the ruling on constitutional grounds shortly afterward.

- In July, the High Court ruled that the MCRA was improperly constituted and ordered its members to stop work. The court found irregularities in President Bingu wa Mutharika's appointments to the agency.

MALI

- In March, Director Diaby Makoro Camara and Editor Oumar Bouaré of the private monthly *Kabako* were sentenced to four-month suspended terms and fined 50,000 CFA francs (US$100) apiece in a defamation suit filed by Planning and Land Development Minister Marimantia Diarra, defense lawyer Amadou Tiéoulé said. The complaint stemmed from an article that described Diarra's alleged attempt to halt the wedding of a young woman.

- Reporter Seydine Oumar Diarra of the independent daily *Info-Matin* was jailed for 13 days and the paper's director, Sambi Touré, received an eight-month suspended sentence and 200,000 franc (US$450) fine for covering a high school essay assignment about a fictitious presidential sex scandal, *Info-Matin* Editor-in-Chief Sékouba Samaké told CPJ. After Diarra's June arrest, three publications reprinted the story as a protest—prompting authorities to arrest the director of each publication. Directors Hameye Cissé of *Le Scorpion*, Birama Fall of *Le Républicain*, and Alexis Kalambry of *Les Echos* each received a four-month suspended sentence and a fine of 200,000 CFA francs, according to local reports.

MOZAMBIQUE

- In February, the Supreme Court rejected appeals by the six hired killers of investigative journalist Carlos Cardoso, upholding their prison sentences and fines. Cardoso was killed on November 22, 2000, after reporting on the 1996 embezzlement of US$14 million from the state-controlled Commercial Bank of Mozambique.

- Reporter Celso Manguana of the private daily *Canal de Moçambique* was arrested during a dispute at a police station in the capital, Maputo, in March. Press reports and local journalists said Manguana had called officers "incompetent" for declining to comment on the detentions of several people after an antigovernment demonstration. He was released after four nights in detention.

SENEGAL

- In a criminal defamation lawsuit brought by a car dealership against the daily *Walf Grand-Place*, a court in the capital, Dakar, sentenced Director Jean Meïssa Diop and reporter Faydy Dramé to six-month suspended prison terms and 10 million CFA francs (US$23,000) apiece in damages on March 8. The charges related to a June 2006 story on a consumer complaint against the dealership.

- In April, Director Ndiogou Wack Seck of the private, pro-government daily *Il Est Midi* was sentenced to six months in prison and ordered to pay damages of 40 million CFA francs (US$90,000) on criminal defamation charges. Seck was barred from working as a journalist for three months and his paper was banned from publication for the same period. The charges stemmed from a story criticizing several figures close to President Abdoulaye Wade over their roles in the 2006 release from prison of embattled former Prime Minister Idrissa Seck.

- Critical comments made during a call-in program led ruling party politician Moustapha Cissé Lô and a dozen supporters to ransack the studios of Radio Disso FM in the town of Mbacké in April. The station filed a complaint with the police, but Lô filed a countercomplaint demanding the closure of the station and 200 million CFA francs (US$452,000) in damages.

SIERRA LEONE

- On February 11, members of the town youth association in Kabala, in Koinadugu District, besieged the premises of Radio Bintumani and forced the community station off the air. The youths evicted the station's staff and demanded the dismissal of Station Manager Jorgoh Barrie, whom they accused of inciting ethnic hatred within the Koinadugu community. No official charges were brought against Barrie, and the station resumed operations the following day.

- In late June, the editor of *The Standard Times*, Philip Neville, was arrested and held in the capital, Freetown, for five days on libel charges. Authorities dropped the charges after the paper retracted a June 27 article that claimed the government did not publicly disclose gifts from Libyan leader Col. Muammar Qaddafi.

- Postelection violence erupted in September as youth supporters of the victorious All People's Congress (APC) party attacked the house of Radio Gbaft journalist Hassan Wai Koroma, according to the director of community radio stations, David Tam-Baryoh. Wai spent one night in protective police custody. APC supporters had accused him of bias in covering a relative who unsuccessfully sought office.

SOUTH AFRICA

- In March, veteran radio presenter John Perlman resigned from the South African Broadcasting Corporation (SABC) in the midst of a high-profile dispute over the public broadcaster's editorial integrity. Perlman did not comment on his departure, but the move was linked to his on-air assertion that outspoken commentators were being muzzled, according to media reports. An internal SABC investigation later confirmed that critical commentators were being hushed.

- Exiled Zimbabwean editor Abel Mutsakani survived a wound from a bullet that lodged near his heart during a July attack by unidentified gunmen near his home in Johannesburg. It was not clear whether the attack was work-related. Mutsakani was editor of the South Africa-based Zimbabwean news Web site *ZimOnline*.

TOGO

- In January, criticism of Rock Gnassingbé, former head of the Togolese soccer association, led authorities to pull Lomé-based Radio Victoire off the air for two weeks. Authorities indefinitely banned from the airwaves French television journalist Jacques Roux, a station contributor, who had criticized Gnassingbé's financial management of the association.

- In March, the government media regulatory body, the High Authority for Audiovisual Communication (HAAC), banned from broadcast the veteran journalist and media activist Daniel Lawson-Drackey. The move was linked to an opinion piece aired on privately owned Nana FM that addressed corruption allegations against Public Administration Minister Arthème Ahoomey-Zunu.

- In June, the HAAC suspended three independent weekly newspapers, citing "violations to journalist ethics." *Le Courrier de La République* was suspended for four months on a complaint filed by an opposition party member about a story alleging corruption; *La Trompette*, for three months on a complaint lodged by a group of University of Lomé academics about a story critical of the faculty; and *Le Perroquet*, for two months on an allegation that it accepted payment for a story about an immigration application.

The editor of *Le Perroquet* denied the charge. The HAAC appeared to have acted beyond its authority. Togo's Press and Communication Code states a publication can be suspended only by court order.

UGANDA

- The state-run Uganda Broadcasting Council removed key equipment used by the independent station NTV Uganda from the state-owned national transmitter in the capital, Kampala, in late January. Authorities cited safety risks associated with the weight of NTV's equipment. The station returned to the air in April.

- In August, the Uganda Broadcasting Council suspended Capital FM presenter Gaetano Kaggwa and producer George Manyali for one week for alleged "unacceptable language" during a debate with a lesbian activist on their morning talk show.

- In October, two assailants, later identified by police as having links to the queen mother of Uganda's western kingdom of Tooro, poured acid over the transmitter of Life FM in the western town of Fort Portal. The attack, which forced the station off the air for five days, was linked to a weekly late-night talk program featuring a panel of local civic leaders who criticized government services in the area. The program had drawn public complaints from President Yoweri Museveni, according to news reports and local journalists.

ANDRES
D 1781-1

MIGUEL OTERO SILVA

1908 - 1985

POLICIA

Preaching Without a Choir

The United States has lost regional influence on press freedom and human rights issues. And that has made for a more dangerous environment for journalists throughout Latin America.

by Carlos Lauría

PHOTOS

Section break: AFP/Juan Barreto — *A police officer in Caracas rushes to a June demonstration protesting the Venezuelan government's shutdown of RCTV. Analysis (next): AFP/ Yuri Cortez — U.S. Secretary of State Condoleezza Rice spoke up for Venezuela's RCTV but found few supporters when the Organization of American States convened in June.*

AMERICAS

PREACHING
WITHOUT A CHOIR

by Carlos Lauría

· ·

AT JUNE'S ANNUAL ASSEMBLY OF THE ORGANIZATION OF AMERICAN
States (OAS) in Panama, U.S. Secretary of State Condoleezza Rice
urged foreign ministers to send the group's secretary-general, José Miguel In-
sulza, to investigate Venezuelan President Hugo Chávez Frías' decision to pull
the plug on the country's oldest private television station, RCTV.

The proposal prompted a strong reaction from the Venezuelan government. Foreign Minister Nicolás Maduro said the OAS should investigate U.S.
rights violations before looking into the situation with RCTV. "If the OAS is
going to name a commission, it first must go to the prisons of Guantánamo ...
or the Mexican border, if it really wants to review human rights and how they
hunt down [migrants]," news reports quoted Maduro as saying.

The dispute forced the countries attending the OAS assembly to take
positions—and the United States was clearly on the losing side. Rice's proposal drew no supporters. While Bolivian, Nicaraguan, and Ecuadoran officials praised Chávez's decision, most countries simply cited Venezuela's
sovereignty and its right to regulate its own airwaves.

"Failure by most Latin American countries to speak out against Venezuela's
censorship of its oldest nationwide television network marked a serious setback
for freedom of the press—and democracy—in the region," wrote Andrés Op-
penheimer, a CPJ board member, in his column for *The Miami Herald*.

As U.S. relations in the region deteriorate, so does its standing as a press freedom leader.

The erosion of U.S. moral authority in criticizing free press violations has made for a more dangerous environment for journalists in Latin America, especially during a period in which several democratic leaders are marginalizing the media. It is a far cry from a decade ago, when the United States spearheaded the creation of the OAS special rapporteur for freedom of expression. The Washington-based Inter-American Commission on Human Rights created the position after discussions with press groups in the United States and Latin America. The special rapporteur was unanimously endorsed by the heads of state attending the 1998 Summit of the Americas in Chile.

But as U.S. relations in the region have deteriorated, so has its standing as a leader in promoting human rights. Most pointedly, by holding two journalists for prolonged periods without formally charging them—one in Iraq and the other at Guantánamo Bay—the United States has damaged its reputation as a leader of democracy, many regional experts say.

In Venezuela, critics say, U.S. credibility was undermined by its support for partisan opposition groups, including one group that briefly deposed Chávez in 2002. "Backing these organizations is inconsistent with the aims of strengthening democratic institutions and fostering reconciliation in such a polarized society," said Michael Shifter, a vice president of Inter-American Dialogue, a U.S.-based policy analysis center, in a March report titled "Hugo Chávez: A Test for U.S. Policy."

Relations between the two nations have only worsened since then, rendering U.S. denunciations ineffective. Chávez has long contended that the Bush administration wants to isolate Venezuela and destabilize the country. Officials have accused Washington of mounting a propaganda campaign via several U.S. and Venezuelan media outlets, and by funding local nongovernmental organizations. Each time the United States criticized Chávez's press freedom record, Venezuela responded by saying the Bush administration lost its moral capacity to point out free press violations, citing detained journalists as evidence.

In particular, Venezuelan government officials were quick to cite the 2005 jailing of former *New York Times* reporter Judith Miller in defending their own decision to restrict news coverage in the name of preserving social order. Other cases in which U.S. journalists were compelled to reveal confidential sources prompted critics in the region to question whether the United States was backing away from the guarantees of free speech in the U.S. Constitution.

AMERICAS

"We have lost influence, and I think that it has to do with the attitude of the United States in its pursuit of foreign policy internationally," said Joy Olson, executive director of the Washington Office on Latin America, a liberal nongovernmental organization that promotes human rights. "An example is the lack of a multilateral approach to the solution of a number of problems. The U.S. is marginalizing itself in Latin America. The presence of long-term prisoners, held without trial in Guantánamo, has caused the U.S. a dramatic loss of credibility on human rights issues in the region."

In the case of Cuba, the U.S. government has little hope of influencing the press freedom environment because of its universal condemnation of Fidel Castro's government and its longstanding economic embargo, political analysts and journalists throughout the region say. These blanket stances divert attention from the island's specific problems, analysts say, such as the lack of free expression and the inhumane treatment of imprisoned journalists.

Many regional leaders avoid debating Cuba's press freedom record because they don't want to be perceived as being aligned with the United States. The annual U.S. resolution before the U.N. Human Rights Council condemning Cuba's human rights record has drawn few supporters. Leftist administrations have traditionally opposed the measure, and a number of other regional leaders abstain because they want to stay out of the Havana-Washington dispute.

The problem does not rest solely in Washington, one analyst noted. "If, by the sole purpose of not wanting to be seen [as] aligned with U.S. policy, Latin Americans are willing to keep their mouths closed and not criticize gross human rights violations, that's their issue," said Susan Kaufman Purcell, director of the Center for Hemispheric Policy at the University of Miami. "This is a case where Latin America in general is willing to accept and even honor a dictator who has been in power for decades."

But U.S. President George W. Bush's policy speeches on Cuba—along with photographs of high-ranking U.S. officials posing with dissidents and their families—usually backfire, analysts believe, by giving Castro and his brother, Raúl, ammunition to claim that their regime is a victim of U.S. aggression. Without any evidence, the Cuban government has insisted that independent domestic journalists are "mercenaries" at the service of the United States. With 24 journalists currently imprisoned, Cuba remains the world's second-leading jailer of journalists, behind only China.

The U.S. government has supported Cuban civil society, including independent journalists, through material assistance and training. The U.S. Agency for International Development has funded action programs to build solidarity with the island's human rights activists and to give voice to Cuba's independent press. Although the United States considers the programs to be transparent, analysts say that the Americans' strong support has played into the Cuban government's strategy to depict dissidents as spies in service of U.S. imperialism.

Even Cuba's independent journalists are wary of American support. "The U.S. stubbornness toward Cuba's foreign policy serves as an argument for many Latin American governments to justify their lack of solidarity with dissidents and independent journalists," prominent Cuban writer and poet Raúl Rivero Castañeda told CPJ. "The embargo policy has no sense and has played into the Cuban government's strategy," said Rivero, a former prisoner who now lives in exile in Spain.

> **Critics say the United States has turned a blind eye to press freedom violations in Colombia.**

So focused on Venezuela and Cuba is the United States, critics say, that it has ignored human rights and press freedom conditions in Colombia. Washington has stated that a central goal of U.S. aid to Colombia is the promotion and protection of human rights. But critics say that the Bush administration has given President Álvaro Uribe Vélez's administration a blank check to fight the war on drugs without creating a system that will require the Colombian government to account for human rights violations, including violence against the press.

While the United States asserts that all aid to Colombia is contingent on improving the country's human rights record, international human rights groups consider the plan seriously flawed by the rise of extrajudicial executions by the Colombian military. Human rights organizations also claim that investigations into cases of human rights abuses by the military have shown little progress.

"It's crucial that the United States, through its government and Congress, exert tighter scrutiny over human rights in Colombia," said prominent Colombian journalist Daniel Coronell, news director for the television network Canal Uno and columnist for the newsweekly *Semana*. Saying U.S. attention has been "sporadic," Coronell urged "a more rigorous and permanent" examination of human rights and press freedom.

Some analysts have also criticized the United States for backing controversial Colombian legislation that grants judicial concessions to members of illegal armed groups. The 2005 Law of Justice and Peace, which offers reduced penalties to right-wing paramilitary fighters in exchange for demobilization and voluntary confessions, was hailed by the Bush administration as an important step toward ending Colombia's civil conflict.

Purcell said U.S. policy toward Colombia should be considered through the lens of recent history. "There has been a significant improvement in the behavior of the armed forces and efforts to demobilize paramilitaries," she noted. "It hasn't been totally successful, but it must be looked at in the context of where Colombia was coming from: an unrelenting guerrilla war that had gone on for decades. Congress has imposed all kinds of restrictions and conditions that President Uribe has been trying to meet."

Still, human rights groups, both international and domestic, have criticized the legislation for failing to ensure a proper level of justice. The Justice and Peace hearings were extremely difficult for the local press to cover, CPJ research shows. Authorities systematically banned reporters from the proceedings, while former paramilitaries threatened journalists and sources outside. As a result, coverage of paramilitary confessions was weak throughout the country, particularly in areas where the paramilitary presence is still strong.

In Mexico and much of Central America, where the United States still exerts considerable influence, there is a perception that Washington has simply lost interest. Since September 11, 2001, as the United States has shifted much of its focus to terrorism and the Arab world, the result has been a lack of U.S. engagement in human rights and press freedom issues. An epidemic of extrajudicial killings in Mexico, including the slayings of reporters, has generated little vocal concern from the Bush administration.

Top administration officials have acknowledged that a shift in priorities has led to an erosion of support in some corners. "People across the world ... were unhappy with some of the decisions that our country has made," said Karen Hughes, former U.S. undersecretary for public diplomacy and public affairs, during a November interview on National Public Radio. Those decisions were made "in the interests of a more secure world," said Hughes, but she acknowledged it will take time to rebuild U.S. influence. "I wish we could snap our fingers and ... change impressions of our country tomorrow. But I don't think that's very realistic. I think that this is patient work, much as it was during the Cold War, and we are in a long ideological struggle."

· · · · · · · · · ·

Carlos Lauría is senior coordinator for CPJ's Americas program. He led CPJ missions to Venezuela, Bolivia, and Argentina in 2007.

••••••••••••••••••• **ARGENTINA** •••••••••••••••••••

Outgoing President Néstor Kirchner's administration dramatically increased its advertising budget, rewarding friendly media with government spots, punishing critics by withholding ads, and, in the process, influencing coverage of the presidential election won by Kirchner's wife, Sen. Cristina Fernández. The manipulation of state advertising undermined press freedom and constituted the single greatest danger to the Argentine press, CPJ found in a special report issued in October. A court ruling that struck down a provincial government's discriminatory advertising practices, however, offered hope that the system might be reformed.

Since Kirchner became president in 2003, the government's advertising budget had jumped more than 350 percent, according to data released in July by the nongovernmental organization Poder Ciudadano (Citizen Power). In the first six months of 2007, the federal government spent 164 million pesos (US$52 million) on official ads, a 63 percent increase over the same period in 2006, according to a report by the nonprofit Asociación por los Derechos Civiles (Association for Civil Rights), or ADC. Federal officials said inflation was a leading cause of the election-year jump, but local journalists noted that the increase far exceeded the inflation rate of 8 percent.

In the October special report "News for Sale," CPJ documented how Kirchner had institutionalized a system of rewards for supportive media and advertising embargoes for critics during his three terms as provincial governor in Santa Cruz and his one term as president. Because national and local governments are not bound by clear rules concerning the placement of advertising, CPJ found, the targeted influx of ad dollars had influenced press coverage.

A provincial media group in Santa Cruz led by Rudy Ulloa Igor, Kirchner's former chauffer and one of his closest advisers, received more than 3 million pesos (US$957,000) in official advertising in 2006, according to María O'Donnell, a well-known journalist and author of *Propaganda K: Una Maquinaria de Promoción con Dinero del Estado* (Propaganda K: A State-Financed Promotional Machinery). Annual ad revenue for the media conglomerate exceeded that of many news outlets with national reach. Records reviewed by CPJ showed the trend continuing in 2007. The Ulloa group regularly featured candidate Fernández in its coverage and consistently portrayed the senator in a positive light.

Elsewhere, news coverage of the presidential election was uneven. A report by Poder Ciudadano showed Fernández receiving about four hours of airtime on state-

• • • • • • • • • •

Country summaries in this chapter were reported and written by Senior Americas Program Coordinator **Carlos Lauría**, Research Associate **María Salazar**, Program Consultant **Marcelo Soares**, and Washington Representative **Frank Smyth**.

AMERICAS

owned Canal 7 in September while opposition candidates drew virtually no coverage during the same period. Argentine Cabinet Chief Alberto Fernández called the report biased.

Government ads publicize services such as hospital and school programs, and they inform citizens of their obligations and rights. In some cases, though, the ads simply highlight the routine activities of officeholders or state institutions. In provinces like Santa Cruz, home of the first couple, official advertising constitutes a large portion of media revenue, in most cases more than 50 percent, according to a 2005 report by the ADC and the New York-based Open Society Institute. With such dependence, managers were under great pressure to avoid critical stories that could hurt their companies financially.

National government advertising has been bound by two regulations that leave officials with broad discretion. Under a 1971 decree, all advertising transactions must be conducted through Télam, the official news agency. A subsequent decree, issued in 1996, makes the national government's press secretary responsible for setting priorities and assigning funds for ad campaigns. Neither decree seeks to ensure an objective, market-based approach to ad placement. Free press advocates have contended that manipulative government advertising violates Articles 14 and 32 of the Argentine Constitution, which bar censorship and guarantee press freedom, respectively; and Article 13 of the American Convention on Human Rights, which bars indirect means of media control.

The Supreme Court of Justice struck a blow to the state advertising system in September, when it ruled against the province of Neuquén. Provincial officials pulled ads from the daily *Río Negro* after the newspaper published a report in December 2002 on corruption in the local legislature. While the court found that "the media have no right to obtain a certain amount of state advertising," it concluded that official advertising cannot be used as a tool to pressure the press. The ruling declared that the state "cannot manipulate official advertising, distributing it or withdrawing it with discriminatory criteria." The government of Neuquén was ordered to present a plan for distribution of official advertising that would follow the decision's guidelines.

"This is a landmark decision in Latin America that protects free press," said Eduardo Bertoni, former special rapporteur for freedom of expression for the Organization of American States. "It is the first time that a supreme court in Latin America found that the media has legal protection against arbitrary allocation of public advertising."

In another closely watched case, the nation's largest magazine publisher, Editorial Perfil, filed suit in July 2006 alleging discrimination in government advertising in retaliation for the group's critical reporting. The case was pending in late year. Roberto Saba, ADC's executive director, said he was optimistic given the *Río Negro* ruling. The most important result, he said, would be clear and transparent legislation that would "limit governments' discretionary authority when allocating official advertising."

The debate prompted Congress to consider several bills aimed at ensuring more objective distribution of official advertising. ADC and Poder Ciudadano have urged that the reforms include moratoriums on state advertising in periods just prior to elections.

Fernández took office in December after handily winning the October 28 presidential balloting. The 54-year-old senator took 45 percent of the vote, nearly double that of her nearest rival and enough to be declared the winner without a runoff. During Kirchner's presidency, the first couple rarely had direct contact with the national news media, saying they would rather speak directly to the people. Kirchner, in fact, never held a formal press conference during his four-year term. Administration officials who felt targeted by critical journalists would block access to official sources and events.

Several journalists told CPJ they believed Fernández would be more open with the press, but they also noted that she has called some news media the opposition. In postelection interviews, Fernández urged the media to act "with responsibility" and examine their own mistakes.

• • • • • • • • • • • • • • • • • •   BOLIVIA   •

Increasing hostility between the government of President Evo Morales and the private media reflected a year of overall tension between Bolivia's indigenous majority and the country's conservative, European-descended opposition. Amid heated debate in December, a constituent assembly approved a proposal for a new constitution that grants more power to the country's indigenous population. Journalists expressed concern about vaguely worded constitutional provisions that could hinder the media in South America's poorest country.

The first-term socialist president repeatedly accused the press, much of it controlled by the conservative elite, of trying to discredit his administration. Morales' aggressive rhetoric—he once called the news media his biggest enemy—was not matched by official persecution of the press. But his constant barrage of criticism created growing difficulties for reporters.

Pro-government supporters have attacked and harassed journalists working for the private press, said Renán Estenssoro, president of the press group Asociación de Periodistas de la Paz, which documented more than a dozen cases of violent attacks since Morales took office in January 2006. After the governor of the central province of Cochabamba announced in January 2007 that he would seek greater political autonomy, at least 11 journalists were harassed by Morales' supporters who had taken to the streets to demand the governor's resignation.

The media faced harassment by antigovernment militants as well. In April, reporter Mario Fernández of state-owned Channel 7 and Radio Patria Nueva was assaulted by union leaders who opposed Morales in the southern city of Tarija, according to the regional press freedom group Instituto Prensa y Sociedad.

The increasing antagonism between Morales and the press exacerbated historic ethnic differences between the capital city of La Paz and Santa Cruz de la Sierra, the opposition stronghold and base of the media and business elite. The rifts became more evident as the constituent assembly debated a new constitution intended to empower the country's long-marginalized indigenous majority. Controversial issues such as regional autonomy, relocation of the capital to the city of Sucre, indefinite presidential re-election, and land reform led to a string of protests. At least five journalists were beaten by Sucre police while covering protests against the new charter in late November. Four people were killed and hundreds injured in the demonstrations.

The new constitution was scheduled to go before voters for approval in a 2008 referendum. Fundamental rights, including freedom of the press, are at the heart of the constitutional debate. Article 107 of the new constitution said that information and opinions expressed through the media must respect the principles of "veracity and responsibility." Journalists and press groups expressed concern about the ambiguity of such terms. They also worried that Article 108—which says the state would support creation of community media—would allow the government to simply amplify its official voice. The provision says nothing about ensuring media plurality and diversity. The same article bars companies from establishing media "monopolies" without defining the term. Some publishers worried that the measure would affect free enterprise.

The escalating confrontation between the private media and the government prompted CPJ to conduct a mission in June to examine press freedom conditions. The CPJ delegation, which included board member Josh Friedman and Americas Senior Program Coordinator Carlos Lauría, met with Morales, Vice President Álvaro García Linera, senior government officials, journalists, editors, media executives, and human rights activists in the capital and in Santa Cruz.

In "Bolivia's Historic Moment," a special report released in September, CPJ concluded that increasing ethnic and class tensions in Bolivian society had fueled resentment between government and media. CPJ called on Morales to exercise greater restraint in his criticism of the news media and to ensure that constitutional reforms do not restrict freedom of the press.

Morales' intolerance toward press criticism resembled the stance of Venezuelan President Hugo Chávez Frías, whose hostility toward the media had become routine. In March, the Venezuelan leader went so far as to bash the Bolivian press, calling it "oligarchic" and "unpatriotic."

Chávez expanded his influence in Bolivia by using funds from his country's oil profits to finance Bolivian state media projects. With a 15 million boliviano (US$2 million) investment from the Venezuelan government, Bolivia launched a network of community radio stations called Radios de los Pueblos Originarios de Bolivia. More than two dozen of these stations were broadcasting to rural and indigenous communities throughout the country in late year. Though the government declared the network did not carry official propaganda, reporters said the stations were specifically designed to give the administration a greater voice.

Like Chávez's Venezuelan regime, the Morales administration had a contentious relationship with the U.S. government. In late August, Juan Ramón Quintana, Morales' top aide, alleged that the United States was paying Bolivian journalists and columnists to create conflict and undermine democracy. Without providing names, Quintana said funds from the U.S. Agency for International Development were used to influence media coverage.

On the domestic front, Morales made clear that media owners were the principal enemy of his administration. The government complained that private media, especially Santa Cruz-based television stations Unitel and Radio Uno, skewed coverage in favor of business or other special interests. As a result, Morales asked his cabinet to hire communications advisers to monitor television and radio news programs to ensure that the official voice was being presented, presidential aide Víctor Orduna told CPJ.

Journalists and press groups acknowledged that politicization of the media had made the press vulnerable to official criticism. "Television in Santa Cruz is sensationalist: News shows frequently use headlines that exaggerate, change, and distort reality," said Carlos Valverde, a prominent radio host in Santa Cruz. Unitel argued that it has always treated authorities the same way. "Our duty is to criticize and report on official wrongdoing," said Unitel News Director José Pomacusi.

Yet many journalists said the polarized environment hindered news gathering and hurt the quality of reporting, sparking a debate within the profession on whether self-regulation could neutralize the excesses of both government and media. Raúl Peñaranda, former editor of the weekly *La Epoca*, said that with so many news outlets openly supporting either the government or the opposition, only a few outlets were considered neutral spaces for debate.

· · · · · · · · · · · · · · · · · · · **BRAZIL** ·

With 15 journalists killed for their work in as many years, Brazil is one of the region's deadliest countries for the press, but court-imposed censorship and official antagonism have also emerged as major issues for the news media. Time and again, local courts issued rulings that barred journalists from reporting on malfeasance, while high-ranking officials routinely assailed the media for their coverage.

"It has become fashionable for politicians and officials to blame the press when caught in irregularities," said prominent reporter Marcelo Beraba, president of the Associação Brasileira de Jornalismo Investigativo. "Instead of responding to the accusations, [politicians] prefer to present themselves as victims of the media."

Journalists in the country's vast interior, where police and government institutions are weak, continued to be targets of violence while reporting on organized crime and corruption. Two reporters were shot; one died and the other quit the profession in fear of further reprisals. In May, unidentified individuals gunned down Luiz Carlos Barbon Filho in the small city of Porto Ferreira, 140 miles (230 kilometers) from São Paulo. The provincial journalist, who had gained national recognition for his reporting on a child abuse case that involved local politicians, was blunt in his criticism of authorities. CPJ is investigating to determine whether the slaying was related to Barbon Filho's work. Several people, police officers among them, were questioned, but no arrests were reported by late year.

Although journalists who work in large urban centers such as Brasília, São Paulo, and Rio de Janeiro enjoy greater security than their colleagues in the interior, they are not immune to violence when reporting on crime and corruption. In September, *Correio Braziliense* reporter Amaury Ribeiro Jr. was shot in the abdomen while investigating a story on organized crime. Ribeiro was investigating possible links between drug trafficking, sexual exploitation of minors, and the killings of teenagers when the attack occurred on the outskirts of Brasília, Brazil's capital. Four men were arrested shortly after the attack. Although police called the shooting an attempted robbery, Ribeiro told CPJ he was targeted for his reporting. He later stopped working as a journalist.

While most crimes against the press have gone unpunished, Brazilian authorities made headway by convicting the mastermind of the 2004 slaying of Samuel Romã, a host and owner of Radio Conquista FM, based in the Paraguayan town of Capitán Bado, just across the Brazilian border from Coronel Sapucaia in the southwestern state of Mato Grosso do Sul. Judge César de Souza sentenced Eurico Mariano, former mayor of Coronel Sapucaia, to 17 years and nine months in prison for hiring the gunmen who shot Romã. The judge concluded that the former mayor ordered Romã's murder to silence his commentary.

Relations between the media and the government of President Luiz Inácio Lula da Silva, known popularly as Lula, became increasingly hostile. Government supporters routinely described the press as "an opposition political party." The antagonism intensified following news coverage of a series of political scandals involving administration officials. On July 31, the ruling Workers Party issued a resolution encouraging its members to oppose "attacks from the right and its allies in the media."

The national newsweekly *Veja* found itself targeted after reporting in May that the president of the Senate, Renan Calheiros, a key Lula ally, had allegedly accepted bribes from a leading construction company. Calheiros denied the allegations and said *Veja* was seeking to force him out of Congress. Brazilian senators rejected in September an ethics committee recommendation calling for Calheiros to be removed from office, although the senator later resigned his leadership position. Calheiros continued to deny corruption allegations against him.

Members of Congress wanted *Veja* investigated, too. Congressman Wladimir Costa, a fellow member of Calheiros' Brazilian Democratic Movement Party, called for an inquiry into commercial links between the Madrid-based telecommunications giant Telefónica and Grupo Abril, *Veja's* publisher. According to his proposal, the inquiry would ensure that the relationship did not harm the free flow of information. Local journalists called the investigation reprisal for *Veja's* reporting on the Calheiros case and official corruption.

Politicians, businessmen, and government officials accused of corruption or incompetence routinely sought court orders to bar news coverage. Local courts were typically sympathetic to such requests, granting injunctions that effectively censored news coverage. The local rulings were quashed on appeal in most cases, but they had the effect of restricting coverage when it was most needed, CPJ found.

"Our judicial system is deeply intrusive and allows censorship—which the constitution does not admit," said lawyer Samuel McDowell de Figueiredo, an expert on media issues. Local judges tended to invoke provisions of the Brazilian Civil Code, which provides strong privacy protection at odds with broader constitutional guarantees of free expression.

In June, a judge in the northeastern state of Bahia banned the Metropóle media group, which includes a magazine, a radio station, and a Web site, from even mentioning the name of João Henrique Carneiro, mayor of the state capital of Salvador. The judge ordered the seizure of 30,000 copies of the magazine *Metropóle*, which criticized local government services and featured a cartoon of the mayor on the cover. In another contentious decision, a judge in the state of São Paulo banned *Folha de Vinhedo*, a weekly in the city of Vinhedo, from publishing an article in which a former official accused local authorities and businesspeople of corruption. The judge ruled that the article would damage the credibility of Vinhedo authorities and ordered "preventive censorship" of two June editions of the weekly.

According to research cited by the magazine *Consultor Jurídico*, which focuses on media legal issues, the range of awards in moral damage suits against the press had quadrupled in four years. The magazine found that compensation increased from an average of 18,200 reals (US$10,400) in 2003 to 73,000 reals (US$41,800) in 2007.

In October, Lula launched a state-owned media group called Empresa Brasil de Comunicación that will run the government-backed broadcaster TV Brasil. Administration officials said the new state-owned channel would be autonomous and would be modeled after European broadcasters such as the BBC. With an initial investment of 200 million reals (US$115 million), the government said TV Brasil would focus on culture, education, and science.

The political opposition and some media outlets criticized the initiative, arguing that TV Brasil had been inspired by Venezuelan President Hugo Chávez Frías' extensive and highly controlled state media system. The influential daily *O Estado de São Paulo* wrote that Lula has created "a system to promote the government's interests."

· · · · · · · · · · · · · · · · · · **COLOMBIA** ·

The national press played a crucial role in exposing illegal paramilitary activities and links between paramilitary leaders and leading politicians. Provincial journalists, working in areas where paramilitaries and other illegal armed groups were prevalent, faced many challenges in trying to report this and other sensitive stories. Paramilitary fighters were behind the majority of documented press freedom violations, CPJ research showed.

The administration of President Álvaro Uribe Vélez was shaken by the so-called "para-politics" scandal, which exposed potential links between far-right paramilitary groups and officials close to the president. The scandal broke in late 2006, after the weekly newsmagazine *Semana* published a series of investigative pieces that forced Colombian authorities to examine the alleged associations. By September 2007, the attorney general and the Supreme Court had investigated 113 government officials and politicians, ordering the detention of more than 50, according to press reports. As the case gained momentum, the Colombian government came under new scrutiny from key foreign allies. With Democrats controlling the U.S. Congress, a free trade agreement with Colombia was put on hold over human rights concerns.

In May, after *Semana* revealed that intercepted telephone conversations showed right-wing paramilitary leaders engaged in criminal activity while in maximum-security prisons, the Colombian government confirmed that members of the police intelligence service had illegally taped the calls and leaked their contents. The government also explained that police had recorded the telephone conversations of people not under investigation, "including government officials, members of the opposition, and journalists," for at least two years. Julio Sánchez Cristo, a veteran radio commentator in Bogotá, was among the journalists whose phones were tapped. CPJ called on authorities to fully investigate illegal electronic surveillance.

Reporters and editors from regions most affected by the para-politics scandal acknowledged that it was extremely difficult to conduct independent investigations. More than a dozen journalists told CPJ that they censored themselves because reporting fully on paramilitary activities could prompt retribution. In Montería and Sincelejo, two northwestern cities where high-ranking officials were jailed because of their paramilitary ties, reporters who investigated received death threats and were accused of being members of leftist guerrilla groups. CPJ research has found that such public claims are often followed by acts of violence. As a result, provincial reporters said they often leaked scoops to their colleagues in Bogotá. Many provincial outlets ran stories on paramilitary activities only after they had been published in the Bogotá-based national media.

Regional authorities also clamped down on the media. Judges in the port city of Barranquilla and on the island of San Andrés issued gag orders preventing local media from reporting on corruption cases. CPJ documented two cases of regional reporters who were beaten and threatened for reporting on police operations in the country's provinces.

The few provincial journalists who dared to report on corruption were also threatened. Geovanny Álvarez, co-director and host of the daily news program "La Verdad" (The Truth) on community radio station La Nueva in the northern city of Sabanalarga, was forced to leave Colombia in late October. Álvarez, who received several anonymous death threats following his reporting on local government corruption, was warned by local police of a possible attempt on his life.

The Revolutionary Armed Forces of Colombia (known by its Spanish acronym, FARC), the most prominent leftist guerrilla movement, also harassed the press, mainly in Colombia's interior, according to the local press freedom group Fundación Para la Libertad de Prensa. Overall in 2007, harassment by leftist guerrillas was less frequent and extensive than that committed by paramilitaries. But some cases involving leftist forces stand out.

CPJ research found that two Colombian reporters were forced to flee their homes following threats from FARC members. In May, Rodrigo Callejas, host of the daily news program "Debate 5" on the local radio station Fresno Estéreo, left his home in the province of Tolima after receiving two telephone calls from an alleged guerrilla commander who warned the journalist to "stop messing with his people" if he didn't want to die. In March, Darío Arizmendi, the Bogotá-based news director for the morning program "6 a.m. Hoy por Hoy" on national Caracol Radio, fled Colombia after hearing of an alleged FARC plot to kill him. FARC members also sent threatening pamphlets to radio stations in Arauca province, warning each that they would become a "military target" if they reported on issues involving public order, local press reports said.

Although journalists in large urban centers were able to work more freely than their colleagues in the provinces, they also faced pressure and intimidation. Three well-known journalists in Bogotá were threatened and forced to flee. Just days after Arizmendi was forced to leave the city, an anonymous e-mail message was sent to

AMERICAS

the offices of the Miami-based daily *El Nuevo Herald* warning that there was an order to kill Gonzalo Guillén, the paper's correspondent in Bogotá, as part of a plan organized by a paramilitary group and members of the local police. After President Uribe, during an October interview on Caracol Radio, accused Guillén of "being a person who has persisted in trying to harm me," the journalist received a second round of death threats that caused him to flee the country.

Hollman Morris, producer of the weekly investigative program "Contravía" for the television network Canal Uno, left Colombia for a month in the fall. Morris, well known for his investigative reporting on the country's civil conflict, had received an e-mail message from a group calling itself the Frente Patriótico Colombiano (Colombian Patriotic Front) stating that he had won a raffle for a coffin.

In June, journalist Daniel Coronell returned to Colombia after two years in exile. Coronell, who directs a news program on Canal Uno and writes a column for *Semana*, had left Colombia in 2005 after receiving two funeral wreaths with cards inviting him to his burial. Coronell had also received e-mail messages threatening the life of his young daughter that were sent from the computer of former Congressman Carlos Náder Simmonds, a close friend of Uribe. Náder later admitted sending one e-mail but claimed it was misinterpreted. The former congressman was not charged, and an investigation by the attorney general's office appeared to be stalled.

On October 9, following publication of a column by Coronell on the Guillén case, the president confronted the journalist on national radio station La FM. Uribe and Coronell engaged in an hour-long discussion on the air, during which the president called Coronell a coward, liar, swine, and professional slanderer. Just hours after the confrontation, Canal Uno received an anonymous threat by e-mail. "We warned you that the next time that you mess with the boss you would dig your own grave," the message read. "All those who attack our president will sign their death sentence." CPJ sent a letter to Uribe on October 11 urging him to publicly retract his comments, to respect dissent in the media, and to abstain from publicly attacking journalists who present critical views.

One journalist was slain in 2007, although the circumstances were unclear. Javier Darío Arroyave, news director for radio station Ondas del Valle, was fatally stabbed in September in Cartago, a city in Valle del Cauca province. Colombia is the world's fourth-deadliest country for the press over the past 15 years, CPJ research shows, although the number of murders has tapered off in the last four years. The government said its press protection program—which offers armored cars, bulletproof vests, and bodyguards to threatened journalists—led to the decline. But CPJ research shows the decline is also related to widespread self-censorship in the news media. Many journalists, especially in the provinces, do not undertake in-depth reporting on drug trafficking, paramilitary activities, or corruption.

While impunity in attacks against the press continued to be the norm, progress was made in the cases of three murdered journalists. In February, a court in the northwestern city of Arauca convicted Andrés Darío Cervantes Montoya, also known as "El Chichi," in the 2002 murder of Efraín Varela Noriega, owner of local Radio Meridiano-70. Cervantes, a former member of the paramilitary group United Self-Defense Forces of Colombia, or AUC, had confessed to Varela's murder in 2006.

Two other former AUC fighters confessed under the controversial Law of Justice and Peace to the murders of provincial journalists. Promulgated by Uribe in 2005 as part of the peace process with paramilitary groups, the legislation granted generous judicial concessions, such as reduced prison sentences, to members of illegal armed groups in exchange for demobilization and full confessions to their crimes.

In May, Juan Francisco Prada Márquez, aka "Juancho Prada," confessed to the 2004 killing of Martín La Rotta Duarte, founder of the San Alberto-based radio station La Palma Estéreo. Pablo Emilio Quintero Dodino, known as "Bedoya," confessed in June to shooting José Emeterio Rivas, the controversial host of the morning program "Las Fuerzas Vivas" ("The Active Forces") on local Radio Calor Estéreo. The journalist was found murdered on a dirt road outside Barrancabermeja in 2003. Two former government officials were detained in September as a result of Quintero's confession.

Hundreds of other demobilized paramilitary fighters confessed to human rights violations in Justice and Peace hearings held in Bogotá, Medellín, and Barranquilla courthouses. But reporting on these statements was severely hindered, CPJ found in an October special report, "Justice, Peace, and Secrecy."

The statements were declared "restricted" by Resolution 3998 of the general prosecutor's office and Decree 315 of the Ministry of Interior and Justice. In practice, the Justice and Peace hearings were open only to the fighter, his lawyer, a special prosecutor, a judge, and a ministry representative. The crime victims, their families, and their lawyers viewed the proceedings via closed-circuit television elsewhere in the courthouse.

Because of the restrictions, reporters had to camp outside the courthouses and rely on secondhand sources. Sometimes, reporters said, they could persuade prosecutors to give short on-the-record briefings. And sometimes, former paramilitaries disseminated informal statements that claimed to describe the courtroom testimony. In most instances, journalists attempted to interview the victims or their representatives following the hearing.

While trying to conduct interviews outside the courthouses, reporters were harassed by paramilitary supporters, who occasionally used intimidation to dissuade victims' families from talking to the press. Journalists in Medellín said demobilized

AMERICAS

paramilitaries had taken photographs of them as they were reporting. And in at least one case, a television reporter claimed a paramilitary fighter came to her office and threatened her directly.

In early August, the Colombian media were shaken by the announcement that a Spanish media group, Planeta, had acquired a majority stake in the country's most influential newspaper, the daily *El Tiempo*. The paper had been one of the few national media outlets not yet owned by foreign investors. According to the agreement, Planeta purchased a 55 percent stake in the company Casa Editorial El Tiempo, a media conglomerate that, in addition to the newspaper, includes a publishing house, a television station, and online media. Planeta's president, José Manuel Lara Bosch, said that the paper would maintain its independence, and that the editorial line would be directed by Colombian staff. While Planeta didn't disclose the cost of the acquisition, press reports said that the group paid close to US$180 million. *El Tiempo* had been the property of the politically influential Santos family since its founding in 1911. Francisco Santos Calderón, Colombian vice president, was once editor of the daily.

· **CUBA** · · · · · · · · · · · · · · · · · · ·

July 31 marked a year without Fidel Castro, whose health remained a "state secret" even though it was the biggest story of the year. Cuba continued to prove itself one of the worst reporting environments in the world as three foreign journalists were expelled from the island and 24 Cuban reporters languished in prison.

Castro, who relinquished power to his younger brother, Raúl, following emergency surgery in July 2006, made no public appearances. His byline, however, was ubiquitous. During the first six months of 2007, dozens of opinion articles appeared under Fidel Castro's name in the Havana dailies *Granma* and *Juventud Rebelde*. His general and often rambling remarks focused on international and historical issues.

The government left intact its 2006 declaration that Castro's health was a state secret. The Cuban media—completely controlled by the Communist Party under the Cuban constitution—barely referred to the condition of the 81-year-old leader. Instead, Cubans learned of it primarily through accounts from foreign leaders such as Venezuelan President Hugo Chávez Frías and Bolivian President Evo Morales. (Independent journalists, filing for overseas Web sites, produced a small number of articles on Castro's health without consequences.)

In April, the sole outlet for critical commentary and analysis within Cuba changed its focus. Citing a lack of resources, the Catholic Church in the western city of Pinar del Río initially announced in April that it would no longer publish the weekly *Vitral*, according to *The Miami Herald*. Instead, however, the weekly continued to publish with a new staff and a different editorial stance that replaced social criticism with coverage of church events. "The end of *Vitral*'s open viewpoint was the hardest blow to the independent press this year," said Oscar Espinosa Chepe, a freelance journalist and paroled political prisoner.

Cubans had limited access to news sources other than the official media, although some listened to shortwave broadcasts of U.S.-based Radio Martí and European radio stations. State control of Internet access remained tight. The general population could log on to the Internet from hotels or government-controlled Internet cafés by means of voucher cards that were expensive and often difficult to find, reporters told CPJ.

Many Web sites were simply not accessible. "Cubans can't visit sites that discuss the dissident movement or Cuban democracy—we can't even visit the CPJ site," said Elizardo Sánchez Santa Cruz, president of the Cuban Commission on Human Rights and National Reconciliation in Havana. Nonetheless, like most commodities in Cuba, Internet access was available on the black market for a high price, independent journalist Guillermo Fariñas said. Cubans could purchase monthly passwords for more than 40 pesos (US$40) that allowed them access to some parts of the Web, he said.

Human rights advocates and independent journalists could also access the Internet at foreign embassies in Havana, said Sánchez Santa Cruz. Overall, the independent Cuban press made significant use of foreign embassy facilities, CPJ research found. Reporters said embassy officials allowed them to read foreign papers and use printers and copiers. Some independent news agencies used embassy equipment to print leaflets with news and commentary, which were distributed among members of the dissident movement, several reporters told CPJ. These rare and unofficial publications were referred to as "clippings."

Independent reporters across the island continued writing and sending news to Web sites abroad. Reporters filed stories via telephone, e-mail, and fax on topics such as the dissident movement, political repression, food shortages, and inadequate transportation. Many told CPJ that official harassment declined in 2007, with fewer detentions and direct threats. Yet a few symbolic cases reminded the world that Cuba remained one of the world's most repressed countries.

Authorities arrested Oscar Sánchez Madan, a freelance reporter, on April 13 at his home in the western province of Matanzas. Sánchez Madan was tried on "social dangerousness" and given the maximum sentence of four years in prison. Authorities had warned the reporter to stop working as an independent journalist after he published an exposé on local corruption, journalist Hugo Sánchez said.

On August 20, Armando Betancourt Reina, a reporter for the independent news agency Nueva Prensa Cubana, was released after 15 months in jail. He had been detained on May 23, 2006, while covering the eviction of poor families from their homes. The journalist was tried and sentenced on July 3, 2007, after being held at the local Cerámica Roja Prison without charge for more than a year. Shortly after his release, Betancourt Reina told the Miami-based group Directorio Democrático Cubano that he observed human rights violations in prison. The journalist said that while he was not attacked, he witnessed guards and hardened criminals beating political prisoners.

After Betancourt Reina's release, the number of imprisoned reporters and editors stood at 24, making Cuba the second-leading jailer of journalists worldwide. The health of 22 of those journalists, most of them jailed in a March 2003 crackdown, deteriorated during the year, CPJ research found. During a series of interviews in June, the families and friends of eight jailed journalists told CPJ that the prisoners' health was suffering amid poor conditions and insufficient health care. Pre-existing ailments worsened in prison, and serious new illnesses arose.

Cuban authorities also intimidated the families of jailed journalists. Laura Pollán, a human rights activist and wife of imprisoned journalist Héctor Maseda Gutiérrez, said police permanently posted an agent outside her house. Police officers searched, harassed, and threatened her visitors, Pollán told CPJ. Yamilé Llanes Labrada, whose husband, José Luis García Paneque, was also imprisoned, told CPJ in June that she and her four young children had been forced to flee Cuba four months earlier after being subjected to continuous harassment. The family moved to the United States.

Authorities continued to use political considerations in granting entry to foreign journalists. In February, the government informed Havana-based correspondents Gary Marx of the *Chicago Tribune*, Stephen Gibbs of the BBC, and César González-Calero of the Mexican daily *El Universal* that their press credentials would not be renewed. The decision, according to international press reports, was based on the government's perception that the journalists had filed negative stories.

• • • • • • • • • • • • • • • • • • ECUADOR • • • • • • • • • • • • • • • • • •

President Rafael Correa regularly bashed the news media after taking office in January, reflecting increasing tensions between his young socialist government and the powerful business groups that control the country's media. Correa immediately called for a new constitution that would expand the power of the executive branch, loosen term limits, and allow for greater government control over the media. In September, Correa's Movimiento Alianza País party took an important step toward those goals by winning an overwhelming majority of seats in the constituent assembly that will rewrite the 1998 constitution.

Ecuador has struggled with instability over the past decade, with eight presidents in as many years, making it the most volatile country in South America. Correa's aggressive move to remake the constitution was met with strong resistance. In March, 57 members of Congress were expelled while trying to block the preliminary referendum that sought permission to modify the constitution. In ordering the expulsion, the Supreme Electoral Tribunal found that the congressmen were trying to obstruct the electoral process. Their removal, which was enforced by police, eased the way for the drafting of a new constitution.

During a radio address in September, Correa called on the constituent assembly to create stronger laws to regulate the country's media, in order to "stop them from being able to manipulate information." The president argued that media outlets, many of them controlled by business conglomerates based in Guayaquil, could not inform Ecuadorans objectively, local news reports said. "The constituent assembly will have to think how the media could rectify erroneous information, as well as better regulate all media, especially when there is so much concentration in a few hands, with powerful interests," Correa said.

Local journalists expressed concern over the president's comments. In his weekly radio show, in interviews, and in press conferences, Correa was aggressive in lambasting journalists as "human misery," "liars," and "incompetents" who "publish trash." Meeting for the first time in November, the constituent assembly seemed eager to take bold action. The assembly suspended Congress until the new charter was drafted; no official press proposals were immediately announced.

Media coverage of the government was critical, although CPJ research found that it was not generally one-sided or biased. Some opinion pieces challenged the president in harsh terms. In a March 9 editorial headlined "Official Vandalism," the Quito-based daily *La Hora* said Correa intended to rule Ecuador "with turmoil, rocks, and sticks," and described the president's behavior as "shameful."

Correa did not take the criticism in stride. He filed a criminal defamation lawsuit against *La Hora* in May, accusing the paper's president, Francisco Vivanco Riofrío, of showing disrespect and causing "moral damage," according to the complaint reviewed by CPJ. The lawsuit was based on Article 230 of the country's penal code, which sets prison penalties of up to two years for "threats or libel that would offend the president." Correa said he would drop the complaint only if the daily's executive publicly apologized. *La Hora* declined.

The lawsuit against *La Hora* sparked controversy. Correa discussed the situation at length during his weekly radio address on May 19, saying that Ecuadorans enjoyed complete freedom of expression but more control was needed. "Freedom implies responsibility, but there's no liberty here. There's only lack of control," said Correa.

Neither free expression nor control was much on display during a discussion on that same program. When guest Emilio Palacio, editor of the Guayaquil-based daily *El Universo*, suggested Correa had shown intolerance to media criticism, the president demanded Palacio leave. "Journalists don't bother me. Mediocrity, incompetence, bad faith, and lies bother me—and there's a lot of that in the press," Correa said. Following the two-hour radio show, an irritated Congress passed a resolution demanding that Correa show respect for freedom of expression. The statement urged the president to "exercise tolerance and respect for divergent opinions."

Critics said that with his aggressive rhetoric against the media, Correa appeared to be emulating allies Hugo Chávez Frías of Venezuela and Evo Morales of Bolivia. In July, Correa announced that he would no longer hold press conferences or interviews (although he did take part in at least one later interview, with a Spanish outlet). All questions for the president must be submitted to his office in writing, he said.

Correa had praised Chávez's decision to pull veteran Venezuelan broadcaster RCTV off the air after accusing the station of conspiracy in a 2002 coup. He later told the Quito-based daily *Hoy* in June that he would cancel the broadcast license of any Ecuadoran television or radio station that conspired against his government. In September, the government announced that it was looking into possible "grave faults" committed by the national broadcaster Teleamazonas, known for its strong opposition views.

Correa is also following in the path of Chávez and Morales by launching a state-owned television channel that will reflect the government's official voice. With a US$5 million grant from the Venezuelan government, Canal Ecuador TV began broadcasting constituent assembly meetings in November.

· **HAITI** ·

Press conditions improved slightly during a year of relative political stability. A decline in gang violence in the capital, Port-au-Prince, allowed reporters to make a cautious return to the city's streets. And, with the strong support of President René Préval, an independent committee was created in August to monitor stalled investigations into a series of journalist murders this decade.

The committee was led by journalist Joseph Guyler Delva, president of the press freedom group S.O.S. Journalistes, and included eight Port-au-Prince reporters from different media outlets. A joint initiative between S.O.S. Journalistes and Préval, the committee was charged with identifying problems in the murder investigations and expediting solutions. Its members had access to official police and court documents in the murders of at least 10 Haitian journalists, Delva said. The committee was tasked with studying the case files, determining how and why the cases stalled, and issuing public reports with recommendations on how to speed the process.

In a meeting with a CPJ delegation in New York on September 26, Préval said political obstacles to justice had been removed. "Haitian politicians and investigators had not been interested in pursuing justice in cases of murdered journalists because some of them were implicated in these crimes," Préval told CPJ. "But now the situation has changed; there is political will, and this will allow us to make progress."

CPJ called on the Haitian government to strengthen the investigations by providing police, judges, and prosecutors with sufficient resources to do their jobs. The long-delayed prosecution of the cases has been characterized by incompetence, corruption, and a lack of official resolve, according to CPJ's analysis.

The committee achieved some early results. On September 15, its members discovered a "missing" courthouse file relevant to the slaying of journalist Brignol Lindor and forwarded it to the investigators handling the case. Lindor, news director of the private Radio Echo 2000, was killed on December 3, 2001, by a machete-wielding mob in the coastal town of Petit-Goâve, 40 miles (64 kilometers) west of the capital. The missing file, which contained most of the investigation's initial findings, set the case in motion. In December, a court convicted two members of Domi Nan Bwa—a local political organization with ties to former president Jean Bertrand Aristide's Fanmi Lavalas party—and sentenced them to life imprisonment in the slaying. The court also issued arrest warrants for five other members.

Prosecutors obtained a conviction in another journalist murder. On August 30, a Port-au-Prince judge sentenced Alby Joseph and Chéry Beaubrun, members of the local Solino gang, to life in prison for the 2005 kidnapping and murder of Jacques Roche. The committee had lobbied for the case to go to trial, Delva told CPJ. Two other gang members were detained in September in connection with Roche's death, he said.

Roche, cultural editor of the Port-au-Prince daily Le Matin, was taken from his car on July 10, 2005. He was found dead four days later, his handcuffed body riddled with bullets and mutilated. According to The Associated Press, Roche's captors demanded US$250,000 in ransom. During their trial, Joseph and Beaubrun said they had been hired to watch Roche but killed him when they didn't receive the full ransom, according to Haitian press reports.

Delva's committee also examined the case of Jean-Léopold Dominique, owner and director of Radio Haïti-Inter and one of the country's most renowned journalists. Dominique was gunned down on April 3, 2000, outside the entrance to his Port-au-Prince station. The case has been politically controversial because of potential links

AMERICAS

to Fanmi Lavalas. In October, as the committee was probing the Dominique case, Delva received a series of threatening phone calls. The anonymous callers warned Delva that he should be careful, that they were tracking his movements, and that they were going to "get him," the journalist told CPJ. Delva fled the country for two weeks, returning after Préval offered him police protection, Haitian press reports said.

Although crime remained high, rampant gang violence and kidnappings tapered off in Port-au-Prince following a major effort by U.N. peacekeeping forces, according to international press reports. The U.N. Stabilization Mission in Haiti, with 7,500 troops on the ground, continued to assist the Haitian government in its attempt to curb gang violence.

Improvement in security conditions gave journalists in the capital more leeway to report without fear of retribution. News managers, who had relied mostly on secondhand information when covering dangerous areas, began sending reporters into the streets again. Richard Widmaier, director of Radio Métropole in Port-au-Prince, said he began allowing his station's reporters to go into high-risk neighborhoods on a limited basis—for example, to cover official press conferences.

In some Port-au-Prince neighborhoods and in the country's interior, gangs continued fighting U.N. troops and one another, according to the Haitian press. One local reporter was killed in relation to his work, CPJ found, while a second was murdered in unclear circumstances.

On January 19, unidentified gunmen killed freelance photographer Jean-Rémy Badio outside his home in Martissant, one of the capital's most dangerous slums. Gangs in Haiti have traditionally allowed only those journalists they deem friendly to report in areas under their control. Badio, a Martissant resident, often photographed gang confrontations in his neighborhood and sold the images to local dailies—a risky proposition, since gang members are averse to having their pictures taken. In a public statement, U.N. security forces said they suspected gang involvement in Badio's murder. By October, authorities had made little to no headway in the investigation, local journalists told CPJ.

In Gonaïves, a city 105 miles (170 kilometers) north of Port-au-Prince ravaged by gang violence, two unidentified men shot and killed radio journalist Alix Joseph in May as he stood outside his wife's house. Joseph was station manager at local Radio-Télé Provinciale, where he also hosted a popular cultural show and a weekly news program. CPJ is investigating to determine whether the slaying was related to his work.

· **MEXICO** ·

Mexican authorities failed again to vigorously pursue the perpetrators of violence against journalists, leaving reporters vulnerable to attacks and the news media resorting to self-censorship. Mexico is one of the most dangerous countries for the press, CPJ research shows, with 13 journalists slain in direct relation to their work and another 14 killed under unclear circumstances in the last 15 years. Three journalists and three media workers were murdered in 2007, and three reporters went missing.

The vicious battle between the powerful Gulf and Sinaloa drug cartels, which had been particularly severe in the northern states since 2004, stretched to almost every Mexican state in 2007. With key shipment routes to the United States at stake, the war between well-financed criminal organizations raised violence to unprecedented levels. The toll was devastating: News reports said that at least 2,000 people were killed in the first 10 months of the year as a result of drug-related violence.

As the violence spread throughout Mexico, journalists covering drug trafficking and crime were increasingly targeted. Rodolfo Rincón Taracena, a reporter for the daily *Tabasco Hoy* in the southern Gulf state of Tabasco, went missing in January after he published an investigative article on local drug trafficking. In late May, the severed head of a local official, wrapped in newspaper, was left outside the daily's offices in an apparent attempt at intimidating reporters.

Danger extended to the central states of Michoacán and Guerrero, and to the southern states of Veracruz and Quintana Roo. In Michoacán, where the administration of President Felipe Calderón deployed thousands of troops to combat drug violence, at least 20 journalists were "picked up" and threatened by rogue police or criminal gangs in 2007, CPJ found in a November special report, "A New Front in Mexico."

The situation in Michoacán diverted attention from the conflict in southern Oaxaca. Although Gov. Ulises Ruiz Ortiz regained control of the state after violent unrest in 2006, journalists continued to be attacked. In October, the reporting staff of the daily *El Imparcial del Istmo* resigned a day after three of the paper's delivery workers were murdered while driving a truck marked with the paper's logo. On October 18, the Mexican army arrested a member of the Gulf cartel in the city of Salina Cruz for his alleged involvement in the crime.

The 2006 murder of U.S. documentary filmmaker Bradley Roland Will remained unpunished. Will was killed in Oaxaca during a street battle between anti-government protesters and armed civilians, many identified by witnesses as working for the local government. On the anniversary of Will's slaying, October 27, CPJ send a letter to Calderón urging him to ensure a rigorous investigation that examined witness accounts and forensic evidence, as well as photographs from the day of the shooting.

The alleged involvement of government agents in the Will slaying was the most egregious example of press attacks believed to be committed by police or military officers. CPJ documented several such cases in 2007. In August, four crime reporters were detained by troops while covering a routine military convoy in Monclova in the state of Coahuila near the U.S. border. One reporter told CPJ that he had been beaten and aggressively questioned by soldiers before being turned over to the state attorney general's office. The journalists, who were initially charged with possession of firearms and drug-related crimes, were exonerated by a federal judge a month later.

Hostility and fear had a disturbing effect on the media, as scores of reporters and many news outlets resorted to self-censorship out of fear of retaliation. In May, the Hermosillo-based daily *Cambio de Sonora* suspended publication after two bomb attacks and repeated threats within a one-month period. In the violent border city of Nuevo Laredo, reports on crime were often published without photographs, analysis, or the names of the criminals, journalists told CPJ. Sensitive topics such as drug trafficking, corruption, human rights abuses, and other problems went uncovered. Journalists expressed concern that the wave of violence was inhibiting citizens' ability to grasp the issues that affect their lives.

Impunity continued to be the norm. Although the Calderón administration pledged to protect journalists who work under the threat of violence, failings in Mexico's judicial system left the media open to attacks. The federal government recognized violence against the press as a national problem by creating a special prosecutor's office in early 2006 to investigate such crimes. But the office has produced no successful prosecutions, in part because of jurisdictional limitations. Murder and assault are state crimes, and the federal government has no automatic jurisdiction to intervene.

In an encouraging sign in September, the attorney general's office promoted legislation that would federalize crimes against the press. The measure would criminalize any attempt to harm, through violence or other means, the right of Mexicans to free expression—a fundamental right enshrined in Articles 6 and 7 of the Mexican Constitution. The bill was pending in late year. CPJ has vigorously advocated in favor of federal legislation giving Mexicans a better legal framework for the protection of free expression.

In a crucial step toward safeguarding journalists, Calderón signed legislation that effectively repealed criminal defamation, libel, and slander at the federal level. All three charges remained civil offenses, subject to monetary damages. The reform did not offer journalists complete protection from criminal defamation complaints, however, since many Mexican states continued to carry criminal libel laws, with penalties of up to four years in prison.

Pressure to repeal criminal defamation provisions had grown after prominent columnist and human rights activist Lydia Cacho was detained in December 2005 and accused of defaming Puebla-based businessman José Camel Nacif Borge. In her book *Los Demonios del Edén* (The Demons of Eden), published earlier that year,

Cacho alleged that a child prostitution ring operated in Cancún with the complicity of local police and politicians. She accused Nacif of having ties to an accused pedophile, an allegation the businessman denied.

In early 2006, the Mexican press exposed the contents of taped telephone conversations detailing a plot by Nacif and Mexican state officials, including Puebla Gov. Mario Marín, to imprison and assault Cacho. All defamation charges against Cacho were ultimately dismissed in January. The Supreme Court of Justice, which had undertaken a lengthy probe into possible violations of Cacho's human rights, decided in November that there was insufficient evidence to pursue criminal charges against the government officials.

·············· UNITED STATES ··············

Editor Chauncey Bailey was gunned down three blocks from his Oakland, Calif., office in August, becoming the first U.S. journalist killed for his work in six years. Bailey, editor-in-chief of the *Oakland Post* and four other weeklies focusing on the San Francisco Bay Area's African-American communities, was targeted after investigating the alleged criminal activities of a local business, Your Black Muslim Bakery. One suspect, bakery worker Devaughndre Broussard, was arrested. He reportedly confessed to killing Bailey with a sawed-off shotgun, although his lawyer said the statement was made under duress. Journalists across the country later formed an ad hoc group to investigate the crime, the first on-duty killing since the 2001 deaths of one journalist in the terrorist attack on New York's World Trade Center and another in a Florida anthrax attack.

Other journalists covering issues involving minority communities came under threat. *Miami Herald* columnist Leonard Pitts Jr. received dozens of threatening phone calls and hundreds of intimidating e-mails in June. After he wrote a column about race, crime, and perceived media bias, Pitts' home address and telephone number had been posted on a Web site featuring swastikas and photos of the Nazi Heinrich Himmler.

Police assaulted several reporters covering a May immigration rights rally in Los Angeles. Patricia Nazario of KPCC Radio, Carlos Botifoll of Telemundo, the Miami-based, Spanish-language television station, and Patricia Ballaz of KTTV-TV were struck with batons. Ballaz suffered a broken wrist. Another journalist, cameraman Carl Stein of KCAL-TV, said police threw him and his camera to the ground. The Los Angeles Press Club protested the attacks in a letter to Police Chief William J. Bratton. The Los Angeles Police Department later issued a report saying police acted improperly; investigations into the actions of individual officers were to be completed in 2008.

In New York, two Urdu-language editors and their publications were targeted. The publisher and editor of the *Urdu Times*, Khalil-ur-Rehman, was threatened on May 23 as he was leaving the newspaper's printing facility; the journalist said he recognized the man as a Pakistani-American with alleged criminal ties. The following day, two men threatened the editor-in-chief of the *Pakistan Post*, Mahammed A. Farooqi, on a Brooklyn street and, just five hours later, in front of the journalist's Long Island home. By then, at least 10,000 copies of each Urdu-language newspaper had been swept up from their distribution racks, the editors told CPJ. Many of the copies were later found illegally dumped. CPJ wrote a letter to New York Mayor Michael R. Bloomberg, urging police to thoroughly investigate the threats and wholesale destruction of the newspapers. Police immediately assigned an Urdu-speaking officer to investigate the case, and a Bloomberg spokesman said that "no one has a right to prevent other people from making their viewpoints known."

Other journalists faced challenges in the courts. Two *San Francisco Chronicle* reporters avoided going to jail in February after a confidential source came forward. Lance Williams and Mark Fainaru-Wada had faced up to 18 months in prison for refusing to name the person who provided them with secret grand jury testimony about alleged steroid use by baseball's home run king, Barry Bonds, and other top athletes. A defense lawyer named Troy Ellerman was later sentenced to two and half years in prison for leaking the transcripts, although the reporters did not confirm that he was the source. Bonds was indicted in November for allegedly lying in his grand jury testimony.

Freelance journalist Josh Wolf was released in April from a federal penitentiary in California after spending 226 days in jail, making him the longest-imprisoned journalist in U.S. history. The independent video blogger was incarcerated after refusing to turn over unedited footage and testify to a federal grand jury investigating vandalism to a police car during a July 2005 protest in San Francisco.

With these and other media subpoena cases in mind, Congressional lawmakers introduced shield legislation that would provide journalists some protection from revealing confidential sources in court. More than 50 media companies and press groups organized by the Newspaper Association of America supported a bill introduced by Sens. Arlen Specter and Charles Schumer, although many journalists said the measure included too many exceptions. Legislation was pending in late year.

U.S. authorities continued to imprison two foreign journalists. Associated Press photographer Bilal Hussein, a member of the AP photography team that won the Pulitzer Prize in 2005, was jailed in Iraq in April 2006 for "imperative reasons of security," according to military officials. The AP said its own investigation found no basis for the detention. In November, the U.S. military said it would refer the case to the Iraqi justice system for possible prosecution. The military cited alleged links between Hussein and Iraqi insurgents but disclosed no evidence to support the accusation.

Sami al-Haj, a Sudanese cameraman for Al-Jazeera, was said to be in deteriorating health as he completed his sixth year in custody. Al-Haj, the only known journalist imprisoned at the U.S. Naval Base in Guantánamo Bay, was first detained at the Pakistani-Afghan border in December 2001 while covering the U.S.-led fight to oust the Taliban. U.S. military officials made vague accusations that al-Haj worked as a financial courier for armed groups and assisted al-Qaeda and extremist figures. Al-Haj's attorneys said the accusations were baseless and that U.S. interrogators were instead focused on obtaining intelligence on Al-Jazeera. Al-Haj refused food for much of the year to protest his treatment; he was force-fed through a tube inserted through his nose.

In May, CPJ and the National Press Club sponsored a panel, moderated by columnist and CPJ board member Clarence Page, to draw attention to the Hussein and al-Haj cases. Numerous national and international news outlets reported on the cases throughout the year.

U.S.-based Internet companies sought to improve their images after the roles they played in helping China identify and, in some cases, imprison online journalists. Press freedom and human rights groups, along with investors, legal experts, and representatives of Yahoo, Microsoft, and Google, worked jointly on a voluntary code of conduct for technology companies that would safeguard free expression and privacy for Web users. No agreement was reached during the year.

The conduct of Internet corporations came under intense scrutiny after China arrested journalist Shi Tao for "leaking state secrets" in an e-mail in which he described an official propaganda directive. A Yahoo subsidiary helped Chinese authorities trace the source of the e-mail. Shi, a 2005 CPJ International Press Freedom Awardee, was convicted and sentenced to 10 years in jail. In November, a Congressional committee harshly criticized Yahoo Chief Executive Officer Jerry Yang and General Counsel Michael Callahan for the company's actions and its failure to disclose all it knew about the case in an earlier hearing on the Hill.

The beleaguered Federal Emergency Management Agency was widely derided in October after staging a "press conference" in which agency workers posed as reporters and asked Deputy Administrator Harvey E. Johnson Jr. a series of mild-mannered questions.

For reasons that were not fully explained, the agency had scheduled the conference on 15 minutes' notice to discuss its response to wildfires in California. With such short notice, no reporters were able to attend, and agency workers filled the breach. The event was carried live on cable news channels. Johnson later apologized "for this error in judgment." Two public relations officials left the administration shortly afterward.

•••••••••••••••••• **VENEZUELA** ••••••••••••••••••

The Venezuelan government's unprecedented decision not to renew the broadcast concession of the country's oldest private television station, RCTV, represented a major setback for free expression and democracy. The decision, aimed at silencing Venezuela's most critical media outlet, was part of President Hugo Chávez Frías' aggressive strategy to challenge the influence of the private press as he expanded the reach of state media. But as Chávez reached for further power in late year, he suffered his first major blow at the polls. Voters narrowly rejected a constitutional overhaul that would have allowed the government to censor the news media.

On May 27, after 53 years of continuous broadcasting, RCTV was forced off the air when the government refused to renew its broadcast concession. The president and top officials accused the station—known for its strident antigovernment views—of violating the constitution and the country's broadcast laws, and of collaborating with planners of a 2002 coup against Chávez. In late March, the Ministry of Communication and Information issued a 360-page document, *El Libro Blanco sobre RCTV* (The White Book on RCTV), to justify the decision. The document asserted that the government had full discretion on whether to renew broadcast concessions first granted to RCTV and other broadcasters for 20-year terms under a 1987 decree. Jesse Chacón, minister of telecommunications, said at a March press conference that the RCTV decision was not a sanction but simply the "natural and inexorable" result of the concession's expiration.

An April CPJ special report, "Static in Venezuela," concluded that the government had failed to conduct a transparent review of RCTV's concession renewal. The report, based on a three-month investigation, found that officials had acted arbitrarily and with political motivations in silencing the station. The government did not follow any discernible application process and provided RCTV no opportunity to respond to the allegations against it, according to CPJ's Carlos Lauría and Sauro González Rodríguez. The report was based on dozens of interviews conducted during a joint mission by CPJ and Instituto Prensa y Sociedad, a regional Peru-based press group.

RCTV filed several appeals to the Supreme Tribunal of Justice to no immediate avail. In May, CPJ wrote a letter to Chávez urging him to allow RCTV to continue broadcasting while its appeals were pending.

Sworn in for a second six-year term in January, Chávez pledged to move Venezuela toward socialism, interpreting his victory in the prior month's election as a mandate to accelerate his agenda. Days after he took office, he announced plans to nationalize companies in the telecommunications and electricity industries. The National Assembly—stacked with government supporters since the opposition boycotted the 2005 legislative elections—unanimously approved a law granting Chávez the power to legislate by decree in key areas for 18 months.

But voters turned back an effort to further strengthen presidential powers in a heated December 2 referendum. By a vote of 51 to 49 percent, Venezuelans rejected a package of constitutional changes that would have eliminated presidential term limits, scrapped central bank autonomy, redefined property rights, and restricted press freedom during states of emergency. The changes would have effectively revoked the 2001 Organic Law on States of Exception, which says that freedom of thought and access to information cannot be restricted even in emergencies. Press freedom advocates said the constitutional changes would have been a great setback.

As the government moved aggressively to silence critical media outlets, it continued to invest in state-owned media, budgeting 362 billion bolívares (US$169 million) for state media in the last two years. Since 2003, the government has financed the startup of ViVe TV, a cultural and educational television network with nationwide coverage; ANTV, which broadcasts National Assembly sessions; and Ávila TV, a regional channel run by the city of Caracas. In July 2005, it launched Telesur, a 24-hour television news channel that has grown into a pan-Latin American broadcaster with the governments of Argentina, Bolivia, Uruguay, and Cuba as minority stakeholders. In late 2006, Telesur acquired Caracas-based broadcast channel CMT in order to expand its domestic reach beyond cable and satellite subscribers. VTV, which had been neglected by previous administrations, received an infusion of technology that allowed the channel to improve the quality and reach of its signal.

In addition, the administration has created a large network of alternative and community media, including television and radio stations, newspapers, and Web sites basically intended to disseminate the official line and discredit critical journalists and media owners, according to CPJ research. It has also filled staff positions with activists and supporters as a means of manipulating content and guaranteeing favorable coverage. Government officials say they believe that, by giving voice to community media, they are ensuring pluralism and diversity.

RCTV's frequency was reassigned to a new public-access station called Televisora Venezolana Social (TVes), which began broadcasting just hours after RCTV went off the air. While the government said it would not dictate the station's editorial line, five of the seven members of the TVes board of directors— including its president—were appointed by Chávez. Analysts said the new station's programming showed a lack of pluralism and diversity. "It can't be called public service television, a station that has [had] an obvious political preference since its launch," wrote Andrés Cañizález, a researcher at Universidad Católica Andrés Bello in Caracas who has been critical of Chávez.

RCTV International, meanwhile, launched a paid-subscription service via cable and satellite on July 16. The station's new signal, carried locally by four cable operators and one satellite provider, offered most of the same programming as before, including news, comedy, and soap operas.

Authorities quickly moved in to say that RCTV must register with the National Telecommunications Commission and comply with the 2004 social responsibility law. The law compels national stations to broadcast a certain amount of state-produced programming and children's shows, and to carry live Chávez's *cadenas*—simultaneous radio and television broadcasts of the president's speeches. RCTV International argued that the station is similar to other international cable channels such as CNN, which are not regulated by the social responsibility law. A stay issued in early August by the Supreme Tribunal of Justice allowed RCTV International and dozens of regional stations to remain on cable temporarily while the government established clear rules as to which stations should be affected by the law.

With RCTV off the public airwaves, there were no national broadcasters left that were critical of the government. Venevisión, led by media mogul Gustavo Cisneros, had removed opinion and news shows that were highly critical of Chávez after Cisneros met with the Venezuelan president in June 2004. Shortly before cutting RCTV's signal, the government announced it was renewing for five years the broadcast concessions of other television stations whose licenses ended on May 27, including Venevisión and state-owned Venezolana de Televisión.

Only local broadcaster Globovisión, whose programs air in metropolitan Caracas and the northern state of Carabobo, remained critical in its coverage. Although the station's concession doesn't expire until 2015, Globovisión executives were nonetheless worried about government intimidation. The day RCTV went off the air, Minister of Communication and Information Willian Lara filed a complaint with the attorney general's office accusing Globovisión of inciting violence against Chávez after the station aired file footage of a 1981 assassination attempt against Pope John Paul II in Rome. Lara said that the broadcast was an incitement to assassinate Chávez, and he accused the network of bias against the administration. Globovisión's director, Alberto Federico Ravell, denied the accusations.

The use of *cadenas* to counter the private media's news coverage exemplified the government's effort to amplify its voice. Since Chávez first took office in 1999, Venezuelan television programming had been pre-empted for more than 1,500 *cadenas*, the equivalent of almost 1,000 broadcast hours, according to AGB Nielsen Media Research. Chávez's weekly radio and TV program, "Aló, Presidente," spanned more than 1,000 hours from its inception in 2000 to the end of 2007. The average duration of the program in 2007 was nearly six hours, AGB Nielsen found.

Telesur President Andrés Izarra put the government's media strategy plainly in a January 8 interview with the Caracas daily *El Nacional*. The administration's aim, Izarra said, is "communication and information hegemony."

BELIZE

- Evan Hyde, host of "Wake Up Belize" on the Belize City-based Krem Radio, found the windows of his Toyota Tacoma smashed and two homemade bombs left on the passenger's seat, the biweekly *Amandala* reported. Local police said someone attempted to light at least one of the explosive devices, according to press reports. Hyde told Channel 5 Belize that he believed the September 28 incident was a work-related reprisal.

- Rufus X, co-host of the political program "Kremandala Show" on local Krem TV and Radio, was passing through the gates surrounding his Belize City home at 10 p.m. on October 2 when an unidentified man beat him with an iron rod, *Amandala* reported. The journalist's arm was broken in two places. In an interview with Channel 5 Belize, he said he believed the attacks were retaliation for Krem's political views. Police were investigating.

CANADA

- At least two individuals attacked Jawaad Faizi, a columnist for the New York-based Urdu-language biweekly *Pakistan Post*, as he was driving to a colleague's home in Toronto on the evening of April 19. Faizi told local reporters that the assailants struck his car with cricket bats and smashed his windshield while screaming at him in Urdu and Punjabi to stop writing about the Muslim group Idara Minhaj-ul-Quran. Faizi had received repeated telephone threats prior to the attack, Muhammed Faruki, New York editor of the *Pakistan Post*, told CPJ.

DOMINICAN REPUBLIC

- On May 2, a court in the southern city of Azua sentenced Vladimir Pujols, leader of the drug trafficking gang Los Sayayines, to 30 years in prison for the 2004 murder of local journalist Juan Emilio Andújar Matos. The court also ordered Pujols to pay 1.3 million pesos (US$39,500) to radio reporter Jorge Luis Sención, who witnessed the attack and was shot during a later ambush. Pujols' lawyers told local reporters that he would appeal his conviction. The Dominican press reported that Ricardo Agramonte, identified as another gang member, was sentenced to five years in prison on a related conspiracy count.

- Erica Guzmán, correspondent in the eastern city of Samaná for the national daily *Hoy* and the national station Radio Popular, told CPJ that on the night of June 11, her daughter received two anonymous calls threatening the journalist and her family with death. According to Guzmán, the caller said the journalist talked too much. Guzmán told CPJ she believed the threats were linked to an article she had recently published on two local officials accused of corruption. Local authorities provided the correspondent with a police escort after she reported the threats.

- Robert Vargas, director of the biweekly *Ciudad Oriental*, was attacked and threatened by a group of people angered by the publication's reporting on prostitution and disorderly conduct in bars in the city of Santo Domingo Este, the journalist told CPJ. At 3 a.m. on December 2, a group of unidentified individuals threw rocks and bottles at Vargas' home, and one of the crowd members threatened to "rip his head off," according to the journalist. The following day, Vargas denounced the attack in an interview with national television station Noticias SIN. Shortly after the interview, another group gathered outside his home, and at least one person fired gunshots in the air, Vargas said. Local police posted a unit outside Vargas' home.

EL SALVADOR

- Salvador Sánchez Roque, a freelance radio reporter, was shot to death on September 20 on a street in Florencia, a town four miles (seven kilometers) from the capital, San Salvador. Sánchez covered social movements and demonstrations, said David Rivas, director of local Radio Mi Gente, for which Sánchez often reported. In the weeks before the murder, Sánchez told Rivas that he had received death threats from the local arm of the Salvadoran gang Mara Salvatrucha, although the callers did not specify a reason for the threats. Salvadoran police arrested José Alfredo Hernández, a member of Mara Salvatrucha, on October 11.

- Borman Mármol, a photographer for the San Salvador-based daily *La Prensa Gráfica*, and Alex Nolasco, a reporter for the national TV station Canal 21, were assaulted in separate incidents while covering an October 25 protest in Cutumay Camones, a small town near the western city of Santa Ana. Protesters attacked Mármol after he refused demands to hand over his camera, the journalist told CPJ. Mármol said he suffered minor injuries. Police roughed up Nolasco as he and cameraman Walter Aparicio attempted to leave the scene in a marked Canal 21 van. Nolasco said he suffered minor injuries. Police said that they believed the van was stolen, according to local press reports.

GUATEMALA

- On the night of February 3, an unidentified gunman aboard a motorcycle fired several times at a car owned by Wilder Jordán, a correspondent for the Guatemala City daily *Nuestro Diario* based in the eastern province of Zacapa, as the journalist was leaving his parents' house. Jordán told CPJ he believed the attack was related to a January 15 article detailing the death of a local man after a car accident. According to the journalist, on the day the article appeared, four of the victim's relatives came to his house and warned him that if he did not write a new piece saying that the man had instead died of a heart attack, he would face consequences. Fearing for his life, Jordán left his home in Zacapa.

- According to press reports, several journalists received anonymous threats directly linked to their coverage of the February 19 murder of three Salvadoran congressmen and their driver outside Guatemala City. Erick Salazar, news director for the program "Guatevisión," which airs on the national television station of the same name, said the program received a threatening e-mail with details about Guatevisión staff and their families, the Spanish news service EFE reported. Reporters from a newspaper and two radio stations based in Guatemala City told the local media they had received similar e-mails and calls to their cell phones.

- Four journalists were assaulted on April 25 while covering a mob's fatal attack on a purported gang member in the northeastern province of Quiché. Rudy Toledo, a reporter for the Quiché-based Televisión Cable Noticias; Oscar Toledo, correspondent for the national daily *Nuestro Diario*; Carlos Toledo, correspondent for the news program "TeleDiario" on the national television station Canal 3; and Oscar Figueroa, correspondent for the national radio station Emisoras Unidas, arrived at the scene at 10:30 a.m. According to Figueroa, heavily armed men punched and kicked the journalists, grabbed their equipment, and fired shots at the group, injuring Rudy Toledo in the left leg. Local police intervened and pulled the journalists out of the mob as protesters continued to fire at their car. Toledo was taken to a local hospital, where he received medical attention before being airlifted to Guatemala City. Toledo, though badly injured, recovered from his wounds.

- At 7 p.m. on May 3, veteran radio producer Mario Rolando López Sánchez was gunned down outside his home in Guatemala City. López produced the political debate program "Casos y Cosas de la Vida Nacional" and various social programs on national privately owned Radio Sonora. According to the journalist's colleagues and family, he had not received any threats prior to the shooting. However, Arnulfo Agustín Guzmán, director of Radio Sonora, told CPJ that the station had been threatened repeatedly.

- Edwin David Hernández, cameraman for the news program "Noti Star" on the national cable channel Star TV, told CPJ that several masked men stopped him on August 27 as he was on his way to cover a protest against the mayor of Cubulco. He was held for three and a half hours, and released after the protest was over. Hernández told CPJ his assailants wanted to stop him from filming the faces of people participating in the protest.

- On September 4, five days before the presidential election, an unidentified individual fired a gunshot into the offices of the Guatemala City-based Radio Nuevo Mundo. Marbin Robledo, director of the radio station, told CPJ the gunshot struck close to one of the station's reporters, but no one was injured. The station's staff believed the shot was meant as intimidation for its critical coverage of the presidential campaign, Robledo said.

HONDURAS

- In May, CPJ wrote a letter to President José Manuel Zelaya Rosales expressing concern over his May 24 proclamation that all radio and television stations would be required to simultaneously broadcast interviews with public officials. Zelaya decreed that 10 official broadcasts would be aired in order "to counteract the misinformation of the news media" about his tenure in office, according to international press reports and CPJ interviews. Regulations established by the National Telecommunications Commission gave Zelaya the authority to pre-empt radio and television programming for emergency broadcasts. Honduran journalists and press freedom advocates said they believed Zelaya's May 24 order contradicted the Honduran constitution and violated the spirit of the American Convention on Human Rights, which guarantees the right "to seek, receive, and impart information and ideas."

- Unidentified individuals shot and killed radio journalist Carlos Salgado on the afternoon of October 18 as he was leaving the offices of Radio Cadena Voces in the capital city of Tegucigalpa. Salgado, 67, host of the radio program "Frijol el Terrible," was known for his satirical criticism of the country's political system. His show mixed humor with coverage of everyday problems in Honduras. Local police arrested Germán David Almendárez Amador in late October after witnesses identified him as the gunman. Dagoberto Rodríguez, director of Radio Cadena Voces, told CPJ he believed the attack was retaliation for the station's investigative reporting on official corruption. Rodríguez said the station had been continuously harassed and threatened over two years. On November 1, Rodríguez himself fled the country after police said his name had appeared on a hit list.

NICARAGUA

- On February 14, three members of the ruling Frente Sandinista de Liberación Nacional (FSLN) approached William Aragón, a correspondent in the northern Madriz province for the Managua-based daily *La Prensa*, and advised him to get a bulletproof vest and a police helmet for his personal security, the journalist told CPJ. According to Aragón, the three men said they had attended a meeting with other FSLN members, during which plans were made to kill the journalist. Aragón said he believed the threat was linked to two articles on alleged government corruption published in *La Prensa* on February 5. Aragón reported the threat to local authorities.

PARAGUAY

- CPJ sent a letter to President Nicanor Duarte Frutos on February 8, expressing concern over the fate of Enrique Galeano, host of a morning news and music program on the Horqueta-based Radio Azotey who disappeared on the afternoon of February 4, 2006, while on his way home from work in the central province of Concepción. Galeano resurfaced in the Brazilian city of São Paulo on July 14, after Paraguayan journalists discovered his whereabouts, according to press reports. Galeano said two unidentified men had kidnapped him, taken him to Brazil, and told him to keep silent or his family would be killed. His captors did not specify their motive, but Galeano said he had received several anonymous death threats after reporting on links between the local government and drug traffickers. Shortly after his reappearance, Galeano relocated to Uruguay, where he requested political asylum, said Vicente Páez, secretary-general of the journalists union Sindicato de Periodistas de Paraguay.

- Oscar Bogado Silva, correspondent for the Asunción-based daily *Última Hora*, told CPJ that he received repeated telephone threats after reporting on local corruption and marijuana production along Paraguay's southern border. On April 18, a car followed the reporter from his house to his wife's office and back, Bogado told CPJ. Anonymous callers later mentioned details about his routine. According to the journalist, on April 24, unidentified individuals broke into his home in the southern city of Encarnación and left all the windows and doors open. A day later, Bogado said, he received a call from an unidentified individual, warning him that he was being watched.

- Tito Alberto Palma, a reporter for the local radio station Radio Mayor Otaño and correspondent for the Asunción-based Radio Chaco Boreal, was gunned down on the night of August 22 as he was having dinner at a friend's home in the southeastern city of Mayor Otaño, according to press reports and CPJ interviews. A Chilean national, Palma often denounced organized crime, illegal smuggling of gas, and local government corruption in the province of Itapúa, a colleague at Radio Chaco Boreal, Erico González, told CPJ. Palma had also reported recently on the existence of illegal radio stations in the area. González told CPJ the reporter had received death threats, which had intensified a month prior to his death. A week before the murder, Palma announced on the air that he was returning to Chile because of the threats. González told CPJ that Palma's colleagues believe he was murdered in retaliation for his work.

PERU

- On March 17, two hooded individuals shot and killed Miguel Pérez Julca outside his home in the northwestern city of Jaén. His wife, Nelly Guevara, was wounded in the attack. Pérez, 38, host of the radio program "El Informativo del Pueblo" (Bulletin of the People) on local Radio Éxitos, covered local crime and allegations of government corruption. One of four suspects originally detained in connection with the murder, José Hurtado Vásquez, remained in custody in late year. According to Peruvian press reports, he was accused of hiring two gunmen to kill Pérez in retaliation for on-air criticism of his girlfriend, the director of a local nonprofit organization. Hurtado denied the accusation. Local colleagues and Lima-based journalists who spoke to CPJ said they were skeptical of the police investigation. According to the national daily *La República*, police had not looked into a claim made by Pérez during his last show that he planned to reveal the names of corrupt local police officers.

- On May 22, the Fifth Criminal Court of Lima convicted Rocío Vásquez Goicochea, director of the weekly *Investigando Chimbote* in the northeastern Áncash region, of criminal defamation, the journalist told CPJ. Vásquez was given a one-year suspended prison sentence and ordered to pay 3,000 soles (US$1,000) to local businessman Samuel Dyer. Dyer filed a defamation suit against Vásquez in 2005 after the reporter wrote a series accusing Dyer's company of illegal fishing practices and corruption. The journalist told CPJ her lawyers had filed an appeal.

- Orlando Rucana Cuba, director of daily news programming on Radio Melodía and Radio Alegría, told CPJ that on May 24 he received an anonymous text message from an undisclosed number threatening him and Manuel Caballero Vidal, a journalist with the television station Canal 13. Rucana told CPJ that he was not sure what coverage could have sparked the threats. The two journalists had covered a violent protest against the local mayor's change in education policies in the provincial capital, Huaraz, the day before the message was sent.

- Five journalists were fired on when they witnessed what appeared to be an illegal occupation of land near the northeastern town of San Julián on June 28, said Paola Lee, a reporter for national América Televisión. The owners of the land had invited Lee; Sandro Chambergo, a reporter for the national daily *Correo*; Perla Polo, a camerawoman for América TV; and Gerardo Pérez and Rafael Rojas, a reporter and a photographer for *La República*. As the journalists and property owners stepped out of their vehicles, unidentified men began to shoot at the group. According to Lee, one of the landowners yelled, "Don't shoot, the press is here," but the gunfire intensified. None of the journalists were injured, but eight of the landowners received minor gunshot wounds.

- José Ramírez, correspondent for the Lima-based daily *La Primera*, was threatened and his companions detained after he tried to photograph graffiti denouncing provincial Gov. César Álvarez in Huari, a city in the northeastern Áncash region. A group of local officials interrupted the assignment, threatened Ramírez, and seized the photographer's three companions. While Ramírez was able to flee, his companions were taken to a local police station, where they were roughed up. Ramírez said he later left Huari after receiving repeated telephone threats. Wilbur Avendaño, a legal representative for the local government, denied the allegations.

- On November 14, the Superior Court of Ucayali sentenced two men in the 2004 murder of Alberto Rivera Fernández, host of the morning show "Transparencia" (Transparency) on the Pucallpa-based Frecuencia Oriental radio station, according to Peruvian press reports. The court sentenced Lito Fasabi to 35 years in prison and Alex Panduro Ventura to 20 years. The court acquitted Luis Valdez Villacorta, former Pucallpa mayor, and Solio Ramírez, a former government official, citing a lack of evidence. Rivera's family appealed the decision to the Peruvian Supreme Court, local press reports said. The Inter-American Commission on Human Rights announced that it would investigate the decision.

- On November 23, two men pointed handguns at Danilo Bautista Hernández, host of the daily news program "El Informativo del Mediodía" (Noon Report) on local Radio California, as the journalist was swimming with family members in the Yuracyacu River in the northern region of San Matín. Hernández told CPJ that witnesses came to the family's aid, forcing the assailants to flee. Officer Robert Llanos Petrel, a spokesman for the local police, told CPJ that an investigation was under way. In March, Hernández received repeated death threats from individuals who identified themselves as members of a local group that had sought education reform. The journalist had criticized the group's tactics.

- A purported hit list containing the names of several journalists and signed by the leftist guerrilla group Sedero Luminoso (Shining Path) was slipped under the door of the mayor's office in Aucayacu, in the central province of Huánuco, according to Ranforte Lozano Panduro, director of local Radio Aucayacu and president of the Center for Press and Communications for the Development of the Amazon. The December 15 list, reviewed by CPJ, contained 15 names in all. The journalists named were Lozano; Novel Panduro Ruíz and Cirilo Velasquez Hilario, reporters for Radio Luz; and Segundo Ramírez Macedo, reporter for Radio Aucayacu and correspondent for the regional daily *AHORA*. Lozano told CPJ that he and his colleagues cover general local news. He said he believes they were targeted because they use local authorities as sources. The national police were investigating.

URUGUAY

- On April 18, the Supreme Court of Justice upheld a three-month suspended prison sentence against Gustavo Escanlar Patrone, host of the satirical television program "Bendita TV" (Blessed TV). The decision let stand a 2006 criminal defamation conviction by a lower court in Montevideo, the journalist's lawyer, Edison Lanza, told CPJ. The case stemmed from a January 2006 interview on the Canal 10 television program "La Culpa es Mía," in which Escanlar referred to a media company owner by using a vulgarity.

ASIA

Amid South Asian Conflict, Remarkable Resilience

Pakistan and Sri Lanka offer a window into the region's surprisingly strong news media. In both nations, professional unity has enabled the news media to survive, even thrive, in the face of upheaval.

by Bob Dietz

PHOTOS

Section break: Reuters – *Photographer Kenji Nagai is left to die on the streets of Rangoon after a Burmese soldier shot him during September protests.* Analysis (next): AP/K.M.Chaudary – *During a June rally in Lahore, Pakistani journalists protest government restrictions.*

ASIA

AMID SOUTH ASIAN CONFLICT, REMARKABLE RESILIENCE

by Bob Dietz

• •

TRAFFIC IS SPARSE DURING A LATE-NIGHT RUN TO THE BANDARANAIKE
International Airport north of the Sri Lankan capital, Colombo. Because
of insecurity caused by war between the Sinhalese-dominated government
and Tamil separatists in the country's north and east, the streets are given over
to police and army checkpoints. On this September night, the air still foggy
from the day's monsoon, reporter Iqbal Athas rides in a rental car, on his way
to catch a Thai Airways flight that would take him to Bangkok. An award-
winning defense columnist for the English-language *Sunday Times*, Athas is
leaving the country for his own safety: His recent reports on arms sales irregularities have drawn threats, harassment, and, on one occasion, an unruly mob
of protestors outside his home. "The harassment and threats have come and
gone in the past," Athas says, "and I have to assume they will again." He would
return to Colombo in less than two weeks.

In Pakistan, Mazhar Abbas walks out of the Karachi Press Club to find
a single 30 mm bullet inside an envelope taped to the windshield of his car.
Several other journalists walk with him in the fading daylight of this May
evening. Two of them find the same "message" waiting when they reach their
own cars. The group returns to the club and drafts a statement to be distributed by the Pakistan Federal Union of Journalists (PFUJ), which Abbas leads as secretary-general. Afterward, most of the journalists go home,

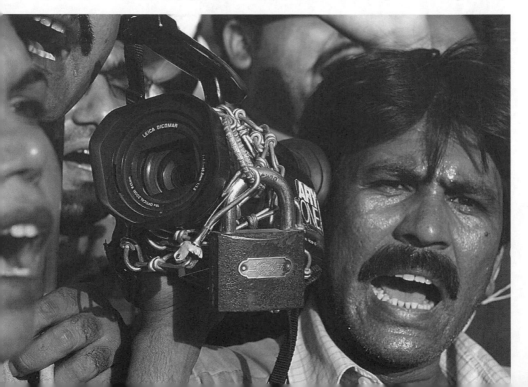

Two nations offer a window into the region's surprisingly strong news media. but Abbas decides to return to work at the Agence France-Presse office where he serves as bureau chief.

Pakistan turned 60 in 2007. Sri Lanka will mark the same anniversary in 2008. Former British colonies, both are fraying democracies, passed over by Asia's economic surge in good part because of internal strife. They have swung between periods of misguided rule and political upheaval since they were born. Sri Lanka is considered one of the world's most politically unstable countries by the World Bank and the Asian Development Bank. Pakistan is ranked 12th on *Foreign Policy* magazine's list of the world's 32 failed states.

Yet in each country, the press, flawed as it is, has survived to serve as a vital forum for free expression. In Pakistan, the media consistently ranks as the most trusted institution in the country. Eighty percent of Pakistanis say they trust the press—a rating higher than that of any other institution, including the judiciary and the military—according to an October poll carried out by the International Republican Institute (IRI), a Washington-based research group affiliated with the Republican Party. The IRI did not conduct a poll in Sri Lanka, but the media's commercial success indicates its importance to the public. While the government controls many broadcasting and publishing operations, there are about 20 privately owned stations and close to 20 privately owned newspapers, most of them dailies. They are avidly consumed.

The conflicts in Sri Lanka and Pakistan are very different, of course, and each country's news media operate in distinctive ways. But the experiences of Iqbal Athas and Mazhar Abbas, both of whom are internationally recognized senior journalists and CPJ International Press Freedom Award winners, provide a window into how the press has persisted, even thrived, in both countries.

They also point to the surprising strength of the press in the region as a whole. Throughout South Asia, amid civil and military turmoil, journalists have shown remarkable resilience and, in many instances, striking displays of professional unity. In Nepal, journalists played a lead role in rallying public opinion against King Gyanendra Bir Bikram Shah Dev when he audaciously seized power in February 2005, ultimately forcing him to cede control to parliament 14 months later. In Afghanistan, several dozen broadcasters and more than 400 newspapers continue their work despite conflict between Hamid Karzai's beleaguered government, militant Islamic groups, warlords, and drug cartels. And in Indonesia, the news media confronted and outlasted the authoritarian Suharto regime to become one of the freest in the region.

S EPTEMBER WAS A TENSE PERIOD FOR IQBAL ATHAS AND HIS FAMILY, but things had been worse. In February 1998, five armed men, including two air force officers, forcibly entered the family's home, pointed a loaded automatic pistol at Athas' head, and threatened him, his wife, and their 7-year-old daughter. Neighbors said there were some 25 armed men waiting outside the house. The family stood their ground, and the intruders left without seriously harming anyone. Athas had recently published a series of exposés on corruption in the Sri Lankan military.

Sri Lankan journalists survive with the support of professional organizations.

This time, the threats followed his investigation into irregularities surrounding a 2006 deal to purchase MiG-27 fighter jets from Ukraine. Immediately after the article appeared, the government withdrew the security detail it had posted around Athas' house after earlier threats. Strangers started following him on the street. A placard-carrying government rent-a-mob demonstrated outside his home. A gunman went to the *Times'* office and threatened the journalist who was about to translate Athas' MiG article for the Sinhalese-language *Lankadeepa*, the largest-selling morning daily in Sri Lanka. In translation, the article would have had far greater reach and caused the government much more embarrassment.

As he makes his way through ticketing at the airport this September night, Athas stays in touch with his friend and editor at *The Sunday Times*, Sinha Ratnatunga, by text message. Athas will continue to write his defense column for the *Times* from outside the country, and soon enough, he'll be back home. The intimidating phone calls, the surveillance, will continue. "The harassment and threats have never been worse," he'll say later.

Fourteen Sri Lankan journalists have been killed in direct relation to their work since 1999, making the country one of the deadliest in the world for the press. The Athas case is, in many respects, an anomaly. Most of the slain journalists in Sri Lanka were Tamil, a minority ethnic group in a majority Sinhalese nation, and their deaths have come in the midst of a 24-year-old civil war. The government's tenuous cease-fire with the Liberation Tigers of Tamil Eelam came undone in 2006 and daily fighting resumed. Not unsurprisingly, the five journalists killed for their work in 2007 were Tamils. Three were killed in a Sri Lankan government air strike.

N. Vithyatharan publishes two Tamil-language dailies, *Uthayan* and *Sudaroli*. For 23 years, *Uthayan* has been printed in Jaffna, the heart of the Tamil secessionist fight, and the staff has learned to cope with the conflict's ebbs and flows. At one point, the paper had about 20 staff members, but the number is down to five or six, with some living in the paper's offices because they fear going out on the street. When newsprint runs short, *Uthayan* has appeared on brown wrapping paper. There is an ancient, hand-fed Heidelberg letterpress standing by should the paper's offset presses be sabotaged. And diesel fuel, always in short supply, is stretched by mixing it five-to-one with vegetable oil to run the paper's generators during the frequent power blackouts. Jaffna has changed hands between Tamil secessionists and the Sri Lankan military several times, and *Uthayan* has incurred the wrath of both sides. Vithyatharan says he is proud of his paper's position and its editorial integrity. Tamil newspapers have long been characterized as practicing partisan journalism, the sort of one-sided reporting bound to draw fire. Vithyatharan disputes this notion. Instead, he says, these newspapers represent the "aspirations of Tamils" in the same way *The New York Times* represents an American viewpoint.

Pakistan and Sri Lanka are among the world's deadliest places for the press.

Sri Lankan journalists have survived with the support of professional organizations, according to Sunanda Deshapriya, who runs the Free Media Movement (FMM), one of five organizations that between them represent almost all of the nation's reporters. The FMM is a small operation with a wide reach, largely because of Deshapriya and his staff's commitment and energy. His office on a dusty side street near the United Arab Emirates embassy compound is up a narrow second staircase on the second floor, a small ill-lit room, the sun partially blocked by a large window-mounted air conditioner fighting a battle with Colombo's heat and humidity. In addition to the FMM, there are the Sri Lanka Tamil Media Alliance, the Sri Lanka Working Journalists Association, the Sri Lanka Muslim Media Forum, and the Federation of Media Employees Trade Union. Their titles reflect their separate ethnic interests, but they have grown increasingly supportive of one another in recent years, due in part to FMM's work.

PAKISTANI JOURNALISTS ARE WELL ORGANIZED, TOO, AND THEY have been for years. Beneath the all-encompassing PFUJ, all major cities and many smaller ones have journalist unions and press clubs. When times are good, the press clubs serve as meeting halls where guest speakers discuss topical issues. When times are bad, journalists seek refuge and support in these same halls.

And journalists do come under frequent attack. In Pakistan, the army steps onto center stage every decade or so, using civil unrest or political ineptitude as an excuse to take control. Gen. Pervez Musharraf's 1999 power grab marked the fifth time the military had seized power in 52 years. And when the military is not in power, dynastic political families feud over the spoils of patronage. Since independence, every legislature has been dominated by fewer than 50 prominent land-owning families. The two principal figures to emerge to challenge Musharraf's ragged military-backed government were Benazir Bhutto and Nawaz Sharif, former prime ministers from powerful families whose governments were recognized for their corruption and ineptitude. After Bhutto was assassinated in December, her son was named leader of her Pakistan Peoples Party.

Pakistani journalists are well organized. All major cities have press clubs.

Maybe it is not surprising that Abbas is part of something of a dynasty, too. In May, several journalists, including Abbas and his two brothers, Zaffar (a former BBC correspondent and now a senior editor at the daily newspaper *Dawn*) and Azhar (Dawn TV's executive director), were identified as "enemies" by the Mohajir Rabita Council—an ethnic political group in Pakistan's southern province of Sindh—because of their reporting on political unrest. The PFUJ called the announcement a "hit list."

The incident was only one in a string that continued throughout the year. Mazhar Abbas could barely tear himself away from Pakistan to make it to New York to accept his 2007 International Press Freedom Award from CPJ in November. In the eight months before he received his award, the government had, among other things, assaulted journalists, swept them up twice in groups of more than a hundred, threatened newspaper owners, and invaded printing plants.

Soon after the bullet threat, Abbas left Agence France-Presse to become the news director at ARY One World TV. It was a promotion, a move to a new medium, but it was not an end to his problems. Not long after he started his new job, ARY was kept off the air for more than two weeks after Musharraf shut down all independent broadcast channels and declared a state of emergency on November 3. Before allowing the stations back on the air, the president forced broadcasters to agree to a new "code of conduct" that made it a crime to criticize the presidency or the military. The crackdown was part of a long-term pattern of attacks on the Pakistani media. Seventeen journalists have been killed in Pakistan in direct relation to their work since 1992, 12 of them in premeditated attacks and nearly all of the cases uninvestigated by the government.

Power-obsessed politicians have failed to suppress the media. And that offers hope.

Despite this deadly violence and legal harassment, the news media are very much alive in Pakistan—a country where the journalism stands out, Abbas says, "because of the struggle of the journalists." After Bhutto's assassination, TV stations defied aspects of the new code of conduct, resuming some live coverage and reviving many of the call-in political shows whose critical commentary had so angered Musharraf. Far from being daunted, the press provided aggressive and exhaustive coverage of the slaying.

Media freedom shrinks and grows in Pakistan, as it does in Sri Lanka and other South Asian nations. The changes can be rapid, depending on leaders' ambitions, the state of the economy, or a worsening security situation. But the media's persistence, resourcefulness, and cohesion have often formed a bulwark against attacks.

Journalists in countries under duress realize that a free and open society is something grander than journalism. They also know that without journalism—even when it is flawed, or biased, or self-censored—a free society cannot truly exist. Power-obsessed politicians know that, too, and that is why in Pakistan and Sri Lanka they have tried to suppress the media. That these politicians have not fully succeeded should give us hope. Failed governments have come and gone. Their executives, legislatures, and judiciaries are easily and regularly corrupted, but South Asian journalists have persevered to uphold a higher ideal.

• • • • • • • • •

Bob Dietz is CPJ's Asia program coordinator. He conducted a CPJ research mission to Sri Lanka and Pakistan in 2007.

················· AFGHANISTAN ··················

Six years after the U.S.-led invasion of Afghanistan, journalists were increasingly pessimistic about the future. The personal tragedies of several Afghan journalists illustrated how much the press situation had worsened amid political disarray, faltering security, and human rights abuses. Despite the adversity, domestic news media remained plentiful and assertive.

Taliban fighters beheaded Ajmal Naqshbandi on April 8 in the Garmsir district of Helmand province, after the Afghan government refused demands to release jailed senior Taliban leaders. Naqshbandi had been abducted on March 4 with *La Repubblica* reporter Daniele Mastrogiacomo and driver Sayed Agha. Naqshbandi, a freelance journalist with several clients, had acted as Mastrogiacomo's fixer on a trip to interview Taliban leaders. Agha, the driver, was beheaded shortly after the abduction; the Italian Mastrogiacomo was released March 19 in an exchange for five Taliban prisoners.

The ugly incident left bitterness all around. Afghan journalists wanted to know why two of their colleagues were so brutally killed while the Italian government had apparently free rein to negotiate with Taliban leaders to save an Italian national.

CPJ had launched an intensive publicity effort to try to win Naqshbandi's freedom. Nearly 300 people signed CPJ's open letter urging his release, including journalists from CNN, The Associated Press, Reuters, *Time*, *The New York Times*, *USA Today*, NBC, ABC, and Al-Jazeera. Naqshbandi's death hit at the very core of one of CPJ's founding realities: Local journalists are the ones most at risk. CPJ research dating to 1992 shows that 85 percent of journalists killed for their work worldwide are local reporters. Many are killed by groups similar to the Taliban—33 percent worldwide have died at the hands of insurgent or political groups.

Another journalist was killed in direct relation to her work, while a third was slain under unclear circumstances. On June 5, unidentified gunmen shot Zakia Zaki in Parwan province, north of the capital, Kabul, in the bedroom she was sharing with her small children. Zaki, 35, had run a private news radio station, Sada-i-Sulh (Peace Radio), since the fall of the Taliban in 2001. The station, which covered women's issues, human rights, education, and local politics, had been threatened repeatedly. Just before the slaying, local warlords warned Zaki to shut down the station.

On May 31, television news presenter Shokiba Sanga Amaaj, 22, was murdered in her Kabul home. Authorities arrested male relatives, but the motive remained unclear and CPJ continues to investigate.

· · · · · · · · · ·

Country summaries in this chapter were reported and written by Asia Program Coordinator **Bob Dietz**, Program Consultant **Shawn W. Crispin**, and freelance writers **Kavita Menon** and **Kristin Jones**.

As killings came to the forefront, harassment and threats remained commonplace. CPJ assisted two Afghan journalists who went into hiding after receiving death threats from extremist groups or gangsters involved in the opium trade. The U.N. High Commissioner for Refugees said it was aware of several other similar cases, although it could not reveal specific information because of privacy issues.

"It is not possible to talk and write freely in such situations," Rahimullah Samandar, head of the Afghan Independent Journalists Association and the Committee to Protect Afghan Journalists, said in a note to CPJ that recounted a series of threats, seizures, and attacks. "The Afghan government should take strong action to stop these acts."

The Taliban were behind several attacks. On August 28, for example, a reporter for Salaam Watandar, a radio syndication service run by Internews, a U.S.-based media training and advocacy organization, was kidnapped by Taliban fighters in the Sayedabad district of Wardak province and interrogated for several hours. The reporter, Mohammad Zahir Bahand, said the Taliban were unhappy about news reports describing a recent arson attack on the Internews-affiliated station Yawali Ghag. Bahand, who had been working for Salaam Watandar for only one month, was told to be sure that the service covered future Taliban actions. Soon after his release, three rockets were fired in Sayedabad and two trucks supplying fuel to NATO forces were burned.

Harassment of the media came from U.S. and government forces. U.S. soldiers deleted journalists' photos and television footage taken in the aftermath of a March 4 suicide bombing in which several Afghan civilians were killed by U.S. fire. Soldiers deleted photos and videos taken by freelance photographer Rahmat Gul, who was working for the AP, and an unidentified cameraman for Associated Press Television News; they also threatened other Afghan television reporters at the scene of the attack. The AP quoted Taqiullah Taqi, a reporter for Afghanistan's largest television station, Tolo TV, as saying that U.S. troops told him: "Delete them, or we will delete you." According to the AP and local reports, Afghans at the scene of the incident in Nanghar province in eastern Afghanistan said U.S. Marines fired at civilians after their convoy was hit by a suicide bomber. In a statement, the military said the troops had come under fire after the explosion.

On the night of April 17, about 50 Afghan police officers raided Tolo TV's main office in Kabul, seized three staff members, and took them to Attorney General Abdul Jabar Sabet's office. Sabet had complained of a clip on Tolo's 6 p.m. news broadcast, which he claimed was inaccurate and misrepresented his comments at an earlier press conference. Four AP journalists who were observing the raid were also detained, some of them kicked and punched by police, the news service reported.

ASIA

The seven were taken to Sabet's office, where they were questioned for about 40 minutes and released without charge. Police provided no basis for the detention.

Tolo's sister station, Lemar TV, was forced to end its retransmission of Al-Jazeera's satellite programming after receiving an order from the Ministry of Information and Culture in April. Minister Abdul Karim Khuram said Al-Jazeera challenged the "cultural and the legal authority of the government." Lemar had argued it had a constitutional right to retransmit the station's programs.

Government intimidation continued in August when Kamran Mir Hazar, editor of the *Kabul Press* Web site and a correspondent for Salaam Watandar, was detained by Afghan secret police. He was released by the end of the day but warned to stop writing articles criticizing Afghan officials. Hazar said he also had been detained and interrogated by members of the National Directorate of Security in July, when he was held incommunicado for five days.

Such actions reflected a running battle by the government against Afghanistan's young and combative press corps. The situation drew the attention of the U.N. mission in Kabul, which expressed its concern in a February press conference about attempts to curb the media in Afghanistan.

Partly in response, the National Assembly withdrew a bill that would have fundamentally changed the country's 2002 press law by inserting language demanding "respect for Islamic values" and giving the government more direct control of broadcast programming. Many see the 2002 press law as the most liberal in the region and a central reason that media were able to grow in the post-Taliban era. Under President Hamid Karzai, six independent television channels had come on the air, as well as dozens of competing radio stations and newspapers.

Although critics in government said that Afghan media had become "un-Islamic," NGOs, foreign donors, and much of the Afghan media saw the bill as a way of stifling criticism.

There were grounds for those fears. Minister of Information and Culture Khuram sacked without explanation 80 Radio Television Afghanistan (RTA) employees who were newly hired by station General Director Najib Roshan. In doing so, Khuram effectively reversed a plan—developed by the government in cooperation with international media advisers and aid groups—to turn RTA into a full-fledged independent public broadcaster.

Journalists told CPJ that they fear the government will eventually impose further constraints. "I think journalists are on the verge of being stripped of their only working weapon, freedom of expression," said Barry Salaam, an independent producer who hosts the popular "Good Morning Afghanistan" and "Good Evening Afghanistan" programs over RTA. "It has not happened yet, but the current policies will lead there if not reversed or diverted."

•••••••••••••••• BANGLADESH ••••••••••••••••

Despite stated commitments to democratic reform and media freedom, Bangladesh's military-backed government dealt a series of crippling blows to what had been one of the freest presses in Asia. Operating under an official state of emergency and faced with a series of written orders and verbal directives governing media coverage, a famously voluble press corps grew increasingly muted.

On January 11, in response to mounting political violence and unrest, President Iajuddin Ahmed declared a state of emergency, announced an indefinite postponement of the parliamentary elections due later that month, and stepped down as head of the caretaker government charged with administering the polls. The next day, Fakhruddin Ahmed, a former central bank governor and World Bank official, was appointed to head a new interim administration.

The Bangladeshi media generally were circumspect in discussing the precise role of the military in the transition, but the international press was free to be more forthright. In an article headlined "The coup that dare not speak its name," *The Economist* noted that, "the army, in the tradition of 'guardian coups' from Fiji to Thailand, has stepped in with the usual list of apparently noble goals" to ensure credible elections, fight corruption, and hold down food prices. "Although the state of emergency has supporters even among some liberal democrats, it is a high-stakes gamble," the London-based weekly concluded.

The abrupt transfer of power, which Bangladeshis referred to as the events of 1/11, bore many of the hallmarks of a coup. On orders from the official Press Information Department (PID), private television stations immediately suspended independent news programming and instead carried broadcasts provided by state-run Bangladesh Television. Officials warned senior journalists and editors to exercise caution in their reporting and not to publish any news critical of the government. Journalists received verbal instructions from the PID that they should consult Inter-Service Public Relations—the office that serves the Ministry of Defense, the army, and other security branches—before publishing any news about the armed forces.

Two weeks after the emergency was first announced, the new caretaker government spelled out its intentions in the sweeping Emergency Powers Rules of 2007. The regulations, which remain in effect, are largely aimed at curbing political and trade union activities, but they also allow the government to censor news deemed "provocative," seize publications, and confiscate printing presses and broadcast equipment. Those violating the restrictions face up to five years in prison.

Over the course of the year, as many as 200,000 people were arrested under the state of emergency, according to local and international human rights organizations. While most of those detained were accused of criminal activities, the arrests were often arbitrary and without adequate judicial oversight. Under the emergency laws,

ASIA

the right to appeal and recourse to bail were routinely denied.

Among those swept up in the anticorruption drive were some of the country's leading politicians—including two former prime ministers—as well as powerful media executives. Local journalists told CPJ that the arrests of media executives, who often had complex business and political dealings, were generally not considered to be press freedom cases. However, their arrests effectively weakened major media outlets by cutting off their primary source of financial support.

The anticorruption drive did provide the pretext for targeting some influential journalists, most notably in the case of Atiqullah Khan Masud, editor and publisher of the popular Bengali-language daily *Janakantha*. In a striking show of force, on March 7, more than 200 army and police personnel raided the newspaper's offices to arrest Khan Masud. Police accused him of corruption, criminal activities, and "tarnishing the country's image abroad" through his paper's reporting, according to local news reports. *Janakantha* was one of the few newspapers to openly question the military's involvement in the caretaker government.

The broad powers exercised by the security forces also led to serious abuses. On May 11, journalist and human rights activist Tasneem Khalil was taken into custody after midnight by men in plain clothes claiming to be members of Bangladesh's "joint task force." The men blindfolded him and took him to an interrogation center later identified as an extension of the military intelligence headquarters in Dhaka, according to Human Rights Watch (HRW). Khalil was tortured and questioned about his work as a journalist, which  included reporting for the *Daily Star* newspaper and CNN, his personal blog, and his research for a 2006 HRW report on torture and extrajudicial killings by members of the security forces. The organization reported that Khalil was forced to make false confessions, both in writing and on video, admitting to acts that could be considered treasonous. At one point, he was photographed with a revolver and some bullets placed before him, suggesting that he was being framed as a criminal and was at risk of being killed in custody, according to HRW. Khalil was released after 22 hours in custody following intense advocacy efforts.

The cases of Atiqullah Khan Masud and Tasneem Khalil were in many ways exceptional, but they provided stark reminders to journalists that they had few protections under the terms of emergency rule. Far more common than arrest or torture were the frequent verbal warnings from officials, including members of military intelligence. "They try to make us understand that they are watching us," one journalist told CPJ.

Journalists working outside the capital, Dhaka, were even more vulnerable to threats and harassment by members of the local administration and security forces. *Daily Star* reporter E. A. M. Asaduzzaman Tipu was arrested on March 21 in the northern district of Nilphamari after reporting on the local government's handling of fertilizer distribution in the area. He was detained for nearly a week on false accusations of extortion. Jahangir Alam Akash, a reporter in the northwestern city of Rajshahi for the television news channel CSB, told CPJ in May that he received death threats from a major with the Rapid Action Battalion (RAB) for his reporting on a raid in which the suspect was shot and wounded. In October, Akash was arrested and beaten in custody, according to his wife, after a local political figure believed to be assisting the RAB accused him of extortion. Local journalists told CPJ that Akash was being targeted for his journalistic work and that he had committed no crime.

The national media faced a major crisis in August, when the government and security forces attempted to restrict news coverage of growing student unrest. Security forces assaulted and detained dozens of journalists reporting on the enforcement of a curfew and on clashes between the police and students calling for an end to emergency rule. In a pointed appeal to broadcasters, Information Adviser Mainul Hosein said, "We request channels to stop televising footage of violence until further notice because this might instigate further violence," according to the BBC. Private television channels in Bangladesh abruptly stopped carrying reports about the street demonstrations and suspended political discussion programs. On August 23, two private television channels—CSB and Ekushey Television—received a written notice from the PID warning them not to broadcast "provocative" news.

Within weeks of that warning, on September 6, authorities took CSB off the air on allegations that the company had forged a document authorizing its frequency allocation. CSB, the country's first private 24-hour news channel, announced its closure in October.

The government allowed the broadcast media to resume talk shows only in mid-September, after senior journalists repeatedly appealed to authorities to be permitted to air discussions on other matters of crucial public interest—including the devastating floods that submerged half of the country and displaced more than nine million people, according to U.N. estimates. On September 17, Hosein summoned TV executives to his office and handed them "informal guidelines" to govern talk shows. The written guidelines, which were not printed on official letterhead and carried no signature, included detailed rules specifying that talk shows must be edited and could not be aired live, that phone-ins and interactive discussions were banned, and that "statements that can create resentment towards the legitimate government of Bangladesh should also be avoided," according to a report published by the newspaper *New Age*.

The government did not directly impose prior censorship of the local print media, but authorities literally ripped out politically sensitive news articles from

ASIA

Himal Southasian, an English-language political monthly published in Kathmandu, and *The Economist* before the magazines were distributed. In both cases, the articles remained accessible online.

Islamist groups demonstrated their still considerable power in September, when they exploited a controversy surrounding the publication of a cartoon that included a play on the use of the name Muhammad. The cartoon, published in the satirical supplement of the country's largest-circulation daily, *Prothom Alo*, featured a small boy referring to his pet as "Muhammad Cat" after being told it was customary to put Muhammad before one's given name. The newspaper fired the cartoonist and the subeditor of the supplement and apologized repeatedly for causing offense. Dhaka police arrested the cartoonist, Arifur Rahman, on September 17 under the provisions of Section 54 of Bangladesh's Criminal Procedure Code, according to the *Daily Star* newspaper. Human rights groups say Section 54 gives the police broad powers to make arrests without a warrant. Islamist groups were not appeased and staged a series of street demonstrations—despite the ban on public protests—calling for the newspaper to be shut down altogether.

While *Prothom Alo* managed to survive the episode, the fact that the country's most powerful daily could be brought to its knees sent a sobering message to the secular press. In October, an imam filed a court case in Jessore, about 170 miles (274 kilometers) west of the capital, against *Prothom Alo*'s publisher, its editor, and the cartoonist Rahman, accusing the three of "sacrilege," according to the news agency United News of Bangladesh. The magistrate hearing the case authorized Rahman's arrest and ordered the newspaper's publisher and editor to appear before the court in early 2008. Rahman remained in prison when CPJ conducted its annual census of imprisoned journalists on December 1.

• **BURMA** •

Burmese journalists came under heavy assault in August and September when covering pro-democracy street protests and the military government's retaliatory crackdown, marking significant deterioration in what was already one of the world's most repressive media environments. The government banned coverage of the uprising and sought to isolate the nation by impeding Internet and phone service. Local and citizen journalists, however, proved innovative and persistent in circumventing the government's electronic blockade.

The ruling State Peace and Development Council's decision in mid-August to remove fuel-price subsidies sparked angry protests across several Burmese cities, including thousands-strong marches in the former national capital, Rangoon. The demonstrations grew into a massive antigovernment movement soon after soldiers used force against protesting Buddhist monks in the religious town of Pakokku on September 6. On September 27, during a march by monks and citizens, a soldier shot and killed Kenji Nagai, 50, a cameraman for the Tokyo-based video and photo agency APF News. Plainclothes police and soldiers arrested six other journalists and assaulted several more.

The Press Scrutiny and Registration Division (PSRD), the state body charged with censoring the local media, imposed a late-August blackout on local news coverage of the protests. Several local newspapers ceased to publish altogether after the Information Ministry demanded they run government-written opinion pieces characterizing the pro-democracy protests as a threat to national security.

Recognizing that electronic communication threatened to expose the crackdown, authorities tried to control or cut off means of communicating with the outside world. On September 8, the Directorate of Military Engineers assigned staff to the main national telecommunications complex in Rangoon to monitor journalists' communications, according to information received by the Burma Media Association, an exile-run press freedom advocacy group. By mid-September, authorities had cut the telephone services of several Burmese journalists, including those who worked as stringers for exile-run and international news organizations. Those affected included Agence France-Presse reporter Hla Hla Htay and freelancer May Thingyan Hein, who received a 2007 Knight International Journalism Award for her exemplary reporting.

Authorities also slowed connection speeds and imposed rolling Internet blackouts, often in late afternoon to coincide with the time journalists usually tried to file their stories. A Reuters photographer had his cameras confiscated by police on August 23 after he attempted to take pictures of plainclothes officials detaining a group of protesters, according to media reports.

Despite the junta's attempt to black out the news, local and citizen journalists managed to send via the Internet reports, images, and video clips of the protests and government crackdown to Burmese exile-run and foreign news organizations. These local and citizen reporters used proxy servers and proxy sites to send news reports, thus circumventing government-administered e-mail blocks. Burmese exile-run publications, including the *Democratic Voice of Burma*, *Mizzima News*, and *The Irrawaddy*, carried in-depth news and images of the protests provided by anonymous stringers based inside the country. *Irrawaddy* Editor Aung Zaw told the Foreign Correspondents Club of Thailand on November 7 that his news site received as many as 100,000 visitors daily at the height of the crisis. The government said in September that anyone discovered cooperating with exile-run media risked a 20-year jail sentence on subver-

ASIA

sion charges, according to a news report by the *Democratic Voice of Burma*.

The brutal crackdown reached a low point on September 27, when Burmese troops opened fire on demonstrators in Rangoon, killing 10 people according to government estimates, and many more according to diplomatic sources cited in news reports. Nagai was among those shot and killed while he was filming near a group of demonstrators in downtown Rangoon. Video footage of his murder later released by Japan's Fuji News Network showed that Nagai was pushed to the ground by a soldier and shot at near point-blank range. He died almost instantly of his injuries. In protest, Japan suspended some of its foreign aid programs to Burma. The United Nations, the Association of Southeast Asian Nations, and many Western governments condemned the junta's onslaught against its citizens. The United Nations pursued mediation aimed at reconciling the military government with the pro-democracy opposition, while the United States imposed a round of financial sanctions aimed at specific junta members.

Authorities detained more than 3,000 people over the course of the crackdown, which continued into October. Six journalists were arrested, one of whom was still being held when CPJ conducted its annual census of imprisoned journalists on December 1. The detention of freelance photographer Win Saing, who was being held on undisclosed charges, brought the total number held by the government to seven, earning Burma the dubious distinction of being the world's sixth-leading jailer of journalists. U Win Tin, the former editor-in-chief of the daily *Hanthawati* newspaper, served his 18th year of a 20-year prison term on trumped-up antistate charges. The 77-year-old reporter has suffered at least two heart attacks while in prison and is one of the longest-serving jailed journalists in the world.

Despite calls from CPJ and others, U Win Tin was not among the 3,000 political prisoners released in a New Year's amnesty on January 3. The authorities did, however, release 2004 CPJ International Press Freedom Awardee Thaung Tun, an editor, reporter, and poet widely known by his pen name, Nyein Thit. He was sentenced to eight years in prison in October 1999 for producing unauthorized video documentaries that included footage of forced labor and impoverished rural areas.

Censorship of the media was pervasive, with no improvement since CPJ ranked Burma as the world's second-most censored country, after North Korea, in a May 2006 special report. All editorial and advertising content still required approval from the PSRD, a time-consuming and often arbitrary process that forced nearly all Burmese newspapers and periodicals to publish as either weeklies or monthlies. On May 21, Aung Shwe Oo and Sint Sint Aung, local journalists working for Japan's *Nippon News Network*, were detained outside Rangoon while covering the docking of a North Korean ship suspected of delivering arms to the junta. The journalists were released on May 23 after undergoing two days of interrogation by local police.

Journalists were banned from reporting favorably on detained opposition leader Aung San Suu Kyi or critically on the junta and its policies. Ross Dunkley, editor-in-chief of the *Myanmar Times*, the country's leading local-language publication, which is run in cooperation with the government, told CPJ in May that PSRD authorities censored about 20 percent of the stories he submitted for publication. He said that included many innocuous articles, including straight news pieces about the construction of a parliament building in the new administrative capital outside Pyinmana.

One subversive advertisement, which ran in the English-language edition of the *Myanmar Times*, slipped by government censors. The Denmark-based satirical group Surrend placed the ad in the paper's July 23 edition to promote tourism among Scandinavian travelers; a Danish-language segment, read backward, said "Killer Than Shwe," a reference to the junta's leading general. In response, the PSRD issued a new ban on all foreign-based advertising in local news publications.

•••••••••••••••••••• **CAMBODIA** ••••••••••••••••••••

Government suppression of a hard-hitting investigative report that implicated senior government officials in illegal logging represented a significant reversal of the modest press freedom gains of the previous two years.

Britain-based environmental watchdog Global Witness released the 95-page report, "Family Trees," on June 1 and several local media groups detailed its findings, which included accusations against Prime Minister Hun Sen's family and personal bodyguard unit. Four days later, the Information Ministry banned and moved to confiscate hard copies of the report, claiming that its conclusions could "incite political problems." Information Minister Khieu Kanarith was quoted in the local media as saying that the confiscation "does not concern the freedom to publish and disseminate information, which the government strongly supports."

Media groups that defied the ban came under threat from officials and unknown assailants. Radio Free Asia (RFA) reporter Lem Pichpisey received an anonymous death threat on his mobile telephone in which the caller said he "could be killed" if he continued reporting on illegal logging. Lem told CPJ that he was routinely followed by plainclothes police officers in the central Kompong Tham province, where he had reported on illegal logging, and in the capital, Phnom Penh. On June 16, fearing for his safety, Lem fled to Thailand, where he lived in exile for more than a month.

Stories like Lem's about Cambodia's illegal logging operations were potentially explosive. Under pressure from foreign donors, which contribute more than half of the country's annual budget, the government had agreed to curb rampant illegal logging. News reports implicating senior officials in the trade were particularly sensitive because they threatened relations with crucial financial supporters.

Although CPJ and other press freedom organizations called on Prime Minister Hun Sen to launch an independent investigation into the threats against Lem, no government action was taken. In response, CPJ conducted a research mission to Cambodia and, in October, published a special report, "Cambodia's Battling Broadcasters," on the government's strained relations with the U.S. government-funded RFA. With its reports on illegal logging, government corruption, and human rights abuses, RFA earned a reputation as one of Cambodia's very few critical news sources.

The print media, meanwhile, came under direct government threat. Soren Seelow, news editor of the French- and Khmer-language daily *Cambodge Soir*, was fired on June 10 for his decision to publish an article that extensively cited the Global

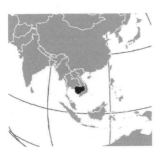

Witness report. News reports at the time claimed that his dismissal was motivated by official pressure. The publication temporarily closed after its journalists went on strike to protest the editor's firing.

A number of Khmer-language newspapers that had serialized RFA's logging reports were directed by the government to stop or face the suspension of their publishing licenses. In particular, officials threatened to close the daily *Sralanh Khmer* if it continued to publish the RFA reports, according to news accounts.

The clampdown marked a worrying departure from what many Cambodian journalists and some press freedom activists had earlier characterized as an improving press freedom environment. Hun Sen came under intense international pressure after his government jailed three journalists between October 2005 and January 2006 over their reports on a controversial border treaty that the premier had struck with neighboring Vietnam.

In early 2006, his government reversed course and released the three men. Several Phnom Penh-based journalists told CPJ that they viewed that event as a watershed for Cambodian press freedom. In June 2006, Hun Sen's government repealed jail terms as penalties for criminal defamation, although journalists may still be imprisoned on broadly written laws governing incitement and disinformation. On August 10, 2007, Hun Sen renewed his 2006 pledge to completely decriminalize defamation through amendment of the country's penal code. The measure was pending in late year, but many Cambodian journalists were optimistic it would be adopted.

At the same time, the administration implemented a new government spokesman system in which all requests for official information were directed to the Information Ministry rather than the relevant ministry or agency. Information Ministry officials presented the new policy as a way to improve government-media relations, according to local journalists. Several journalists who spoke to CPJ in Phnom Penh said the new system had narrowed the flow of information and complained about the spotty availability of Information Ministry officials with clearance to speak to the press.

There were also doubts about the quality of the information dispensed by the ministry. In an exclusive interview with the English-language bimonthly *Phnom Penh Post*, Information Minister Khieu Kanarith articulated his strategy for communicating to Western journalists. "You have to understand: Cambodians know the song you want to hear, and we can sing it for you. ... When you ask a question, we know what kind of answer you want to hear."

On May 3, the Cambodian Center for Human Rights issued a statement calling for the elimination of the Information Ministry, which it referred to as "an obstacle to freedom of the press" and a relic of the country's former "authoritarian regime." Other press freedom advocates continued to push for new legislation barring politicians from owning media outlets.

Of the country's 20 regularly published Khmer-language newspapers, all but two were heavily slanted in favor of Hun Sen's ruling Cambodian People's Party (CPP). Several publications were owned and editorially steered by senior CPP politicians, while others were managed by their close business associates, including the country's largest circulation daily newspaper, *Rasmei Kampuchea*. One critical newspaper, *Khmer Amatak*, saw its license suspended for one month beginning on October 8, when its director refused an Information Ministry order to print a correction to an article critical of Deputy Prime Minister Nhiek Bun Chhay. The paper stood by the accuracy of its story and said it was willing to fight its case in court before the suspension was handed down.

A similar situation prevailed in television news. All 11 stations were either owned or run by politicians or their business proxies, and all reported fawningly on Hun Sen and his CPP-led government. One television news analysis program, "Thursday Talk," aired by privately held Cambodian Television Network and hosted by popular broadcaster Soy Sopheap, did begin to earn a reputation for tackling low-level corruption.

Soy Sopheap told CPJ that "over the past 15 years we have seen big improvements" in the press freedom situation for television reporters, but that the situation was "still less free compared with most Western countries." He said that criticism of Hun Sen, CPP members, and senior military officials was still off-limits. The reporter spoke from personal experience: In November 2006, he received an anonymous death threat connected to his program's reports on military corruption. "Watch out for yourself when you criticize the stars. It means death," said the Khmer-language letter, invoking the term "stars" to mean senior generals. The threat came shortly after Soy Sopheap aired a report on corruption allegations against senior military figures.

In remote provinces, meanwhile, journalists continued to work in a hostile and often lawless environment. On May 2, Gen. Pol Sinuon, a senior military official based in the western Battambang province, threatened to shoot *Kampuchea Thmey* newspaper reporter Chim Chenda after Chim addressed him by his name rather than a term

ASIA

of respect reserved for senior members of the military. The general later retracted his statement, claiming he made the threat in jest, according to the Cambodian Association for the Protection of Journalists, a local press freedom advocacy group.

Other attacks on provincial reporters arose from anonymous sources. On August 9, *Chbas Kar* reporter Phon Phat received a threat from an anonymous caller who said he would deliver a "gift" to the reporter because of his accounts of illegal logging in western Porsat province. The following night, at around 4 a.m., unknown assailants set Phat's house on fire. He and his family escaped without injury, and the blaze was quickly extinguished.

Boeng Khnar Commune Police Chief Sann Ly was quoted in the local press saying that the attack was likely in "revenge" for Phat's reporting on illegal logging. District Police Chief Youk Yoen told reporters that his investigation team was approaching the case as "an attack on the free press." One week later, on August 17, Phat's house was attacked again by unknown arsonists.

· · · · · · · · · · · · · · · · · · · **CHINA** ·

In a year of internal political wrangling and further emergence on the global stage, Chinese leadership under President Hu Jintao showed a keen awareness of public opinion at home and abroad. But the result was not greater freedom for the press. The administration undertook a clumsy effort to woo the foreign press corps while simultaneously tightening control over the flow of information and commentary within China.

To mark the one-year countdown to the start of the 2008 Olympic Games in Beijing, CPJ sent a delegation to the capital in August to release a special report, "Falling Short," outlining China's failure to live up to its promise of expanding media freedom in advance of the Summer Games. The 79-page report pointed up Chinese authorities' continued control and abuse of journalists, particularly the domestic press. For the ninth consecutive year, China was the world's leading jailer of journalists, with 29 imprisoned when CPJ conducted its annual census on December 1.

January 1, 2007, brought the implementation of a rule that appeared designed to appease international critics of China's press freedom record in the run-up to the Games. The new regulations lifted a requirement that foreign journalists—as well as those from Hong Kong and Macau—obtain official permission for interviews.

"We are encouraged to see an increasing number of reports by foreign journalists, which now cover every aspect of our society," said Liu Jianchao, head of the Foreign Ministry's Information Department, in an interview with the state-run *China Daily*. Liu stated that the new regulations gave the international press free access. "China has followed up on its pledge to facilitate the work of foreign journalists," he said.

The changes, however, were mostly cosmetic, since journalists had widely ignored the old rules. Foreign journalists told CPJ that they still experienced surveillance and harassment, particularly while traveling outside of major cities. The continued imprisonment of Hong Kong journalist Ching Cheong, China correspondent for the Singapore-based daily *Straits Times*, demonstrated the ongoing risk for foreign-employed journalists.

The gesture of increased freedom did not extend to the mainland press. Rather, leaders in Beijing displayed a heightened sensitivity in 2007, apparently related to the convening of the Communist Party's National Congress in October to determine, among other things, a line of succession for Hu. Instead of relying on a technologically sophisticated system of information control, authorities chose their bluntest tool and shut down Internet communication in advance of the Congress. Public security officers in several regions shuttered Internet data centers, which house servers, for hosting even a single Web site deemed politically offensive, according to news reports and industry sources.

One of the country's biggest data centers, Waigaoqiao, was ordered to suspend operations on September 3, affecting 30 servers, according to bloggers and industry sources. Other data centers were ordered to disable interactive features such as bulletin boards and comment sections during the Congress. Thousands of Web sites were shut down or became otherwise unavailable to Internet users.

The suppression of news and commentary belied statements Hu made in an address to the Congress, pledging to solicit public opinion in drafting new laws and to improve public oversight of governance. "We need to carry out democratic elections, decision-making, administration, and oversight in accordance with the law and safeguard people's rights to be informed, to participate, to express, and to oversee," Hu said.

Throughout the year, the people's right to be informed took a backseat to official efforts to control public opinion, particularly as it was expressed online by the country's 137 million Internet users. Hu emphasized the goal of Internet control at a Politburo meeting in January, according to the official Xinhua News Agency. The president urged the party's Central Committee members "to build online fronts of ideology and public opinion … actively employing new technologies to strengthen positive propaganda, and fostering positive and uplifting mainstream public opinion."

Three Internet journalists were imprisoned during the year, making for a total of 18 jailed for online work. In May, Sun Lin, a reporter for the U.S.-based Web news service *Boxun News*, and his wife, He Fang, were arrested in Nanjing. Sun, who used the pen name Jie Mu, had filed audio, video, and written news reports that were harshly critical of party and government policies. In one of his most recent reports, filed from Tiananmen Square, Sun described his unsuccessful efforts to gain accreditation to cover the Olympic Games. Both Sun and He were charged with illegally possessing weapons.

In June, journalist Qi Chonghuai was arrested after writing online posts that defended news reports of official corruption in the northern province of Shandong. Initially accused of holding a forged press card, Qi was later charged with extortion. Police severely beat the veteran journalist during interrogations, his lawyer told CPJ.

Another journalist was imprisoned for "inciting subversion of state authority," a charge commonly used to suppress criticism of party or government leadership. Lü Gengsong was detained in the eastern city of Hangzhou in August. A freelance writer, political activist, and frequent contributor to overseas Web sites, Lü wrote about corruption, land grabs, organized crime, and human rights abuses. The day before he was detained, he reported the handing down of a two-year sentence in the trial of activist Yang Yunbiao. Authorities did not clarify the specific reasons for Lü's arrest.

Party leaders continued to exert control over print and broadcast media by shuffling editorial personnel and by issuing frequent communiqués from central and local propaganda departments. All print and broadcast media in mainland China are state-owned and subject to the ideological whims of party cadres. The human cost of a policy of censorship encompasses far more than the journalists demoted, transferred, or jailed for crossing the line. In 2007, unreported or underreported topics included fatal coal mining accidents, rural protests against corrupt local officials, serious problems with the supply of food and drugs, and environmental degradation, as well as a host of trivial topics that local officials deemed embarrassing or inflammatory.

During the summer, a wave of international recalls and bans on Chinese exports brought a flurry of bad press worldwide. The deaths of American dogs and cats from tainted pet food from China prompted further inquiries into product safety. In the months that followed, importers discovered lead-paint-covered toys, toxic toothpaste, and contaminated seafood from China. In Panama, mass poisonings from cough syrup in 2006 were linked to an industrial solvent imported from a Chinese firm that mislabeled it as glycerine.

In Beijing, a July news report showing steamed buns being filled with cardboard pulp made international news. Within a few days, however, Beijing TV issued an apology, saying that the story was fabricated. The arrest of Zi Beijia, the freelancer responsible for the report, only raised more questions. Was Zi targeted for making up news, or because he exposed another embarrassing flaw in the food supply? In less than a month, Zi was sentenced to a year in prison for the unusual crime of "infringing on the reputation of a commodity."

Whatever the real reasons for Zi's arrest, authorities used it as the basis for a further crackdown on the press. News reports on product quality became noticeably tamer, and in August the National Anti-Pornography and Anti-Piracy Office announced a fresh campaign to stop the spread of "illegal" news. Office Director Liu Binjie, who is also director of the General Administration of Press and Publication, vowed to increase inspections of newspapers and periodicals, and "to clamp down on illegal news coverage and eliminate any spread of false news," according to Xinhua. Targeted publications included newspapers imported without authorization, "illegal political newspapers," and "illegal military newspapers and magazines that leak state secrets."

Prison conditions for journalists remained harsh. After visiting her husband in a prison in Hebei province, the wife of jailed Internet writer Guo Qizhen told CPJ that her husband was covered in bruises and that he was not receiving adequate medical attention for injuries that included a fractured right leg. Guo, who was detained in May 2006, is serving a four-year sentence for his online political writings. Internet journalist Zhang Jianhong, convicted of "subversion" in March 2007, described in a letter to his lawyer a debilitating nerve disorder that threatened to paralyze him. His appeals for release on medical grounds were denied, and Zhang continued to serve out his six-year term.

The revolving prison door also released some journalists in 2007, including *New York Times* researcher Zhao Yan, who was imprisoned for three years after the newspaper exposed a high-level leadership shift. Li Minying, former editor of the Guangzhou-based daily *Nanfang Dushi Bao*, was released in February after serving half of a six-year prison sentence handed out during a crackdown against the paper for its aggressive reporting. Li's colleague Yu Huafeng remained in jail.

In November 2007, CPJ honored journalist Gao Qinrong with an International Press Freedom Award. Gao, a former reporter for Xinhua, was imprisoned in 1998 after exposing a scam irrigation project in his home province of Shanxi. He was sentenced to prison on a grab bag of trumped-up charges that included embezzlement and fraud. After his release in December 2006, he refused to stay silent, instead giving interviews about his experiences to international and domestic news organizations. In an interview with CPJ in Beijing, Gao said he hoped to get the charges against him erased so that he could return to work as a journalist.

"I am not afraid because my conscience is clear," Gao said. "I didn't do anything wrong or hurt anyone. Everything I do, I do under the sun."

· **INDIA** ·

The famously freewheeling press in the world's biggest democracy operated largely without interference from the central government but nevertheless faced significant challenges, from the threat of violent assault to legal harassment. The dangers confronting journalists varied tremendously across regions, with those working in conflict areas or outside the major urban centers at greatest risk. With no national organization systematically tracking press freedom violations, cases involving jour-

ASIA

nalists working for small media outlets rarely drew wide attention.

Subir Ghosh, a media analyst and editor of the Web site *Newswatch India*, told CPJ that he had come across a surprising number of unreported press freedom violations while doing his own work. "There is tremendous scope for research," he said. "Journalists' solidarity is just not there."

The threat of physical violence was most acute in conflict areas such as those in the North-Eastern States, the central Indian state of Chhattisgarh, and the disputed territory of Kashmir. The media in Manipur, in northeast India, faced perhaps the most severe pressures in 2007, balancing official restrictions on the publication of statements made by "unlawful organizations" against the competing demands made by more than a dozen insurgent groups involved in separatist activity or factional fighting. Local journalists said they were caught in an impossible situation, facing physical reprisal from militants on the one hand and government prosecution on the other. Twice during the year, Manipuri print media shut down their presses for days on end to protest the severe threats against them.

Deadly violence also flared in unexpected corners, such as the comparatively stable southern state of Tamil Nadu. Three media workers died in a gasoline bomb attack on the offices of the Tamil-language daily *Dinakaran* in the Tamil Nadu city of Madurai. The victims were identified as computer engineers M. Vinod Kumar and G. Gopinath, and security guard K. Muthuramalingam. India's Central Bureau of Investigation took charge of the investigation, as the prime suspect behind the attack was the chief minister's elder son, M. K. Azhagiri, according to local news reports. *Dinakaran* staffers said that Azhagiri was apparently angered by an opinion poll published by the paper that showed his brother had more popular support as a future leader of the state. Azhagiri, who was awaiting trial on an unrelated murder charge, denied the allegations.

In a case that drew national and international attention, a group of men who identified themselves as members of the Shiv Sena, a Hindu nationalist party, vandalized the Mumbai offices of the English-language newsmagazine *Outlook*. The assailants were apparently angered by the political journal's depiction of their founder, Bal Thackeray, as a "villain" in its August 20 issue. The attack followed warnings by a Shiv Sena spokesman that there would be "repercussions across the state" if the government revived attempts to prosecute Thackeray and others indicted for their roles in the 1992-93 communal riots in Mumbai.

The Indian judiciary continued to use contempt-of-court provisions to silence critics and shield the institution from public scrutiny. The highest-profile contempt case involved the sentencing of four journalists from the New Delhi edition of the daily newspaper *Mid-Day* to four months in prison apiece for a series of articles and a political cartoon accusing a former chief justice of official misconduct. The journalists were freed on bail and filed an appeal with the Supreme Court, which was due to consider the case in early 2008. India's parliament had passed an amendment to the Contempt of Courts Act in 2006 that introduced truth as a defense. Local journalists said the *Mid-Day* case marked the first known test of that new provision.

Members of the press were sometimes targeted or subjected to arbitrary actions by police and government agents. In April, about 20 Indian police and two municipal officials raided the office of Mizzima, a nonprofit news agency established by a group of Burmese exiles. Reporters were refused entry and the office was sealed off with padlocks, according to a Mizzima editor who spoke with CPJ. Authorities claimed that Mizzima was illegally conducting commercial activities in a residential area, a charge denied by the organization. Mizzima was allowed to reopen after two days, following protests by national and international journalists' organizations. It was not clear why the news agency was targeted, although one editor said his sources indicated that Indian intelligence agencies may have been behind the raid.

For better and for worse, the Indian media were obsessed with the sting. Debates swirled about the ethics of these undercover investigations to expose corruption or wrongdoing, which have become a staple of the country's booming television news industry. Many media commentators feared that, in the absence of any effective self-regulatory framework for the broadcast media, the government would step into the breach to control content.

The most infamous case of the year involved a sting operation conducted by the Live India news channel, which on August 30 broadcast a report accusing a New Delhi teacher of pushing schoolchildren into prostitution. An angry mob besieged the school and assaulted the teacher, stripping and beating her, according to local and international news reports. Within 24 hours, she was dismissed by the Department of Education, arrested, and charged with human trafficking. And then, it turned out, the police discovered that the sting was staged, allegedly organized by a businessman to whom the teacher owed money and starring an aspiring young reporter playing the role of a victimized former student.

The Live India episode became an ugly symbol of all that was wrong with the country's hypercompetitive news industry, with more than 40 all-news channels battling for viewers. Analysts lamented the prevalence of "stink journalism" and "babloid" television, and tallied the costs of the media's loss of credibility. "The timing could not have been worse," wrote NDTV Managing Editor Barkha Dutt, one of the country's most prominent television journalists, in a column in the national daily *Hindustan Times*. "On a day when television journalists were all set to wrestle the government to the ground over its imperious and inane Broadcasting Bill, along comes our own moment of ignominy and shame." The draft legislation proposed by the government

ASIA

included content controls that were bitterly opposed by the broadcast media, which began work to formulate their own set of voluntary guidelines. The issue stalled in late year amid the political storm over the India-U.S. nuclear deal, but it appeared likely to resurface.

Broadcast liberalization also led to positive developments, including the growth of community radio stations addressing the concerns of the rural poor, who still make up India's vast majority but who are largely ignored by the mainstream media. Sevanti Ninan, editor of the media-monitoring Web site *The Hoot*, said that there is a kind of self-censorship in India.

"Poverty does not get reported because upwardly mobile readers are presumed to be not interested," she wrote in an e-mail to CPJ. "Or because the market wants only upbeat stories, or because the editor or proprietor has certain holy cows that the journalists know they are expected to avoid."

Tehelka magazine took on sacred cows across the western state of Gujarat with its undercover investigation into who orchestrated the wave of violence in 2002 that claimed the lives of more than 2,000 people, mostly Muslims, according to local news reports. "This was no uncontrived, unplanned, unprompted communal violence. This was a pogrom. This was genocide," wrote reporter Ashish Khetan in his introduction to the 108-page exposé, published in the magazine's November 3 edition. As evidence, *Tehelka* pointed to videotaped interviews with politicians and Hindu activists describing their roles in the violence and the involvement of the state government.

Tehelka launched the exposé even before the magazine hit the newsstands, releasing video excerpts to television channels on October 25. That same day, a senior official in the state capital of Ahmedabad, District Collector Dhananjay Dwivedi, ordered cable television operators to block news channels carrying the *Tehelka* story on the grounds that the footage could inflame communal tensions between Hindus and Muslims, according to local media reports. Among those channels taken off the air in Gujarat were Aaj Tak, Headlines Today, CNN-IBN, and NDTV. The state election commission said it was looking into the circumstances of the ban order, and normal broadcasting resumed after two days.

A state government lawyer featured in the sting publicly resigned from his post but went on to say he had been framed by reporters, who he claimed had given him a script to read. He later registered a complaint with police accusing the Gujarat bureau chief of the television news channel Aaj Tak, which broadcast *Tehelka*'s video of his testimony, of "criminal breach of trust, conspiracy, and fraud." Aaj Tak denied the allegations.

Tehelka stood by the story. The magazine, in its introduction to the report, stated that the reporter had elicited the testimonies by posing as a student researching the Hindu resurgence, "armed with nothing but two button-sized cameras." The editors defended their use of undercover tactics, arguing that "extraordinary stories need extraordinary methods."

· · · · · · · · · · · · · · · · · · · **PAKISTAN** ·

The December 27 assassination of opposition leader Benazir Bhutto plunged the nation into further turmoil after months of violent unrest and a bitterly contested state of emergency. An aggressive domestic press corps was in the middle of the momentous events, questioning government assertions and being targeted by government censorship.

Leaving a political rally in Rawalpindi in the waning days of the parliamentary campaign, Bhutto's vehicle was attacked by a gunman and a suicide bomber. The government tried to claim that Bhutto died by hitting her head on the car's sunroof, but Pakistani news media published images of a gun-wielding assassin just feet from the former prime minister. Bhutto supporters blamed the government for lax security at the rally and even complicity in the killing.

The assassination punctuated a year of growing conflict and plummeting popularity for Pervez Musharraf, the general who had led Pakistan through eight years of military-backed rule. On November 3, Musharraf tightened his hold on power by declaring a state of emergency, suspending the constitution, dissolving the Supreme Court, and shutting all independent broadcasters. Musharraf later stood down as head of the army and lifted the emergency order in moves designed to assuage international concerns. But the parliamentary elections scheduled for early January were postponed following Bhutto's assassination.

The crisis peaked in late year after months of anti-Musharraf demonstrations, mounting deaths from the militant Islamic insurgency, and clashes between the president and the Supreme Court. Musharraf declared the emergency just as the high court was due to rule on challenges to his new term as president. Members of the national and provincial assemblies had elected Musharraf president on October 6, but opposition politicians argued that he was ineligible to run while remaining as army chief. With the court dissolved, a new one hand-picked by the president, and the media muzzled, however, Musharraf had cleared away obstacles to a new term.

Under the emergency order, Musharraf imposed a series of restrictions on press coverage, but television broadcasters were his primary target. He had apparently come to view the country's 50 cable stations as a major threat to his rule. In March, when Musharraf sacked Supreme Court Chief Justice Iftikhar Muhammad Chaudhry in a dispute over the release of 61 terrorism suspects, the stations' live coverage of the ensuing demonstrations, their free-ranging political commentary, and their animated call-in programs had been the president's main media challenge.

It was a strange situation. The cable broadcasters, as well as other parts of Pakistan's expanding media universe, were in large part Musharraf's own creation.

Having allowed the stations, many of them owned by large media groups, to blossom under his rule, he appeared surprised and angered when they decided to pursue independent journalism rather than do the government's bidding. As the broadcast ban continued through November—only state-run Pakistan TV remained on the air—the independent stations lost millions in advertising.

With the shutdown taking a financial toll on stations, the government pressured owners to sign a 14-page "code of conduct" before they could return to the air. The code prohibits material that "defames or brings into ridicule the head of state" and imposes jail terms of up to three years for journalists who violate the ban. Geo TV, owned by the Jang Group, and ARY One World TV, an Urdu- and Hindi-language news channel, were among the longest holdouts. But the stations were undercut by the Dubai government, which discontinued their satellite retransmission under intense pressure from Musharraf's administration. Though the two stations' broadcasts could not be seen in Pakistan during the shutdown, they had continued to reach global audiences via the satellite services of Dubai Media City, a state-sponsored, regional media hub.

Most independent television stations were back on the air by mid-December—and they soon leapt into wall-to-wall coverage of the Bhutto assassination.

Musharraf's antimedia policies did not appear to have cost him U.S. backing, although U.S. Ambassador Anne Patterson did visit the shuttered TV stations and express support for press freedom. By the time the emergency was lifted, the Bush administration and other Western governments did not seem eager to pressure Musharraf to ease media restrictions. Talat Hussain, a popular talk-show host whose program was canceled, told *The New York Times* in December that Musharraf was "getting away with it, really, because the Western support is there again. ... There isn't enough pressure."

Owais Aslam Ali, who runs the media support group Pakistan Press Foundation in Karachi, said he understood why broadcasters bore the brunt of Musharraf's ire: "The government has to control 50 or more channels now, and, given the competition, the news teams don't miss stories. They tend to drive national media coverage." With overall literacy at about 50 percent, according to U.N. figures, television and radio broadcasts reach a wider audience than Pakistan's many vernacular newspapers and magazines. But Ali also saw a downside to the predominance of television: "Because the electronic media are so young ... there were laxer standards. They were showing body parts and all sorts of shocking pictures after terrorist bombs, for example."

The power of television had become evident to Musharraf in the spring, when citizens joined thousands of lawyers who had taken to the streets to protest his sacking of Chief Justice Chaudhry. The privately owned Royal TV, which broadcast in Islamabad, was the first to fall victim; government regulators ordered the station off the air in April after coverage of the demonstrations.

The same month, the Pakistan Electronic Media Regulatory Authority (PEMRA) threatened to close Aaj TV after it aired programming critical of the government's role in the Chaudhry dispute. That did not happen, but on May 12, amid violence between anti- and pro-government groups in Karachi, Aaj's studios came under gunfire from what media reports identified as pro-government supporters. No injuries were reported, and the station remained open.

It was around this time that the government's tactics appeared to be shifting: Rather than targeting individual journalists as it had in the past, it began aiming directly at media houses, harassing them legally, financially, and through attacks on their facilities. On March 16, riot police used tear gas and batons against staff as they swept through the Islamabad offices of the Jang Group, which houses Geo TV, Pakistan's leading private TV station, and the newspapers the *Daily Jang* and *The News*. The raid came less than a day after the government ordered Geo not to air coverage of street protests sparked by Chaudhry's ouster.

The Supreme Court had its own hand in media repression in May, when it issued a directive to print and electronic media to avoid "any interference" in the Chaudhry dispute. Violations would be considered "contempt of court," the official Associated Press of Pakistan (APP) reported. For an institution sworn to uphold Pakistan's constitution, the court's censorship order was shockingly broad. "Discussions, comments, or write-ups that are likely to interfere with the legal process, ridicule, scandalize or malign the court or any of its judges, or that touch on the merits of the case are strictly prohibited," the APP quoted the court's directive as saying. Under Pakistani law, a contempt citation could lead to imprisonment.

The Federally Administered Tribal Areas along the Afghan border remained virtually off-limits to foreign journalists. Local reporters at the Peshawar Press Club, a traditional jumping-off point to the tribal areas, told CPJ that conditions had worsened, and that even the most experienced journalists had curtailed their activity. Reporters remained under assault from government security forces, criminals, and foreign elements—usually Taliban or al-Qaeda fighters who had moved into the area from Uzbekistan, Chechnya, or Afghanistan.

Sohail Qalander, Peshawar editor for the *Daily Express*, the country's second-largest Urdu-language newspaper, was abducted in January and held for seven weeks by "criminal and tribal elements" in the Khyber Agency of Pakistan's lawless North-West Frontier Province, the newspaper's managing editor, Abid Abdullah, told CPJ. In April, foreign militants killed the brother, father, uncle, and cousin of *Inkishaf* reporter Din Muhammed at the family home in South Waziristan, colleagues told CPJ. The attack was an apparent reprisal for Muhammed's reporting in the town of Wana—a place so dangerous that few journalists dared to enter.

Another story with potentially long-term implications continued to play out, as Islamic militant influence spread from the tribal areas into adjacent regions. After a

ASIA

four-month truce with the government ended in late September, militant Islamists took over most of the Swat Valley, once a tourist attraction known for its natural beauty and skiing, located about 100 miles (160 kilometers) north of Islamabad. The Tehreek-e-Nafaz-e-Shariat-e-Mohammadi (Movement for the Enforcement of Islamic Law), led by cleric Maulana Fazlullah, had been in open rebellion against the Pakistani government for years. By November, the militants had set up a "parallel government," with Islamic courts imposing Sharia, or Islamic, law in at least 59 villages. Fazlullah had used a string of pirate FM radio stations to build his power base over several years.

All of these attacks—from the government, from political factions, from the judiciary, from Islamic militants—led CPJ to rank Pakistan among the world's worst backsliders on press freedom. Twelve Pakistani journalists have been killed since the death of American reporter Daniel Pearl in 2002. Only Pearl's death was thoroughly investigated, the findings publicly reported, and the perpetrators brought to trial. At least 15 more journalists were abducted in that time, with the government's own Directorate of Inter-Services Intelligence suspected in many of the cases. In 2007, five journalists were killed in direct relation to their work:

- Mehboob Khan, 22, a freelance photographer, died on April 28 in a suicide bomb attack in Charsadda that was aimed at Interior Minister Aftab Sherpao. Khan had started working as a journalist just a few months before.

- Noor Hakim Khan, a correspondent for *Daily Pakistan*, was among five people killed by a roadside bomb in the Bajaur region of the North-West Frontier Province on June 2. Khan was traveling in an official convoy that might have been targeted.

- On July 3, crossfire between government forces and students from the Lal Masjid (Red Mosque) in Islamabad took the life of Javed Khan, a journalist with *Markaz* and DM Digital TV. He was shot in the chest and neck. The source of the fatal shots was not clear.

- Muhammad Arif, a cameraman for ARY One World TV, was among 139 people killed in an October 19 bombing during a Karachi political rally celebrating Bhutto's homecoming.

- Zubair Ahmed Mujahid, correspondent for the national Urdu-language daily *Jang*, was shot in the southern province of Sindh on November 23. Local journalists believed their colleague was slain because of his investigative reporting.

•••••••••••••••••• **PHILIPPINES** ••••••••••••••••••

ASIA

Supreme Court Chief Justice Reynato S. Puno told a visiting CPJ delegation in July that he would personally seek justice for the unsolved killings of journalists and use his judicial authority to better protect press freedom. "The fact that the killings remain unsolved heightens public distrust in our system of justice," Puno told CPJ. The senior judge was fresh off a national summit that he had convened to examine a rash of extrajudicial killings committed nationwide in recent years.

Puno's pledge follows President Gloria Macapagal Arroyo's move in 2004 to create a special police task force dedicated to investigating journalist murders. Police investigators said they had identified suspects in nearly half of the 27 cases they examined, but they had managed convictions in only two cases since the task force was created.

According to CPJ research, at least 32 journalists have been killed in direct relation to their work in the Philippines since 1992, making it the world's fifth-deadliest nation for journalists during that time period. The impunity rate in these cases is more than 90 percent, CPJ research shows. This record, in part, prompted CPJ to launch a new global campaign against impunity; the effort will initially focus on the Philippines and Russia, two of the worst nations in solving crimes against the press.

Much of the aggression has followed a sadly familiar pattern: Journalists, usually in a provincial town, take on a local corruption issue and wind up being attacked or killed. Often, journalists have political affiliations of their own, making the motive for the attack difficult to determine.

The violence dipped in 2007, when two journalists were slain under unclear circumstances, CPJ research shows. Hernani Pastolero, 64, editor-in-chief of the community newspaper *Lightning Courier Weekly*, was shot twice in the head in front of his home in Sultan Kudarat township, on the southern island of Mindanao. His unidentified assassin escaped on foot, according to local media reports. Local Police Superintendent Joel Goltiao said his office compiled a list of suspects in the February 20 slaying, but he declined to comment on a possible motive. Local media reported that investigators were exploring Pastolero's connection to a dispute between residential lot owners and a large private landholder.

In another emblematic case, gunmen killed commentator Ferdinand Lintuan in downtown Davao City, Mindanao, on December 24. Lintuan, 51, was a "block time" broadcaster—an independent commentator who leased airtime from local radio station DXGO—and a columnist for the regional English-language daily *Sun Star*. Two masked, motorcycle-riding assailants shot Lintuan as he was driving his

Volkswagen with two radio station colleagues as passengers. The passengers were uninjured in the attack, and no motive was immediately established. Well-known for his criticism of local politicians, Lintuan had recently decried alleged corruption in a local development project and illegal logging activities. The *Sun Star* said that Lintuan had survived an August 1987 attack inside another Davao radio station. Three people died in that attack.

The 2007 slayings each drew an immediate national response, with Arroyo dispatching the Philippine National Police and the National Bureau of Investigation to assist in the probes. CPJ is investigating to determine whether the slayings were work-related.

Attacks on journalists did not come in isolation. Early in the year, the human rights group Karapatan (Rights) counted 832 extrajudicial killings since 2001, when Arroyo came to power. Few, if any, had been investigated by the police, allowing an air of impunity to flourish.

In February, Arroyo was hit with a one-two blow. Philip Alston, U.N. Human Rights Council special rapporteur on extrajudicial, summary, or arbitrary executions, ended a 10-day mission by demanding that an undisclosed government report on the killings be released. Forced into a corner, the administration publicly issued a report that found "elements in the military" were responsible for many of the extrajudicial killings. The report was compiled by a government-backed commission headed by retired Philippine Supreme Court Justice Jose Melo.

These reports, while not addressing journalists specifically, highlighted the inability of local governments to conduct thorough, effective, and unbiased investigations—despite pressure from central authorities. CPJ's own research has found a longstanding pattern in which local officials are implicated in journalist murders but are protected by corrupt provincial police and judges.

In an October special report, "The Road to Justice," CPJ board member and veteran Philippine journalist Sheila Coronel described this culture of impunity and pointed to one of the rare exceptions—the successful prosecution of three men in the 2004 murder of columnist Marlene Garcia-Esperat. Advocates used several techniques effectively in the Garcia-Esperat case: hiring a private attorney to assist prosecutors, securing a change in venue from a corrupt local court, providing protection to witnesses, and drawing wide public attention to the crime. CPJ joined with Philippine press groups in 2007 to push prosecutors to go further in the case by filing charges against two agriculture department officials accused of ordering the murder.

Despite its poor record in fighting these crimes, the government did not shy away from bringing new legal pressure against journalists. On February 14, Arroyo's government filed incitement to sedition charges against the *Daily Tribune* Publisher Ninez Cacho-Olivares and two columnists, Ramon Seneres and Herman Tiu-Laurel, in Manila's Metropolitan Trial Court. Prosecutor Philip Kimpo said that articles published in the paper were designed to "lead or stir up the people against the lawful authorities, namely, the president of the Philippines, and disturb the peace of the community." The case was pending in late year.

Arroyo's government had a history of harassing the *Daily Tribune*, which frequently published articles critical of her administration. Police raided and confiscated materials from the newspaper's offices in February 2006, soon after Arroyo declared martial law to clamp down on an alleged coup attempt by her political opponents. The Supreme Court later ruled that the raid was in violation of the Philippine Constitution, citing provisions in the charter that protect press freedom.

Journalists faced new uncertainties when, on July 15, the government enacted antiterrorism legislation. A top Justice Ministry official told reporters the law would, in certain instances, allow the government to wiretap journalists if they were "suspected of co-mingling with terror suspects." The Human Security Act broadly defines terrorism and calls for the arrest of any accomplices to terror-related crimes. CPJ and local press freedom groups expressed concerns that the law leaves open the possibility that journalists could be considered accomplices to terrorism if they merely interviewed or reported the statements of those considered to be terror suspects.

Criminal defamation cases also made news in 2007. The outcomes for journalists were mixed.

On March 7, Gemma Bagauaya, editor of the online magazine *Newsbreak*, was arrested on a criminal libel complaint filed by Luis Singson, governor of Ilocos Sur province. She posted 10,000 pesos (US$230) in bail and was released the same day. *Newsbreak* Managing Editor Glenda Gloria and Editor-in-Chief Marites Vitug were also charged but not detained. The charges stemmed from a February 12 article written by Gloria that identified Singson as one of five key people who helped Arroyo survive the political fallout from an election-rigging scandal that broke out in 2005.

But on May 3, World Press Freedom Day, First Gentleman Jose Miguel Arroyo announced in a government-released statement that he would drop a rash of pending defamation complaints related to the scandal. A new outlook on life apparently drove the decision: Arroyo said he withdrew the cases because he was "grateful for surviving a delicate open-heart surgery." Arroyo had filed 46 different complaints against 11 journalists and was pursuing a total of 70 million pesos (US$1.6 million) in damages in related civil suits. More than 40 journalists had filed a countersuit, accusing Arroyo of using the courts to harass the media.

• • • • • • • • • • • • • • • • • SRI LANKA • • • • • • • • • • • • • • • • • •

In May, senior journalist Iqbal Athas wrote to CPJ warning that press freedom conditions had deteriorated under President Mahinda Rajapaksa. By September,

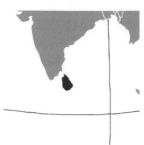

Athas, a well-known defense correspondent for *The Sunday Times* of Sri Lanka and a 1994 CPJ International Press Freedom Award winner, had to leave the country temporarily in fear for his safety after angering officials with a story about the corruption-ridden purchase of MiG-27 fighter jets from Ukraine. That departure was not the first time Athas had fled Sri Lanka for his safety, but it was indicative of the pressures facing journalists who dared to take on the government.

The Athas incident galvanized the political opposition and the rest of the media, although most other attacks on the press drew little attention. Ethnic Tamil journalists faced the direst threats, with local and less prominent journalists the most likely to be targeted, Sunanda Deshapriya, a leader of the press freedom group Free Media Movement, told CPJ. In August, CPJ conducted a research mission to Sri Lanka, speaking with journalists about the extent and nature of the threat. Swept up in a 24-year-long conflict between the Sinhalese-dominated government and Tamil separatists, the nation is among the world's deadliest for the press.

CPJ recorded the deaths of five journalists in 2007, all ethnic Tamils. On April 16, Subash Chandraboas, editor of the Tamil-language monthly magazine *Nilam*, was shot in his home near Vavuniya. In addition to his work for *Nilam*, Chandraboas was head of an alternative media network and was known as a poet. Vavuniya, 162 miles (260 kilometers) north of Colombo, had been the site of a number of killings in 2007, at least 25 in April alone. The targets, there and elsewhere, were usually Tamil journalists whose assailants were virtually never prosecuted.

On April 29, Selvarajah Rajeewarnam, a reporter for the Tamil-language daily *Uthayan*, was riding his bicycle to an assignment when he was shot by unidentified motorcycle-riding gunmen about 600 feet (180 meters) from a military checkpoint, according to *Uthayan* staffers. Rajeewarnam was a crime reporter who had recently switched jobs from the pro-Tamil Jaffna daily *Namathu Eelanadu*, which closed after its managing editor, Sinnathamby Sivamaharajah, was gunned down in August 2006.

Three journalists for the Voice of Tigers radio station in Kilinochchi—announcer Isaivizhi Chempiyan and technicians Suresh Linbiyo and T. Tharmalingam—were killed in a Sri Lankan Air Force air strike on November 27. Fighter jets dropped a dozen bombs on the station shortly before Velupillai Prabhakaran, leader of the separatist Liberation Tigers of Tamil Eelam (LTTE), was due to broadcast a statement. At least five other people were killed in the strike against the LTTE-run station, according to local media reports.

Tamil-language media have taken the brunt of the government-led assault on the press, particularly in the north and east, where Tamil separatist groups have sought territory. A joint press freedom mission in October 2006—which included representatives from the International Federation of Journalists, the International Press Institute, and the International News Safety Institute—produced a highly critical report in January. The report found "a serious deterioration in the security situation for the Sri Lankan media with threats, abductions, and attacks committed by all parties to the conflict, and particularly paramilitary and militia groups." Titled "The Struggle for Survival," the report stated that "media practitioners are prevented from reporting freely and as a direct consequence press freedom and freedom of expression are severely restricted." The media situation, the report said, is complicated by the fact that many journalists are openly partisan, favoring a particular side or faction within the conflict.

Threats, abductions, and attacks on journalists come from all sides. In the Tamil conflict areas, armed men from the government or rival Tamil groups, both in and out of uniform, operate with virtual impunity.

In the capital, Colombo, roving government agents and paramilitaries are usually behind the violence. Their vehicles of choice are often vans with tinted side glass and no license plates, driven by men in plain clothes. One reporter, Parameswaree Maunasámi, dared to write about the vans and the abductions in November 2006. Maunasámi, a Tamil writing for the Sinhalese-language weekly *Mawbima* (Motherland), was arrested and accused of associating with a young woman alleged to be a Tamil suicide bomber. Maunasámi, held for five months in a darkened cell infested with vermin and roaches, was eventually released with no charges brought against her. Though frightened, Maunasámi continued to pursue the abduction story and was soon followed for a time by a white van. She filed a complaint with the police, but no apparent investigation was launched.

In areas of conflict, publications that supported negotiated peace with the government were labeled traitorous and threatened by militant groups such as the LTTE. It was common for journalists to back away from their jobs and go into hiding, particularly when their families had been threatened. But threats did not have to come at street level, as they did for Maunasámi. In April, Champika Liyanarachchi, editor of the prominent *Daily Mirror*, told CPJ that Defense Secretary Gotabhaya Rajapaksa called her to complain about the paper's coverage of sectarian fighting in Pottuvil in Ampara district. Rajapaksa was angered by an article that said Tamil rebels belonging to the breakaway Karuna faction of the LTTE were freely moving weapons within the government-controlled area. Liyanarachchi said Rajapaksa told her "that she should not expect any security from the government to protect her" against possible retaliation from the rebels.

Such intimidation is not likely to subside as long as the country remains at war. The LTTE started its rebellion in 1983 with the goal of establishing a separate state for the country's 3.2 million Tamils. Before the government and rebels signed a cease-fire in 2002, some 65,000 people died. The situation grew more complicated

ASIA

in March 2004, when the LTTE split into two factions after a rebel leader known as Colonel Karuna formed his own rival army in eastern Sri Lanka. The LTTE accused the Sri Lankan army of supporting Karuna's rebellion.

Emergency regulations from 2005 give the government wide powers to control the media. As in other countries, Sri Lankan authorities employ a vaguely worded "state secret" law to harass troublesome journalists against whom they do not otherwise have a case.

In June, the government proposed reinstating a criminal defamation law—repealed in 2002—that would include a two-year prison term and fine for anyone convicted of the offense. Justice Minister Dilan Perera introduced the resolution at a cabinet meeting with the backing of President Mahinda Rajapaksa, but three cabinet ministers dissented and the resolution was quietly taken off the table. It was, however, an indicator of the Rajapaksa government's intention of silencing its critics.

The Free Media Movement's Deshapriya cited two encouraging developments in 2007. During a three-day visit in May, U.S. Assistant Secretary of State Richard Boucher publicly identified attacks on journalists as an area of concern. The United States, a major donor of food and economic and military assistance, has considerable influence with the country's leadership. Boucher's visit, coupled with the January release of the press freedom mission's report, lent credibility and publicity to the issue of media freedom, Deshapriya said.

Still, Deshapriya and others said that press freedom problems were significant. "Some of us feel personally threatened," Deshapriya wrote in an e-mail in November. Said Athas: "The harassment and threats have never been worse. This is easily the darkest chapter in my 42-year career in journalism."

• • • • • • • • • • • • • • • • • • • THAILAND • • • • • • • • • • • • • • • • • • •

Fallout from the September 2006 military coup cast a chill over Thailand's media throughout 2007, as the junta maintained martial law over nearly half the country's provinces and used its discretionary powers to censor broadcast news, seize control of the country's only privately run television station, and pass new legislation that severely curtailed free expression on the Internet.

Voters in an August national referendum adopted a new constitution that in letter and spirit upheld, and even extended, some of the press freedom guarantees enshrined in the progressive 1997 charter. The provisions included a ban on politicians' owning media outlets and a renewed legal commitment to strengthen public broadcasting. At the same time, however, the military-appointed National Legislative Assembly passed new laws that effectively sustained the government's powers to curb free expression and press freedom for ill-defined reasons of national security.

A new Computer Crime Act, enacted on July 18, included some of the most restrictive and potentially punitive measures for governing the Internet anywhere in the world, including possible prison terms for people who use proxy servers to access government-restricted material.

The legislation gave Thai authorities broad discretionary powers to filter content deemed threatening to national security or insulting to the monarchy. Before the legislation was passed, the military-appointed Information and Communications Technology (ICT) Ministry had moved on dubious legal authority to block several politically oriented Web sites.

That included the May 27 blocking of two Web sites—*Hi-thaksin* and *Saturdayvoice*—that reported favorably on exiled former prime minister Thaksin Shinawatra and posted critical commentary on the ruling Council for National Security (CNS) junta. Access to both sites was barred after they posted an interview the ex-premier gave to several local community radio stations in mid-May.

On April 3, the ICT Ministry blocked access to popular video-sharing Web site YouTube in response to an unknown contributor who, using the pseudonym "Paddidda," uploaded clips lampooning King Bhumibol Adulyadej. Internet users in Thailand who tried to log on to YouTube received an "access denied" message written in Thai and administered by the ministry. Thai officials said the postings violated the country's strict lèse-majesté laws, which bar any media criticism of the Thai royal family and carry possible 15-year jail terms. Rather than filtering only the perceived objectionable content, Thai authorities censored the entire site.

The government lifted the ban on August 30 after reaching an agreement with YouTube's owner, Google, to block any video clips considered offensive to Thai citizens or in violation of Thai law. ICT Minister Sittichai Pookaiyaudom told the local press that YouTube had created a program to bar sensitive video clips from being accessed by Thai Internet service providers.

Another worrying development came on August 24, when a blogger and a Web administrator were arrested under Article 14 of the new Computer Crime Act, which broadly restricts the posting online of "forged" or "false" information that impinges on national security. Both were released on bail after spending several days in detention. State prosecutors, for unknown reasons, failed to press formal charges by an October 12 deadline.

The CNS also maintained hard curbs on the broadcast media. After launching its September 2006 coup, the military positioned tanks and troops at the country's six main television stations, which were initially barred from airing news that portrayed the former premier or criticized the military. In early January 2007, the CNS

ASIA

summoned senior Thai broadcast representatives and urged them not to broadcast comments made by Thaksin, his lawyer, or his former political party members.

On January 15, military officials instructed local cable television provider United Broadcasting Corporation to block domestic broadcasts of an interview that U.S.-based CNN conducted with Thaksin in Hong Kong. The interview was replaced with a rerun of a sports program; scheduled rebroadcasts were replaced with still images of Hollywood movie stars.

In March, the government-run Public Relations Department (PRD) took control of iTV, the country's only privately owned and managed television news station. The CNS claimed that Thaksin's government had illegally amended its original 30-year operating concession with the prime minister's office and as a result owed more than 100 billion baht (US$3.2 billion) in fines, unpaid broadcasting license fees, and overdue interest payments. Prime Minister's Office Minister Khunying Dhipavadee Meksawan had said the station would be shuttered on March 6, but backtracked in the face of protests and kept the station running, using government funds, under the new name Thailand Independent Television.

The seizure put under direct government control all six of Thailand's main television broadcasters, including one channel directly managed by the army. Attempts to break the government's monopoly through the use of new technologies were firmly rebuffed by authorities. A group of former government officials and journalists on March 1 attempted to launch a pro-Thaksin news station, People's Television (PTV), via satellite. The state-run Communications Authority of Thailand and the Telephone Organization of Thailand, which together control the country's telecommunications infrastructure, declined to give PTV the Internet access it needed to launch. (PTV needed to connect to an uplink station in Hong Kong, where its signal could be beamed to Thai customers with satellite dishes.) To bypass the state agencies, PTV joined with Star Channel MV1, one of 18 satellite broadcasters in the country. But authorities blocked its maiden broadcast on March 18—just hours after the station aired its first news reports.

PTV co-founder Jakrapob Penkair, a former government spokesman and veteran broadcast journalist, told CPJ that plainclothes police officers frequently followed him and other senior PTV executives when they left their studios, which were situated on the top floor of a shopping mall. He said the station hired private security guards to oversee staff members' automobiles after unknown people were observed apparently conducting surveillance.

In May, CPJ issued an investigative report, "Thailand at a Crossroads," that found the CNS maintaining sharp curbs on privately run provincial radio stations several months after the initial coup. A number of station managers who spoke with CPJ said that PRD officials had continued to enforce blanket restrictions on news reporting, including strict bans on any news portraying Thaksin in a favorable light, and orders to broadcast government-prepared news three times per day.

On May 16, government authorities raided and closed three different community radio stations—Taxi Driver Community Radio FM 92.75, Confidante Radio FM 87.75, and the Internet-based station run by the opposition group Saturday Voice Against Dictatorship—after they each had broadcast an interview with Thaksin, who spoke from London. PRD head Pramoj Rathavinij said the following day that the three stations had been shut down for national security reasons and for operating without licenses. All three were later allowed to resume broadcasting while their appeals were pending.

There were no reports of direct government censorship or harassment of the local print media, which regularly published critical reports about the CNS and their appointed interim government. However, several mysterious bomb threats and attacks signaled that print publications were not necessarily immune to the unresolved political conflict between the military and Thaksin's supporters.

The Nation Group, which publishes several Thai- and English-language newspapers, was forced to evacuate its Bangkok offices in early January after receiving an anonymous bomb threat by telephone. The threat came soon after a string of unclaimed bombs killed three and injured 40 on New Year's Eve 2006 in Bangkok. Later in January, a small grenade exploded in the office compound of the Thai-language *Daily News*. Nobody was injured in the blast, and no group claimed responsibility for the attack.

Some print journalists were heartened by the August 30 passage of a new Printing Act, which effectively repealed decades-old legislation that allowed police officials to censor publications for reasons of national security. The new legislation scrapped the draconian 1941 Printing and Publishing Act, which local journalists and press freedom advocates had long campaigned to abolish.

Still, the government continued to closely monitor foreign media coverage, particularly in relation to any reports that referred to the monarchy and any analysis that touched on the institution's possible involvement in the coup. Foreign Affairs Ministry officials called individual reporters throughout the year to remind them to avoid discussion of the monarchy in their political reporting, CPJ sources said. The CNS sent letters to several accredited foreign correspondents detailing the military's official explanation of the coup and a return letter the correspondents were supposed to sign to indicate they had read the document.

ASIA

AUSTRALIA

- Proposed legislation would give the federal police commissioner power to unilaterally block Internet content that he or she "has reason to believe … is a crime or terrorist related." The bill was introduced in the Senate on September 13 by Helen Coonan, a congresswoman and Australia's minister for communications. Its sponsors argued that the bill was aimed mainly at controlling pornography and criminal activities on the Web, but critics said it would give federal police broad discretionary power to consider whether online information threatened national security. The bill defined offending content as that which "encourages, incites or induces" or is "likely to have the effect of facilitating" an offense against the commonwealth. Police would be empowered to order the Australian Communications and Media Agency to censor specific Web sites and require individual Internet service providers to "take reasonable steps" to block content blacklisted by the authorities.

EAST TIMOR

- Unidentified men attacked the office of the country's leading daily, *Suara Timor Lorosa'e*, on August 4. The precise motive behind the attack was unclear, although the Timor Lorosa'e Journalists Association said the newspaper may have been targeted by political partisans. *Suara Timor Lorosa'e* was perceived to favor the party of independence leader Xanana Gusmao. Political tensions were running high in the country after parliamentary elections in June ended with no party winning an absolute majority.

- A report on the June elections issued by the Solidarity Observer Mission for East Timor (SOMET), a nonpartisan association of local and international nongovernmental organizations, expressed concern about the climate for press freedom. "Some Timorese journalists at times felt pressured to cover (or not to cover) certain political issues or to advance a particular political perspective," according to SOMET.

INDONESIA

- In September, the Supreme Court ordered *Time* magazine to pay more than US$100 million in damages and to print apologies to the family of former President Suharto. In May 1999, the magazine, owned by Time Warner Inc., ran a cover story alleging Suharto and his family had amassed a fortune of around US$15 billion, which Suharto and his family denied. *Time* had prevailed in lower courts.

- In November, an Australian coroner's inquest found that five Australian journalists were deliberately killed in 1975 by Indonesian armed forces seeking to prevent them from reporting on Indonesia's invasion of East Timor. The killings may qualify as war crimes under the Geneva Conventions and Australian law, according to the report by Dorelle Pinch, deputy coroner for the state of New South Wales. Pinch referred the case to Australian Attorney General Philip Ruddock. The Indonesian government said the journalists were accidentally killed in crossfire.

MALAYSIA

- Police interrogated popular Internet-based writer Raja Petra Kamarudin, founder of the *Malaysia Today* news Web site, for eight hours on July 25. United Malays National Organization officials said the site had published material the government perceived as an insult to Islam and an attempt to stir racial tensions. Raja Petra said police questioned him not about the articles he had written but about reader comments posted on his site. "The bottom line is, what you post in the comments section may get me sent to jail under the Sedition Act," the journalist wrote to his readers.

- On August 24, the government ordered the monthlong closure of *Makkal Osai*, a Tamil-language newspaper, for publishing a picture of Jesus holding a cigarette and what appeared to be a can of beer. The Internal Security Ministry suspended the paper's publication permit after the Malaysian Indian Congress (MIC), a predominantly Hindu Tamil political party that is part of the ruling coalition, called for strong action against the paper. *Makkal Osai* had been critical in its coverage of the MIC, which owns a rival paper. *Makkal Osai* published the illustration on August 21, as part of the daily's regular "Thought for the Day" feature, which highlights famous quotations from world leaders and philosophers. The accompanying quote read: "If someone repents for his mistakes, then heaven awaits him." The newspaper said that it had printed the illustration mistakenly, and it published a front-page apology the next day.

MALDIVES

- The criminal charge of "disobedience of an order" against *Minivan Daily* Deputy Editor Nazim Sattar was dropped on May 3, World Press Freedom Day, and charges against editor Aminath Najeeb were reduced. The two were facing trial on a criminal complaint related to an August 2005 article quoting opposition activist Ahmed Abbas, whose statements were alleged to have incited violence against the police; Abbas was jailed in connection with the statement. Najeeb still faced jail time on the pending charge.

NEPAL

- Attacks and threats against journalists by protesters in southern Nepal in January and early February inhibited coverage of unrest in the area. Several journalists were forced from their homes because of the harassment. The ethnic Madheshi people, who live in the southern plains, accused the media of biased coverage. The Madheshi People's Rights Forum threatened Bedraj Poudel, a correspondent for the daily *Kantipur*, by phone, saying the group would kill him, the paper reported. Several journalists were beaten during protests, including photojournalist Ram Sarraf in the city of Birgunj, the Federation of Nepali Journalists said.

TAIWAN

- On June 19, CPJ wrote to U.N. Secretary-General Ban Ki-moon, calling on him to review a U.N. policy that refuses accreditation to journalists from states not recognized by the General Assembly. Journalists from Taiwan, who are most affected by the policy, were excluded from covering the World Health Organization annual assembly on May 14. On June 24, when asked at a U.N. press briefing about CPJ's letter, Michele Montas, a U.N. spokeswoman, said the policy reflected the wishes of the General Assembly.

VIETNAM

- Journalist Nguyen Vu Binh was freed on June 9 after nearly five years in prison. CPJ and other international organizations had appealed for Binh's release based on his deteriorating health. The release was announced as part of an amnesty orchestrated by Vietnamese President Nguyen Minh Triet prior to a meeting with U.S. President George W. Bush. According to state media reports, Binh was jailed because he had "written and exchanged, with various opportunist elements in the country, information and materials that distorted the party and state policies." He was also accused of communicating with "reactionary" organizations abroad. Binh had worked for almost 10 years at the official publication *Tap Chi Cong San* (Journal of Communism).

- Authorities detained French journalist Nguyen Thi Thanh Van and three activists with the pro-democracy Viet Tan party for nearly four weeks. She and the others were arrested by security officials during a meeting with local democracy activists at a private residence in Ho Chi Minh City, according to a source associated with the Viet Tan party. The four were released on December 12 after international protests. Thanh Van, also known by her pen name Thanh Thao, is a journalist for the exile-run monthly *Viet Nam Dan Chu* (Vietnam Democracy) and a regular contributor to the Japan- and U.S.-based "Chan Troi Moi" (Radio New Horizon) program. She and the political activists had been held on terrorism-related charges.

УКРАЇНО
тобі не соромно?

Георгій Ґонґадзе
21/05/1969 – 16/09/2000

EUROPE AND CENTRAL ASIA

PHOTOS

Section break: Reuters/Konstantin Chernichkin — *A September vigil marks the
seventh anniversary of the murder of Ukraine journalist Georgy Gongadze.* Analysis
(next): AFP/Denis Sinyakov — *Russian President Vladimir Putin's annual press
conference is televised in February.*

EUROPE AND CENTRAL ASIA

REWRITING THE LAW TO MAKE JOURNALISM A CRIME

by Nina Ognianova

IN ITS 17 YEARS ON THE AIR, MOSCOW-BASED EKHO MOSKVY RADIO has enjoyed, by Russian standards, extraordinary editorial independence. Nearly alone among Russian broadcasters in its critical approach, the station employs some of the country's most outspoken journalists, who produce in-depth reporting on the most sensitive issues of the day. But in the run-up to the March 2008 presidential election, even the unshakable Ekho has begun to feel a shudder of apprehension.

Ekho received a series of letters in midyear—15 in all—from Moscow prosecutors, the Federal Security Service, the prosecutor general's office, and the state media regulator Rosokhrankultura, after the station gave airtime to Garry Kasparov and Eduard Limonov, leaders of the Other Russia coalition and organizers of the so-called Dissenters' Marches in several major cities. In the letters, authorities informed Ekho that its April programs featuring Kasparov and Limonov were being investigated for carrying "public calls to extremism." The authorities demanded the station provide transcripts of the programs and said that host Yuliya Latynina, one of Russia's sharpest politi-cal commentators, had been placed under investigation as well.

"Extremism" is an evolving and expanding term in Russian law. In suc-cessive years, parliament has sharply contracted the boundaries of accept-able reporting by redefining laws against extremism. Criticizing public of-

Restrictive Russian laws contribute to a climate of self-censorship. ficials and covering dissenting views are now outside the limits of permissible journalism. In pursuing this tactic—rewriting laws to restrict critical commentary—Russia has taken a regrettable lead in the region. Uzbekistan has rewritten laws to drastically limit the activities of foreign media, while Tajikistan has taken aim at Internet commentary by making much of it illegal.

The trend began in 2006, when the Russian parliament passed a measure broadening the definition of extremism to include media criticism of public officials. The measure, which President Vladimir Putin signed into law over the objections of media and human rights groups, said extremist activity includes "public slander directed toward figures fulfilling the state duties of the Russian Federation"—the sort of catchall terminology used by the Soviets to prosecute critics in the past.

In 2007, parliament approved a series of amendments to the criminal code that were ostensibly designed to counter the growing nationalist and neo-Nazi movements. The amendment package, also signed into law by Putin, classifies "public justification of terrorism" as extremism and gives law enforcement officials broad authority to suspend noncompliant media outlets. The new law pointedly avoids defining "justification," leaving critics to say that it will be interpreted very broadly.

"This law I compare to a surgical scalpel," said Karen Nersisian, a prominent Russian lawyer known for defending journalists' rights. "It is only to be used against those who criticize—inconvenient individuals, inconvenient politicians, and, particularly, inconvenient journalists. The moment a journalist makes the decision to pick up a pen and write about a sensitive issue, he will be already at risk. This is why today, journalists are more and more cautious to write about hot subjects."

Masha Lipman, editor of the Carnegie Moscow Center journal *Pro et Contra,* called the extremism legislation one more tool in the Kremlin's now-bulging tool kit. Its greatest threat to press freedom, she said, lies not in its actual use but in its contribution to an existing climate of self-censorship. "The law is designed to contribute to an environment in which every writer, every editor, every [media] owner would not forget that we can only exercise our freedom of expression because the Kremlin is permissive," Lipman told CPJ. "The more instruments there are, the more authors would weigh it up, thinking, 'Maybe I should be more cautious, maybe I should censor myself.' That is the point."

Several details in the 2007 amendments are of particular concern. One requires media to label as "extremist" in their reports any organization that the

In Russia, extremism has come to mean criticism of public officials.

government has banned as such. Another bans the production and distribution of "extremist" material but does not specify what constitutes such material, even as it introduces new penalties for journalists, media outlets, and printers found guilty of the offense. The measure also expands the definition of extremism as a crime motivated by "hatred or hostility toward a certain social group" without clarifying the term "social group." This purposely vague language is expected to have a chilling effect on the coverage of public officials, businesspeople, and law enforcement officials.

"The effect of the new amendments could be compared to a cold shower on political journalism," said Andrei Richter, director of the Moscow-based Media Law and Policy Institute. Since the extremism laws were first adopted in 2002, Richter said, the list of concepts that fall under its definition has grown long. And if a "cold shower" were not enough, authorities emphasized the point by moving quickly to initiate criminal proceedings against Kremlin critics. In September, state prosecutors brought charges against prominent political analyst Andrei Piontkovsky over statements in his 2006 book *Unloved Country*, a collection of political essays critical of Putin and his policies. The prosecutor in Piontkovsky's case, who spoke briefly to *The Washington Post* after the hearing but refused to elaborate or give her name, said *Unloved Country* incited "inferiority among people of Jewish, American, Russian, and other nationalities."

On September 25, the court ordered that *Unloved Country* be subjected to a linguistic analysis to determine whether it contains extremist content. Piontkovsky and his lawyers said the accusations were utterly baseless. "There are no calls to extremism in my political diary," Piontkovsky told CPJ. "Absolutely none. This book is very critical of Putin, yes, but the accusations against me are a laughing matter." But Piontkovsky, who is now a visiting scholar at the conservative Washington-based Hudson Institute, is pessimistic about the potential verdict. "The court sent my book to undergo a linguistic [analysis] at the Institute of the Ministry of Justice. So you can imagine how 'independent' the expertise will be. ... It will be independent only of sound logic."

Piontkovsky's case is the first to be tried under the newly amended law on fighting extremism. He faces up to five years in prison if convicted.

"In the world, as a rule, the concept of extremism is linked to terrorism. But in Russia, it is used to describe critics of the powerful," said Oleg Panfilov, director of the Moscow-based media watchdog Center for Journalism in Extreme Situations.

Uzbekistan and Tajikistan broaden their own restrictions.

Russia has been unmoved by Western criticism of its backsliding on press freedom and democracy; instead, authorities have warned against what they call "foreign meddling" in their country's internal affairs. Emboldened by the defiant attitude of their strong neighbor, authorities in the former Soviet states of Uzbekistan and Tajikistan have broadened their own restrictions against reporters. In other ex-Soviet countries—such as Azerbaijan—authorities have employed existing laws with new creativity and fresh vigor.

"I don't think anyone can imitate what Russia is doing exactly because no one is as sophisticated as the Kremlin," said Lipman, who also noted that Russia still allows greater press freedom than most other former Soviet states.

Still, Lipman said, Russia is clearly pulling former Soviet states back into its orbit of influence through political initiatives such as the Shanghai Cooperation Organization—a regional security alliance that includes China, Kazakhstan, Kyrgyzstan, Tajikistan, and Uzbekistan. "And there is no doubt," she said, "that these countries feel more secure having Russia by their side." The regime of Uzbek President Islam Karimov, after all, might not have survived international outrage over the mass killings in the city of Andijan in May 2005 had it not been for the Kremlin's public support.

A year after the killings—in which government troops fired on civilian demonstrators—Uzbek authorities further restricted the small independent press by passing a new law regulating the work of journalists for international media. With domestic media entirely under state control, international broadcasters such as the U.S. government-funded Radio Free Europe/Radio Liberty, the BBC, and the German public broadcaster Deutsche Welle—all of which support local-language services—have served as important alternatives for independent news. International broadcasters lost their bureau accreditations and were forced to leave Uzbekistan in the months immediately after Andijan, but they retained informal networks of local stringers who continued to contribute to them at the risk of official harassment. Since the passage of the 2006 law, however, not only has reporting for international outlets become risky—it has also become illegal.

The new regulations give the Uzbek Ministry of Foreign Affairs wide discretion to issue formal warnings to foreign correspondents, revoke their accreditation and visas, and expel them. Among other vaguely worded bans, foreign correspondents were barred from "interfering in the internal affairs of the Republic of Uzbekistan, harming the honor and dignity of citizens of the Republic of Uzbekistan, interfering in their private lives, and committing other actions that provide for legal accountability." The broad language of the measure does not define what constitutes interference in Uzbekistan's internal affairs or in the private lives of citizens, nor does it specify "other actions" that are prohibited.

Interpretation of this law, like the Russian antiextremist measures, is left to state agencies. And, as in Russia, the law spreads and sustains a climate of fear and self-censorship. "The sense is that you can be attacked at any moment and placed under criminal investigation," said Galima Bukharbaeva, a prominent exiled Uzbek journalist and 2005 recipient of CPJ's International Press Freedom Award. "Any journalism but that of state media is outlawed."

Putting the new regulations to immediate use, the Uzbek Foreign Ministry issued official reprimands to several Deutsche Welle correspondents, forcing one to quit journalism and another to flee Uzbekistan to escape legal threats.

In Tajikistan, authorities are expanding restrictions to the Internet. In July, the Tajik parliament passed amendments to the country's Criminal Code that broaden defamation provisions to include Internet publications. The bill, which President Emomali Rahmon signed into law in October, effectively criminalizes critical reporting and commentary online, and extends existing penalties for criminal insult and defamation to the Internet. Penalties include fines and prison terms of up to two years.

The Internet-specific amendments are significant for Tajikistan, where no daily newspapers circulate, independent weeklies are suppressed, and foreign broadcasters are barred from the airwaves. With the scarcity of available independent information, Central Asia news Web sites such as *Ferghana* and *Centrasia*, as well as Tajikistan-specific opposition sites such as *Charogiruz* and *Tajikistan Times*, have grown popular. The new amendments are expected to cause wide self-censorship among Web site contributors, according to CPJ sources in the region.

Mukhtor Bokizoda, director of the Dushanbe-based press freedom group Foundation for the Memory and Protection of Journalists, told CPJ that officials tend to interpret criticism as libel, and that a politicized court system invariably sides with the government.

Tajikistan criminalizes critical online reporting and commentary.

This is a common refrain. In Russia and other former Soviet states, journalists have little confidence in the independence of their justice systems. "State agencies create a myth of a formal procedure," Russian lawyer Nersisian told CPJ. "They choose the opponent, they put together a case, and the law acts as a guided missile against him."

Said Panfilov: "Russian authorities are setting an example for those governments who want to re-create Soviet authoritarianism."

One such country is Azerbaijan, where, in the words of Emin Huseynov, director of the Baku-based Institute for Reporters' Freedom and Safety (IRFS), authorities are following "a Russian scenario" in regard to critics. "Azeri authorities are now moving away from using defamation charges and [toward] more serious articles of the criminal code, such as terrorism," he told CPJ. Because terrorism is such a grave charge, the crime is less likely to be challenged by the public, Huseynov said. "In Russia, few journalists report on the Chechen war," he said, "because that could be assessed as a support of terrorism."

Now Azerbaijani authorities are starting to use a similar approach, he told CPJ. Huseynov noted the October 30 conviction of Eynulla Fatullayev, the embattled editor of two popular independent newspapers that were forced to shut down after authorities imprisoned him in April. Fatullayev, convicted of terrorism and incitement of ethnic and religious hatred, was sentenced to eight and a half years in jail because of a critical piece on President Ilham Aliyev's foreign policy regarding Iran. Authorities are growing more inventive, Huseynov said. "Today, it's terrorism charges. Tomorrow, it will be revealing state secrets or extremism. … It's no longer only defamation. The practice is shifting."

The climate is changing in the region, too. Aleksei Simonov, head of the Moscow-based Glasnost Defense Foundation, said Russian journalists have not yet been marginalized as dangerous dissidents. "Not yet, not yet, not yet," he said. "But the climate is changing very rapidly."

Toward what? He paused and said: "Toward winter."

• • • • • • • • •

Nina Ognianova is program coordinator for Europe and Central Asia. She led a mission to Moscow in 2007.

EUROPE AND CENTRAL ASIA

•••••••••••••••••• AZERBAIJAN ••••••••••••••••••

Ignoring international opinion, the authoritarian government of President Ilham Aliyev clamped down on opposition and independent media and became the world's fifth-leading jailer of journalists, with nine reporters and editors behind bars when CPJ conducted its annual census on December 1. On May 3, World Press Freedom Day, CPJ ranked the oil-rich Caspian Sea state as one of the world's worst backsliders on press freedom.

In cracking down, Aliyev and his government were simultaneously emboldened by Azerbaijan's growing energy profits and apprehensive about a "color" revolution of the kind that had toppled corrupt regimes in Georgia, Ukraine, and Kyrgyzstan. Taking a cue from the region's leader, Russia, Azerbaijani officials shrugged off criticism of their steady assault on the press, confident that the West's need for energy would outweigh human rights concerns. Aliyev, who was expected to seek

another term as president in the October 2008 election, essentially inherited the office from his father, Heydar Aliyev, who stepped aside in 2003 due to failing health. (The 2003 presidential election, which the young Aliyev won amid vote-rigging allegations, was largely seen as symbolic.) Like his father, Ilham Aliyev has ruled with an iron hand, using politicized courts and loyal law enforcement agencies to crush dissent. A fragmented political opposition, beset by bickering and mistrust, has been unable to gain traction.

Responding to deteriorating press conditions in Azerbaijan, CPJ Program Coordinator Nina Ognianova testified in August before the U.S. Commission on Security and Cooperation in Europe. Ognianova said the spike in imprisonments had resulted in pervasive self-censorship, and she urged the commission to make press freedom issues a priority in Azerbaijan and other former Soviet states.

While law enforcement officials devoted time and resources to imprisoning critical journalists, they reported no progress in solving the 2005 murder of Elmar Huseynov, editor and founder of the opposition newsweekly *Monitor*. Instead, authorities launched an intensive campaign of persecution against the slain journalist's former colleague Eynulla Fatullayev, editor of the now-shuttered independent Russian-language weekly *Realny Azerbaijan* and Azeri-language daily *Gündalik Azarbaycan* in Baku, whose published reports questioned the competence and independence of the murder probe.

•••••••••••

Summaries in this chapter were reported and written by Program Coordinator **Nina Ognianova**, Research Associate **Muzaffar Suleymanov**, and freelance writer **Alex Lupis**.

Starting in early March, when he published his own investigation into the murder of Huseynov, Fatullayev was threatened, criminally charged, sentenced, and imprisoned; while he was in custody, authorities harassed his staff and closed his papers. By the end of an eight-month-long ordeal, a politicized court system had branded him a terrorist and slapped him with prison terms totaling 11 years.

Fatullayev's case was extreme in its severity but emblematic of the tactics that authorities used to prevent journalists from pursuing sensitive subjects. The embattled editor's saga started on March 6, when he received a death threat—an anonymous call at home that warned his elderly mother that, as a "wise woman," she should "talk sense into him" or else, the caller said, "we will send him to Elmar"—a reference to the slain Huseynov. The threat came four days after Fatullayev published an article in *Realny Azerbaijan* accusing authorities of ordering Huseynov's killing and obstructing the investigation.

Fatullayev reported the threat to both police and Interior Minister Ramil Usubov and asked for personal protection. Instead, he found himself in the crosshairs of law enforcement officials. In April, a Yasamal District Court judge found Fatullayev guilty of defaming Azerbaijanis in an Internet posting that the journalist said was falsely attributed to him. The posting, published on several Web sites, said Azerbaijanis bore some responsibility for the 1992 killings of residents of the restive Nagorno-Karabakh region, according to local press reports. Fatullayev, ordered to serve 30 months, was jailed immediately after the proceedings, the independent news agency Turan reported.

With Fatullayev jailed, authorities evicted *Realny Azerbaijan* and *Gündalik Azarbaycan* from their Baku offices, citing purported fire safety and building code violations. (Both papers later stopped publishing.) More charges against Fatullayev followed. On October 30, a judge in the Azerbaijani Court of Serious Crimes found Fatullayev guilty of terrorism, incitement to ethnic hatred, and tax evasion. The journalist was sentenced to eight years and six months in prison, to be served concurrent to the 30-month term. The terrorism and incitement charges stemmed from a *Realny Azerbaijan* commentary, headlined "The Aliyevs go to war," that sharply criticized President Ilham Aliyev's foreign policy regarding Iran.

Emin Huseynov, director of the Baku-based Institute for Reporters' Freedom and Safety, said authorities have started to use retaliatory charges such as terrorism, extremism, drug possession, and hooliganism to target critics. The Fatullayev prosecution and the November jailing of opposition editor Geniment Zakhidov illustrated this new government tactic. Zakhidov, editor of the daily *Azadlyg*, was placed in pretrial detention on a spurious charge of hooliganism.

The use of criminal defamation charges, long the government's favorite method of silencing critics, drew increasing criticism from international bodies such as the Organization for Security and Co-operation in Europe, the pan-European election,

EUROPE AND CENTRAL ASIA

human rights, and security monitoring organization. Five of the nine journalists behind bars when CPJ conducted its annual census were serving time for insult or defamation; in four of those cases, the charges were filed by government officials.

In January, Faramaz Novruzoglu of the independent weekly *Nota Bene* was sentenced to two years in prison on charges of defaming Interior Minister Ramil Usubov in a series of articles that focused on corruption in the ministry. In May, a Baku court handed 30-month sentences to Editor-in-Chief Rovshan Kebirli and reporter Yashar Agazadeh of the opposition daily *Muhalifet* on charges of defaming Jalal Aliyev—the president's uncle and a member of parliament—in an article about the Aliyev family's business activities. And in November, a Baku court sentenced Nazim Guliyev, editor-in-chief of the pro-government daily *Ideal*, to two and a half years in prison on charges of defaming the head of the Interior Ministry's traffic department. After international protests, President Aliyev pardoned Novruzoglu, Kebirli, Agazadeh, and 100 other political prisoners on December 28. An appeals court freed Guliyev after voiding his conviction.

Official harassment and lawlessness in the Nakhchivan Autonomous Republic made it difficult for independent journalists to do their jobs. In September, Nakhchivan authorities seized, beat, and imprisoned Hakimeldostu Mehdiyev, regional correspondent for the opposition daily *Yeni Musavat*. In articles preceding the official actions, Mehdiyev had criticized authorities for recent gas and electricity shortages. He had also reported on corruption and human rights abuses by local officials, and had given radio interviews on political and social issues in Nakhchivan. In late September, Ministry of National Security agents abducted Mehdiyev, beat him, and warned him to stop his critical reporting. The next day, police raided Mehdiyev's home and arrested him on charges of disobeying law enforcement; the same day, a local court summarily tried and sentenced Mehdiyev to 15 days in prison. No defense lawyer was present at the hearing, and the reporter's family was not allowed to visit him in prison. Shortly after he was jailed, local authorities leveled the family's teahouse and store, leaving them without income. Mehdiyev's home was placed under police surveillance and the family's phones were tapped, according to local CPJ sources.

• • • • • • • • • • • • • • • • • • • BELARUS • • • • • • • • • • • • • • • • • •

Authorities moved aggressively to control the Internet, introducing sweeping new restrictions that allow the government to monitor citizens' use of the Web. President Aleksandr Lukashenko's administration continued its practice of suppressing dissent—but paid a price in May when the U.N. Human Rights Council (UNHRC) denied Belarus a seat following international criticism of the country's poor human rights and press freedom record.

The Council of Ministers adopted regulations in February that require Internet café owners to maintain records of Web sites accessed by customers, and to make those logs available to law enforcement agencies. Belarusians were already required to present identification in order to use Internet cafés, and authorities have long blocked opposition and critical Web sites.

Ostensibly designed to control violent and sexually explicit content, the new regulations include vague language about "forbidden" Internet activities that leaves interpretation to the state security agency. The agency, known as the KGB, appeared ready to enforce the new rules. "The regulation has a pre-emptive character. Those who wish to use anonymity with illegal purposes would not want to do so now," KGB spokesman Valery Nadtochayev told the Belarusian news agency Belapan.

Belarusian television and radio broadcasters provide virtually no independent news coverage of politics or sensitive issues, CPJ research shows. With broadcast media under their thumb, authorities continued to focus their attention on what remains of the independent print press. The opposition newsweekly *Vitebsky Kuryer* fought off a government-inspired eviction effort in March only to see its printer, the state-run Vitebsk Publishing House, terminate its contract, according to local news reports. The editorial staff used office printers to produce the paper for about a month, until the weekly was able to renegotiate its contract with the state printer, the Minsk-based human rights group Charter 97 reported. CPJ research shows a pattern of government harassment against *Vitebsky Kuryer*. In 2006, the newspaper faced defamation charges and was twice forced to change its location after receiving eviction notices.

The government also used its distribution powers to harass the independent press. The Belarusian Association of Journalists (BAJ), a press freedom group based in the capital, Minsk, said the state-owned postal service Belpochta and distribution agency Soyuzpechat had stopped providing service to 16 independent newspapers, including the popular newspapers *Narodnaya Volya*, *Tovarishch*, *Nasha Niva*, *Svobodnye Novosti Plyus*, and *Brestsky Kuryer*. The papers switched to private vendors and volunteer distributors, prompting authorities in the cities of Brest, Vitebsk, and Gomel to arrest and threaten those distributors. In June, Brest city council deputy chairman Vyacheslav Khafizov sent letters to local independent newspapers ordering them to stop distributing their publications, BAJ reported.

Authorities wielded search-and-seizure powers, too. In August, Lenin District Court officials raided the offices of Belarus' largest opposition newspaper, *Narodnaya Volya*, confiscating computers and production equipment. Officials cited the paper's failure to pay a 2006 fine as the reason for the raid, Charter 97

EUROPE AND CENTRAL ASIA

reported. The next month, Minsk police entered the offices of *Tovarishch*, the official newspaper of the Belarusian Communist Party, and confiscated 10,000 copies of its latest issue, claiming they were not printed at the publishing house named on the paper's banner. The printing house rule is one of many arcane and selectively enforced regulations designed to obstruct the independent press, CPJ research shows. The seized edition of *Tovarishch* was dedicated to an upcoming opposition rally in the city of Minsk, BAJ said.

Throughout the year, KGB security agents and police officers arrested journalists on spurious charges that ranged from the petty, such as lack of accreditation and "hooliganism," to the very serious, such as treason. Contributors to the U.S. government-funded Radio Free Europe/Radio Liberty, German public broadcaster Deutsche Welle, Warsaw-based Radio Polonia, and the private Belarusian station Radio Racyja were among those detained on supposed accreditation violations, according to local reports. In March, CPJ protested the arrest of Igor Bantsyr, correspondent for the independent Polish-language *Magazyn Polski na Uchodzstwie*, after a Grodno city court sentenced the journalist to 10 days in prison for "uncensored swearing" in public. Grodno police filed the same charges when officers detained Bantsyr and independent journalist Ivan Roman at an opposition rally on October 10, local press reports said.

Reporter Valery Shchukin and photographer Yury Dedinkin with the daily *Narodnaya Volya*, the country's largest opposition newspaper, were forced out of polling stations in Vitebsk and Minsk while covering local elections in January. In March, Minsk police arrested Shchukin as he was covering unapproved opposition rallies marking a brief period of Belarusian independence in 1918. On June 8, the Vitebsk Pervomaisky District Court found Shchukin guilty of "insulting electoral committee members" and fined him 1,490,000 rubles (US$700), BAJ reported.

Authorities reported no progress in investigations into the July 2000 disappearance of Dmitry Zavadsky, a cameraman for the Russian television channel ORT who is presumed dead, and the October 2004 slaying of Veronika Cherkasova, a reporter for the Minsk opposition weekly *Solidarnost*. In October, Minsk prosecutor Mikhail Ivanov told journalists the investigation of Cherkasova's murder had been suspended due to a lack of suspects. Cherkasova, who had written articles about KGB surveillance and alleged arms sales to former Iraqi president Saddam Hussein, was found dead in her apartment with multiple stab wounds.

In May, heeding concerns over Belarus' poor human rights record, the UNHRC rejected the country's bid for a seat on the council. BAJ was among the press freedom groups that had opposed the bid. In its letter to the UNHRC preceding the vote, BAJ stated: "Electing a representative of Belarus to the U.N. Human Rights Council will mean a devaluation of this body and will make it impossible for the council to carry out the role of protecting the human rights and freedoms entrusted to it."

The international community continued calling on Lukashenko to introduce political and economic reforms and to stop harassing opposition party members and independent journalists. René van der Linden, president of the Council of Europe's Parliamentary Assembly, aired his concerns in a January meeting with Vladimir Konoplyov, speaker of the Belarusian parliament. Van der Linden also called for an international fact-finding mission into what opposition leaders called Belarus' growing ranks of political prisoners, RFE/RL reported. The Vienna-based Organization for Security and Co-operation in Europe, a pan-European human rights body, expressed its concerns over the fate of political prisoners and young opposition activists detained and arrested on falsified charges.

The year also saw a shift in the country's international relations. In January, Russia temporarily cut off oil and gas supplies after Belarus balked at price increases of more than 100 percent. The move triggered an eight-month-long dispute, raised questions about Russian-Belarusian cooperation, and prompted Lukashenko to announce a search for alternative energy resources. In May and June, Lukashenko hosted leaders of two energy-rich states: President Mahmoud Ahmadinejad of Iran and President Hugo Chávez Frías of Venezuela. Lukashenko signed energy and military-supply contracts with both countries, announced an agreement to develop an oil field in Iran, and vowed joint cooperation against "Western pressure," according to international press reports.

GEORGIA

Facing a week of massive protests in the capital, Tbilisi, President Mikhail Saakashvili stunned Western allies in November by imposing a state of emergency, banning broadcast news reporting, closing two television stations, and deploying police to forcefully disperse demonstrators. Saakashvili defended the November 7 crackdown, saying that the protests were orchestrated by Moscow with the intention of overthrowing his government. After acceding to opposition demands for early presidential elections, Saakashvili lifted the state of emergency and the news-gathering ban nine days later. But by then, he had damaged his own reputation as a pro-Western reformer.

Protests began on November 2, when an estimated 50,000 demonstrators descended on the capital. Their initial demands for early elections and electoral changes granting more proportional representation quickly escalated into calls for Saakashvili's resignation. Imedi TV, founded by presidential opponent Badri Patarkatsishvili, emerged as the main platform for opposition demands, and carried direct calls for the public to join in the demonstrations.

Though the size of the protests diminished daily, an angry Saakashvili lashed out by shutting down Imedi and the local pro-opposition station Kavkaziya. While coverage on other television stations was largely pro-government, the administration barred all independent broadcasters from airing news reports. As the clampdown took hold, police broke up protests in front of parliament, using tear gas, rubber bullets, batons, and water cannons, according to international news outlets. More than 500 people were injured and 32 were detained, The Associated Press reported. Local press reports said police roughed up four journalists for the television channel Obshchestvenny Veshchatel.

It was a remarkable turnaround for Saakashvili, the U.S.-educated leader who swept into office in the elections that followed the 2003 democratic uprising known as the Rose Revolution. Western allies moderated their criticism but were clearly taken aback. Washington warned that the actions could hurt Saakashvili's plan to integrate the former Soviet republic into the European Union and NATO. Adam Michnik, the renowned Polish newspaper editor deployed by Western nations to help resolve the crisis, said that keeping Imedi off the air would be "a threat to democracy in Georgia." Imedi resumed broadcasting in December only to suspend its own operations the same month amid internal dissent over Patarkatsishvili's dual role as presidential challenger and media owner. Saakashvili claimed victory based on early results of the January 5, 2008, poll.

The tumult featured a fascinating cast of characters, not least of them the U.S. media baron Rupert Murdoch, whose News Corporation became a partner in Imedi in 2006. Murdoch publicly rebuked the Georgian government, telling the AP that he was "shocked and horrified that, in what was allegedly a democratic country, something like this could happen."

Saakashvili came to power with promises of democratic reform. Following a brief honeymoon with the press, the administration's intolerance of criticism, its bureaucratic secrecy, and its failure to reform a weak judiciary undermined many of the press freedom gains that followed the revolution. Public dissatisfaction with low standards of living and continued corruption caused its approval ratings to plunge.

As a result, the Saakashvili government closely scrutinized and sought to influence television reporting, the country's most popular and influential source of news. It found success in the gradual decline of Rustavi-2 from a leading broadcaster that rallied Georgians during the Rose Revolution to a pro-Saakashvili station emphasizing entertainment. The evolution culminated in 2006, when management hired government loyalists in a staff shakeup, merged the station with two others, and sold the entity to a little-known holding company named Geotrans LLC. In October,

Geotrans appointed Rustavi-2 Advertising Director Irakli Chikovani to head the station, moving the broadcaster even further from its news reporting roots, according to local news reports and CPJ research.

The government expanded its direct influence over the airwaves in September when the Defense Ministry financed the launch of a new television channel, Georgia, that was designed to promote patriotism and advocate for closer military ties with NATO, local press reports said.

Throughout the year, Imedi TV was the only private channel with national reach that directly criticized the government. Some senior politicians boycotted the channel, reflecting the administration's view of the media as either friend or foe. In some cases, government officials obstructed Imedi journalists from reporting on politically sensitive issues. In September, police officers confiscated a camera from an Imedi crew filming the corruption-related arrest of the country's influential former defense minister, Irakli Okruashvili. The arrest occurred two days after Okruashvili announced during an interview on Imedi that he was forming a new opposition party, according to local and Russian news reports.

Regional media outlets that criticized local authorities faced retaliation and harassment. Throughout 2007, the Trialeti television company in the central city of Gori faced a campaign of harassment because the station criticized regional governor Mikhail Kareli, according to local press reports. Journalists and media executives from Trialeti received anonymous telephone threats, were barred from local government buildings, and stopped receiving government press releases, while their appeals for protection to police and prosecutors were ignored, the reports said. Trialeti also lost several advertising contracts, and its headquarters was vandalized.

Georgia has progressive press laws—such as a 2004 measure decriminalizing libel—but authorities have not consistently followed the letter or the spirit of these laws. Government officials, for example, effectively ignore the freedom of information law, with uncooperative press officers and outdated Web sites making it hard for journalists to obtain basic information about the work of state agencies, according to local press reports. Journalists reported that the powerful Defense Ministry is particularly secretive, and often bars critical journalists from press conferences.

The Georgian National Communications Commission—a media regulatory body whose senior members are appointed by the president—and the pro-government human rights organization Liberty Institute drafted a Broadcasters Code of Conduct in 2006 that proved controversial because of its vague and restrictive guidelines for journalists, according to the news Web site *EurasiaNet*. The proposal—which sought to regulate reporters' dress, language, use of anonymous sources, and ability to broadcast live footage of demonstrations—was abandoned amid protests from journalists and media rights groups.

Despite these difficulties, the media continued to successfully publicize and rally public opinion against some government abuses. Such was the case when officials in Tbilisi ordered a series of unlawful apartment evictions and building demolitions, according to local press reports and *EurasiaNet*.

Local authorities in two Russian-backed separatist regimes in northern Georgia—Abkhazia and South Ossetia—regularly harassed, restricted, and detained local journalists and foreign correspondents. This resulted in limited news coverage of these self-proclaimed republics. In July, a group of independent journalists in Abkhazia sent a letter to local authorities complaining that police surveillance, bureaucratic obstruction, and harassment by prosecutors had reached "Soviet-era proportions," the U.S. government-funded Radio Free Europe/Radio Liberty reported.

· · · · · · · · · · · · · · · · · KAZAKHSTAN · · · · · · · · · · · · · · · · · ·

President Nursultan Nazarbayev and his administration played down the country's troubling press freedom and human rights record as they successfully pursued chairmanship of the Organization for Security and Co-operation in Europe (OSCE), the Vienna-based human rights monitoring body.

In a divided decision on November 30, the ministerial council overseeing the OSCE named Kazakhstan to the 2010 chairmanship. Russia and former Soviet bloc nations backed Kazakhstan's bid, while Western countries were split. The ministers delayed the country's chairmanship by a year—Kazakhstan had sought the 2009 slot—as a compromise that would enable Nazarbayev to implement democratic reforms. Greece was chosen for 2009.

Nazarbayev benefited from the European Union's Germany-driven Central Asia strategy. German Chancellor Angela Merkel, whose country presided over the EU in the first half of the year, declared as early as mid-January that Central Asia would be a priority for her state's EU presidency and singled out Kazakhstan as a potential economic partner. Anxious to diversify its oil and gas resources to reduce reliance on Russia, as well as balancing the regional clout of Russia and China, the EU declared its intentions to develop better energy, economic, and political ties with Central Asia.

Germany repeatedly assured rights defenders that it had a "two-track" plan for developing relations with the region, one that would not sacrifice human rights for energy interests. The United States, too, adopted an accommodating tone on Kazakhstan, tolerating the administration's nepotism, its total control of influential broadcast media, and its record of unpunished attacks on the press. After a February 27 meeting with Nazarbayev in Kazakhstan's capital, Astana, U.S. Assistant Secretary of State Richard Boucher called the oil-rich state a "strategic partner" and emphasized the importance of security, economic, and antiterrorism cooperation between the two states. He did not mention press freedom and human rights.

Only a day later, during his annual address to parliament, an emboldened Nazarbayev said regional economic integration remained a priority for his country, and declared that Kazakhstan will pursue its "own Kazakh way" of political reforms, which the country would implement gradually.

A joint session of the Kazakh parliament approved a constitutional amendment on March 18 that abolished term limits for the country's first post-Soviet president—giving Nazarbayev the right to remain in office for life. Nazarbayev, who had run Kazakhstan for a total of 18 years (two before the Soviet Union's collapse and 16 since), signed the amendment into law on May 22. Though he previously said he would not remain in office after his current term expired in 2012, the amendment sparked considerable speculation—especially in the absence of a strong potential successor. The constitutional change was part of a package that included a reduction in presidential terms from seven to five years after 2012, and the transfer of some presidential powers to the parliament. Despite intense criticism from the Kazakh opposition, the U.S. State Department lauded the reforms. At a press briefing on May 22, State Department spokesman Sean McCormack said: "It's a step, ultimately, when you look at the balance of these things, in the right direction." He added: "Is it all that the rest of the world would like to see? No, it's not. But again, this is a country that … we have high hopes for, that we're working closely with, [and] they have a lot of potential." An outraged Kazakh opposition accused the United States of employing double standards.

Amid tolerant signals from abroad, critical journalists continued to suffer retribution from authorities at home.

On January 22, a judge in Almaty sentenced Kaziz Toguzbayev, staff reporter for the independent biweekly newspaper *Azat* and contributing writer for the news Web site *Kub*, to a two-year suspended prison term under Article 316 of the criminal code for "insulting the honor and dignity" of the president. The Committee for National Security of the Republic of Kazakhstan had charged Toguzbayev in August 2006, after he wrote two commentaries critical of the government for *Kub*. Defamation laws remain part of the criminal code in Kazakhstan, and authorities readily use them against critical journalists.

From December 2006 to mid-January 2007, three printing companies consecutively refused to print the independent biweekly *Uralskaya Nedelya*—a popular newspaper based in western Kazakhstan that had recently published a series of articles exposing local government corruption. Editor-in-Chief Tamara Yeslyamova told CPJ that sources at Poligrafservis, the local printer that had produced *Uralskaya Nedelya* since 2001, informed her that local officials had threatened the company with closure if it continued to produce the paper. *Uralskaya Nedelya* was forced to seek an alternative printer outside the region.

Little attention, domestic or international, was paid to the first case of a missing journalist since the country declared its independence from the Soviet Union in 1991.

Oralgaisha Omarshanova, an investigative reporter for the Astana-based independent weekly *Zakon i Pravosudiye* (Law and Justice), went missing on March 30. Omarshanova headed the paper's anticorruption department. At the time of her disappearance, she was in Almaty, on a business trip with several colleagues. The colleagues said they last saw her getting into a jeep, the Moscow-based news agency Regnum reported. Four days before her disappearance, Omarshanova had published an article in *Zakon i Pravosudiye* about ethnic clashes between rival Chechen and Kazakh residents in the Almaty-region villages of Kazatkom and Malovodnoye. The clashes, which took place on March 17 and 18, claimed at least five lives, according to local and international press reports. In her article, Omarshanova identified the instigators of the unrest and mentioned their alleged connection to the government and local businesses, the Almaty-based press freedom group Adil Soz reported.

In February, *Zakon i Pravosudiye* published an investigative report by Omarshanova that described the dangerous working conditions of miners in the central city of Zhezkazgan. At an April press conference, the journalist's brother, Zhanat Omarshanov, told reporters that in the weeks prior to her disappearance, Omarshanova had received several telephone death threats, Regnum reported. Despite the threats and the journalist's sensitive beat at the paper, Kazakh prosecutors announced in September that Omarshanova's disappearance had nothing to do with her work and was likely connected to a personal matter. They did not provide a rationale for their conclusion.

In May, a television station and a newspaper found themselves caught in the middle of a political scandal. An Almaty court suspended Kommerchesky Televizionny Kanal (KTK) and the weekly *Karavan* for unspecified violations of Kazakh media laws. Prosecutors accused KTK of broadcasting predominantly in Russian in violation of what is commonly known as the "language law," a 1989 provision requiring that half of all programming be in Kazakh, according to local and international press reports. Authorities had not applied the law to KTK before. Authorities also suspended for three months the Russian-language weekly *Karavan* for violating unspecified media regulations.

The suspensions came a day after Rakhat Aliyev, the owner of both media outlets and then-son-in-law of President Nazarbayev, was charged with kidnapping and assaulting two senior employees of Nurbank, a commercial bank he partly owned. Aliyev had denied involvement in the disappearance of the two men. Local journalists attributed suspension of the outlets to their coverage of the Nurbank scandal and tensions between members of the presidential family. Aliyev was at the time married to the president's eldest daughter, Dariga, who owns several major media outlets and has been seen as a possible presidential successor. The couple divorced in June.

Shortly before the suspension, the Almaty prosecutor's office sent KTK and *Karavan* letters warning them not to cover details of the Nurbank employees' disappearance without permission of law enforcement agencies, according to local and international press reports. In August, the original *Karavan* was forced to close, and was replaced by a paper similar in format and carrying the same name—but owned by Zhanai Omarov, a former Nazarbayev press secretary. Authorities called it a "restructuring," *The Washington Post* reported.

The August 18 parliamentary elections brought an absolute victory for Nazarbayev's ruling Nur Otan party, which got all 98 contested seats in the Mazhilis, Kazakhstan's lower house of parliament. None of the opposition parties managed to pass the 7 percent bar required to enter the Mazhilis, leaving Kazakhstan with a one-party system for the first time since the Soviet era. Nazarbayev called the elections free and fair, but international observers disagreed. OSCE monitors said the vote did not meet international standards with its opaque ballot-counting system and high bar for parties to enter the legislature. In two years, Kazakhstan will be in charge of such monitoring.

· · · · · · · · · · · · · · · · · **KYRGYZSTAN** · · · · · · · · · · · · · · · · · ·

One prominent editor was slain and other journalists faced escalating government harassment, violent attacks, and lawlessness amid intense political rivalry between President Kurmanbek Bakiyev and opposition parties in parliament. In the face of recurring protests, Bakiyev periodically made political concessions to the opposition, only to withdraw or undermine the agreements after demonstrators had gone home. Seemingly focused on political obfuscation, the administration was unable to effectively tackle widespread crime, corruption, and poverty, and Bakiyev became steadily more reliant on authoritarian policies to keep the upper hand with opposition parties, civil society activists, and independent journalists.

After coming to power in the March 2005 "Tulip Revolution"—a populist revolt against the corrupt rule of former President Askar Akayev—Bakiyev continued to bog down in bickering with opposition parties about the constitutional balance of power. While Kyrgyzstan remained the only genuinely pluralistic country in Central Asia, with an active parliament, dynamic media, and truly competitive political system, the intense political rivalry polarized the country and allowed organized crime groups to flourish, making independent news reporting increasingly dangerous.

Reflecting Bakiyev's increasingly authoritarian style, his government overreacted to sympathetic coverage of the major opposition rallies of November 2006. During late 2006 and early 2007, prosecutors and National Security Committee (KNB) officers summoned senior managers of the independent television station NTS for questioning about its coverage of the rallies, according to local press reports. Bakiyev's ultimate rejection of a November 2006 constitutional powers agreement—and the ensuing harassment of the media—angered the political opposition during the winter of 2007.

Journalists in the capital, Bishkek, and in the countryside faced periodic harassment, threats, and violent attacks in reprisal for their news reporting as tensions between Bakiyev and the opposition escalated in early 2007. In February, unidentified individuals broke into the editorial office of the Bishkek-based opposition newspaper *Kyrgyz Rukhu* and set the premises on fire, according to local press reports. The newspaper had recently published several articles criticizing presidential aide Kurmanbek Temirbayev.

In October, an unidentified gunman in the southern city of Osh shot and killed Alisher Saipov, the 26-year-old editor of the independent Uzbek-language weekly *Siyosat* (Politics) and a stringer for the U.S. government-funded Voice of America and several other foreign news organizations. Prior to his murder, Saipov had received telephone threats, was followed by several men who appeared to be Uzbek security agents, and was smeared in the Uzbek state media in retaliation for his reporting on politically sensitive human rights abuses in Uzbekistan. Kyrgyz authorities opened a criminal investigation amid speculation that Uzbek agents were behind the slaying. (In Uzbekistan, state-controlled Internet service providers blocked access within their borders to articles describing Saipov's murder.) In November, CPJ met with Zamira Sydykova, the Kyrgyz ambassador to the United States, to urge a thorough and transparent investigation into Saipov's slaying.

Even journalists with the more cautious Kyrgyz National Television and Radio Corporation (KTR) were targeted for reporting on politically sensitive issues. In March, KTR reporter Kairat Birimkulov sustained serious head injuries in an attack by two unidentified men outside Bishkek, according to local press reports. The assault occurred after the journalist reported on allegations of negligence and corrupt business practices against the director of the Bishkek railway company Kyrgyz Temir Zholu. In the weeks prior to the attack, Birimkulov had received telephone threats, and the railway company's director, Nariman Tyuleyev, had filed a defamation lawsuit against the journalist. Birimkulov continued receiving telephone threats following the attack, prompting him to move to Switzerland in October, the U.S.

government-funded Radio Free Europe/Radio Liberty (RFE/RL) reported.

On March 27, little more than a week after the attack on Birimkulov, four un-identified men abducted NTS news anchor Daniyar Isanov in Bishkek, drove him to the outskirts of the city, beat him unconscious, and shouted "this is for NTS," accord-ing to CPJ research. Isanov found himself on the street after regaining consciousness the following morning; he was hospitalized with a broken nose and facial bruises.

During large opposition protests in mid-April, nearly 10,000 demonstrators marched daily to the presidential palace in Bishkek, calling for Bakiyev's resignation. At least five local and foreign journalists were assaulted during the protests, but it was not always clear whether the attackers were opposition activists or pro-government provocateurs. Interior Minister Bolotbek Nogoibayev dismissed the attacks, stating that "our staff usually reach the conclusion that it was a coincidence, but journalists use it as PR to draw attention to themselves," according to the London-based Insti-tute for War and Peace Reporting.

On April 19, the ninth day of protests in the capital, police violently dispersed the crowd and mobilized prosecutors and KNB security officers to censor oppo-sition media. The following morning, some 30 KNB officials raided an indepen-dent printing house in Bishkek and confiscated the print runs of four opposition newspapers—*Agym, Kyrgyz Rukhu, Apta*, and *Aykyn*—as well as the electronic files containing the editions of those newspapers, according to press reports. The raid, though directed by prosecutors, violated laws requiring a court order for the seizure of journalistic material, according to the country's independent media ombudsman, Shamaral Maichiyev.

The harassment of NTS managers following the November 2006 protests and the crackdown on opposition newspapers in April 2007 reflected Bakiyev's growing reliance on prosecutors, KNB security officers, and police to intimidate and silence critical news reporting. In May, *Novy Kyrgyzstan* newspaper editor Artyom Petrov was summoned to KNB headquarters in Bishkek to answer questions about his relation-ship with opposition party members, according to local press reports. In October, po-lice officers in Bishkek confiscated 2,500 copies of the independent newspaper *Alkak* that contained an article criticizing a proposal by Bakiyev that would weaken the pow-ers of the parliament. (The changes were approved by voters at a referendum. Bakiyev then dissolved parliament and called a December election, won by his party.)

Throughout the year, Bakiyev and parliamentary allies delayed or undermined var-ious media reforms, including efforts to transform state broadcaster KTR into an inde-pendent public broadcast network. Bakiyev approved in March a long-delayed law to reform KTR—but then appointed a director by presidential decree, undermining the KTR supervisory board that was supposed to be responsible for such appointments, according to local press reports. In late March, parliament began debating a measure to decriminalize libel, but the proposal remained stalled at year's end, RFE/RL reported.

The intense and sometimes confrontational political divide between Bakiyev and primary political opponent Felix Kulov—a former KNB colonel and prime minister—reinforced longstanding factionalism. As a result, independent and opposition journalists were increasingly stranded between Kulov's allies, who represent the more Russified, prosperous north, and Bakiyev's supporters, who represent the more religious, impoverished, ethnically Uzbek south.

Pyramid—the country's first influential independent television station, known for its critical reporting of Bakiyev—was mired in lawsuits over ownership rights that left the station's headquarters impounded and its bank accounts frozen for much of 2007, the local press reported. With advertising revenue scarce, some media owners sought to use their outlets to advance political interests instead, leaving frontline journalists vulnerable to pressure, according to an assessment conducted by the Washington-based media training organization IREX.

Authoritarian neighbors such as Uzbekistan, Russia, and China encouraged Bakiyev to abandon Western-style pro-democracy reforms. In August, Bishkek hosted a meeting of the multilateral Shanghai Cooperation Organization, an alliance of repressive governments in Eurasia seeking to counterbalance the U.S. military presence in the region. Bakiyev forged closer ties with leaders from Tashkent, Moscow, and Beijing, while subtly distancing himself from democratic aspirations and ties with the United States and the European Union.

• • • • • • • • • • • • • • • • • • • RUSSIA • • • • • • • • • • • • • • • • • • •

Constitutional constraints posed little problem for a term-limited President Vladimir Putin, who appeared certain to hold power long after his tenure was due to end in 2008. The popular, two-term president hopped into the parliamentary race in the fall, topping the dominant United Russia ticket that took 64 percent of the vote in a December 2 election. Eight days later, Putin endorsed First Deputy Prime Minister Dmitry Medvedev to be his successor, smoothing his protégé's road to the March 2008 presidential election. Medvedev returned the favor by announcing that, as president, he would name Putin prime minister—a post likely to carry greater powers given United Russia's control of parliament.

The parliamentary campaign offered plenty of alarming signs for the press and civil society. Authorities cracked down on dissent, moved aggressively to limit news coverage of any party other than United Russia, and harassed the few news outlets that tried to cover the opposition. In an unambiguous signal that Russia would not tolerate outside scrutiny, the Central Election Commission slashed by three-quarters the number of international election observers allowed to monitor the vote. A mere 300 observers were allowed to monitor roughly 100,000 polling stations.

Putin's plans were shrouded in secrecy for most of the year, but his government's determination to muzzle critics was pronounced and clear. Three journalists were behind bars when CPJ conducted its annual census on December 1. Two journalists committed "suicide" under mysterious circumstances. Critical media outlets and nongovernmental groups were harassed or closed altogether. Journalists took fewer risks in covering sensitive subjects such as corruption, organized crime, and human rights abuses. Authorities applied new extremism charges, bureaucratic harassment, and Soviet-style forced psychiatric detention. And they deployed special forces to disperse peaceful opposition demonstrations and to prevent journalists from covering the protests.

Despite an increasingly repressive climate, authorities made progress in three high-profile journalist murders—those of Igor Domnikov, Yuri Shchekochikhin, and Anna Politkovskaya, all reporters with the fiercely independent Moscow newspaper *Novaya Gazeta*. Five men were convicted in August in the 2000 murder of Domnikov—the first convictions in a reporter's slaying obtained during Putin's eight-year tenure. The landmark verdict was followed by another encouraging sign. A newly formed investigative committee under the jurisdiction of the prosecutor general's office announced in November that it had opened a separate probe into the masterminds of Domnikov's murder. The committee, created in September, was charged with overseeing major criminal cases.

Prosecutor General Yuri Chaika announced on August 27 the arrests of 10 suspects in the 2006 murder of Politkovskaya. Chaika told reporters that the suspects included current and former officials from the Interior Ministry and Federal Security Service (FSB), as well as members of a criminal gang headed by an ethnic Chechen. Two days later, a spokeswoman for the Moscow City Court announced that a warrant had been issued for an 11th suspect, a former police officer with the Moscow Directorate for Combating Organized Crime. Authorities provided no details on the suspects' alleged involvement.

In October, the prosecutor's investigative committee said it would open a criminal probe into the mysterious July 2003 death of Yuri Shchekochikhin, deputy editor of *Novaya Gazeta*, who died from a purported "acute allergy." At the time of his death, Shchekochikhin was uncovering high-level corruption involving top officials with the FSB and the prosecutor general's office. Colleagues, who had repeatedly sought a criminal investigation, said they believe the 53-year-old journalist was poisoned to stop his reporting. The sudden illness that befell Shchekochikhin during a June 2003 business trip initially had flulike symptoms, which quickly grew into full-fledged organ failure. Hospital authorities sealed—even from Shchekochikhin's family—his medical tests and autopsy, labeling the documents "medical secrets."

EUROPE AND CENTRAL ASIA

The courage displayed by *Novaya Gazeta* journalists was recognized in November, when CPJ honored Editor-in-Chief Dmitry Muratov with an International Press Freedom Award. Muratov spoke of the heavy price the paper has paid for its independent editorial stance and aggressive investigative reporting.

Fourteen journalists have been slain in direct relation to their work during Putin's tenure, making Russia the world's third-deadliest nation for the press. A CPJ delegation traveled to Moscow in January to meet with Foreign Ministry officials and the president's Council on Human Rights. Expressing grave concern at the lack of progress in journalist murder investigations, the delegation called on Putin to stop the cycle of violence by bringing the perpetrators to justice.

A week later, Putin issued his first public pledge to protect Russia's press corps and noted the importance of Politkovskaya's journalism. "The issue of journalist persecution is one of the most pressing," Putin told the hundreds of reporters gathered in the Kremlin's Round Hall for the annual presidential press conference. "We realize our degree of responsibility in this. We will do everything to protect the press corps." He described Politkovskaya as "a rather sharp critic of authorities," adding, "This is good." His remarks were in sharp contrast to his initial reaction to the murder, in October 2006, when he downplayed the significance of Politkovskaya's work and said "her influence on political life in Russia was minimal."

Putin's pledge to protect the press, though welcomed, was undercut by events that followed. The retrial of two suspects in the 2004 murder of *Forbes Russia* Editor Paul Klebnikov stalled in March because one suspect went missing. Ivan Safronov, a prominent military correspondent for the business daily *Kommersant*, died that same month after falling from an upper-floor window in his Moscow apartment building. Prosecutors termed the death a suicide, citing unspecified personal reasons. In a special report in November, "Another Mystery in Moscow," CPJ spotlighted numerous questions that investigators left unanswered.

Safronov, 51, plunged to his death just days after returning from a reporting trip to Abu Dhabi, United Arab Emirates, where he had covered an international gathering of defense manufacturers. He left no suicide note, had no evident personal or professional problems, had no life-threatening illness, and was expecting his first grandchild. Just before he supposedly took his own life, he had dropped by a grocery store and picked up some oranges. The fruit was found strewn on the landing between the building's fourth and fifth stories.

Colleagues said Safronov had just obtained sensitive information about Russian arms sales to Syria and Iran—a story that would have embarrassed authorities. He told colleagues that he had been warned not to publish the information, and that the FSB would charge him with disclosing state secrets if he did. For weeks after Safronov's death, authorities did not question reporters or search the journalist's computer or his notes. Ilya Bulavinov, Safronov's editor, told CPJ that authorities appeared uninterested in examining his journalism as a possible motive for murder.

Another journalist's death was also termed a suicide. Vyacheslav Ifanov, 29, a cameraman for the independent television station Novoye Televideniye Aleiska in the Siberian city of Aleisk, was declared the victim of self-induced carbon monoxide poisoning in April. Yet Ifanov had received death threats, and family members found wounds on his body. On the night before his death, he was featured in a television report that described an earlier attack against him. In the April 4 broadcast, Ifanov said he hoped to identify his attackers soon with the help of police, the Moscow-based daily *Izvestiya* reported. Ifanov was referring to a January incident in which a group of unidentified men wearing camouflage attacked him after he filmed them gathering in the center of Aleisk, according to local press reports. After realizing they were being filmed, the men broke Ifanov's camera, destroyed his footage, and severely beat him. During the attack, the men told the journalist, "We warned you that military reconnaissance works here, but you didn't listen," the Novosibirsk State Television and Radio Company quoted Ifanov as saying. The journalist sustained a concussion in the attack and spent several days in the hospital, according to local press reports.

CPJ highlighted violence against Russian journalists in August testimony before the U.S. Commission on Security and Cooperation in Europe. "As violence against these messengers goes unpunished, fewer journalists are willing to risk their lives in pursuit of difficult stories, the press is forced to compromise its role as a watchdog, and the public is kept in the dark about important issues," CPJ Program Coordinator Nina Ognianova told the commission.

Ognianova also noted that, as elections approached, authorities were cracking down on opponents with vigor. Special police forces broke up rallies, or "Dissenters' Marches," organized by Other Russia, the opposition coalition led by former world chess champion Garry Kasparov and nationalist writer Eduard Limonov. Journalists who tried to cover the protests were harassed. In March, for example, police detained nine Russian and international journalists as they covered a Dissenters' March in the central Russian city of Nizhny Novgorod. Three of the journalists were beaten. In April, police in St. Petersburg seized thousands of copies of an opposition paper destined to be transported to Moscow ahead of a Dissenters' March planned in the capital the next day. In May, police detained three foreign journalists from leading news outlets as they prepared to fly from a Moscow airport to a Dissenters' March in the southern city of Samara. And on the eve of the December vote, police in the northern city of Arkhangelsk seized the entire press run of the local independent newspaper *Arkhangelsky Obozrevatel*, the independent radio station Ekho Moskvy reported. The issue carried articles critical of United Russia and local authorities.

In a disturbing move, Putin signed into law a package of amendments expanding the definition of extremism to include even the public discussion of such activity, and giving law enforcement officials broad authority to suspend media outlets that do not comply. Ostensibly designed to fight extremism—including the growing nationalist and neo-Nazi movements—the new measures have already restricted the independent press and critical writers. Ekho Moskvy received 15 letters from the FSB, prosecutors, and media regulators, all warning the station against carrying "extremist" statements. Authorities launched an official probe of prominent political analyst Andrei Piontkovsky, author of the critical 2006 political diary *Unloved Country*, for making public appeals to extremism. Several regional newspapers faced similar charges and possible closure.

Also disturbing was the resurrection of forced psychiatric confinement—a measure used during Soviet times to silence dissidents. Two cases were particularly egregious. Vladimir Chugunov, founder and editor of the now-defunct newsweekly *Chugunka* in the town of Solnechnogorsk, was arrested in January on a spurious charge of "threatening to murder or cause serious health damage." He spent more than four months in state custody, shuttling between prison cells, hospital wards, and psychiatric wards. Chugunov had long angered local authorities with articles criticizing the Solnechnogorsk government and judiciary.

Writer Larisa Arap, an activist affiliated with Kasparov's United Civic Front party, was held in a Russian psychiatric hospital for 46 days. The forced hospitalization came after the party's newspaper, *Dissenters' March*, published her comments on abusive treatment of patients at the Murmansk regional psychiatric hospital in the northern city of Apatity. Arap said hospital personnel tied her to her bed, beat her, tried to smother her with a pillow, and injected her with undisclosed drugs. On August 13, an independent psychiatric evaluation, ordered by Ombudsman for Human Rights Vladimir Lukin, concluded that Arap had been illegally hospitalized. Even so, it took an international outcry, including statements from CPJ, to persuade authorities to honor the independent evaluation and release Arap on August 20.

Provincial authorities used spurious charges such as infringing on copyright law and using counterfeit software to shutter independent and opposition outlets ahead of national elections. In November, just weeks before the parliamentary elections, authorities in Samara suspended publication of the local edition of *Novaya Gazeta*. Local police raided the paper's bureau, seizing computers and financial documents and placing editor Sergei Kurt-Adzhiyev under criminal investigation for violating copyright law. An earlier raid against the bureau had occurred in May. Although copyright infringement is pervasive in Russia, Kurt-Adzhiyev faced up to six years in prison. The paper had regularly covered the activities of the Other Russia coalition.

Authorities continued to stifle news about Russia's volatile North Caucasus region. To promote an image of stability, Putin elevated Chechnya's notorious prime minister, Ramzan Kadyrov, to president of the Chechen republic in February. Human rights abuses committed by Kadyrov and his military forces have been well documented.

Two reporters who had long covered Russia's North Caucasus for international news outlets were forced to resettle in the United States in the spring after enduring intense official retaliation for their work. Yuri Bagrov and Fatima Tlisova, former correspondents for The Associated Press and Radio Free Europe/Radio Liberty, joined CPJ in speaking to the U.S. Congressional Human Rights Caucus in late June. They told the caucus of harassment, obstruction, and attacks they had endured at the hands of the FSB because of their reporting on civilian abductions, illegal detentions, torture, and human rights abuses by officials in Chechnya and other parts of the North Caucasus.

Imprisonment became a risk once again for critical journalists in Russia. In late year, authorities held three journalists behind bars because of their work: Boris Stomakhin, editor of the monthly newspaper *Radikalnaya Politika* in Moscow; Anatoly Sardayev, founder and editor of the independent weekly *Mordoviya Segodnya* in Saransk; and Nikolai Andrushchenko, co-founder and an editor of the weekly newspaper *Novy Peterburg* in St. Petersburg.

• • • • • • • • • • • • • • • • • • • TAJIKISTAN • • • • • • • • • • • • • • • • • • •

Beginning his 16th year as head of state, President Emomali Rahmonov promoted policies to foster "national identity." He abolished Russified endings from Tajik surnames—and started by cutting the suffix "ov" from his own surname and decreeing that he be called President Rahmon. The newly renamed president went on to prohibit students from driving cars to school and to admonish the public for what he called lavish spending on weddings and funerals. In his annual address to parliament, Rahmon called for the development of a new press policy in which "Tajik mass media will be expected to raise patriotism with the public."

The president's call for a "patriotic" press did not immediately lead to new legislation, but the country's poor overall press situation has drawn international and domestic criticism. The National Association of Independent Media of Tajikistan (NANSMIT), a press freedom group based in the capital, Dushanbe,

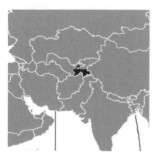

said government officials have consistently denied independent and opposition reporters access to public information and failed to notify reporters of official press conferences—despite a 2005 presidential decree that obliges authorities to hold quarterly press conferences and grant journalists access. But the greatest indicator of press conditions is the dearth of independent news sources. No daily newspapers circulate in the country, independent weeklies are suppressed, and foreign broadcasters are barred from the airwaves. In a country where the average monthly salary is about US$45, few have access to the Internet or satellite television. Broadcast television, the primary source of news, is dominated by three national state-run stations: Tajik, Soghd, and Khatlon.

Authorities have long relied on politicized investigations and regulatory actions to obstruct the independent media. The newspapers *Ruzi Nav, Nerui Sukhan*, and *Odamu Olan*; the television stations Somonien and Guli Bodom; and BBC radio all saw their licenses pulled for alleged administrative violations between 2004 and 2006. (Somonien TV regained its license in 2007.)

The government, which had already blocked domestic access to critical Internet news sites, moved in 2007 to impose greater criminal liability against them as well. Parliament, dominated by the pro-presidential People's Democratic Party, approved amendments to the criminal code that added Internet-based publications to the mass media that can be charged with criminal defamation. CPJ and others called on Rahmon to veto the amendments, which effectively criminalize critical reporting and commentary on popular news Web sites such as *Ferghana* and *Centrasia* and opposition sites such as *Charogiruz* and *Tajikistan Times*. Existing penalties include a fine of 20,000 somoni (US$5,800)—hundreds of times a citizen's normal monthly income—and two years in prison. Rahmon signed the measure into law on October 20.

The Vienna-based Organization for Security and Co-operation in Europe (OSCE)—a pan-European human rights monitoring group—expressed its concern about the expansion of criminal defamation and the poor overall press situation. Miklos Haraszti, the OSCE representative on media freedom, called on the Tajik government to "bring its legislation in line with its OSCE commitments by revoking recent criminal code amendments that restrict freedom of speech. Whether published on the Internet or in any other media, only explicit incitement to violence or discrimination should be criminalized; the rest of the verbal offenses should belong to civil courts."

Already, the fear of criminal persecution leads Tajik reporters to practice widespread self-censorship, NANSMIT reported. One high-profile case, pending in late year, was closely watched by journalists. In July, popular Tajik singer Raikhona Rakhimova filed a defamation complaint against Editor-in-Chief Saida Kurbonova and reporters Mukhaiye Nozimova and Farangis Nabiyeva of the newspaper *Ovoza* over a story that purported to describe details of the singer's personal life.

One positive development came in September, when Tajik authorities brought to justice Aslan Usmonov, an accomplice in the 1995 killing of prominent Tajik journalist Muhiddin Olimpur. The Supreme Court of Tajikistan sentenced Usmonov to 15 years in prison in a maximum-security penal colony on September 28, *Ferghana* reported. Olimpur, head of the BBC's Persian Service in Tajikistan, was found dead near the University of Tajikistan in Dushanbe with a gunshot wound to the head.

He was among 16 journalists killed during the Tajik civil war, which lasted from 1992 to 1997. According to CPJ research, two other accomplices in the Olimpur murder were convicted in 2003; the suspected mastermind, a field commander with the United Tajik Opposition, died during the war.

Nongovernmental organizations, or NGOs, especially those receiving foreign funding, encountered new restrictions in 2007. A vaguely worded measure approved by parliament and enacted in February increased state control over the NGO sector, introducing a number of procedural and licensing hurdles that appear designed to obstruct the work of NGOs, according to the London-based Institute for War and Peace Reporting.

•••••••••••••••• TURKMENISTAN ••••••••••••••••••

The sudden death of President-for-Life Saparmurat Niyazov in December 2006 marked an end to an eccentric and authoritarian rule, raising modest hopes for social, economic, and political reform. Gurbanguly Berdymukhammedov, a deputy prime minister and Niyazov loyalist, was named interim leader and then became president in a government-orchestrated "election" in February.

Pledging limited changes, Berdymukhammedov made limited improvements: opening Internet cafés but blocking access to critical news sites, restoring 10-year compulsory education but retaining Niyazov's propaganda-filled guide for living as required reading, traveling widely abroad while insisting his country was free. The circumstances surrounding the 2006 death in state custody of journalist Ogulsapar Muradova remained unaddressed, despite repeated calls by international human rights and press freedom groups for an investigation.

The outcome of the February presidential election was predetermined. The country's highest legislative body, the People's Council, named six candidates including Berdymukhammedov, all members of the ruling party. In the run-up to the balloting, Berdymukhammedov vowed to restore pensions abolished by Niyazov, to improve the educational system, to provide public access to the Internet, and to honor the country's energy contracts. At the same time, he said he would continue the political course set by his tyrannical predecessor, and that the election would "conform to Niyazov's concept of democracy," according to local and international press reports.

As a testament to those words, Turkmen authorities did not allow any exiled opposition members to return to the country and participate in the balloting, Radio Free Europe/Radio Liberty (RFE/RL) reported. On February 14, Berdymukhammedov was sworn in as president after receiving 89 percent of the vote.

The new leader immediately introduced a number of changes, but he stuck to Niyazov's policy principles. Within a day of his swearing-in, Berdymukhammedov

EUROPE AND CENTRAL AS A

 signed a decree reversing his predecessor's reduction of compulsory education from 10 to nine years. In March, he abolished an obligatory two-year period of work before citizens could enroll in a university. At the same time, however, Berdymukhammedov kept the *Rukhnama* (Book of the Soul), a 400-page guide written by Niyazov, as a must-read in all spheres of Turkmen society—from elementary schools to government offices. The Ministry of Education stated that the *Rukhnama* would be a core subject in schools, raising questions about the validity of any educational reforms. Rife with historical inaccuracies and nationalist hyperbole, the *Rukhnama* denies any influence from other cultures on Turkmenistan's development and claims that Turkmen invented writing.

On February 16, authorities opened Turkmenistan's first Internet café, in the capital, Ashgabat—a landmark for a country whose access to information had long been strangled by the state. RFE/RL quoted Berdymukhammedov as saying that "Internet cafés are starting to open in Ashgabat and other cities. At this moment, we are working on a program to extend Internet access to every school." This new accessibility, however, was marred by a variety of limitations: The cafés were initially guarded by armed soldiers, connections were uneven and the per-hour fee costly, and authorities monitored or blocked access to certain Web sites. RFE/RL reported in April that authorities had blocked the regional news sites *Ferghana*, *EurasiaNet*, and *Centrasia*, as well as opposition Web sites.

The government recoiled after taking a tentative step toward interactive communication with its citizens. RFE/RL reported in October that Turkmen authorities had allowed the public to post comments on the official Altyn Asyr (Golden Age) Web site. Just four days later, after comments criticizing the government were posted, the feature was removed without explanation.

In May, state media trumpeted a presidential initiative to provide national television broadcasters—all government-run—with the latest technological equipment. Content, though, remained under tight control. In June, the president sacked Minister of Culture Enebai Atayeva, who had been reprimanded for being too liberal in loosening controls on television broadcasts, according to CPJ research. As the news Web site *EurasiaNet* pointed out in a May analysis: "The state owns all domestic media, appoints all editors, and approves all content. Imports of print news are limited, so residents seeking more comprehensive coverage must either add to the country's mushrooming number of satellite dishes or tune in to foreign-funded radio programming." Satellite dishes might not remain so plentiful. In a November 30 televised statement, Berdymukhammedov said he ordered his Communications Ministry to remove satellite dishes from apartment buildings in Ashgabat. He said removal of the dishes would beautify the capital, RFE/RL reported.

The Russian agency ITAR-TASS was the only foreign news organization to maintain a bureau in Turkmenistan in 2007, journalists said. Prior to the presidential election, Turkmen authorities placed restrictions on foreign and domestic journalists covering the vote, prompting protests from CPJ and others.

Oguljamal Yazliyeva, director of RFE/RL's Turkmen service, said harassment of the news network's stringers continued under the new leadership. Authorities cut off their land-line and mobile phone service, placed them under close surveillance, and harassed their families, Yazliyeva said.

The U.S. government-funded RFE/RL was the only other international broadcaster maintaining even an informal network of correspondents in Turkmenistan. Long harassed by the government, RFE/RL lost its Ashgabat correspondent in September 2006. Ogulsapar Muradova died in state custody after being sentenced to a six-year term on spurious charges in a closed-door trial. More than a year after authorities handed over Muradova's battered body to her family, the circumstances surrounding her death remain unexplained. The government continued to resist international calls for an independent investigation and failed to release official autopsy results. Neither did it release any information on Annakurban Amanklychev and Sapardurdy Khadzhiyev—the two human rights activists who had been sentenced to seven years each in the same closed trial.

Speaking as if Muradova's killing had never happened, Berdymukhammedov insisted during a visit to the United States in September that Turkmen citizens enjoy free press and free speech. In a talk given at Columbia University in New York, he stated that "there was never in Turkmenistan any pressure on the press," RFE/RL reported. Protesting the press freedom conditions in Turkmenistan, CPJ urged U.S. Secretary of State Condoleezza Rice to include Muradova's case on the agenda for her meeting with Berdymukhammedov, who was in New York to address the U.N. General Assembly. In a written response to CPJ, the U.S. State Department said the case, as well as other press freedom and human rights issues, were on the American agenda.

· · · · · · · · · · · · · · · · · · **UKRAINE** ·

Intense political rivalries among a trio of powerful leaders created a chaotic and highly politicized environment in which journalists were vulnerable to a variety of abuses. Parliamentary elections in September and negotiations to form a new government in the succeeding months intensified pressure on journalists to take sides. In November, Ukraine's two pro-Western parties formed a fragile coalition that returned Orange Revolution leader Yulia Tymoshenko to the prime minister's post she once held.

EUROPE AND CENTRAL ASIA

Viktor Yanukovych, the pro-Russian politician who was prime minister for more than a year, found himself the odd man out, but it was uncertain how long Tymoshenko's alliance with President Viktor Yushchenko could last.

The growing domestic economy created a surge in media advertising revenue (about 20 percent since 2005), an expanded readership for news Web sites, and a greater demand for business-oriented media, according to international press reports. But these gains were offset by widespread corruption and a dysfunctional criminal justice system that regularly failed to protect journalists from threats, harassment, and violent crimes.

The Ukrainian press continued to adapt to a period of political tumult that began four years earlier. The public's frustration with the corrupt, authoritarian rule of President Leonid Kuchma erupted in late 2003, when widespread voter fraud and media restrictions sparked the massive Kyiv protests that came to be known as the Orange Revolution. Elections for Kuchma's successor were eventually won by the reformist Yushchenko, who ended the Kuchma administration's practice of sending editorial instructions, called *temnyki*, to news media and who committed his government to solving the 2000 murder of Internet journalist Georgy Gongadze. But the electoral success of the Orange Revolution was undermined by Yushchenko's intense rivalry with Tymoshenko, the popular prime minister in the first post-revolution government, who pushed for more radical political and economic reform. Yushchenko effectively fired Tymoshenko, creating an opening for Yanukovych and his conservative Party of Regions (PRU) in the March 2006 parliamentary elections.

Yanukovych's ruling coalition of conservative, pro-Russia parties did what it could to curtail the influence of the news media. In an effort to take greater advantage of state media, the Yanukovych government appointed political loyalist Eduard Prutnyk to head the State Committee for Television and Radio Broadcasting. In March 2007, state-run Channel 1 of Ukrainian National Television canceled its only current affairs debate program, "Toloka," a day after Tymoshenko appeared on the program and drew high approval ratings during a call-in segment. In April, the PRU tried unsuccessfully to oust the chairman of the parliamentary Committee on Freedom of Speech and Information, Andriy Shevchenko, a widely respected media rights lawyer and Tymoshenko ally. Shevchenko had urged state media reform and had criticized attempts to restrict independent journalists.

Some members of the PRU were overtly hostile toward the media. In April, PRU activists tossed television crews from NTN and Novy Kanal off a train after the journalists tried to film the leader of the party's Crimean branch as he traveled to Kyiv for pro-Yanukovych rallies, the Moscow-based human rights news agency Prima reported. In Kyiv, prosecutors decided in July not to file charges against Oleg Kalashnikov, a PRU loyalist and member of parliament, in a 2006 case in which he allegedly attacked two STB TV journalists who had filmed him without permission. The prosecution cited a lack of evidence.

A weak and politicized criminal justice system left journalists throughout the country vulnerable to harassment from politicians, businessmen, and organized-crime groups. Abuses remained so widespread that one-third of the journalists attending a media conference in the southeastern city of Donetsk in April reported having received threats, while half said they had experienced other kinds of pressure in response to their work, the local news Web site *Obkom* reported.

The political deadlock in Kyiv stalled efforts to transform the government's network of television and radio stations into an independent public broadcasting system, leaving these media outlets in the hands of officials allied with either Yanukovych or Yushchenko. In effect, the two political camps divided control of the state media apparatus. Most government agencies remained secretive, regularly denying requests for basic public information and sometimes obstructing journalists—for example, by creating cumbersome rules for accreditation.

The media operated in a complex environment that reflected the nation's cultural divisions: predominantly pro-European, Ukrainian-language regions in the west and north; predominantly pro-Russian, Russian-language regions in the south and east. Reporters, editors, and media owners periodically faced pressure to align their editorial policies with one of the dominant political forces in the country—Yanukovych, Tymoshenko, Yushchenko, or regional politicians. These powerful figures and their allies provided some protection for the press but demanded that journalists report the news in ways that would advance their interests.

Despite Yushchenko's stated commitment in 2004 to solve the Gongadze case, the government's investigation focused on low-level suspects and made limited progress. The trial of three senior Internal Affairs Ministry officials accused of murdering Gongadze opened in January 2006 but was adjourned in July 2007 for court-mandated medical examinations of the suspects. A fourth ministry official wanted for the murder, Gen. Aleksei Pukach, fled Ukraine in 2000 and remained on Interpol's list of wanted fugitives.

Gongadze's family and press freedom advocates continued to criticize prosecutors for not pursuing those who ordered the murder and for ignoring credible evidence—most notably, secretly recorded audiotapes in which Kuchma is heard instructing Internal Affairs Minister Yuri Kravchenko to "drive out" Gongadze and "give him to the Chechens." Gongadze, a pioneer among Ukrainian journalists because he published his articles on the Internet, wrote highly critical reports detailing corruption in Kuchma's administration. "There are people who are trying to cover up for their colleagues," Gongadze's widow, Myroslava Gongadze, told reporters on the seventh anniversary of the murder in September.

EUROPE AND CENTRAL ASIA

· · · · · · · · · · · · · · · · · UZBEKISTAN · · · · · · · · · · · · · · · · ·

In power for nearly two decades, President Islam Karimov had little trouble
securing another seven-year term in office. He faced three candidates but no genu-
ine opposition in a December election that international observers said was neither
free nor fair. Though constitutional term limits seemed to constrain the president
from seeking re-election at all, the Central Election Commission cleared Karimov
for another run without bothering to explain its reasoning. Throughout, the regime
continued to suppress dissent and independent voices.

Tashkent urged the European Union to lift sanctions imposed after the bloody 2005 crackdown on antigovernment protesters in the eastern city of Andijan. But
Karimov's authoritarian regime did not change its course
on press freedom and human rights, many EU sanctions
remained in place, and the divide separating Uzbekistan
and the West continued to widen. Foreign Affairs Minister Vladimir Norov said during a March meeting with
his German counterpart, Frank-Walter Steinmeier, that
his country's sovereignty should be respected and that

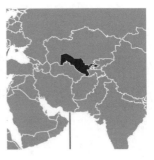

Europe should not lecture Uzbekistan on human rights and democracy issues, the
U.S. government-funded Radio Free Europe/Radio Liberty (RFE/RL) reported.
Rather, "it is necessary to take into consideration the countries' national traditions,
history, and the mentality of our peoples," Norov said.

Independent journalists affiliated with Western media outlets were singled out
for harassment. Umida Niyazova, who reported on politics and human rights for
RFE/RL and the independent Central Asia news Web site *Oasis*, spent three and
a half months in detention and endured daily interrogations that lasted up to 15
hours, according to reports issued by news and human rights organizations.

Niyazova, who also contributed reporting to international groups such as Human Rights Watch and Internews Network, was arrested in January after arriving at
the Tashkent airport from Kyrgyzstan. She was charged with carrying and distributing subversive literature—human rights reports about Andijan that she had saved on
her laptop—and crossing the border illegally. On May 1, according to press reports,
Niyazova was convicted and sentenced to a seven-year prison term following a trial
riddled with procedural problems. The proceedings, despite being billed as open to
the public, were closed to reporters and diplomats, reports said. Only one family
member was allowed in the courtroom, and observers were forbidden from taking
notes.

Following an international outcry, including protests from CPJ, a Tashkent appellate panel suspended Niyazova's jail term on May 8, effectively setting her free but

leaving intact her conviction. The release appeared to be timed to EU discussions on the Andijan sanctions. On May 9, CPJ sent a letter to the EU urging that it consider Uzbekistan's appalling press freedom record when making its decision.

The EU had imposed an arms embargo and a travel ban on senior Uzbek officials after Tashkent resisted calls for an independent inquiry into the killing of hundreds of civilians in Andijan in 2005. Meeting in mid-October, EU foreign ministers partially lifted the travel ban but left the embargo in place. "After six months we want to see some improvement in the human rights situation in Uzbekistan," said Deputy Dutch Foreign Minister Frans Timmermans, the *International Herald Tribune* reported. The travel ban, lifted against four officials, remained in place for eight others, he said.

A week later, a prominent Kyrgyz journalist of Uzbek ethnicity was slain in the southern Kyrgyz city of Osh, across the border from Andijan. Alisher Saipov, editor of the Uzbek-language weekly *Siyosat* (Politics), was shot three times by an unidentified gunman as he left the newspaper's offices on October 23. In its six months of publication, *Siyosat* had grown popular in the Uzbek-dominated eastern end of the Ferghana Valley. Saipov, 26, also covered Uzbekistan's political and social issues as a stringer for RFE/RL, Voice of America, and the Central Asia news Web site *Ferghana*. An active supporter of Andijan refugees and the exiled Uzbek opposition, he had received numerous anonymous threats prior to his death.

Kyrgyz authorities opened a criminal investigation amid speculation that Uzbek agents were behind the slaying. While the international journalist community denounced Saipov's killing, the Uzbek state-controlled media waged a smear campaign against the journalist, calling him a traitor who tried to destabilize the country with his reporting. Authorities blocked domestic access to independent Web sites that reported on the case, according to the Germany-based exile news site *Uznews*.

Uzbekistan held five reporters behind bars in late year, making it the region's second-leading jailer of journalists, behind only Azerbaijan. The lengths to which authorities have gone to silence dissent were illustrated by the case of Dzhamshid Karimov, former correspondent for the London-based Institute for War and Peace Reporting (IWPR) and a nephew of the president. Karimov disappeared in the eastern city of Jizzakh on September 12, 2006, and was later discovered in a psychiatric clinic in the neighboring city of Samarkand, CPJ sources said. He had been forcibly hospitalized by local authorities after a secret court hearing; government officials did not release any information about the court proceedings or permit independent experts to examine Karimov, according to international press reports. *Uznews* reported that his family was unable to find a defense lawyer willing to take on the case.

Authorities also targeted correspondents working for the German public broadcaster Deutsche Welle, one of the last foreign news agencies with stringers operating in the country. Natalya Bushuyeva and Yuri Chernogayev were among a number of Deutsche Welle contributors who were accused of tax evasion, concealing income, and working without accreditation. Bushuyeva fled the country after authorities confiscated her banking records, interrogated her at length about Deutsche Welle's news practices, and filed criminal charges against her in March. Chernogayev stopped reporting, according to CPJ sources.

Authorities also tightened their grip on the Internet. While Karimov continued to proclaim that the Internet was impossible to monitor, his government regularly blocked domestic access to regional independent news Web sites such as *Ferghana*, *Centrasia*, *Gazeta*, *Lenta*, and *Vesti*, as well as sites maintained by Western broadcasters such as the BBC and RFE/RL, according to CPJ research.

The government took an aggressively resistant stance toward international human rights organizations. Authorities consistently refused to accredit Human Rights Watch staff, and in April, U.N. High Commissioner for Human Rights Louise Arbour was denied a visa during her tour of the region. According to the IWPR, officials in Tashkent told Arbour they would be unable to meet with her because the timing of her visit was inconvenient.

Further distancing itself from the West, the Uzbek government strengthened its ties with Russia and China through oil and natural gas contracts and economic cooperation agreements. Energy cooperation with these two powers was further expanded during the Shanghai Cooperation Organization (SCO) annual meeting in Kyrgyzstan in August. Initially founded as the Shanghai Five group in 1996, the SCO is a regional association that includes China, Kazakhstan, Kyrgyzstan, Russia, Tajikistan, and Uzbekistan. In 2007, the SCO focused on energy and security cooperation, and the year ended with the parties signing an agreement "on neighborly relations." The agreement states that the SCO will create a "unified energy market," distributing its resources of natural gas and oil to member countries that need them and exporting reserves to the global energy market, the news Web site *EurasiaNet* reported.

EUROPE AND CENTRAL ASIA

BULGARIA

- On February 9, two unidentified men threatened *Politika* reporter Mariya Niko-laeva in the newsroom of the Sofia-based weekly. The men warned her not to do follow-up reporting on a piece that alleged improper local government in-volvement in real estate developments in Strandzha, a mountainous region in the southeast. "You know what happens to female journalists who know a lot: They have acid splashed on them," one of the men told Nikolaeva—an apparent reference to a 1998 acid attack in which *Trud* crime reporter Anna Zarkova lost her left eye. Despite the threat, Nikolaeva wrote a follow-up story for *Politika's* February 16 edition. The issue never reached readers in Strandzha: Unknown people bought out the entire regional allotment from the paper's local distribu-tor in the city of Burgas.

- On February 23, about 100 people led by Ataka party leader Volen Siderov stormed the offices of the newspapers *24 Chasa* and *168 Chasa* in the capital, Sofia. Siderov was angered by the publication of a financial document that al-legedly showed Ataka had received financing from another party, the Movement for Rights and Freedoms, according to news reports. Nikolai Penchev, editor-in-chief of *168 Chasa*, told the Bulgarian press that Ataka party member Kostadin Kostov had threatened him. "We will extract your liver," Penchev quoted the party member as saying. Editor-in-Chief Venelina Gocheva of *24 Chasa* told local reporters that she had assigned security to several of her reporters. Siderov denied he had stormed the building and said he had a right to contest "slanders," the news Web site *Mediapool* reported.

CROATIA

- Robert Valdec, anchor of the popular weekly program "Istraga" (Investigation) on Zagreb's independent Nova TV, received numerous phone and e-mail death threats from December 2006 to March 2007. The anonymous messages did not specify particular broadcasts, but colleagues believed they were in response to "Istraga" reenactments of crimes committed during the Croatian conflict of the 1990s. The threats against Valdec graphically described the manner in which he was to be executed. "Istraga" is known for its coverage of organized crime, wrongful imprisonments, and domestic violence. Police began investigating the threats against Valdec in January, but no arrests were made.

FRANCE

- Officers with the Directorate of Territorial Security, a counterespionage agency, searched the Paris home of Guillaume Dasquié, a reporter for the daily *Le Monde*, and detained the reporter for 48 hours. Magistrate Philippe Coirre filed preliminary charges against Dasquié on December 6, alleging that the reporter had published intelligence secrets related to the September 11, 2001, terror attacks. The probe stemmed from an April 16 article that said French intelligence agents had warned U.S. counterparts of the terrorist plot, according to international news reports. The article contained excerpts from what *Le Monde* described as a 328-page classified report. Dasquié faced five years in prison.

GERMANY

*   German prosecutors said in August that a criminal investigation had been launched against 17 journalists from a number of leading national publications, including the Hamburg-based newsmagazine *Der Spiegel*, the Munich-based daily *Süddeutsche Zeitung*, the Hamburg-based weekly *Die Zeit*, and the Berlin-based daily *Die Welt*. The journalists were accused of publishing information from classified documents related to CIA rendition flights and suspected misconduct by German secret service agents in Baghdad during the 2003 U.S.-led invasion of Iraq. A parliamentary committee assembled to examine the alleged misconduct had apparently leaked the documents to the press, according to international press reports. Investigations against the 17 journalists were led by local prosecutors in Munich, Hamburg, and Berlin. By September, the Munich prosecutor's office had dropped its investigation against journalists with the local *Süddeutsche Zeitung*, but Berlin and Hamburg prosecutors did not immediately follow suit.

HUNGARY

*   On the evening of June 22, unknown assailants abducted investigative journalist Iren Karman in the outskirts of the capital, Budapest, according to international press reports. The assailants pushed Karman into a car, tied her up, and severely beat her before leaving her on the banks of the Danube River, where she was found by a fisherman, the Hungarian News Agency (MTI) reported. Karman was hospitalized for more than a week and underwent surgery for internal bleeding, MTI said. The 40-year-old journalist had recently published a book, *Facing the Mafia*, detailing illegal oil sales in the 1990s, and was working on a related documentary at the time of the assault. The book describes the practice of "oil bleaching"—removing a characteristic red dye from government-subsidized heating oil in order to sell it as diesel at a higher price. Shortly before the attack, Karman had complained on an Internet blog that she had been receiving e-mail and telephone threats.

IRELAND

- Police in Dublin detained freelance reporter Mick McCaffrey on February 21 in connection with an August 2006 article in the Dublin-based *Evening Herald* about police mishandling of a 1997 murder case that led to the jailing of an innocent man. In his article, McCaffrey cited an internal police probe. Detectives pressed McCaffrey to reveal his sources, but he refused, according to the *Sunday Times* of London. Detectives also seized the reporter's itemized phone records, the *Times* said. McCaffrey was released the same day.

SERBIA

- In April, the neo-Nazi group National Formation made death threats against Dinko Gruhonjic, head of the Vojvodina branch of the independent news agency BETA and chairman of the Independent Journalists' Association of Vojvodina. The threats, posted on National Formation's Web site, stemmed from Gruhonjic's coverage of the group, the journalist told CPJ. Among other things, the coverage described a 2005 attack in which members armed with crowbars attacked people marking the anniversary of Kristallnacht, a pogrom launched against Jews throughout Germany and parts of Austria in 1938, according to local and international press reports. National Formation leader Goran Davidovic had threatened Gruhonjic in the past, denouncing him as a traitor and an enemy of the Serbian people.

- One of two hand grenades planted on a windowsill outside the bedroom of Dejan Anastasijevic, an investigative reporter and editor for the Belgrade newsweekly *Vreme*, exploded at around 3 a.m. on April 13, Anastasijevic told CPJ. The explosion caused extensive damage to the journalist's apartment and several cars parked outside but did not harm Anastasijevic or his wife, who were asleep in the bedroom at the time. In addition to his work as an investigative reporter for *Vreme*, Anastasijevic had written extensively about torture, abuse, persecution, and harassment of Croats, Muslims, and other non-Serbs during the Bosnia and Croatia wars of the 1990s. Eight former Serbian paramilitaries were briefly detained, but no charges were filed.

- Stefan Cvetkovic, editor-in-chief of the independent broadcaster TNT in Bela Crkva, received anonymous death threats by phone in August. Cvetkovic said he believed the threats could be in response to his station's coverage of a police scandal. Six months before, TNT broadcast a hidden-camera video showing two Bela Crkva police officers snorting a white powder off a café tabletop. The two officers were later fired, according to the Belgrade-based Association for Independent Electronic Media (ANEM). TNT had also reported on a variety of other sensitive topics, ANEM said, including local corruption and economic and social issues.

- On October 16, an unidentified assailant stormed into the home of Vesna Bojicic, a Serbian-language correspondent for Voice of America, beating and threatening her in connection with her reporting. The attacker cited Bojicic's purported "bias in favor of Albanians" and said he would kill her and abduct her child if she did not stop reporting, the Belgrade-based Association of Independent Electronic Media said. Bojicic told VOA she would continue reporting in Kosovo "regardless of what Serbs or Albanians think." According to local press reports, Bojicic had been attacked previously. Her house was set on fire during ethnic unrest between the Albanian majority and Serbian minority in March 2004.

SPAIN

- National Court Judge Jose Maria Vazquez Honrubia found artist Guillermo Torres and writer Manel Fontdevila guilty of defaming Crown Prince Felipe in a cartoon published in the satirical weekly *El Jueves*. The judge fined the journalists 3,000 euros (US$4,400) apiece in the November 13 ruling, according to international press reports. The cartoon, which ran on the front page of *El Jueves'* July 18 issue, showed the prince and his wife, Princess Letizia, in a graphic sexual position—an apparent reference to government efforts to boost the birth rate by offering families financial incentives. In July, a judge ordered *El Jueves'* entire 70,000-copy press run taken off newsstands because the cartoon insulted the royal family.

SWITZERLAND

- On April 17, a Swiss military tribunal in St. Gallen acquitted Christoph Grenacher, editor-in-chief of the Zurich-based weekly *SonntagsBlick*, and two of his reporters, Sandro Brotz and Beat Jost, on charges of publishing classified intelligence about purported CIA prisons in Eastern Europe, according to international press reports. Swiss prosecutors had charged the journalists in 2006, after *SonntagsBlick* published the contents of a fax from Egyptian Foreign Minister Ahmed Aboul Gheit to the Egyptian Embassy in London. The fax pointed to the existence of a CIA prison in Romania and suggested there were other such prisons in Bulgaria, Kosovo, Macedonia, and Ukraine, according to The Associated Press.

THE MIDDLE EAST AND NORTH AFRICA

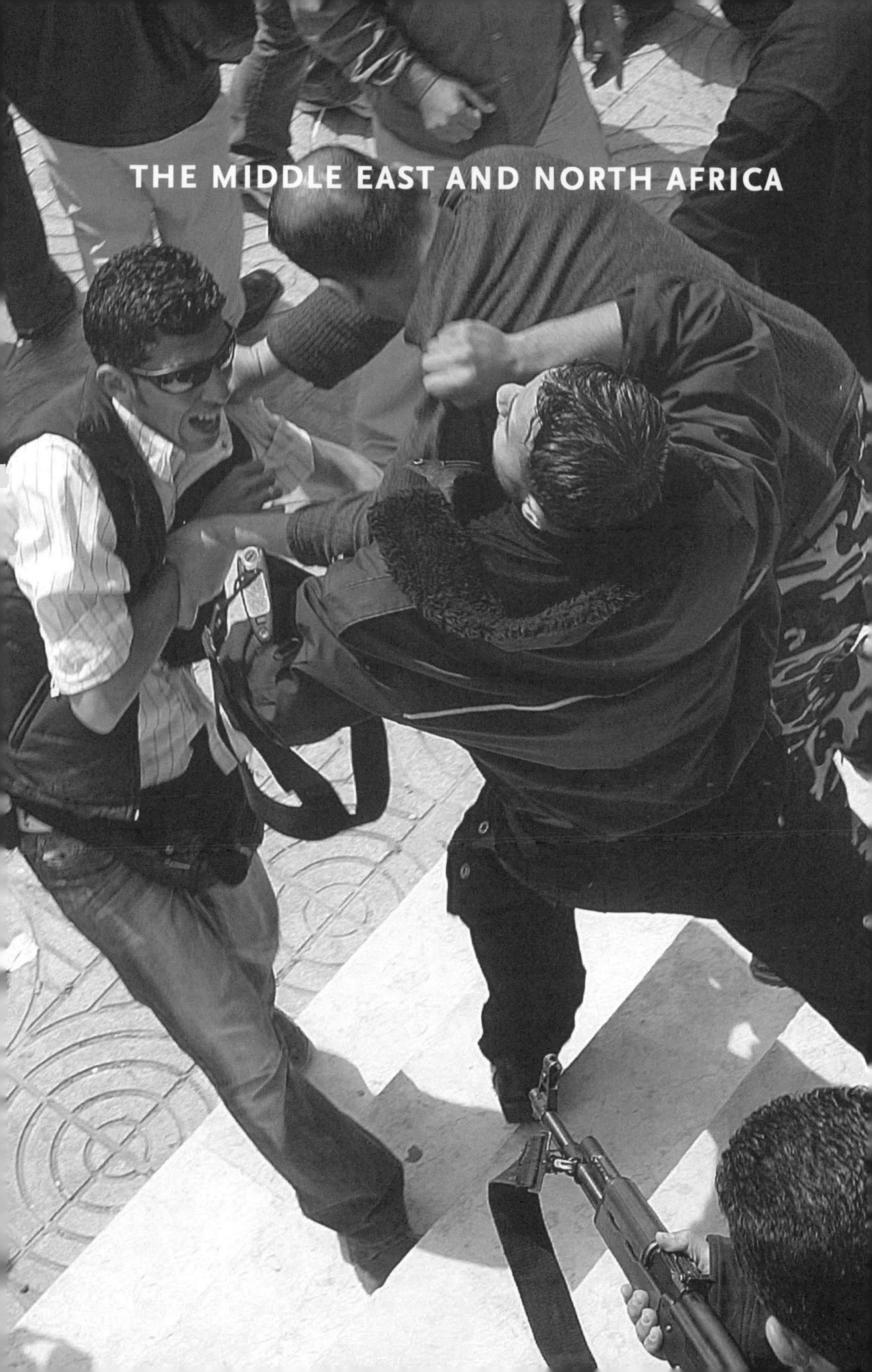

PHOTOS

Section break: Reuters/Mohammed Salem — *Palestinian police rough up
a photographer during an April rally calling for the release of abducted BBC
correspondent Alan Johnston.* Analysis (next): Reuters/Khaled Abdullah — *Yemeni
editor Abdel Karim al-Khaiwani faces charges in a State Security Court in Sana'a.*

THE MIDDLE EAST AND NORTH AFRICA

UNDER THE RADAR, A NEW KIND OF REPRESSION

by Joel Campagna

• •

ON A WEDNESDAY AFTERNOON LAST JUNE, YEMENI SECURITY AGENTS stormed the home of outspoken editor Abdel Karim al-Khaiwani and dragged him before a State Security Court in the capital, Sana'a. A prosecutor questioned al-Khaiwani and later rang him up on charges of belonging to a secret terrorist cell—charges that carry a possible death sentence. The arrest shocked Yemeni journalists, and some wondered aloud whether their colleague, known for his incendiary columns attacking the Yemeni government and its battle with rebels in the northwestern city of Saada, might have been involved in something nefarious. CPJ issued guarded statements of concern, unsure whether the charge had substance.

But as al-Khaiwani's court case unfolded over several weeks, it became clear that the editor was no terrorist. Instead, the meager "evidence" that prosecutors revealed turned out to be photographs, news articles, and interviews found in al-Khaiwani's home during a search. Al-Khaiwani, it seemed, was being railroaded for his unsparing criticism of President Ali Abdullah Saleh, whom he blamed for the war in Saada and whose government he had accused of widespread corruption. It was the same kind of criticism that had landed the editor in prison three years earlier, an episode that garnered Yemen international condemnation and helped scuttle millions in U.S. aid. In the earlier case, al-Khaiwani was jailed explicitly for his work; by 2007, Yemeni officials had apparently learned to take an indirect tack.

Governments have learned that blunt repression costs them international standing and investment.

By obliterating the line between reporting on government foes and being a foe, Yemeni authorities sought "to weaken solidarity" among journalists, al-Khaiwani told CPJ.

Al-Khaiwani's ordeal is typical of the oblique tactics Arab governments increasingly use to stifle independent media while minimizing international censure. In today's interconnected world, where information on rights abuses can travel the globe in minutes, governments can no longer afford to run roughshod over human rights as they did as recently as the 1990s. Aware that blunt repression could cost them international standing, foreign aid, and outside investment, they have fashioned themselves as democratic reformers while resorting to stealthy forms of media control. Manipulating the media, they have found, is more politically palatable to the international community than outright domination.

"In recent years, a new model of authoritarian governance has emerged in a number of key Arab states," American political scientist Steven Heydemann wrote in an October 2007 Brookings Institution report. "A product of trial and error more than intentional design, Arab regimes have adapted to pressures for political change by developing strategies to contain and manage demands to democratize."

In terms of the media, governments have built new strategies to contain the assertive journalists who have emerged over the last decade in countries such as Algeria, Jordan, Morocco, Saudi Arabia, and Yemen. Job dismissals, behind-the-scenes threats, third-party defamation suits, and trumped-up terrorism charges like those brought against al-Khaiwani have replaced the torture, enforced disappearances, and open-ended incarcerations that were the hallmarks of the previous era. Image conscious governments have also become masters of spin, championing cosmetic media reforms designed mainly for public consumption.

To be sure, outright repression of the media hasn't vanished. Security forces still brutalize street reporters in places like Egypt and Tunisia, but such brazen suppression has become more selective, and governments more calculating.

Morocco, which has burnished an image as a country in democratic transition, typifies this trend. There, authorities have relied on third-party lawsuits, launched by individuals ostensibly independent of the government, to punish the country's most independent journalists through extraordinary monetary damages that threaten to put their publications out of business. In February, Aboubakr Jamaï, publisher of the leading independent newsmagazine *Le Journal Hebdomadaire*, was forced to leave the country as judicial authorities prepared to seize his assets following a record-breaking defamation judgment. A Moroccan court upheld damages in the amount of 3 million dirhams (US$395,000) against Jamaï— the second record judgment against the publisher—in a suit brought by the head of a Brussels-based think tank who claimed *Le Journal* had defamed him in an article questioning the independence of the organization's report on the disputed Western Sahara. A palace source told the magazine that the judgment was in fact reprisal for an unflattering 2005 cover photo of King Mohammed VI. In recent years, other similarly extraordinary libel judgments have been handed down against independent publications such as the popular weekly *TelQuel*. The verdicts, along with other forms of harassment, have had the desired effect of banishing critical journalists and promoting self-censorship.

Job dismissals and politically motivated lawsuits have replaced torture and abductions.

"Surely we became far more cautious, understanding that anything, even the less harmful writings or pictures, could lead us to court trials—and God only would know the outcome," remarked Ahmed Reda Benchemsi, publisher of *TelQuel*.

In Algeria, Mohamed Benchicou, outspoken editor of the now-defunct daily *Le Matin*, was sent to prison for two years in 2004 on alleged currency violations. Few journalists doubted that the real reason for Benchicou's jailing was his criticism of President Abdelaziz Bouteflika, whom he had labeled an "Algerian fraud" in a book published earlier that year. In neighboring Tunisia, the government jailed human rights lawyer Mohammed Abbou in 2005 for defaming the judiciary and assaulting a fellow lawyer during an argument—bogus charges that were tacked on to Abbou's conviction for writing an online article comparing Tunisia's prisons to Iraq's infamous Abu Ghraib.

For all of the region's press freedom casualties, authoritarian governments are less intent on silencing critical media than they are bent on controlling them through the use of carrots and sticks. "You have to understand the equation that the regime is playing with the press in Morocco," Jamaï said. "On the one hand, they hate us; on the other hand, they need us. If you went to Morocco and you visited the Royal Cabinet and you told the guys there, 'You are an autocratic regime,' do you know what they would say? They would say, 'Look at *Le Journal*, look at this crazy Aboubakr Jamaï and what he is writing. How can you say we are not a free country?' So we serve them, in a sense."

Arab governments have also manipulated the media reform process. Regimes from Egypt to Yemen have touted cosmetic amendments to media laws that have long been used to control journalists. With great fanfare, Tunisia's parliament passed a series of meaningless amendments to its press code in 2001, excising an ambiguously worded article prohibiting "defaming public order," eliminating prison penalties for violating advertising regulations, and decreasing the period of time the government can suspend newspapers. It has had no practical effect: At least four journalists have been jailed for their work in Tunisia since 2001, and independent media remain under siege.

In Jordan, the government championed successive revisions of the country's press law as a major step toward democracy because they eliminated prison penalties for journalists. Yet most journalists and dissidents jailed over the last decade have been put away not under the press law, but under the country's restrictive penal code, which, along with other repressive legislation, remains intact. Recent amendments to the law prescribe severe fines that can easily be used to stifle independent reporting. And in Morocco, where four journalists have been jailed

Regimes from Algeria to Yemen tout cosmetic media reforms that have no practical effect.

in the last five years, officials touted as a major step forward a 2007 press bill that would reduce the number of prohibitions against what could be written. But the bill, pending in late year, left intact a range of other restrictive provisions that could land journalists in jail or bankrupt them with heavy fines.

More critically, governments have fostered the illusion of change in the important electronic media sector, which remains a bastion of state control. Syria and Tunisia have hyped moves to privatize radio and television, yet licenses are doled out selectively to regime cronies. Syria launched private radio stations in 2004, but the outlets were barred from airing news or political content. In September, while a long line of other applicants waited and fumed, the Tunisian government allowed President Zine al-Abidine Ben Ali's son-in-law to launch a new radio station. Tunisia's first private television station, licensed in 2004, is owned by a pro-regime businessman, and its programming differs little from that of Tunisian state television.

Pan-Arab satellite stations such as Al-Jazeera have dented state monopolies on electronic media, of course, but they are no substitute for domestic broadcast outlets that can cover local news and deliver it to mass numbers of people.

Arab governments have had success in keeping independent journalists at heel by stunting media development, or, in countries like Egypt, Morocco, and Yemen,

THE MIDDLE EAST AND NORTH AFRICA

by chipping away at press freedom gains through periodic crackdowns. Despite the democracy-promotion statements of the United States and, to a lesser extent, the European Union, Western donors have provided little inducement for governments to make meaningful reforms. In Yemen, for example, the Millennium Challenge Corporation, a U.S. government aid agency, suspended the country's participation in its programs in November 2005, citing the absence of democratic reform and press freedom. Yet the nation's status was reinstated in 2007, allowing the flow of millions in development aid. And as Morocco pursued its media crackdown in 2007, Millennium Challenge approved a five-year, US$697.5 million economic aid package—the agency's largest grant since it was formed in January 2004. Elsewhere in the region, aid money continued to flow, some of it to support media under the thumb of the state or paralyzed by

> *Syria and Tunisia hype efforts to diversify the airwaves, then dole out licenses to regime cronies.*

government control. In Persian Gulf countries, where Western financial assistance is minimal or nonexistent, allies such as Saudi Arabia and Oman have retained strong bilateral relations even as they clamped down on media freedom.

Donors, human rights groups, and those involved in promoting democracy need to rethink their strategies to account for the new tactics employed by authoritarian governments. "[Arab regimes] have adapted by reorganizing strategies of governance to adjust to new global, regional, and domestic circumstances," Heydemann wrote in the Brookings report. "Autocrats have not simply fallen back on coercion to fend off pressures for change—though repression remains a visible and potent element in the arsenal of Arab governments. Regimes have turned instead to a process that can best be described as 'authoritarian upgrading.' These emerging strategies of governance have undermined gains achieved by democracy promotion programs, and will continue to blunt their impact in the future."

For their part, press freedom groups must raise the political and economic costs for governments that trample on press freedom. They can start by exposing empty media reforms, unmasking stealth attacks on the press, and lobbying policymakers to develop meaningful criteria for change. The islands of media freedom in the region will vanish if journalists do not meet this new challenge.

• • • • • • • • •

Joel Campagna is CPJ's senior program coordinator responsible for the Middle East and North Africa. He led a CPJ mission to Morocco and Egypt in 2007.

• • • • • • • • • • • • • • • • • • •   EGYPT   •

The government clamped down on political opposition, tried to suppress speculation about the health of President Hosni Mubarak, and waged a steady offensive against critical journalists, bloggers, and foreign media workers. By year's end, a full-fledged crackdown was under way, with Egyptian courts aggressively prosecuting several of the country's leading independent editors and writers. Authorities appeared bent on setting tighter boundaries for the independent press and for bloggers, whose numbers and influence have grown. In 2007, CPJ designated Egypt one of the world's worst backsliders on press freedom, citing a dramatic increase in attacks on the press.

In January, Al-Jazeera producer Howayda Taha Matwali was detained in connection with her work on a documentary about torture in Egyptian police stations. On May 1, a court in Cairo sentenced Matwali in absentia to six months in prison and a fine of 20,000 Egyptian pounds (US$3,600). She was found guilty of "harming Egypt's national interest" and "falsely depicting events." Matwali was free on appeal at year's end.

In February, Egyptian authorities convicted and imprisoned a blogger for the first time. A criminal court in Alexandria sentenced 22-year-old Abdel Karim Suleiman, widely known by his online name, Karim Amer, to four years in prison on charges that included "spreading information disruptive of public order and damaging to the country's reputation," "incitement to hate Islam," and "defaming the president of the republic." Over the previous two years, several bloggers had been harassed and detained briefly by state security forces for exposing government torture, nepotism, and corruption.

Suleiman, a former student at Cairo's Al-Azhar University, the preeminent institution of higher education in Sunni Islam, had accused the school of promoting extremist ideas and had called Mubarak a dictator. Suleiman's jailing was prelude to a similar prosecution. In mid-April, Abdel Moneim Mahmoud, another young blogger, was arrested and detained for several weeks. His apparent crime was using his blog, *Ana-Ikhwan* (I Am a Brother), to expose the torture of civilians by Egyptian security forces and to denounce the country's practice of trying civilians in military courts. Authorities charged him with defaming the government and belonging to the Muslim Brotherhood, the country's largest opposition group, which had been banned in 1954 but long tolerated as a behind-the-scenes political force. Throughout the year, the government continued to round up members of the Muslim Brotherhood in an intensifying clampdown.

• • • • • • • • •

Country summaries in this chapter were written by Senior Program Coordinator **Joel Campagna**, Research Associate **Ivan Karakashian**, and Regional Representative **Kamel Eddine Labidi**.

THE MIDDLE EAST AND NORTH AFRICA

In late summer, authorities turned their attention to the country's boisterous independent press, which has been a source of growing concern among top government officials. Its vitality and rising popularity have come at the expense of state-run papers, which "are held back by their own sluggishness ... and financial corruption," according to *Al-Ahram* columnist Salama Ahmed Salama.

Independent journalists speculated about Mubarak's health in August after the 79-year-old president was not seen in public for several days and his administration offered no explanation. The state security prosecutor charged Ibrahim Eissa, editor of the independent weekly *Al-Dustour*, with publishing reports on Mubarak's health that were "likely to disturb public security and damage the public interest." Official media and local rights groups reported that Eissa was to appear before an emergency state security court on October 1. CPJ expressed its deep concern, noting that such courts were notorious for not issuing acquittals or allowing appeals. Authorities later moved Eissa's case to a Cairo misdemeanor court, where it was pending in late year.

Many journalists saw the prosecution of Eissa as a settling of scores with one of the most vocal critics of Mubarak's 26-year rule: *Al-Dustour*. The paper was banned in 1997 but resurfaced in 2004 amid government promises to open up the political system. (That same year, Mubarak promised to reform laws that set prison penalties for journalists, a pledge that has gone unfulfilled.)

While prosecutors moved against Eissa, the state-backed press launched an intensive campaign against independent journalists who raised questions about Mubarak's health.

Mursi Atallah, board chairman of the state-owned *Al-Ahram*, told his newspaper that Egypt's "enemies" were resorting to rumor and exploiting "the chaos that prevails in the journalistic field." He added that it was this "chaos which allows, under the deceitful cover of press freedom, traditions, ethics, and norms to be trampled and red lines to be crossed."

First Lady Suzanne Mubarak also issued an unusual rebuke in an interview with the satellite television station Al-Arabiya, stating that her husband's health was "excellent" and that "there must be punishment either for a journalist, a television program, or a newspaper that publishes the rumors." The government-controlled Supreme Press Council, which issues licenses and guidelines to newspapers, announced it had formed two commissions to assess press coverage of Mubarak's health and to "decide what legal measures should be taken."

Eissa was among four independent and opposition editors convicted in a separate, "false information" case. Wael al-Abrashy of the weekly *Sawt al-Umma*, Adel Hammouda of the weekly *Al-Fajr*, and Abdel Halim Kandil, former editor of the opposition weekly *Al-Karama*, were also convicted. The four men had published articles denouncing Mubarak's comments about the Lebanese Shiite group Hezbollah and criticizing high-level officials that included the president's son, Gamal.

The controversial case was initiated by lawyers affiliated with the ruling National Democratic Party (NDP), which is headed by the elder Mubarak and guided by the son, seen by many as the country's next president. The verdict prompted widespread condemnation among journalists and human rights defenders in Egypt and other Arab countries. "It looks like the government no longer tolerates the customary margin of freedom available for the press and NGOs and is planning to confiscate this margin," a coalition of 33 civil-society groups said in a joint statement.

Speaking at a September 20 rally in Cairo, during which journalists and political rights activists decried the prosecutions, Eissa sarcastically thanked Mubarak for bestowing on him what he called "the honor of being among his top opponents" and for planning to jail him. "The long night of Egypt must end and the shackles broken," Eissa said. "Many went to prison to help Egypt on the road to freedom."

At the same rally, Galal Aref, then head of the Egyptian Journalists' Syndicate (EJS), warned against what he called "the attacks which were not only targeting a few journalists, but democracy and the whole political and cultural life." And Hossam Eissa, a prominent legal expert, called the court ruling against the four editors "nonsense." He said the editors were brought to trial simply because they stood against corruption and the perceived plan to pave the way for Gamal Mubarak to rule Egypt.

But the circle of journalists prosecuted for doing their jobs kept widening. On September 24, three editors with the opposition daily *Al-Wafd* were convicted of criminal libel and sentenced to two years in prison, the paper reported. Editor-in-Chief Anwar al-Hawari, Deputy Editor-in-Chief Mahmoud Ghalab, and Politics Editor Amir Salem were charged under Article 102 of the penal code, which allows for the detention of anyone publishing news "liable to disturb public security, spread horror among the people, or cause harm or damage the public interest." The three men were freed pending appeal.

NDP lawyers were behind that criminal complaint as well, accusing the journalists of "publishing false news and erroneously attributing it to the minister of justice, harming the Egyptian judiciary and judges," the independent daily *Al-Masry al-Youm* reported. In a January article, *Al-Wafd* had described Justice Minister Mamdouh Marei's appearance before a parliamentary committee, during which he questioned the competence of lower court judges.

In October, 22 independent and opposition newspapers went on a one-day strike to protest the rising attacks on independent journalism. Sheikh Mohammed Sayed Tantawi, the grand imam of the Al-Azhar mosque in Cairo, used the occasion to criticize the independent press. "The Islamic Sharia [law subjects] all the people to be equally punished for the crime of libel, which is a flagrant aggression on the virtuous men and women," The Associated Press quoted him as saying.

THE MIDDLE EAST AND NORTH AFRICA

The EJS said on October 11 it was shocked by Tantawi's remarks. The syndicate said he appeared to be "taking part in the escalating campaign of incitement against the press, the journalists, and opinion holders."

• IRAN •

Iran's troubled economy weakened President Mahmoud Ahmadinejad's power at home, with protests spilling into the streets and intellectuals, activists, and students expressing dissent in the media. Silencing the uproar became essential for Ahmadinejad, prompting authorities to intensify a media crackdown that had been waged by conservative forces for a decade. Iran became the world's fourth-leading jailer of journalists in 2007, with one writer on death row and 11 other journalists imprisoned when CPJ conducted its annual census on December 1.

Journalists had to tread carefully in their reporting to avoid arrest or the closure of their publications. Most adhered to official orders banning coverage of the riots that followed the government's abrupt decision in June to restrict fuel supplies for six months. Explicit restrictions on coverage of the ailing economy, antigovernment demonstrations, and nuclear development—coupled with prevailing self-censorship— left little room for independent news reporting. Minister of Culture and Islamic Guidance Mohammad Hossein Saffar-Harandi went so far as to accuse the press of a "creeping coup" to overthrow the regime, the Iranian Student News Agency reported.

The government imprisoned more than 20 journalists during the year, some without charge, for periods ranging from days to months. Adnan Hassanpour, former editor for the now-defunct Kurdish-Persian weekly *Aso*, faced a death sentence handed down in mid-July. A Revolutionary Court convicted him of endangering national security and engaging in propaganda against the state, one of his attorneys, Sirvan Hosmandi, told CPJ. Hosmandi said the charges against Hassanpour were not proved in court and were supported with merely a report from security officials. An appeals court upheld the conviction, finding that Hassanpour had engaged in espionage. Hassanpour's sister, Leyla, told CPJ that she believed his critical writings were the reason for the charges.

The longest detained was Mohammad Hassan Falla-hiyazadeh, a reporter for the state-run Arabic-language sat-ellite channel Al-Alam and several other Arab media outlets. Authorities arrested Fallahiyazadeh on November 1, 2006, in connection with his reports on the government's harsh treatment of Iranian Arab protestors in the Khuzestan provincial capital, Ahwaz, according to the organization Human Rights Activists in Iran (HRAI). A Revolutionary Court gave

Fallahiyazadeh a three-year prison sentence in April for distributing propaganda against the Islamic regime and communicating with opposition groups abroad, according to HRAI and Amnesty International. Fallahiyazadeh, who belongs to Iran's Arab minority, was denied access to a lawyer, HRAI said.

Parnaz Azima, a journalist with the U.S.-backed Radio Farda, was among four people of dual Iranian-American citizenship who were detained during the year. Authorities confiscated her passport upon her arrival at Tehran's airport on a trip to see her ailing mother in late January. By May, the Special Security Bureau of the Revolutionary Court's Public Prosecutor's Office had charged her with disseminating propaganda against the Islamic Republic, Azima's lawyer, Mohammad-Hossein Aghasi, told CPJ. Radio Farda, broadcasting from Prague, Czech Republic, is jointly run by the U.S. government-funded Radio Free Europe/Radio Liberty (RFE/RL) and Voice of America. Officials ordered Azima to post US$550,000 in bail, which the journalist paid by putting up her mother's Tehran home as collateral. Authorities unexpectedly returned Azima's passport in early September, allowing her to leave Iran later that month, according to RFE/RL.

The government retaliated against those journalists who seemingly threatened Iran's insularity with their reporting for foreign news services or their travel abroad for work-related events. Supreme Leader Ayatollah Ali Khamenei claimed that the United States was using such journalists to overthrow the regime.

In late January, security officials at Tehran's airport arrested freelance journalists and women's rights activists Mansoureh Shojai, Talat Taghinia, and Farnaz Seifi as they waited to board a flight to India for a journalism training workshop, according to news reports. Human rights lawyer and Nobel Peace Prize Laureate Shirin Ebadi said authorities charged them with acting against national security and released them on bail, Reuters reported.

All three women supported a campaign that seeks to amass a million signatures urging the reform of Iranian laws that discriminate against women. Authorities responded to such efforts with intolerance, beating and arresting women's rights activists during peaceful demonstrations. In November, an Islamic Revolutionary Court charged online journalist and women's rights activist Maryam Hosseinkhah with disturbing public opinion, engaging in propaganda against the regime, and spreading false news, according to the Web site *Change for Equality*. Defense lawyer Ebadi told *Change for Equality* that her client was jailed because of her articles on women's rights for online sites and newspapers.

The government also targeted ethnic Kurdish journalists for arrest. Along with Hassanpour, at least three others were imprisoned for their work, according to CPJ research. In July, for example, plainclothes security officials arrested journalist and Kurdish human rights activist Mohammad Seddigh Kaboudvand at his Tehran office, according to Amnesty International and CPJ sources. Authorities accused

Kaboudvand, head of the Human Rights Organization of Kurdistan and managing editor of the weekly *Payam-e Mardom*, with acting against national security and engaging in propaganda against the state, according to his organization's Web site. Kaboudvand had published articles about torture in Iranian jails and human rights abuses against Iran's Kurdish minority.

As dissenting Web sites and blogs continued to rise in popularity, the government was quick to shut them down. The popular conservative news Web site *Baztab* was blocked twice inside Iran for criticizing Ahmadinejad's policies, particularly his handling of the economy, Reuters reported. On September 23, a court ordered *Baztab*'s offices closed after staff continued to update the site for users abroad, according to news reports. The Iranian Labor News Agency was blocked inside Iran in July for reporting on demonstrations by workers and activists and their arrest, Reuters said. Savvy Internet users such as the group calling itself Iran Proxy have responded to the government's filtering system by providing online methods to circumvent site restrictions, RFE/RL reported.

The regime also cracked down on pro-reform student journalists. In May, authorities jailed three student journalists at Amirkabir University of Technology in Tehran following the distribution of newsletters carrying articles deemed insulting to Islam, according to news reports. The three students—Majid Tavakoli, Ehsan Mansouri, and Ahmad Ghassaban—said they had had no involvement in the publications and that a hard-line conservative student group had fraudulently used the names and logos of legitimate student publications as a dirty trick, news reports said. The students, who received sentences of two to three years following a closed court session in November, were subjected to torture during their six-month detention, according to news reports that quoted their families. The school's administration banned all student publications in the aftermath of the incident.

Critical journalists found themselves prone to violent attacks. In early November, two journalists were stabbed by unknown assailants in separate incidents. Two perpetrators stabbed Reza Avazpour, editor-in-chief of the sports weekly *Varzeshi*, as he was leaving the paper's offices in the southeastern city of Kerman, according to news reports. Avazpour was seriously wounded and needed several hours of surgery. The attack came after he had received a number of threats made by a group identifying itself as Allah's Soldiers, according to the news agency Adnkronos International. *Varzeshi* had published investigative articles that were critical of the directors of Iran's football federation, the agency said. The attackers accused Avazpour of being a "servant of the Americans," the agency reported, and scolded him for being critical of Ahmadinejad. Assailants also stabbed Abaselat Abed, managing editor of the daily *Mardomsalari* (Democracy) in Karaj, a city west of Tehran, in front of the paper's offices, *Mardomsalari* reported.

The government continued to suspend publications because of their critical reporting or pro-reform slant. CPJ research showed that authorities closed at least 11 publications, some of them indefinitely. The Press Supervisory Board, under the Ministry of Culture and Islamic Guidance, suspended the pro-reform daily *Ham-Mihan* and revoked the license of the daily *Mosharekat* in early July. Iran's leading critical daily, *Shargh*, was shut down in August for publishing an interview with Saqi Qahreman, an exiled Iranian poet accused by the regime of supporting homosexuality, according to news reports. *Shargh* had just resumed publication in May, when a previous suspension lapsed.

• • • • • • • • • • • • • • • • • • • IRAQ • • • • • • • • • • • • • • • • • • •

The war in Iraq, the deadliest conflict for journalists in recent history, kept the country at the top of the world's most dangerous places for the press. Thirty-two journalists and 12 media support staffers were killed during the year, bringing the record toll to 174 media personnel killed in the line of duty since the U.S. invasion of March 2003. Improving security conditions in parts of the country in 2007 may have had an effect on media deaths, as most occurred in the first seven months of the year.

The vast majority of victims continued to be Iraqis, most of whom were singled out by armed groups and murdered with impunity. Since the war began, nearly nine in 10 media deaths have been Iraqi journalists working for the numerous local media outlets that sprouted after the toppling of Saddam Hussein, or serving as frontline reporters for international media organizations.

Armed groups such as Sunni insurgents, Sunni and Shiite militias, and other, unidentified armed assailants were responsible for most of the killings. The motives were typically murky. The disorder that prevailed in much of the country made it difficult to determine whether the victims were singled out for their work, their sect, or their political allegiances—or were simply caught up in the general violence. In some cases, journalists may have been targeted because of their past work as translators for the U.S. military, complicating the task of determining a motive.

Still, there was ample evidence of armed groups and militias ruthlessly targeting journalists because of their reporting or editorial views. Working for a Western news organization, where Iraqis might be suspected of being spies, or for a news outlet deemed hostile to a certain group, could mean a death sentence. Threats have forced many Iraqi journalists to live clandestinely, leave the profession altogether, or flee the country.

In a case emblematic of the danger, Sahar Hussein Ali al-Haydari, a correspondent for the National Iraqi News Agency (NINA) and the independent news agency Aswat al-Iraq and a contributor to a number of other Iraqi media outlets, was slain by gunmen in her hometown of Mosul in June. Al-Haydari was shopping in Mosul's

THE MIDDLE EAST AND NORTH AFRICA

Al-Hadbaa neighborhood when four unidentified men got out of a vehicle, shot her, and fled the scene, taking her cell phone with them. Al-Haydari had been covering a suicide attack on a police station in the nearby town of Al-Rabiya, according to NINA. When a police captain called later that day to give her more information on the story, the killers answered her phone and said: "She went to hell." Al-Haydari had received multiple death threats. In an e-mail to CPJ on March 22, al-Haydari said her name was fourth on a death list composed of journalists and police officers. The list had been circulated throughout Mosul and posted on the door to her home. According to Aswat al-Iraq, it was issued by the "Emir of the Islamic State in Mosul," the local leader of the al-Qaeda-affiliated Islamic State in Iraq.

Abductions continued to plague the press, as they did for much of the population at large. Radio Free Iraq correspondent Jumana al-Obaidi, for example, was held by kidnappers for nearly two weeks after gunmen seized her from a car taking her to an assignment at the Ministry of Environment on October 22. Her driver was slain.

Due to the perilous situation in Baghdad, the number of foreign correspondents continued to dwindle, and those who remained were often heavily circumscribed in their movements for fear of abduction or attack. For many, the only way to visit parts of the country was to embed with the military or travel with considerable calculation and the aid of security details. The danger eroded the ability of journalists—especially the more conspicuous television crews—to report from the field, and it forced news organizations to rely increasingly on Iraqis for news and information from areas deemed too dangerous for Westerners.

The heightened role of Iraqi journalists as frontline correspondents took a toll. Khalid W. Hassan, 23, a reporter and interpreter for *The New York Times*, was slain in July while driving to work in the south-central Seiydia district of Baghdad. That same month, Reuters photographer Namir Noor-Eldeen, 22, and his assistant, Saeed Chmagh, were killed in eastern Baghdad during what witnesses described as a U.S. helicopter attack. And in May, ABC News cameraman Alaa Uldeen Aziz and soundman Saif Laith Yousuf were shot and killed in an ambush on their way home from the network's Baghdad bureau.

Some international news organizations have found it difficult to find local journalists willing to work for them. Former *New York Times* Baghdad Bureau Chief John F. Burns told the *New York Observer* that "the pool of available people is shrinking," and noted that "working for an American institution in Iraq—whether the embassy, armed forces, or media organizations—carries with it a considerable hazard." Burns said that numerous Iraqi staff members had fled to Jordan and Syria.

Deaths of foreign reporters have become less frequent as these journalists keep lower profiles and step up security precautions. One foreign journalist was killed in 2007. On May 6, Dmitry Chebotayev, a Russian freelance photographer embedded with U.S. forces, was killed along with six American soldiers when a roadside bomb struck a U.S. military vehicle in Diyala province, northeast of Baghdad.

The U.S. military poses another threat to journalist safety. At least 16 journalists have been killed by U.S. forces' fire since March 2003. The July attack that killed the Reuters photographer and his assistant—as well as nine other Iraqis in the Al-Amin al-Thaniyah neighborhood—came during an American air strike. The military said in a statement that troops had come under fire and "were clearly engaged" with hostile forces when the Reuters employees were killed. In July, Reuters demanded an investigation after it said new evidence had emerged that contradicted the U.S. description of events. According to eyewitnesses, Reuters said, the U.S. forces fired indiscriminately.

The U.S. military has failed to fully investigate or properly account for the killings of journalists in Iraq, CPJ found. After a CPJ Freedom of Information Act request, the Pentagon disclosed its 2004 investigation exonerating U.S. troops in the killings of two Al-Arabiya journalists at a Baghdad checkpoint that year. The report failed to address contradictory witness reports, including statements from Al-Arabiya employees, that at least two U.S. soldiers fired directly on the journalists' vehicle. Neither did it address testimony from Al-Arabiya employees that a U.S. tank may have briefly collided with the press vehicle moments before soldiers opened fire. The report also failed to reconcile the military's conclusions with statements by Al-Arabiya employees that the checkpoint was poorly illuminated.

Elsewhere, U.S. forces harassed or obstructed the work of journalists in a number of instances. In February, the U.S. military raided the headquarters of the Iraqi Journalists Syndicate and ransacked the premises while briefly detaining staff, according to local journalists. The military continued its practice of open-ended detentions of journalists. In April, Pulitzer Prize-winning Associated Press photographer Bilal Hussein marked his one-year anniversary in U.S. military custody without charge.

Hussein was taken by U.S. forces on April 12, 2006, in the western city of Ramadi and placed in a U.S. prison in Iraq for "imperative reasons of security." But he was not tried or charged with a crime, and the military disclosed no evidence of criminal wrongdoing. U.S. officials have since made numerous, shifting allegations against the journalist. U.S. military officials accused Hussein of having prior knowledge of insurgent attacks, but they did not substantiate the accusation. According to the AP, officials at one point alleged that Hussein was involved in the insurgent kidnapping of two Arab journalists in Ramadi—a claim the AP said it had investigated and discredited. The two journalists had not implicated Hussein in their abduction; they had instead praised him for his assistance when they were released. The military's only evidence supporting its claim, according to the AP, appeared to be images of the journalists, taken after their release, that were found in Hussein's camera. The AP said it believed Hussein was being held because of his photographic work documenting combat in Anbar province. Finally, in November 2007, the U.S. military said it would refer Hussein's case to the Iraqi justice system because "new evidence [had] come to light." That evidence remained a secret in late year.

Hussein's detention was not an isolated incident. Dozens of journalists, mostly Iraqis, have been detained by U.S. troops, according to CPJ research. While most have been released after short periods, in at least eight cases documented by CPJ, Iraqi journalists were held for weeks or months without charge or conviction. In all of those detentions, the journalists were released without charges being substantiated.

The Iraqi government continued to commit a wide range of press freedom abuses that included censorship, arbitrary detentions, threats, physical attacks, and harassment. On January 1, the Iraqi Ministry of Interior, which operates a special unit charged with monitoring coverage for "inaccurate" news, ordered the closure of Al-Sharqiya TV's Baghdad office for fomenting sectarian violence and reporting false news. The ban followed Al-Sharqiya's coverage of Saddam Hussein's execution on December 30, 2006, during which the presenter wore black clothing in mourning for the former Iraqi president. The channel referred to Saddam as "president," while state-owned television broadcasts called him a "tyrant" and a "criminal." The satellite channel had already decided to close its Baghdad bureau because of security concerns but continued broadcasting from its Dubai headquarters.

Officials again obstructed the press on May 13, when Brig. Gen. Abdul-Karim Khalaf, a spokesman for the Ministry of Interior, announced that journalists would be barred from the scenes of bomb attacks for one hour. Khalaf said the ban would protect journalists from a second bomb attack at the same site. "We do not want evidence to be disturbed before the arrival of detectives," he said, adding that he did "not want to give terrorists information that they achieved their goals." Journalists told CPJ they viewed the ban as an attempt to limit coverage of the violence. Iraqi police enforced the order two days later, when they prevented journalists from covering the aftermath of a twin bomb attack at Baghdad's Tayaran Square. Camera operators and photographers who sought to report at the scene were met by Iraqi police, who fired shots in the air to disperse the press. The restrictions remained in place and continued to be enforced in late year.

Throughout the year there were numerous reports that security forces harassed journalists by physically assaulting them, seizing their footage, interrogating them, and expelling them from press conferences or from official offices.

On February 25, Ministry of Interior forces raided the Baghdad offices of Wasan Media and detained 11 employees. The ministry claimed that Wasan, which provides technical support to news organizations, supplied the banned satellite station Al-Jazeera with footage of an Iraqi woman who alleged she was raped by three Iraqi police officers. Wasan denied supplying footage to Al-Jazeera and noted that the interview was filmed by several news organizations and was widely available. The Wasan workers were charged with incitement to terror under Iraq's antiterrorism law, but a criminal court in Baghdad dismissed the charges and freed the men several months later.

Iraq's Kurdistan region has been spared much of the violence that has consumed other parts of the country, and independent journalists have carved out space for critical reporting. But in 2007 outspoken writers were plagued by several violent attacks perpetrated by suspected government agents, as well as criminal lawsuits filed by thin-skinned politicians. In one October attack, four armed men wearing military uniforms abducted and assaulted Nasseh Abdel Raheem Rashid, a Halabja-based journalist who writes for the expatriate online news site *Kurdistanpost*. The men, driving a Nissan truck, placed a sack over Rashid's head, handcuffed him, tied his legs with a scarf, and drove him around for two hours before stopping in a remote area. There, the men began to punch, kick, and threaten him. In his writings for *Kurdistanpost*, Rashid had frequently criticized Kurdish authorities and the practices of the Kurdish security forces, known as Asayish.

In November, a CPJ delegation to the northern city of Arbil expressed alarm over the attacks and concern about a press bill before the Kurdistan parliament. A bill passed in late year would set fines of up to 10 million dinars (US$8,200) for vaguely worded offenses such as disturbing security, spreading fear, or encouraging terrorism, according to local journalists. Given the tenuous financial situation of independent papers—several operate at losses or barely break even—the elastic language could be exploited to put critical publications out of business. The bill would also allow the government to suspend newspapers and jail journalists under other criminal code provisions. Masoud Barazani, president of the regional government, said in December that he would veto the bill and send it back to parliament for revision.

· ISRAEL AND THE OCCUPIED PALESTINIAN TERRITORY ·

A bitter power struggle between the Palestinian factions Hamas and Fatah left journalists vulnerable to harassment and attack, with the slayings of two local media workers and the abduction of BBC correspondent Alan Johnston underscoring the risk. Journalists covering Israeli military operations in the West Bank and Gaza also had to contend with perennial abuses at the hands of Israeli forces.

The press was under constant suspicion—and danger—because of perceived partiality in news coverage. The popular pan-Arab satellite channels Al-Jazeera and Al-Arabiya were threatened from opposite directions: Hamas accused Al-Arabiya of bias, while Fatah alleged favoritism in Al-Jazeera's coverage. A bomb exploded outside the entrance to Al-Arabiya's office in Gaza City on January 22, causing heavy damage, journalists told CPJ. And throughout the year, Fatah officials called for the closure of Al-Jazeera in the West Bank and Gaza, according to news reports.

THE MIDDLE EAST AND NORTH AFRICA

Amid a week of heavy factional fighting in May, a newspaper journalist and a manager were slain in Gaza. On May 13, presidential security forces stopped a taxi carrying Suleiman Abdul-Rahim al-Ashi, an editor for the Hamas-affiliated daily *Palestine*, and Mohammad Matar Abdo, a distribution manager for the paper, in a Fatah-controlled area southwest of Gaza City, Editor-in-Chief Mustafa al-Sawaf told CPJ. After being questioned by the Al-Aqsa Martyrs Brigade, a militant Fatah group, the two were taken to a public street near Fatah's Ansar security compound and shot, according to Abdo's brother, Hamid.

Two days later, masked gunmen seized, bound, and interrogated a proofreader for the Islamist weekly *Al-Risala*, the journalist and his editor said. The proofreader, Osama Abu Musameh, said the men took him to a street near the presidential compound, accused him of working against them, and shot him twice in the legs at close range.

Dozens of journalists were under siege on May 16, when Fatah gunmen took over the roofs of the Shawa and Hosari Tower and Al-Johara Tower, which house local and international media outlets such as Al-Jazeera and the BBC. Journalists told CPJ that the Fatah gunmen skirmished with Hamas fighters who were on the ground, trapping the journalists in the middle of heavy fire. Journalists covered the fighting live from inside the building; no injuries were reported.

The shaky truce that followed would last less than a month, giving way to fresh factional violence in Gaza and parts of the West Bank. At least 116 Palestinians, mainly militants, were killed and hundreds more injured as Hamas routed Fatah forces in Gaza during five days of intensive fighting in mid-June. Palestinian President Mahmoud Abbas dissolved the Palestinian government, firing Prime Minister Ismail Haniya of rival Hamas and ending three months of tenuous power sharing. Abbas set up an emergency government in the West Bank, with Salam Fayyad as prime minister. Hamas took full control of Gaza, with Haniya as its de facto leader.

This split between the West Bank and Gaza had a ripple effect on the Palestinian media, with increasing factionalism within the media and the targeting of media seen as aligned with specific groups. In June, Hamas gunmen in Gaza stormed the facilities of the official Palestinian broadcasting outlets, Palestine TV and Voice of Palestine, seizing equipment and burning transmission facilities, said Mohammed al-Dahoudi, head of the television station. The stations had operated under Abbas' jurisdiction. The Hamas government later issued a statement banning Palestine TV from broadcasting in Gaza, al-Dahoudi told CPJ.

In the West Bank, Fatah forces engaged in their own crackdown on pro-Hamas media. On June 12, members of the Presidential Guard attacked the Hamas-operated Al-Aqsa TV office in Ramallah, confiscating equipment and detaining three employees, Reuters reported. By September, security forces shut Al-Aqsa altogether in the West Bank. The same month, Palestinian security forces and Fatah gunmen burned copies of pro-Hamas newspapers—the daily *Palestine* and the Islamist weekly

Al-Risala—in the West Bank city of Ramallah, the papers' editors told CPJ. Fatah Information Minister Riyad al-Maliki later banned distribution of the newspapers.

Renegade groups took advantage of the chaos in Gaza to kidnap foreign journalists as a means of pressuring authorities to accede to their demands. The Johnston kidnapping and the one-week abduction of Agence France-Presse photographer Jaime Razuri spotlighted the trend.

Eager to show that it could control splinter groups and restore security, Hamas leaders actively sought Johnston's release by pressuring the powerful Dughmush family. One of the clan's members, Mumtaz Dughmush, is believed to head Jaish al-Islam, the little-known Palestinian group that held Johnston, according to news reports and CPJ sources. For their part, local and foreign journalists staged numerous demonstrations seeking the reporter's release. On July 4, the militant group released Johnston unharmed. The Dughmush clan denied involvement.

Palestinian security services had suspected the same militants of being behind the kidnapping of Razuri in early January, according to news reports and CPJ sources. Razuri, a Peruvian national, was seized by a group of armed men as he was entering the news agency's bureau in Gaza City, AFP reported. He was released unharmed after a week in captivity.

Since 2004, at least 16 journalists have been abducted in the Gaza Strip, CPJ research shows. All were released unharmed. The abductions appeared to be the work of armed splinter groups. Often formed with personal goals in mind, such as the release of imprisoned relatives or the securing of government jobs, these groups have resorted increasingly to the abduction of foreigners, including journalists, for use as bargaining chips.

As Hamas sought to restore security in Gaza in late summer, it clamped down on protests and coverage of dissent. On several occasions in August and September, Hamas forces harassed, beat, and arrested journalists covering demonstrations by Fatah supporters in Gaza. In mid-August, Hamas gunmen stormed several Gaza media outlets, including Al-Arabiya, where they seized footage of a pro-Fatah protest, The Associated Press reported. Later that month, Hamas gunmen roughed up Reuters cameraman Abed Rabbo Shanah as he filmed a demonstration, according to news reports.

In November, the Hamas Interior Ministry in Gaza ordered that all journalists carry a Hamas press card, the AP reported. Several journalists told CPJ that they refused to comply and threatened to ignore Hamas news events; Hamas did not appear to enforce the order vigorously.

The Israeli army continued its incursions into the West Bank and Gaza, as it has done regularly since the second intifada in September 2000. In several instances, Palestinian journalists alleged that they were deliberately targeted by Israeli military fire—a charge the Israel Defense Forces (IDF) denied. During an Israeli search-and-seizure raid in the West Bank city of Ramallah in January, soldiers shot two journalists. AFP photographer Abbas Momani told CPJ that he and *Al-Ayyam* photographer Fadi al-Aruri were among a group of journalists covering the clashes between Israeli forces and Palestinian militants. An Israeli soldier fired several shots from less than 10 yards (nine meters), severely wounding al-Aruri, Momani said.

Al-Aruri, who was not wearing a bulletproof vest, sustained severe injuries that led to the loss of a kidney, *Al-Ayyam* reported. Momani was shot in the chest but escaped serious injury because he was wearing a vest. Momani said he and the other journalists were wearing clothing clearly marked "Press" and were standing in a sheltered area. He said the Israeli soldier appeared to have deliberately shot at them since there were no Palestinian militants in their immediate vicinity. An IDF spokesman said the military could not determine whether al-Aruri was struck by Israeli or Palestinian fire; the spokesman said the military was unaware that Momani had been hit. Momani said he had suffered head injuries in May, when he was struck by a rubber bullet fired by an Israeli soldier in the West Bank village of Bilein. The IDF said an investigation was pending in the May incident.

One of the more troubling incidents came in early July during an incursion in the eastern part of the Bureij refugee camp in central Gaza. Israeli tank soldiers shot Imad Ghanem, a cameraman for the Hamas-affiliated Al-Aqsa TV, and then shot him twice more in the legs after he had fallen to the ground, journalists at the scene told CPJ. Sameer al-Bouji, a cameraman for the Pal-Media news agency, filmed the incident, which was broadcast on Al-Jazeera. The footage showed Ghanem dressed in black clothes similar to those worn by Hamas gunmen. An eyewitness, who requested anonymity, told CPJ that some armed residents of the camp were in the vicinity when Ghanem was shot, but the clip indicates that they were not firing at that moment. Both of Ghanem's legs were amputated.

An Israeli army spokesman who reviewed the footage said the incident was being investigated, but it was unclear who shot the cameraman, *The New York Times* reported. An Israeli military source quoted by international news organizations, including the *Times* and Reuters, said that Israel does not recognize cameramen working for the Hamas-affiliated channel as journalists.

On several occasions, journalists said, Israeli forces and border police intimidated, harassed, and obstructed them by firing tear gas and stun grenades. In mid-February, Israeli soldiers fired tear gas at several cameramen and photojournalists covering clashes between Israeli soldiers and Palestinian stone-throwers near the West Bank city of Hebron, according to the AP's Nasser Shiyoukhi and other journalists at the scene. Shiyoukhi told CPJ he was overcome by the gas and that colleagues brought him to a hospital in Hebron.

On March 8, Rami al-Faqih, a correspondent for local Al-Quds Educational Television, and Iyad Hamad, an AP cameraman, said they were each hit by stun grenades while covering a peaceful march marking International Women's Day at the Qalandia Israeli military checkpoint between Jerusalem and Ramallah. Israeli National Police spokesman Micky Rosenfeld told CPJ that border police used minimum force to disperse protesters who had tried to enter an off-limits area.

Bilein, west of Ramallah, remained a flashpoint; several journalists were injured by Israeli forces dispersing weekly demonstrations against Israel's border security barrier. Al-Jazeera correspondent Shireen Abu Aqleh told CPJ that she was delivering an on-air report on August 10, when an Israeli soldier fired a bullet at the front window of the channel's uplink vehicle. No injuries were reported.

Over the course of the year, Israeli forces raided several Palestinian television and radio stations in the West Bank and confiscated equipment during military operations. They also often interrupted the signals of local television and radio stations to broadcast orders for residents to turn in or provide information about wanted Palestinians, local journalists told CPJ.

Two journalists were being held by Israeli forces when CPJ conducted its annual census on December 1. Walid Khalid Hassan Ali, *Palestine*'s West Bank bureau chief, was taken into administrative detention on May 18, the journalist's wife told CPJ. According to court documents obtained by CPJ, an Israeli military judge found Ali had a "recent propensity for military activity." Ali's attorney, Tamar Pelleg, said she believed Ali's work at *Palestine* played a role in the detention. Israeli authorities did not detail the factual basis for the detention, and the evidence remained secret.

Israeli authorities arrested Syrian journalist Atta Farhat in the Golan Heights northern village of Baqaata on July 30, according to the Syrian Center for Media and Freedom of Expression and the Paris-based International Federation of Human Rights. The groups said they believed Farhat was suspected of "collaborating with an enemy state," but noted that Israeli authorities had not disclosed the reasons for the detention. The center said it suspected the allegation was directly related to Farhat's journalism for Syrian media. Farhat is editor-in-chief of the daily news Web site *Golan Times* and a correspondent for the Syrian daily *Al-Watan* and state-run Syrian TV.

• • • • • • • • • • • • • • • • • • • MOROCCO • • • • • • • • • • • • • • • • • • •

Press freedom continued its downward slide, belying Morocco's carefully burnished image as a liberalizing country with a free press. Outspoken journalists found themselves in court, in prison, or out of work following a rash of politicized court cases, while the government of King Mohammed VI unveiled a restrictive new press bill. On May 3, World Press Freedom Day, CPJ designated Morocco as one of

THE MIDDLE EAST AND NORTH AFRICA

the world's worst backsliders on press freedom.

Media repression picked up where it left off in December 2006, when then-Prime Minister Driss Jettou suspended for two months the independent Arabic-language weekly *Nichane* for running a 10-page cover story analyzing popular jokes about religion, sex, and politics. In January, a Moroccan court handed down a three-year suspended prison sentence to Driss Ksikes, then director and editor of the magazine, and to reporter Sanaa al-Aji for denigrating Islam, an offense under Morocco's press law of 2002. The journalists were also fined 80,000 dirhams (US$10,400) each. The prison terms could be imposed if either journalist were convicted of a future offense. Ksikes later resigned from the magazine citing, in part, concern that the suspended sentence could be reactivated if he were swept up in another press case.

The government response was set in motion when an Islamist Web site attacked *Nichane* for publishing "un-Islamic" material. Word of the *Nichane* story quickly spread to Kuwait, where the country's political opposition in parliament seized the moment to embarrass Emir Sabah al-Ahmed al-Jaber al-Sabah, who was traveling in Morocco at the time, and criticize him for visiting a country that showed no respect for Islam. Moroccan officials defended the *Nichane* ban and the suspended prison sentences for Ksikes and al-Aji as a way to outflank the country's powerful Islamist opposition. Some journalists, however, said the case was a means of striking back at Ksikes, who had published stories critical of the monarchy.

Officials used other judicial tactics to crack down on dissident journalists. In February, the country lost its leading independent publisher when Aboubakr Jamaï, of the weekly newsmagazine *Le Journal Hebdomadaire*, left the country as judicial authorities prepared to seize his assets in the wake of a record-breaking defamation judgment in 2006. Jamaï and a colleague were ordered to pay 3 million dirhams (US$395,000) to the head of a Brussels-based think tank, who claimed *Le Journal Hebdomadaire* had defamed him in a six-page article questioning the independence of the organization's report on the disputed Western Sahara. The judgment was widely billed as political retribution for Jamaï's uncompromising coverage of the king and powerful political interests. A palace source told the magazine that officials had been incensed by an unflattering 2005 cover photo of the king, triggering the exorbitant damages.

Moroccan journalists remained vulnerable to a stable of prohibitions outlined in the country's restrictive press code, which criminalizes offending the king, "defaming" the monarchy, insulting Islam or state institutions, and offending Morocco's "territorial integrity" (the last being code for the country's claim to the Western Sahara). Maximum penalties include up to five years in jail; the government also has the power to revoke publication licenses, suspend newspapers, and confiscate editions deemed threatening to public order.

The government unveiled a press bill that would keep in place tough criminal penalties and possibly open the door to other restrictions on the news media. Though touted by officials as a step forward, the draft legislation left intact most existing restrictions, retained prison penalties for many so-called press offenses, and increased maximum fines tenfold, from 100,000 dirhams (US$13,000) to 1 million dirhams (US$130,000). It also called for the creation of a "national press council," whose 15 members would be appointed by the king, journalists, and publishers. One version

of the measure would grant the council the power to ban journalists from working in their profession, and to levy economic sanctions against newspaper journalists who violate a yet-to-be-drafted ethics code. Press syndicate head Younes Moujahid said some provisions were being eased as work on the draft continued. The bill was pending in late year.

In response to the country's plummeting press situation, a CPJ delegation traveled to Rabat and Casablanca in April, spending 10 days meeting with Moroccan journalists and top government officials. In meetings with CPJ, then-Prime Minister Jettou and then-Communications Minister Nabil Benabdallah denied government involvement in a string of excessive libel judgments against independent journalists dating to 2005, and claimed that the court case against Jamaï "fell from heaven" and was "in the hands of the judiciary." "The four or five problems we had to face were each time handled by the judiciary," Jettou said. "We abide by the rule of law in this country."

But government officials, including those who met with CPJ, openly acknowledged problems with the independence of the country's judiciary. Abbas al-Fassi, then minister of state without portfolio, admonished judges in February "to listen to the voice of their conscience, not to instructions given through their cellular phones." Officials continued to emphasize that press freedom was strong compared to the past and to prevailing conditions in the Arab world. "We have never sought to cause prejudice to our newspapers or journalists," Jettou told CPJ. "We are proud to have the freest and the most dynamic press in the region." Benabdallah pledged to CPJ that "the days of imprisoning journalists in Morocco are over."

Their words, however, were contradicted by their government's actions. As September parliamentary elections approached, outspoken Moroccan journalists were targeted for government reprisals. On August 4, police seized copies of the beleaguered *Nichane* from newsstands and confiscated copies of its sister weekly, the French-language *TelQuel*, as it came off the press. The seizures came after *Nichane* published an editorial that questioned the point of legislative elections since King Mohammed VI controlled all facets of government. *TelQuel* Publisher Ahmed Benchemsi, who wrote the editorial, was charged on August 6 with failing to show "due respect to the king" under Article 41 of the Moroccan Press and Publication Law. He faced between three and five years in prison and a fine of up to 100,000 dirhams (US$13,000).

One week later, Publisher Abderrahim Ariri and journalist Mustafa Hormatallah of the Moroccan weekly *Al-Watan al-An* were convicted by a criminal court in Casablanca of "possession of stolen items" under the Moroccan Penal Code. The men were charged shortly after the paper reproduced a secret government document detailing the security service's monitoring of jihadist Web sites. Hormatallah was sentenced to eight months in jail, while Ariri received a six-month suspended sentence. They were each fined 1,000 dirhams (US$130). Hormatallah was released in September, pending an appeal.

As the summer press crackdown reached its height, Benabdallah continued to spin the country's press freedom record. "There are no red lines. However, insolence and press freedom do not form a rhyme," he told the daily *L'Economiste* in August. He added, "There are no taboos, provided one abides by the required forms of decency."

Moroccan journalists said the wave of criminal prosecutions further dissuaded journalists from tackling sensitive topics such as the monarchy and powerful political personalities. The deteriorating conditions did not spur close allies, including the United States, to publicly express disapproval. In fact, just a week before Ariri and Hormatallah were convicted, the U.S. government-backed Millennium Challenge Corporation (MCC) approved a five-year, $697.5 million economic aid package to Morocco—the largest grant since the agency was formed in January 2004. MCC is a self-described U.S. government corporation "based on the principle that aid is most effective when it reinforces good governance, economic freedom, and investments in people that promote economic growth and elimination of extreme poverty."

· · · · · · · · · · · · · · · · · · **SUDAN** · · · · · · · · · · · · · · · · · ·

Despite free speech protections built into Sudan's 2005 interim constitution, authorities operated as if a state of emergency were still in force. Newspaper suspensions, criminal charges, and detentions were a routine part of working as a journalist in Sudan. When trying to cover one of the world's biggest stories—the genocide in Darfur—reporters faced high barriers.

The Arab janjaweed militias backed by the government have killed more than 200,000 people and displaced 2.5 million others over the last four years in the Darfur region of western Sudan, according to international news reports. One rebel group, a faction of the Sudan Liberation Movement led by Minni Arcua Minnawi, signed the Darfur Peace Agreement with the Sudanese government in 2006. The agreement was intended to stop three years of fighting in Darfur, but it was made largely moot by the refusal of other rebel groups to join. The government allowed a joint U.N. and African Union peacekeeping force to deploy in the region, but the violence continued—as did the struggle to cover the story.

Al-Musalimi al-Bashir al-Kabashi, Khartoum bureau chief for Al-Jazeera, told CPJ that local and foreign journalists were able to travel from the capital to Darfur unhindered by authorities. But once there, he said, insecurity in the western region often prevented journalists from traveling freely. Criminal gangs taking advantage of the chaos, he said, posed a particular threat.

Even when not reporting from the center of the crisis, Sudan's television and radio broadcasters remained under the tight control of President Omar Hassan al-Bashir's government. The country's print press—composed of independent, opposition, and pro-government dailies and weeklies—had greater latitude. Independent newspapers such as *Al-Sahafa* and *Al-Sudani* produced daring coverage of sensitive topics such as government corruption and security service actions. The pan-Arab satellite channels Al-Jazeera and Al-Arabiya also reported aggressively on the government's actions.

Sudan emerged from a decades-long civil war between the north's Arab-Muslim elite and the south's impoverished non-Muslim Africans with the signing of the Comprehensive Peace Agreement in January 2005. The longstanding state of emergency lapsed as the ruling Islamist National Congress Party and the Sudan People's Liberation Movement formed a national unity government led by al-Bashir. In early July 2005, Sudan adopted an interim national constitution that guaranteed freedom of expression and the press. But al-Bashir's government has not always lived up to its word.

Despite constitutional guarantees, the Justice Ministry and prosecutors often invoked Article 130 of the 1991 Code of Criminal Procedure to suspend newspapers for covering subjects such as popular unrest, the security services, the justice minister and other officials, and certain criminal investigations. Journalists maintained that the legal provision did not apply to the press, since it specifically deals with "crimes relating to safety and public health."

In February, a state prosecutor suspended indefinitely the prominent Arabic-language daily *Al-Sudani* for covering the murder of Mohammed Taha Mohammed Ahmed, the *Al-Wifaq* editor beheaded in September 2006. The prosecutor said he imposed the ban under Article 130 to "prevent any influence" on the investigation. *Al-Sudani* Editor-in-Chief Mahjoub Erwa told Reuters the paper exerted no such influence since the investigation had already been completed. The suspension was overturned on appeal, and the ban was soon lifted.

Prosecutors charged 19 Darfuris, including two women and a 16-year-old boy, in the editor's brutal murder. Taha had angered Islamists by running an article about the Prophet Muhammad, and he had written critically about armed groups operating in Darfur. A Khartoum criminal court dismissed the case against nine of the defendants in August, citing insufficient evidence, but handed down death sentences to the remaining 10 in November, The Associated Press reported. Some of the defendants complained of coerced confessions and torture by Sudanese security services. Journalists expressed skepticism that the investigation had uncovered the people responsible for masterminding the murder.

In May, authorities suspended *Al-Sudani* again under Article 130 for allegedly libeling Justice Minister Mohamed Ali al-Mardi. Osman Mirghani, a reporter at the paper, told CPJ he wrote a critical article calling on the minister to resign for his handling of a money-laundering case. Mirghani and Erwa were detained for several days but never charged. Following an intensive campaign by local journalists, the government allowed the paper to resume publication on May 23, according to news reports. Yielding to mounting pressure, al-Mardi said Article 130 would not be used against the press again.

The National Press and Publications Council (NPPC), Sudan's official press regulator, kept in place stringent requirements for licensing newspapers. The NPPC also ordered a two-day suspension of the daily *Al-Watan* following a February interview in which two religious militants threatened to kill foreigners in Sudan. The paper was accused of "provoking hatred against the state" and violating journalistic responsibilities, Deputy Editor-in-Chief Adil Sid Ahmed told CPJ.

Government officials regularly filed criminal complaints against newspapers and journalists for publishing purportedly false information. Editors told CPJ that the prosecutor's office vigorously pursued their papers and staff. The independent daily *Al-Ayam* has been named in five criminal cases filed by government institutions or officials, according to its editor-in-chief, Mahjoub Mohamed Saleh. *Al-Watan*'s Sid Ahmed said his paper was facing 10 separate trials over its news coverage. Beyond the heavy fines levied against papers in several cases, editors told CPJ that their work was hindered by the amount of time they had to spend in court.

When it was not filing lawsuits, the government was busy seizing newspapers and censoring stories. Security officers confiscated the press run of the opposition daily *Ra'y Al-Shaab* on August 21, a journalist at the paper told CPJ. Later that month, authorities seized an entire press run of the opposition weekly *Al-Midan* without providing a reason.

In mid-June, the government tried to black out coverage of a deadly clash in the northern village of Furaig between Sudanese forces and several thousand Nubian demonstrators angered by construction of the Kajbar Dam. While authorities did not issue an official ban, they actively prevented journalists from reaching the area and arrested those who managed to report on the confrontation. About 300,000 Nubians, an ethnic group with a distinct culture and language, live in villages along the Nile River north of Khartoum. The government's planned construction of dams in their region would flood around 30 villages, the AP reported, forcing many residents to relocate. The government's crackdown on protesters left four civilians dead and 19 injured, according to CPJ sources.

Authorities detained reporters on several occasions. In one egregious case, *Ra'y Al-Shaab* reporter Mujahid Abdallah was detained for two months for violating a ban on covering the Kajbar Dam story. He was released without charge on August 19 after signing a pledge not to write anything negative about the project.

Journalists on assignment also faced physical harassment at the hands of the Sudanese security services. The most alarming example was the beating and detention in March of Nichola Dominic Mandil, a Sudanese producer for the U.S. government-funded Sudan Radio Service (SRS). Mandil had gone to an area northwest of Khartoum to report on clashes between security forces and the rebel Minawi faction, the station reported. The security forces prevented several journalists, including Mandil, from reporting the story. As he waited for a taxi to leave the area, he told the SRS, members of the security services forced him into a car. The officers blindfolded and severely beat him, he said. Mandil was accused of "being a foreign agent in Sudan promoting American ideology" and held for five days, the SRS reported.

Foreign journalists trying to tell the Darfur story were obstructed. The External Information Council (EIC), a press liaison office, issued an exit visa in March to BBC correspondent Jonah Fisher, forcing him to leave the country within one month, the journalist said. The EIC told Fisher's lawyer that the Interior Ministry had deemed his reporting "hostile." That reporting had included a November 2006 piece about the government working closely with the janjaweed militias. Fisher left Sudan in April.

Reporters who wanted to enter the Darfur region had to obtain permission from both the bureaucracy-laden EIC and military leaders who imposed travel restrictions, Fisher said. The expenditure of time and money for uncertain results deterred some journalists from parachuting in for short periods to cover the conflict. On top of that, the presence of security forces and informants in refugee camps made residents hesitant to talk freely with the press.

For the local press, self-censorship of government atrocities or those carried out by the janjaweed was heavy, even at independent newspapers. English-language papers had more leeway and often reprinted reports carried in the Western press. More often than not, however, a significant portion of the citizenry remained in the dark about the extent of the violence.

· · · · · · · · · · · · · · · · · · **TUNISIA** ·

In a July 25 speech marking the 50th anniversary of the Tunisian Republic, President Zine El Abidine Ben Ali proclaimed that his government had "enriched the information and communication landscape and offered opportunity for the expres-

THE MIDDLE EAST AND NORTH AFRICA

sion of different opinions." It was an Orwellian moment in a year in which the Ben Ali administration stepped up attacks on independent journalists and blocked numerous online news sites.

The Tunisia Monitoring Group, a coalition of 18 organizations that belong to the International Freedom of Expression Exchange, said in April that it witnessed "serious deterioration in the conditions related to freedom of expression," and cited a list of banned writers, books, and Web sites. The coalition, established to monitor conditions before and after Tunisia hosted the World Summit on the Information Society in 2005, had already called on U.N. Secretary-General Ban Ki-moon to help assure that "the right to establish media outlets is not solely reserved to individuals or groups close to the [Tunisian] government." The group highlighted the need for Tunisia to establish a "fair and transparent procedure for the award of broadcast licenses through an independent regulatory body" and to protect "the right to access Internet cafés and to freely surf the Web."

OpenNet Initiative, an academic partnership that studies Internet censorship issues, found Tunisia to be among the worst nations in blocking Web content. In a global survey of government filtering techniques that was released in May, OpenNet Initiative placed Tunisia alongside Burma, China, Iran, Syria, and Vietnam as a nation deeply engaged in "politically motivated filtering."

In one disturbing case, Omar Mestiri, managing editor of the online magazine *Kalima*, appeared in a Tunis court in August on defamation charges brought by Mohammed Baccar, a lawyer with close connections to state authorities. The case stemmed from a September 2006 article in which Mestiri criticized the Tunisian Bar Association's decision to lift Baccar's disbarment. The prosecution did not question the accuracy of the story in *Kalima* (a site blocked domestically) but insisted that Mestiri reveal his sources. Baccar unexpectedly withdrew his complaint on August 30. A day later, unknown arsonists torched the office of Ayachi Hammami, the human rights lawyer who had defended Mestiri.

In July, CPJ welcomed the release from prison of human rights lawyer and writer Mohammed Abbou. Abbou was jailed for 28 months because of online articles he wrote criticizing Ben Ali's autocratic rule. Plainclothes police harassed Abbou's wife and children throughout the imprisonment, CPJ research shows. Ben Ali granted Abbou and 21 other political prisoners conditional pardons as part of events marking the republic's 50th anniversary. The government said the freed prisoners would have to serve out their terms if they were ever charged with new offenses.

Tunisian law does not restrict the movements of pardoned prisoners, but police turned Abbou away from the Tunis Carthage Airport on August 24, preventing him from taking part in a talk show on free expression at the London bureau of Al-Jazeera. He was also prevented on October 22 from traveling to Cairo to monitor the trial of Egyptian editor Ibrahim Eissa for a local human rights group.

Two other freed journalists, one released in 2002 and the other in 2006, continued to be denied freedom of movement and the right to earn a living. Abdallah Zouari, a reporter for the now-defunct Islamist weekly *Al-Fajr*, saw his virtual house arrest, more than 300 miles (480 kilometers) from his wife and children in Tunis, arbitrarily extended for an additional 26-month period. A military court sentenced Zouari in 1992 to 11 years in prison and five years of "administrative surveillance" for "belonging to an illegal organization" and "planning to change the nature of the state." Several weeks after his release in June 2002, he was arrested and forced to move to the outskirts of the southern city of Zarzis, where he was put under continuous police surveillance.

Hamadi Jebali, editor of *Al-Fajr* and one of the leading figures in the banned Islamist Al-Nahda Movement, also remained under constant monitoring. Jebali spent more than 15 years in prison for publishing an article on the constitutionality of military tribunals, for his membership in an illegal organization, and for "planning to change the nature of the state."

Local journalists and rights activists said Al-Jazeera reporter Lotfi Hajji, co-founder of the independent Tunisian Journalists Syndicate, was under near-constant siege by police. Hajji, they said, was assaulted, detained, and prevented from working as a journalist. In September, plainclothes police blocked Hajji from entering the offices of the opposition Progressive Democratic Party (PDP) in Tunis, where its secretary-general, Maya Jribi, and the managing director of the weekly *Al-Mawkif*, Ahmed Nejib Chebbi, were on hunger strike to protest administrative and judicial attacks on free expression and assembly.

Many reporters said they were followed and even assaulted in the streets of Tunis. They included Slim Boukhdhir, whose stories on human rights violations and the increasing influence of Ben Ali's relatives on the country's economy have made him a favorite target of plainclothes police. In November, authorities detained Boukhdhir on charges of "aggression against a public employee" and "violation of public morality standards." Boukhdhir was sentenced to a year in prison after a trial that observers called a sham. Lotfi Hidouri of *Kalima* and Aymen Rezgui, a young reporter for the Italy-based satellite channel Al-Hiwar Tunisi, were both assaulted by police; the director of the channel, Tahar Ben Hassine, was briefly detained.

This unrelenting campaign against government critics has led more than 100 journalists to go into exile since Ben Ali seized power in 1987, according to the Tunisian Journalists Syndicate. One of the latest victims of this forced migration was Mohamed Fourati, former contributor to different media outlets, including *Al-Mawkif*. He settled in Qatar at the end of 2006 as a reporter for the daily *Asharq.*

THE MIDDLE EAST AND NORTH AFRICA

On March 9, the Court of Appeals in the southern city of Gafsa, nearly 220 miles (350 kilometers) southwest of Tunis, sentenced Fourati in absentia to 14 months in prison for "belonging to an unauthorized association" and "raising funds without authorization," even though he had twice been acquitted of the charges. The prosecution was triggered by two articles Fourati had written nearly seven years ago for the online magazine *Aqlam*.

Government attacks on the press targeted independent journalists and the private media. In January, as the first issue of the new French-language magazine *L'Expression* went to the printer, the privately owned Dar Assabah group, which owns the magazine, received government instructions to delay the launch until further notice. Managing Director Raouf Cheikhrouhou later said Tunisians would be provided with "independent, but responsible information." The first issue of the weekly was published on October 19.

Al-Mawkif, published by the PDP, was a regular target. On October 1, a Tunis court evicted the newspaper from its longtime offices in a case that was widely seen as a political reprisal. Three times during the year, Editor Rachid Khechana said, plainclothes police removed copies of *Al-Mawkif* from newsstands—once when the paper ran an opinion piece by Jebali, again when it ran a front-page photo of a schoolmaster hospitalized after a police attack, and a third time when the paper covered the hunger strike by Jribi and Chebbi. The *Muwatinoon* (Citizens) weekly, launched in January by the opposition Democratic Forum for Labor and Liberties, also reported police harassment.

The attacks occurred despite several visits to Tunisia by U.S. congressmen and government officials. "Our development would have impressed you far more if Tunisians were free citizens," journalists Sihem Ben Sedrine and Neziha Rejiba wrote in an open letter to a May delegation of U.S. congressmen led by Rep. John Tanner. "The examples of other Mediterranean countries such as Greece and Portugal, which have lived through political situations similar to what Tunisia now endures, attest to the extraordinary metamorphosis that can occur as soon as the totalitarian yoke is cast off."

• • • • • • • • • • • • • • • • • • • TURKEY • • • • • • • • • • • • • • • • • • •

The murder of an outspoken newspaper editor underlined a troubling year in which journalists continued to be the targets of criminal prosecution and government censorship.

Hrant Dink, the Turkish-Armenian editor of the bilingual weekly *Agos*, was gunned down outside his newspaper's Istanbul office on January 19. Dink had received numerous death threats from nationalist Turks who viewed his iconoclastic journalism, particularly on the mass killings of Armenians in the early 20th century, as an act of treachery. In a January 10 article in *Agos*, Dink said he had passed along a particularly threatening letter to Istanbul's Sisli district prosecutor, but no action had been taken. Dink's murder rekindled memories of the not-too-distant past, when murders of journalists were common in Turkey. In the 1990s, 18 Turkish journalists were killed for their work, many of them murdered, making it the eighth-deadliest country in the world for the press. Few of the cases were solved.

The slaying of a well-known editor in broad daylight on the streets of Istanbul jolted both the news media and the public, drawing attention to the rising tensions between hardline nationalists and the press. A headline in the daily *Milliyet* proclaimed "Hrant Dink is Turkey," while the daily *Hürriyet* asserted, "The killer is a traitor to his nation." Thousands thronged the streets for demonstrations honoring Dink and calling for justice.

Prime Minister Recep Tayyip Erdogan condemned Dink's death as an attack on Turkey's unity and promised to catch those responsible. A day later, police arrested the alleged triggerman, 17-year-old Ogün Samast, who confessed to the crime. Erhan

Tuncel and Yasin Hayal, described as ultranationalist Turks opposed to Dink's political views, were accused of conspiring with Samast to carry out the murder. In all, 19 people went on trial beginning in July.

As the case unfolded, though, suspicions arose of possible police complicity. Photos emerged before the trial showing Samast posing with police officers in the Black Sea city of Samsun. And a recorded phone call between Tuncel, who had been a police informant, and an officer indicated that police may have had prior knowledge of the murder plot, according to Turkish press reports. (In one exchange, the reports said, Tuncel seemed to suggest that the gunman had not followed plans to stay at the murder scene.) As the trial progressed in late year, police claimed the recording had been lost, according to news reports. Many independent journalists told CPJ that the full truth of the murder may never be known.

Dink's death helped focus attention not only on the threats facing dissident journalists in Turkey, but also on the country's restrictive press freedom climate, one buttressed by an arsenal of repressive laws that can be used to punish critical speech. Before his death, Dink himself faced a possible prison sentence in cases brought by nationalist Turks objecting to his writings about the Armenian killings, his criticism of lines in the Turkish national anthem that he considered discriminatory, and even his public comments on the court cases filed against him.

The Turkish press freedom group BIA documented dozens of criminal cases brought against print and broadcast journalists in 2007 under controversial penal code provisions that criminalize expressions deemed insulting to the Turkish identity, that represent pro-Kurdish political sentiments, or that criticize the military and state

THE MIDDLE EAST AND NORTH AFRICA

institutions. Article 301 of the penal code, which prohibits insults to Turkish identity and sets penalties of up to three years in prison, was the most commonly used weapon against the press. Dink's son, Arat, who took over the paper after his father's death, was found guilty by a Turkish court in October under Article 301 and sentenced to a one-year suspended term. In effect, the son was prosecuted for the father's supposed offense: The charge stemmed from an interview Hrant Dink gave to Reuters in July 2006 about the Armenian killings, which was later reprinted in *Agos*.

BIA said that at least 100 prosecutions were brought against journalists under Article 301 in the first six months of the year alone.

The European Union urged Turkey to reform its laws and eliminate such prosecutions. Turkey began accession talks with the EU in 2005, but concerns about the country's human rights and press freedom record have lingered. In October, the EU again urged reform of Article 301 and other repressive laws. "We regret the lack of progress that has been made. ... There have to be substantial changes to Article 301 and also to other articles worded in similarly vague terms," Portugal's European affairs minister, Manuel Lobo Antunes, said on behalf of the EU.

President Abdullah Gül, the former prime minister who took office in August, said he would seek reforms. "We know there are problems with regard to Article 301. There's still room for improvement, and there are changes to be enacted in the period ahead," he said in October. Gül and his governing AK Party, a moderate Islamist party, have overseen the start of constitutional and legal reforms to ease repressive free-expression laws.

Despite the rash of criminal prosecutions, few members of the press were imprisoned as they were during the 1990s, when Turkey was the world's leading jailer of journalists. As a result of legal reforms to the country's penal code in recent years, prison penalties were often dismissed, suspended, or converted to fines. However, the mere presence of repressive laws stifled debate. And jailings, while rare, were still in evidence in 2007.

In May, muckraking journalist Sinan Kara, formerly of the newspaper *Datca Haber*, served five months in prison for allegedly defaming local political officials, according to BIA. Short-term detentions of journalists were more common. In June, journalists Sait Bayram and Firat Avci of the newspaper *Söz* were arrested by security forces in the southeastern city of Diyarbakir and held for two days over a story alleging that a local judge took bribes.

Courts continued to suspend newspapers, mainly pro-Kurdish titles, over objectionable political content. Just before parliamentary elections in July, a court ordered the pro-Kurdish daily *Gündem* suspended for two weeks for allegedly disseminating "terrorist propaganda," according to BIA. Officials had objected to an article describing popular sympathy for Kurdish guerrillas. When the paper attempted to republish under another name, *Günceli*, the court reissued the ban.

Police violence against journalists was a recurring problem. Sinan Tekpetek, who works for the newspapers *Özgür Hayat* and *Yüzde 52 Öfke*, said he was abducted in downtown Istanbul by police officers who dragged him into a waiting car, BIA reported. Tekpetek, who filed a complaint, alleged that police threatened him and broke his ribs in the July incident. BIA said the case could have been related to the journalist's work or his scheduled appearance as a witness in a police brutality case.

Radio and television stations abound in Turkey, but the Supreme Radio and Television Board, the main regulatory body, continued to impose punitive sanctions against media outlets accused of violating any number of vague restrictions about morals and ethics. Several broadcast stations or their programs were temporarily ordered off the air for violating these proscriptions, especially election coverage deemed to be biased in favor of a political campaign.

While the Internet is mostly unregulated, in recent years the courts have ordered the censorship or banning of Web sites deemed in breach of Turkish law. In the year's most publicized instance, a court ordered Internet providers to block the popular Web site YouTube because of postings deemed to offend the memory of Mustafa Kemal Atatürk, the founder of modern-day Turkey. The order was reversed two days later.

· · · · · · · · · · · · · · · · · · YEMEN ·

Journalists covering a rebel insurgency and government corruption were subjected to a frightening array of violent attacks and politically motivated court cases. Threats against independent journalists continued at an alarming rate, taking on an almost routine air. Perpetrators, for the most part, went unpunished.

Since 2004, the government has been combating a regional insurgency led by tribal and religious figures in the northwestern Saada region. Until a tenuous cease-fire was reached in June, hundreds of civilians had been killed and thousands displaced during the three-year conflict. Yemeni authorities continued to respond aggressively toward journalists who tried to report independently on the fighting. Government forces prevented journalists from entering the region to cover the conflict, effectively imposing a media blackout.

At least one journalist became ensnared in the government's attempt to stop coverage of the conflict. In June, in one of the year's most troubling press freedom incidents, Yemeni authorities stormed the home of Abdel Karim al-Khaiwani, editor of an opposition news Web site and former editor of the online newspaper *Al-Shoura*. Al-Khaiwani was hauled before a State Security Court on vague terrorism charges that carried a possible death penalty.

In court, the government made a slew of unsubstantiated accusations, reinforcing the belief among Yemeni journalists and political observers that the editor's arrest was an attempt to punish him for his unrelenting criticism of the fight against rebels in Saada, as well as his writing about government nepotism. The preliminary evidence against al-Khaiwani consisted of photographs of the fighting in Saada, an interview and contact with a rebel leader, and news articles, including one written by al-Khaiwani that criticized President Ali Abdullah Saleh.

Al-Khaiwani's case took a dangerous twist in July when, following his release pending trial, several gunmen abducted him as he attempted to hail a taxi. The assailants threatened him, beat him, and tried to break his fingers, CPJ sources said. The gunmen also threatened to kill the journalist and his family if he wrote another word against the president or the country's national unity, those sources said.

A spike in attacks against journalists corresponded with the independent media's increasing assertiveness. During the last three years, opposition newspapers have smashed political taboos by criticizing rampant government corruption, the war in Saada, Saleh's policies, and the president's perceived plan to have his son Ahmed succeed him. Though small in circulation, these papers represent one the few avenues of dissent in Yemen, where political parties are weak and electronic media are firmly under the state's control.

Editor-in-Chief Naif Hassan of the independent weekly *Al-Sharaa* told CPJ that, in August, several armed men in two army jeeps with military license plates stormed the paper's offices and threatened to kill him. It was unclear what prompted the raid, although journalists at the paper suspect it was connected to a recent criminal complaint filed by the Yemeni Ministry of Defense over *Al-Sharaa*'s coverage of the conflict in Saada.

In March, armed men accosted freelance columnist Mohamed al-Maqaleh on a street in the capital, Sana'a, holding him at gunpoint and warning him against criticizing the government in his writings. On September 2, Omar Bin Fareed, a columnist for the Aden-based daily *Al-Ayyam*, was abducted by gunmen as he sat at a restaurant eating dinner; the assailants grabbed Fareed, shoved him into a waiting car, and beat him for several hours before dumping him in the desert in the early hours of the morning. *Al-Ayyam* reported that it traced one of the cars used in the assault to the office of a local military commander. Fareed said he believed the abduction was in reprisal for his writings about local officials.

The government has been under increasing domestic pressure, with a debilitated economy, a restive rural population, declining living standards, and high unemployment. Police attacked or barred journalists trying to report on the rising number of public protests. As in past years, Yemeni officials failed to issue public expressions of concern over these violent attacks against the press. On the contrary, it denied any problems existed.

Columnist al-Maqaleh, Abdullah al-Wazeer, editor-in-chief of the weekly *Al-Balagh*, and Saddam al-Ashmouri, a freelance reporter for the English-language weekly *Yemen Times*, were assaulted by security forces in October while covering an opposition rally in Sana'a. *Al-Ayyam* reported a spike in attacks on its journalists beginning in May, with several reporters beaten, detained, and threatened. Security forces seized cameras from its reporters and barred them from covering protests. In May, municipal security guards visited *Al-Ayyam* reporter Abdul Hafez Mugab at his office and threatened him over his coverage of alleged financial corruption in the local government.

Those who abducted and attacked journalists enjoyed widespread impunity for their actions, as they had in the past. In January, CPJ wrote to Saleh one year after his government pledged to a CPJ delegation visiting Sana'a that it would investigate the brutal assaults against the press. A year later, however, those responsible for the attacks continued to evade justice. Government investigations have been incomplete or not seriously pursued, CPJ research shows. In only two of the five cases that CPJ brought to the government's attention did authorities identify suspects and initiate legal action. One of those cases was dismissed, and the other was pending in late year, with the suspects free.

Outspoken journalists continued to face the threat of judicial harassment in politically motivated court cases. Yemen's judiciary—which is headed by the president—is not independent, and outspoken journalists are often at the mercy of politicized judges. Under Yemen's harsh press law, penal code, and other statutes, journalists face prison terms, fines, and professional bans in connection with their published work. Coverage of corruption and nepotism frequently triggers judicial retaliation.

In an unusual move, one case was referred to the prosecutor's office specializing in national security and terrorism cases. On July 7, the Ministry of Defense filed a complaint against the weekly *Al-Sharaa* after the paper published a controversial series on the conflict in Saada that alleged, among other things, that a known terrorist group was fighting alongside the Yemeni army and training tribal volunteers to fight in the conflict. An editor and two reporters faced several years in jail.

The government retained its firm grip over the influential broadcast media, which continued to strictly reflect government views. Cyberspace became a forum for independent news, but the government increasingly censored content. Authorities banned several news sites and chat forums during the year. According to the Yemeni Journalists Syndicate, authorities blocked access to the news sites *Al-Shoura* and *Aleshteraki* because of their reports on the conflict in Saada. The daily *Al-Ayyam* reported that access to its Web site was briefly blocked within Yemen on September 2.

Critical bloggers, including those based outside the country, were also censored. Access to U.S. journalist Jane Novak's Web site, *Armiesofliberation*, which is frequently critical of the Yemeni government, was repeatedly blocked inside Yemen.

THE MIDDLE EAST AND NORTH AFRICA

ALGERIA

- Anis Rahmani, managing editor of the Arabic-language weekly *Echourouk*, told CPJ that he and reporter Naïla Berrahal received death threats in June from what they suspected was an al-Qaeda-affiliated group. "They threatened to kidnap and kill me if I did not stop writing articles they deemed against al-Qaeda and Islam," he said. Rahmani told CPJ that on August 1, he received a letter from the General Directorate of National Security in Algiers informing him that, "based on the confessions made by a detained terrorist," armed terrorist groups were targeting the editor.

BAHRAIN

- In October, the High Criminal Court convicted three journalists on charges of libeling Fatima Buali, former director of Dar al-Manar for Elderly Care, according to news reports. Saleh al-Amm, editor of the now-banned online newspaper *Al-Sahafa*, and journalists Fareed al-Shayeb and Muath al-Meshari were each fined 200 dinars (US$533) and ordered to pay 50 dinars (US$133) in damages, according to the Bahrain Center for Human Rights. The journalists wrote several articles that alleged mismanagement of Dar al-Manar, according to news reports.

- Municipalities and Agricultural Affairs Minister Mansour Bin Rajab filed a criminal libel complaint against blogger Mahmood al-Yousif in February, according to news reports. In a December 2006 posting, the blogger took issue with Bin Rajab's positive characterization of the ministry's response to recent flooding. The minister withdrew his complaint in May after al-Yousif apologized, according to news reports.

JORDAN

- The prosecutor's office in the northwestern town of Ain al-Basha charged Khaled al-Khawaja, a reporter for the leading pro-government daily *Al-Rai*, with assaulting a public security officer, according to the journalist's lawyer. The officer, Mohammad Qudah, filed his complaint after al-Khawaja accused him of assault, the journalist's lawyer told CPJ. Qudah and two other public security officers insulted and severely beat al-Khawaja while he was on assignment covering the municipality's distribution of meat to impoverished residents of Ain al-Basha in late January, the lawyer said.

- An amended press law took effect in May, increasing fines tenfold, to a maximum of 20,000 dinars (US$28,000), for "defaming any religion protected under the constitution," "offending the prophets," causing "insult to religious sentiments and beliefs, fueling sectarian strife or racism," or committing "slanders or libels," Agence France-Presse reported. Parliament considered but did not act on more extensive use of prison penalties. Journalists can still be imprisoned under Jordan's penal code.

- Four public security officers assaulted Aubaida Dammour, a reporter for Al-Ghad TV, and Fady Ramhy, a cameraman for the fledgling station, while the journalists were attempting to cover a bus drivers' strike in Jordan's capital, Amman, in early April, according to the Jordanian human rights organization Arab Archives Institute. The officers forcibly seized and destroyed Ramhy's camera and briefly detained both journalists. The station filed an official complaint with the Public Security Directorate.

- Authorities banned the April 30 edition of the weekly *Al-Majd*, Fahd al-Rimawi, editor of the paper, told CPJ. He said that security agents intervened because of a front-page story about a "secret plan" devised by the United States and unnamed Arab parties to oust the Hamas-led Palestinian government. Later that week, al-Rimawi reached an agreement with authorities to place the story on an inside page, he said.

- On April 18, the Jordanian government seized a taped Al-Jazeera interview with former Crown Prince Hassan bin Talal. Al-Jazeera's Ghassan Benjeddou told CPJ that intelligence officers stopped his producer at Amman's Queen Alia Airport and confiscated the videotape of the interview. In the interview, Hassan spoke critically of Saudi Arabia and U.S. policies in the Middle East, Benjeddou said.

KUWAIT

- On August 18, state security officers arrested Bashar al-Sayegh, an editor for the daily *Al-Jarida*, in Kuwait City, his lawyer said. Jassim al-Qames, another editor at the paper, told CPJ he photographed the arrest, prompting the officers to detain and beat him. Al-Qames was released the following day without charge. The prosecutor's office accused al-Sayegh of insulting the emir of Kuwait, which violates both the penal code and the press law and carries a five-year prison sentence. The accusation stemmed from a comment made in an open forum on the *Al-Ommah* news Web site hosted by al-Sayegh. Web site administrators removed the comment several hours after it was made. The person who posted the comment was arrested on August 21.

LEBANON

- The Lebanese Army restricted public access to the Nahr el-Bared refugee camp near Tripoli, in northern Lebanon, the day after fighting broke out between Fatah al-Islam—an extremist group in Lebanon—and the Lebanese Army on May 20. Officials initially told journalists it was for safety reasons. Journalists told CPJ at the time that they suspected the army was attempting to hinder coverage of the humanitarian crisis inside the camp, where, according to news reports, more than a dozen civilians were killed and 12,000 refugees forced to flee.

- Crews from three different television stations came under attack from civilians while covering the aftermath of a bomb blast in the mountainous town of Aley, to the east of Beirut, on the night of May 23. A crew from the Lebanese satellite-television channel New TV was interviewing residents and filming the site of the explosion when young men suspected of being loyal to anti-Syrian leader Walid Jumblatt attacked them, cameraman Ghassan al-Hagg told CPJ. New TV correspondent Christine Habib said she had been overheard saying that Lebanese residents were severely beating Syrian workers in the area in retribution for bombings. Crews from Iran's state-run Arabic-language satellite channel Al-Alam and Hezbollah's Al-Manar channel escaped unharmed.

- Photographer Wael al-Ladifi of the Lebanese daily *Al-Akhbar*, photographer Asad Ahmad of the Lebanese daily *Al-Balad*, photographer Ramzy Haidar of Agence France-Presse, and cameraman Ali Tahimi of the Iranian satellite channel Al-Alam said they were beaten by members of the Lebanese Army on May 24. The journalists told CPJ they were covering the exodus of thousands of Palestinian refugees from Nahr el-Bared to the nearby Beddawi camp when Lebanese soldiers warned them not to take pictures. The Lebanese Army Command-Orientation Department later called the journalists to apologize and assure them that those behind the beatings would be punished, the journalists said.

- On May 30, the U.N. Security Council established an international criminal tribunal to prosecute the masterminds behind the assassination of former Lebanese Prime Minister Rafiq al-Hariri, who was killed along with 22 others in a Beirut bombing in February 2005. The resolution gives the tribunal jurisdiction over the cases of several journalists targeted for assassination prior to and following al-Hariri's murder. They include Gebran Tueni, *Al-Nahar* managing director and columnist, and Samir Qassir, a prominent columnist for the daily, who were killed by bombs planted in their cars in 2005; and May Chidiac, a political talk-show host with the Lebanese Broadcasting Corporation, who lost an arm and a leg in a car bomb explosion in September of that year. All were strong critics of the Syrian regime, which was alleged to have been involved in al-Hariri's assassination. Their cases remain unsolved.

LIBYA

- A Tripoli court sentenced to death three suspected murderers of freelance journalist Daif al-Ghazal al-Shuhaibi, the journalist's brother told Agence France-Press in mid-July. Al-Ghazal's body was found in a suburb of Benghazi, about 620 miles (1,000 kilometers) east of Tripoli, in early June 2005. He had been a journalist for the government-owned daily *Azahf al-Akhdar* and a contributor to the London-based Web sites *Libya al-Youm* and *Libya Jeel*. Al-Ghazal had publicly criticized Libyan officials in his articles for the Web sites, accusing them of corruption and "stealing the public's money." Details of the prosecution were scant, prompting concern among rights groups about whether the true perpetrators had been brought to justice.

SAUDI ARABIA

- In August, the Saudi government banned the distribution and sale of the popular London-based daily *Al-Hayat* for four days due to coverage of sensitive issues in the paper's local edition, a source at the paper told CPJ. An *Al-Hayat* source told Reuters that the Information and Culture Ministry had set "conditions" for lifting the ban, but the paper refused to comply. The Associated Press reported that the ban may have been triggered by an article about a Saudi member of the al-Qaeda-affiliated Islamic State of Iraq and his close connection to clerics in the kingdom. The pan-Arab paper is owned by Prince Khaled Bin Sultan, the eldest son of Crown Prince Sultan bin Abdul Aziz.

SYRIA

- The government issued regulations in July that require Web site administrators to identify individuals posting material on their sites. The effort appeared to be aimed at deterring critical commentary. Communications Minister Amr Salem ordered all of the country's Web administrators to show "the name and e-mail of the writer of any article or comment," Human Rights Watch reported.

JOURNALIST DEATHS
HIT DECADE PEAK
. . . .

Journalists were killed in unusually high numbers in 2007, making it the deadliest year for the press in more than a decade. Worldwide, CPJ found 65 journalists were killed in direct connection to their work in 2007—up from 56 a year earlier—and it is investigating another 23 deaths to determine whether they were work-related. CPJ has recorded only one year with a higher death toll: 1994, when 66 journalists were killed, many in conflicts in Algeria, Bosnia, and Rwanda.

For the fifth straight year, Iraq was the deadliest country in the world for the press. Its 32 victims account for nearly half of the 2007 toll. Most of the victims were targeted and murdered, such as *Washington Post* reporter Salih Saif Aldin, who died in Baghdad from a single gunshot wound to the head. In all, 25 deaths in Iraq were murders and seven occurred in combat-related crossfire.

Unidentified gunmen, suicide bombers, and U.S. military activity all posed fatal risks for Iraqi journalists. All but one of the 32 journalists killed were Iraqi nationals. They worked mainly for local media, although nine worked for international news organizations such as *The New York Times*, ABC News, Reuters, and The Associated Press. The 2007 toll in Iraq is identical to that of 2006, when 32 journalists died.

Twelve media support workers, such as bodyguards and drivers, also died in Iraq. Since the beginning of the war in March 2003, 125 journalists and 49 media workers have been killed, making it the deadliest conflict for the press in recent history. More than one-third worked for international news organizations.

Somalia was the second-deadliest country for the media in 2007, with seven journalist deaths. Among them were the back-to-back assassinations of two prominent journalists. Mahad Ahmed Elmi, director of Capital Voice radio in Mogadishu, died after being shot four times in the head. Hours later, a remotely detonated landmine took the life of HornAfrik Media co-owner Ali Iman Sharmarke as he left Elmi's funeral.

Deaths spiked in Africa overall, from two in 2006 to 10 in 2007. Two journalists died in Eritrea and one in Zimbabwe in 2007.

Beneath the terrible numbers, CPJ documented some positive developments: No work-related deaths were reported in Colombia for the first time in more than 15 years, and none in the Philippines for the first time in eight years.

Murder is the leading cause of work-related deaths for journalists worldwide. Consistent with previous years, about seven in 10 journalist deaths in 2007 were murders. (Combat-related deaths and deaths in dangerous assignments account for the rest.) CPJ announced a global campaign against impunity in November to seek justice in journalist murders. The campaign focuses on the Philippines and Russia, two of the deadliest countries for the press over the past 15 years. Despite recent convictions in both countries, the impunity rate in each remains at about 90 percent.

In every region of the world, journalists who produced critical reporting or covered sensitive stories were silenced. In both Pakistan and Sri Lanka, five journalists were killed for their work. Suicide bombers caused three of the five fatalities in Pakistan, including the death of Muhammad Arif of ARY One World TV, who was among the 139 people killed when bombs exploded during the October homecoming of former Prime Minister Benazir Bhutto. In Sri Lanka, air force fighter jets bombed the Voice of Tigers radio station, killing three employees. One slaying occurred in the United States, where a masked gunman shot *Oakland Post* Editor-in-Chief Chauncey Bailey as he walked to work. Police moved quickly to apprehend the suspected gunman.

Millions of people around the globe watched the apparently deliberate killing of Japanese photographer Kenji Nagai by Burmese troops during the crackdown on antigovernment demonstrators in Rangoon. No apparent moves were made to bring his killer to justice.

The assassination of Turkish-Armenian editor Hrant Dink outside his newspaper office in Istanbul sent shock waves through the Turkish press and the international community. In Kyrgyzstan, ethnic Uzbek independent journalist Alisher Saipov was shot and killed at close range, and in Peru, popular radio commentator Miguel Pérez Julca was gunned down in front of his family.

Nepal, the Occupied Palestinian Territory, Haiti, Honduras, and Russia also made the list of places with journalist fatalities.

Media support workers were increasingly at risk; for the first time, CPJ has compiled a list of media worker deaths. Worldwide, 20 translators, fixers, guards, and drivers were killed in 2007. The victims included three Mexican newspaper delivery workers slain by drug traffickers seeking to silence their employer.

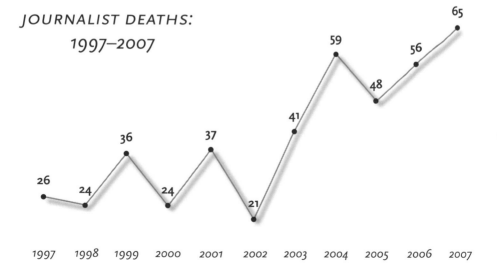

JOURNALIST DEATHS:

1997–2007

26 24 36 24 37 21 41 59 48 56 65

1997 1998 1999 2000 2001 2002 2003 2004 2005 2006 2007

Journalists who disappeared or were abducted are not included in this report. Details of those cases are available on CPJ's Web site. Five journalists were classified as missing in 2007, three of them in Mexico.

CPJ, founded in 1981, compiles and analyzes journalist deaths each year. CPJ staff applies strict criteria for each entry on the annual killed list; researchers independently investigate and verify the circumstances behind each death. CPJ considers a case work-related only when its staff is reasonably certain that a journalist was killed in direct reprisal for his or her work; in crossfire; or while carrying out a dangerous assignment.

If the motives in a killing are unclear, but it is possible that a journalist died in direct relation to his or her work, CPJ classifies the case as "unconfirmed" and continues to investigate. CPJ's list does not include journalists who died from illness or were killed in accidents—such as car or plane crashes—unless the crash was caused by hostile action. Other press organizations using different criteria cite higher numbers of deaths than CPJ.

A database of all journalists killed since 1992 is available at *www.cpj.org/deadly*.

65 JOURNALISTS KILLED: MOTIVE CONFIRMED

AFGHANISTAN: 2

Ajmal Naqshbandi, freelance
April 8, 2007, Helmand province

Taliban fighters beheaded reporter Aj-mal Naqshbandi in the Garmsir district of Helmand province after the Afghan government refused demands to free jailed Taliban leaders in exchange for the journalist's release.

Naqshbandi was abducted on March 4 with *La Repubblica* reporter Daniele Mastrogiacomo and the group's driver, Sayed Agha, in Helmand province. Agha was slain a few days after the ab-duction, while the Italian Mastrogiaco-mo was released March 19 in exchange for five Taliban prisoners.

Naqshbandi, a freelance journalist with several clients, was accompanying Mastrogiacomo on a trip to interview Taliban leaders when the kidnapping took place.

Zakia Zaki, Sada-i-Sulh
June 5, 2007, Parwan province

Unidentified gunmen shot Zaki seven times after storming into the bedroom of her home north of Kabul, according to colleagues. Zaki's six children were unharmed in the attack, which occurred near midnight. Her husband was not at home.

Zaki, 35, had launched Sada-i-Sulh, or Peace Radio, soon after the fall of the Taliban in 2001. Sada-i-Sulh became a partner in 2002 with the U.S.-based media nonprofit Internews, which had seen several of its stations come under attack. She was also a prominent lo-cal leader who was critical of warlords and represented Parwan in the national tribal assembly. She had recently been warned by local warlords to shut down the station, Rahimullah Samander, head of the Afghan Independent Jour-nalists Association, told international reporters.

Sada-i-Sulh was the only indepen-dent radio station in Parwan province. Under Zaki's direction, it covered women's issues, human rights, educa-tion, and local politics. Zaki had re-ceived several death threats over the years, and her staff had become accus-tomed to being harassed. Threats came from local community and religious leaders opposed to her political views and to the concept of a female station manager. Station staff and Internews colleagues said they were convinced that she was killed because of the stances Sada-i-Sulh had taken.

BURMA: 1

Kenji Nagai, APF News
September 27, 2007, Rangoon

Nagai, 50, who was working for the To-kyo-based video and photo agency APF

News, was killed by Burmese troops cracking down on antigovernment demonstrations in Rangoon, according to official Japanese state-run television.

Nagai appeared to be deliberately targeted by a Burmese soldier, according to video footage shown on Japan's Fuji News Network. The footage shows Nagai filming near a group of demonstrators before being pushed to the ground and shot at near point-blank range. The Japanese embassy in Burma confirmed the killing and said that the path of the bullet through Nagai's body was inconsistent with Burmese authorities' claims that Nagai died as a result of a stray shot.

The journalist had entered Burma just three days before, according to media reports.

According to the Burma Media Association and Burmese exile-run news sources, the military government disconnected nearly all mobile phone services in Rangoon on September 27. The cuts took place at 3 p.m., coinciding with the time when security forces confronted and opened fire on Buddhist monk demonstrators at Sule Pagoda in central Rangoon.

Ten people were killed in the September 27 crackdown, according to the government; diplomatic sources cited in news reports said the death toll was higher.

Troops were seen clearing demonstrators from the streets, telling protestors to leave within 10 minutes before they would open fire.

ERITREA: 2

Fesshaye "Joshua" Yohannes, *Setit*
Date unknown (death disclosed
February 2007), location unknown

Yohannes, a publisher and editor of the defunct weekly *Setit* and a recipient of CPJ's International Press Freedom Award in 2002, died in prison, several sources in the Eritrean diaspora disclosed to CPJ in February 2007. Yohannes was among 10 independent journalists rounded up in a massive 2001 government crackdown that shuttered the nation's private press.

Several sources said Yohannes died on January 11, 2007, after a long illness in an undisclosed prison outside Asmara; one source said the journalist may have died much earlier in a prison in Embatkala, 21 miles (35 kilometers) northeast of Asmara.

In a June 2007 interview, Eritrean Information Minister Ali Abdu told CPJ that he had nothing to say about Yohannes. "I don't know," he said. "This is an Eritrean issue; leave it to us. I have nothing to say."

Yohannes went by the name of "Joshua" among family and friends. Formerly a member of the guerrilla movement fighting for Eritrean independence from neighboring Ethiopia, he turned to journalism when Eritrea became a state in 1993. In November 1997, he joined *Setit* as co-owner and board member, a former colleague told CPJ. He became a popular writer, and *Setit* grew into the nation's largest-circulation newspaper.

Setit's staff tackled tough issues in the young nation, including poverty, prostitution, and Eritrea's lack of infrastructure for handicapped veterans of the 30-year independence struggle. The weekly's criticism angered the government, and by May 2001, Yohannes asked CPJ to help him create a journalists' union to improve press freedom conditions.

He and other journalists never got the chance. President Isaias Afewerki's government launched a crackdown on all critical voices, including those in the press, just one week after the September 11, 2001, attacks on the United States had diverted the world's attention. Under the pretext of combating terrorism, the government shut down every independent media outlet and arrested independent journalists on sight.

At the time, he and other imprisoned journalists still had contact with the outside world. In May 2002, Yohannes and several other colleagues staged a hunger strike in hopes of spurring their release. Instead, government officials transferred the journalists to undisclosed locations. Online news reports, which have not been confirmed, suggest that as many as three other journalists also may have died in government custody. The other jailed journalists continued to be held incommunicado in secret jails throughout 2007, according to CPJ research.

Paulos Kidane
Eri-TV and Dimtsi Hafash
June 2007, northwest Eritrea

Kidane, a presenter with the Amharic service of state broadcaster Eri-TV and state Radio Dimtsi Hafash (Voice of the Broad Masses), died in unknown circumstances after setting out on foot to cross into Sudan with a group of seven asylum-seekers, according to several CPJ sources. Kidane sought to leave Eritrea because of years of professional repression, according to family, colleagues, and personal notes he sent out of the country that were reviewed by CPJ.

Kidane's companions were forced to leave him in the care of residents of a village in northwest Eritrea after the journalist collapsed from seven days of walking in temperatures of more than 100 degrees, according to a woman who traveled with him and who spoke with CPJ through an interpreter. He was suffering from severe foot blisters and had an epileptic seizure, she said. Kidane's condition was not critical when the group left him, the woman insisted, saying that even in the event of complications, he would have survived had he received proper medical care. She believed Kidane may have been captured by government security forces. The village in which he was left is believed to be populated by government informants.

In a telephone interview with CPJ in August, Eritrean Information Minister Ali Abdu acknowledged that the journalist died while attempting to leave the country, but he offered no information about the circumstances. "We don't know," he said.

Kidane's passions for sports, particularly soccer, and poetry had led him to begin his journalism career as a freelance sportswriter in his native Ethiopia in the mid-1990s, according to his brother. In May 1998, at the outbreak of the border war, he was among more than 65,000 people of Eritrean descent deported from Ethiopia. He became the sports editor of the now-defunct independent weekly *Admas* in the Eritrean capital, Asmara, according to exiled *Admas* founder Khaled Abdu. In 2000, authorities exploited his skill in Amharic and knowledge of Ethiopia by conscripting him into state media service to broadcast anti-Ethiopian propaganda, and as a film and stage actor playing the roles of villainous Ethiopian military officers. In November 2006, he was among nine state media journalists summarily detained for several weeks without charge, according to CPJ research.

Kidane, 40, was survived by a wife and infant daughter, according to his brother.

HAITI: 1

Jean-Rémy Badio, freelance
January 19, 2007, Port-au-Prince

Badio, a freelance photographer, was gunned down outside his home in the southern Port-au-Prince neighborhood of Martissant, Haitian press freedom advocate Guyler Delva told CPJ. Gang members were suspected in the shooting, said Fred Blaise, a U.N. spokesman.

Badio photographed gang confrontations in Martissant, where he lived with his family, and sold them to local dailies, including the Port-au-Prince newspaper *Le Matin*. Badio was a member of Delva's press group, SOS Journalistes, and the Haitian Association of Photojournalists.

Rival gangs had been battling in Martissant for months, The Associated Press reported. According to the Port-au-Prince-based Radio Métropole, the escalating gang violence made Martissant one of the most dangerous neighborhoods in the Haitian capital. Delva said gang members seldom allow journalists to take their pictures for fear of being identified by local authorities. According to colleagues interviewed by CPJ, Badio had received threats from local gang members beginning in October 2006.

Prime Minister Jacques Edouard Alexis said he had authorized U.N. peacekeepers to increase patrols in Martissant. Still, Badio's wife and children were forced to flee their home after receiving further threats from Martissant's gangs, Delva told CPJ.

HONDURAS: 1

Carlos Salgado, Radio Cadena Voces
October 18, 2007, Tegucigalpa

Unidentified individuals intercepted Salgado, host of the radio program "Frijol el Terrible," as he was leaving the studios of Radio Cadena Voces at 4 p.m.

The assailants shot Salgado at close range at least seven times and sped away in a gray Toyota 4Runner, according to witnesses quoted in local press reports.

Dagoberto Rodríguez, director of Radio Cadena Voces, said he believed the killing was in retaliation for the station's critical reporting on official corruption. The Honduran Commissioner of Human Rights, Ramón Custodio López, told CPJ no other motive had come to light. Police said Salgado's murder was unrelated to his work, but they did not disclose any other motives, local press freedom advocate Thelma Mejía told CPJ.

Salgado, 67, was noted for his satirical criticism of the country's political system, according to Rodríguez. His show combined humor with coverage of everyday problems, such as the prices of food and transportation. "Frijol el Terrible," which was on the air for more than 20 years, reached a nationwide audience, Rodríguez said. He described Salgado as respected by his colleagues and admired by his listeners.

Rodríguez told CPJ that Radio Cadena Voces had been harassed continuously for its reporting on government corruption. Over the last two years, he said, hackers had repeatedly erased information on the radio station's Web site, the staff had received anonymous telephone threats, and at least one journalist had been attacked by a local government official. Rodríguez and his family were themselves forced to flee Honduras on November 1, after police informed the journalist that his name had appeared on a hit list, Custodio told CPJ.

Sandra Aguilar, the victim's wife, described Salgado as a quiet man who divided his time between the radio station and his small study at home. Aguilar told CPJ her husband had never had problems or received any threats. Several days after Salgado's murder, hundreds of journalists protested in the streets of Tegucigalpa. They called on local authorities to ensure justice.

On October 26, authorities arrested German David Almendárez Amador after witnesses identified him as the gunman, the Tegucigalpa-based daily *El Heraldo* reported. Almendárez was not immediately charged but was placed in preventive detention. Almendárez and his family insisted that he was innocent and had an alibi, local news reports said.

IRAQ: 32

Ahmed Hadi Naji
Associated Press Television News
January 5, 2007, Baghdad

Naji, 28, a cameraman for Associated Press Television News, was found in a Baghdad morgue with a gunshot wound to the back of the head, six days after he had gone missing.

The journalist left his home in southwest Baghdad's Ashurta al-Khamsa district for work on the morning of December 30, 2006, AP reported. His wife, Sahba'a Mudhar Khalil, reported him missing that evening, the news agency said. The circumstances surrounding his death were unclear, according to AP. A coroner's report could not pinpoint a date of death, a CPJ source said.

The source said Naji had received telephone threats a year previous, prompting him to move his family to a safer location. Naji also worked as a messenger for the news agency.

Naji was the second AP employee killed in less than four weeks. On December 12, 2006, Aswan Ahmed Lutfallah, 35, was gunned down by insurgents while filming clashes between Iraqi police and insurgents in the northern city of Mosul.

Falah Khalaf al-Diyali, *Al-Sa'a*
January 15, 2007, Ramadi

Several gunmen in a car followed al-Diyali, a photographer for the Baghdad-based newspaper *Al-Sa'a*, and then shot him in Ramadi's central neighborhood of Malaab, a journalist familiar with the case told CPJ. Al-Diyali died at the scene, the journalist said.

Just before he was killed, al-Diyali photographed damage to the central mosque in Ramadi caused by a U.S. bombardment the previous day, the source said. Witnesses said al-Diyali was being watched while he was taking photographs. The gunmen caught up with al-Diyali after he drove away from the mosque, the source told CPJ.

Al-Sa'a was established immediately after Saddam Hussein's overthrow in 2003. It is a political and social weekly owned by prominent Sunni cleric Ah-

mad Kubeisi. Al-Diyala also contributed photographs on a freelance basis to the state-run daily *Al-Sabah*, the source said.

Hussein al-Zubaidi, *Al-Ahali*
January 28, 2007, Baghdad

Gunmen abducted al-Zubaidi, an editor for the independent weekly *Al-Ahali*, in early morning in Baghdad's eastern neighborhood of Al-Saleekh, a source at the paper told CPJ. Although there are conflicting dates for al-Zubaidi's death, the source said he was killed on January 28. People identifying themselves as the abductors contacted al-Zubaidi's family and demanded $20,000 but could not provide proof that the journalist was alive, the source said. Iraqi police notified the family the following day that al-Zubaidi's body had been found.

Two sources at the paper told CPJ that they believed al-Zubaidi was targeted for his work. One of them said that the journalist was active in his profession, carrying a press card and frequently visiting government ministries and civil society organizations. The other source said no other motive for his killing was evident.

Al-Zubaidi, who was born in 1953, specialized in investigative reporting, a source at the paper said. He also covered civil society organizations and higher education, and worked as head of information at Baghdad University's College of Dentistry.

Abdulrazak Hashim Ayal al-Khakani
Jumhuriyat al-Iraq
February 5, 2007, Baghdad

Iraqi police discovered the body of al-Khakani, 45, an editor and news presenter at Jumhuriyat al-Iraq radio, and that of his cousin, in Baghdad's western neighborhood of Al-Jihad. The bodies had several gunshot wounds, al-Khakani's brother, Majid, told CPJ.

Gunmen abducted the two on February 4.

The family identified the journalist on February 19 in Baghdad's Al-Tib al-Adli morgue. The abductors had taken his identification cards, the brother said.

The kidnappers spoke several times with the family using al-Khakani's cell phone. Majid al-Khakani told CPJ that the kidnappers told him they killed al-Khakani because he was a journalist who was harming Iraq. They identified themselves as belonging to al-Qaeda in Iraq.

Al-Khakani had returned to Iraq in 2003 after spending 21 years as a prisoner of war in Iran following his capture in 1982 during the Iran-Iraq war. Al-Khakani presented a news show for the radio station that addressed government and politics, Majid al-Khakani told CPJ.

Radio Jumhuriyat al-Iraq is part of the state-run Iraqi Media Network. Insurgents have frequently targeted state-run media because of their ties to the U.S.-supported Iraqi government.

Jamal al-Zubaidi
As-Saffir and Al-Dustour
February 24, 2007, Baghdad

The body of al-Zubaidi, 56, an economics editor for the Baghdad-based dailies As-Saffir and Al-Dustour, was identified by his family in a Baghdad morgue. Al-Zubaidi's son, Riyah, told CPJ that police found the editor's body with gunshot wounds to the head in Baghdad's southwestern neighborhood of Al-Aamal.

Al-Zubaidi's identification cards and cell phone were taken by the gunmen. He was last seen leaving As-Saffir's offices in the central Karada neighborhood around 1 p.m. on February 24.

Al-Zubaidi had worked for As-Saffir and Al-Dustour for three years. Two journalists for As-Saffir were killed by gunmen in September 2005 in Mosul. Another was kidnapped and held for ransom for nearly three weeks in March 2006.

Mohan Hussein al-Dhahir
Al-Mashreq
March 4, 2007, Baghdad

Several gunmen in two vehicles attempted to abduct al-Dhahir, 49, managing editor of the Baghdad daily Al-Mashreq, at 8:30 a.m. while he waited outside his home in Baghdad's Al-Jamia neighborhood for the paper's car to pick him up for work, according to sources at the paper. After a struggle, the sources said, the gunmen shot al-Dhahir six times in the back and once in the head.

Al-Mashreq is a privately owned, widely read Baghdad newspaper that publishes commentary critical of the government, according to local journalists. The paper had received numerous warnings to stop publishing, local journalists said. Al-Dhahir worked nearly four years for the paper.

Yussef Sabri, Biladi
March 7, 2007, Baghdad

Sabri, 26, a cameraman for the Biladi satellite channel, was among several journalists filming pilgrims traveling southwest from Baghdad to the Shiite holy city of Karbala, according to sources at the station. Iraqi security forces had set up checkpoints to safeguard the way for the pilgrims. Sabri and other journalists were traveling in a convoy with Brig. Gen. Qassim Atta al-Mussawi, Iraqi spokesman for the Baghdad security plan, who was reviewing the checkpoints.

Sources at the station told CPJ that an explosives-laden car appeared from a side road in the Al-Saydiya neighborhood of Baghdad's Al-Rasheed district and fired at the convoy. The car accelerated, hit the last vehicle in the convoy, and blew up. Sabri and the others in the vehicle were killed in the blast, the sources said. The U.S. military said 12 Iraqi soldiers were killed, according to The Associated Press.

Al-Qaeda in Iraq was suspected of carrying out the attack since it controlled the Al-Rasheed district, a hotbed of violence. Sabri had worked for six months at Biladi, an independent channel with a pro-government editorial line established by former Iraqi Prime Minister Ibrahim al-Jaafari.

Hamid al-Duleimi, Nahrain
March 17, 2007, Baghdad

Gunmen abducted al-Duleimi, a producer for the privately owned Nahrain satellite channel, as he left work in Baghdad's Al-Aamel neighborhood, a source at Nahrain told CPJ. He had driven only about 650 feet (200 meters) from the station when he was seized.

Late that night, eyewitnesses saw his body being thrown on a pile of garbage in a neighborhood alley, according to the station source. Family and colleagues identified al-Duleimi two days later at a Baghdad hospital morgue. The source said al-Duleimi had several gunshot wounds to the head, and his body showed signs of torture, including multiple burns and broken hands, legs, and neck.

Al-Duleimi, born in 1977, was survived by his then-pregnant wife and three children, another source at the station said. Al-Aamel neighborhood was controlled by the Mahdi Army, led by radical Shiite cleric Muqtada al-Sadr, a local journalist told CPJ.

Thaer Ahmad Jaber, Baghdad TV
April 5, 2007, Baghdad

A suicide attacker driving a garbage truck packed with explosives set off a blast near the main entrance of Baghdad TV's offices on April 5, killing Deputy Director Jaber and injuring 12 employees, according to CPJ sources and a statement by the Iraqi Islamic Party.

The Journalistic Freedoms Observatory, an Iraqi press freedom organization, reported that the attackers fired at the station's guards, clearing the way for the truck. The front of the building, which housed the Sunni Iraqi Islamic Party-owned Baghdad TV and Radio Dar al-Salam, was destroyed along with several station and employee vehicles, according to news reports. The main transmission equipment was damaged, briefly interrupting broadcasts.

Jaber often helped CPJ document attacks against journalists in Iraq. CPJ learned of Jaber's death after calling his cell phone and being informed by a family member that he had been killed.

Khamail Khalaf, Radio Free Iraq
April 5, 2007, Baghdad

Radio Free Iraq reporter Khalaf, who was kidnapped April 3 from Baghdad's Yarmouk district, was found dead in the city's Al-Jamia neighborhood on April 5, according to Radio Free Europe/ Radio Liberty and CPJ sources. Police received an anonymous call informing them that there was a body on the street. They came under heavy fire by unidentified assailants when they went to retrieve the body, according to RFE/ RL and CPJ sources.

RFE/RL reported that an unidentified caller used Khalaf's cell phone to contact her family, but no demands for ransom were made. Khalaf had received prior threats, according to RFE/RL. It was not clear if the threats were directly work-related.

Khalaf had reported on social and cultural life in Iraq for Radio Free Iraq since 2004, according to a statement by RFE/RL. Radio Free Iraq is the Arabic language service of RFE/RL in Iraq, broadcasting from the network's headquarters in Prague, Czech Republic.

Othman al-Mashhadani, Al-Watan
April 6, 2007, Baghdad

The body of al-Mashhadani, 29, was found by Iraqi security forces in Baghdad's northwestern district of Al-Shoula three days after he was abducted.

Al-Mashhadani, a reporter for Saudi Arabia's daily newspaper Al-Watan, was abducted on his way home from work between the northwestern Baghdad districts of Al-Shoula and Al-Ghazaliya, according to CPJ sources. Colleagues told CPJ that al-Mashhadani was on assignment covering the Baghdad security plan and its effects on the Mahdi Army, led by radical Shiite cleric Muqtada al-Sadr.

Al-Mashhadani was shot in the head and chest; his body showed signs of torture and the fingers on his right hand were broken, according to CPJ sources and the Journalistic Freedoms Observatory, an Iraqi press freedom organization. His captors called his family hours after his abduction demanding a ransom, but there was no further communication, the organization reported.

The Mahdi Army had a stronghold in Al-Shoula while the predominantly Sunni district of Al-Ghazaliya was under the control of the Islamic Army, the largest Sunni insurgent group.

A colleague told CPJ that al-Mashhadani reported on the activities of the Islamic Army and other militias. Al-Mashhadani began work for *Al-Watan* in October 2006, according to an article published by the paper. He had also worked as a freelance reporter for the prominent pan-Arab weekly magazine *Al-Watan al-Arabi* since 2005.

Khaled Fayyad Obaid al-Hamdani
Nahrain
April 12, 2007, Abu Ghraib

Al-Hamdani, a producer for the privately owned Nahrain satellite channel, was killed in a shooting that involved U.S. military forces, according to a station source and a relative. Al-Hamdani was driving at high speed from his home in Abu Ghraib to work in Baghdad when troops opened fire, the relative told CPJ. The source said al-Hamdani had often driven at high speed to minimize danger; the military patrol was apparently alarmed by the rate of speed. The road, a main access to Baghdad, was so notoriously dangerous that it was called the Highway of Death.

The relative told CPJ that his account was based on conversations with U.S. military personnel and eyewitnesses. A U.S. military spokesman said the military had no record of the shooting.

Al-Hamadani, 36, prepared documentary and cultural programs for the channel. He was survived by a wife and children.

Dmitry Chebotayev, freelance
May 6, 2007, Diyala

Chebotayev was the first Russian journalist to be killed in Iraq after the U.S.-led invasion of March 2003. A freelance photographer embedded with U.S. forces, Chebotayev was killed along with six American soldiers when a roadside bomb struck a U.S. military vehicle in Diyala province, northeast of Baghdad.

Chebotayev was on assignment for the Russian edition of *Newsweek* magazine, reporting on the efforts of U.S. forces to control roads in Diyala province, Leonid Parfyonov, the edition editor, told CPJ. Chebotayev, 29, had freelanced for several news agencies, including the German-based European Pressphoto Agency and the independent Moscow daily *Kommersant*. He had been in Iraq for more than two months.

Raad Mutashar, Al-Raad
May 9, 2007, outside Kirkuk

Gunmen riding in an Opel without a license plate intercepted a vehicle carrying Mutashar, 43, owner and director of a media company, on a road southwest of Kirkuk at around 2 p.m., a company source told CPJ. The source said the gunmen shot Mutashar, driver Imad Abdul-Razzaq al-Obaid, and passengers Nibras Abdul-Razzaq al-Obaid and Aqil Abdul-Qadir. The Associated Press first reported the attack.

Mutashar's company, Al-Raad, published a weekly newspaper, *Al-Iraq Ghadan*, and a related institute operated a news agency and a media education center. A CPJ source said Mutashar was a prominent writer, poet, and journalist who started the company four years earlier.

The CPJ source said Mutashar's son was kidnapped more than a year previous but was released after a ransom was paid. The kidnappers told Mutashar that his journalistic work had prompted the abduction, the source said.

Imad Abdul-Razzaq al-Obaid and Nibras Abdul-Razzaq al-Obaid were Mutashar's brothers-in-law.

Alaa Uldeen Aziz, ABC News
Saif Laith Yousuf, ABC News
May 17, 2007, Baghdad

Gunmen in two cars ambushed and killed cameraman Aziz, 33, and soundman Yousuf, 26, on their way home from the network's Baghdad bureau, ABC News reported. ABC said Aziz was survived by a wife and two daughters, while Yousuf was set to marry his fiancée.

Nazar Abdulwahid al-Radhi
Aswat al-Iraq and Radio Free Iraq
May 30, 2007, Al-Amarah

Al-Radhi, 38, a correspondent for the independent news agency Aswat al-Iraq and Radio Free Iraq, was gunned down in the southern city of Al-Amarah in Maysan province. Three men wearing white uniforms and riding in a pickup truck killed al-Radhi outside the Al-Arusa Hotel in the city's center, Saad Hassan, an eyewitness and reporter for the daily newspaper *Al-Sabah*, told Aswat al-Iraq.

Al-Radhi had finished covering a journalism workshop for Radio Free Iraq, according to a statement by its parent, the U.S. government-funded Radio Free Europe/Radio Liberty (RFE/RL). Hassan told Aswat al-Iraq that al-Radhi was talking to a workshop leader when the gunmen began firing. RFE/RL said al-Radhi was shot four times and died at the scene; several other journalists were injured. Eyewitnesses said nearby Iraqi police did not intervene during the attack, Aswat al-Iraq reported.

RFE/RL reported that al-Radhi had received prior threats because of his work for a "foreign agency." Radio Free Iraq is the Arabic-language service of RFE/RL in Iraq, broadcasting from the network's headquarters in Prague, Czech Republic.

Mohammad Hilal Karji, Baghdad TV
June 6, 2007, Yusufiya

Karji, a correspondent for the Jordan-based satellite channel Baghdad TV, and his cousin were traveling to Baghdad for work when they were stopped at an Iraqi Army checkpoint in the town of Yusufiya, about 12 miles south of Baghdad, according to a source at the station who requested anonymity. The two were handed over to armed men who claimed to be security officers and who were in a car stationed by the checkpoint, the source said.

Karji and his cousin tried to escape, but only the cousin was able to flee, the source said.

The gunmen were suspected members of the Mahdi Army, a militia led by radical Shiite cleric Muqtada al-Sadr, according to the source at the station. The source said that Karji was shot in the head and that the body showed signs of torture.

Karji was believed to be killed because of his affiliation with Baghdad TV, where he worked for two years, the source told CPJ. The channel, owned by the Iraqi Islamic Party, a large Sunni political group, had lost at least seven other employees since June 2005. The channel had been attacked by a truck laden with explosives in one incident and shelled by insurgents in another. The attacks forced the channel to relocate its main headquarters to Jordan.

Sahar Hussein Ali al-Haydari
National Iraqi News Agency and Aswat al-Iraq, June 7, 2007, Mosul

Al-Haydari, 44, was shopping in Mosul's Al-Hadbaa neighborhood when four unidentified gunmen got out of their vehicle, gunned her down, and fled the scene, taking her cell phone with them, local journalists told CPJ.

Earlier, she had been reporting news of a suicide attack on a police station in the nearby town of Al-Rabiya, according to the National Iraqi News Agency. When a police captain called to give her more information, the killers answered her phone, telling him, "She went to hell," according to a local journalist who spoke with the captain.

Al-Haydari had previously told CPJ that she had received many death threats. In early 2006, she was twice targeted for abduction; one attempt failed, and she was rescued the other time. In March 2006, al-Haydari told CPJ she had been shot, requiring surgery. In August 2006, gunmen killed her daughter's fiancé.

In her final e-mail to CPJ, on March 22, al-Haydari said her name was on a death list composed of journalists and police officers. It had been circulated throughout Mosul and posted on her house door. According to the independent news agency Aswat al-Iraq, the list was issued by the "Emir of the Islamic State in Mosul," the local leader of the al-Qaeda-affiliated Islamic State in Iraq.

Al-Haydari was a correspondent for the National Iraqi News Agency and Aswat al-Iraq, and a contributor to a number of other Iraqi media outlets. She also was a journalist trainee and correspondent for the London-based Institute for War and Peace Reporting, an organization that trains local journalists in war coverage. She visited CPJ's offices in New York in late 2005, and CPJ helped relocate her husband and four children to Damascus, Syria, after she received death threats.

Aref Ali Filaih, Aswat al-Iraq
June 11, 2007, Al-Khalis

Filaih, correspondent for the independent news agency Aswat al-Iraq, was killed by a roadside bomb while driving to an assignment south of Al-Khalis in Diyala province, Aswat al-Iraq reported. Filaih, 32, had worked as Aswat al-Iraq's correspondent in the violence-plagued province since December 2006, the news agency said.

Filaih Wuday Mijthab, *Al-Sabah* June 17, 2007, Baghdad

Mijthab's body was found in Baghdad's main morgue four days after he was abducted by armed men. Mijthab, who worked with the government-run daily *Al-Sabah*, suffered bullet wounds to the head, the independent news agency Voices of Iraq reported. There was no claim of responsibility.

Insurgent and other armed groups have frequently targeted *Al-Sabah* and other state-run media because of their ties to the U.S.-supported Iraqi government. *The New York Times* reported that Mijthab could have been targeted by Shiite groups because of his past work for state-run media under the former Iraqi leader Saddam Hussein. Mijthab, like many of the newspaper's employees, had received numerous telephone threats while working at *Al-Sabah*, the paper reported.

Gunmen in three vehicles intercepted Mijthab, 53, as he was traveling to work in Baghdad's eastern Shiite neighborhood of Al-Habibiya. Mijthab, who was with his eldest son and a driver, was ordered out of the vehicle at gunpoint, according to the Journalistic Freedoms Observatory, an Iraqi press freedom organization. Mijthab was taken to an un-

known location; his son and the driver were not seized.

Hamid Abed Sarhan, freelance June 26, 2007, Baghdad

A car carrying several gunmen intercepted Sarhan, a freelance journalist and a public relations director at Baghdad's municipal secretariat, while he was driving home from work in Baghdad's Al-Saydiya neighborhood, a local journalist familiar with the case told CPJ. The gunmen shot the journalist and sped away.

Iraqi police were about 1,000 feet (300 meters) from the shooting and responded quickly to the scene, the source said. Police called Sarhan's sons, who identified the body.

Several CPJ sources familiar with the case said that Sarhan's work was the only plausible motive for his killing. Sarhan was a well-known journalist who worked as a managing editor at the Iraqi News Agency until the U.S.-led invasion of Iraq in March 2003, according to CPJ sources. Since then, he worked as managing editor for the independent daily *Al-Mashriq* and the now-defunct weekly *Al-Wihda al-Wataniya*. He was the editor-in-chief of the now-defunct weekly *Iraqiyoun*. In 2005, Sarhan became the managing editor of Baghdad's municipal secretariat weekly *Sawt Baghdad*. He later became a public relations director for the secretariat.

Sarhan freelanced for several national and international Arabic-language newspapers, including the Iraqi dailies

Azzaman and *Al-Mashriq*, according to the CPJ source. He also appeared as an analyst on several programs for Iraqi satellite channels such as Al-Baghdadia and Al-Sharqiya. He regularly wrote articles and reports for *Sawt Baghdad* as part of his job for the secretariat, the source said.

Al-Saydiya, located in the Al-Rasheed district controlled by al-Qaeda in Iraq, was a hotbed of violence at the time.

Sarmad Hamdi Shaker, Baghdad TV
June 27, 2007, Baghdad

Shaker, 43, a correspondent for the satellite channel Baghdad TV, left his home in Baghdad's Al-Jamia neighborhood for work on the morning of June 27. He was waiting on the street for a friend to pick him up, a source at the station told CPJ, when a car carrying several gunmen came alongside and two armed occupants asked him to get in for questioning, the source said. His body was found on the street in the same neighborhood that afternoon, according to the source.

Shaker's wife and three children fled the neighborhood and moved north of Baghdad.

The source said the gunmen were suspected members of al-Qaeda in Iraq, and that Shaker was killed because he worked for Baghdad TV, a moderate Sunni channel that has been repeatedly targeted by both Sunni and Shiite extremist groups, according to staff.

Shaker worked at Baghdad TV for two years, the source told CPJ. The channel, owned by the Iraqi Islamic Party, a large Sunni political group, had lost at least seven other employees since June 2005.

Namir Noor-Eldeen, Reuters
July 12, 2007, Baghdad

Photographer Noor-Eldeen, 22, was killed in eastern Baghdad during what witnesses described as a U.S. helicopter attack. The strike claimed the lives of 10 other Iraqis in the Al-Amin al-Thaniyah neighborhood, Reuters reported, citing a preliminary Iraqi police report. The victims included Noor-Eldeen's driver and camera assistant, Saeed Chmagh.

Witnesses told Reuters that Noor-Eldeen and Chmagh arrived in the neighborhood about the time a U.S. helicopter fired on a minivan. Video footage showed that the minivan was destroyed, Reuters reported. Initial reports suggested that the air strike took place during clashes between U.S. forces and insurgents, but witnesses later said there were no clashes, according to Reuters.

The Multi-National Force-Iraq press desk in Baghdad did not respond to CPJ's telephone and e-mail inquiries seeking comment. Four other Reuters employees had been killed on assignment in Iraq, among the largest losses suffered by an international news organization in the conflict, CPJ research shows.

Khalid W. Hassan
The New York Times
July 13, 2007, Baghdad

Khalid W. Hassan, 23, a reporter and interpreter, was shot while driving to work in the south central Seiydia district, the newspaper reported. He had called the bureau to say that he was taking an alternative route because his usual way was blocked by a security checkpoint, the newspaper said. The *Times* reported that the journalist called his mother a half hour later to say, "I've been shot." The family notified the newspaper that Hassan later died.

An Iraqi of Palestinian descent, Hassan had worked for the *Times'* Baghdad bureau since fall 2003, the newspaper said. He was survived by his mother and four sisters. He was the second *New York Times* employee killed on assignment in Iraq, CPJ research shows. *Times* reporter Fakher Haider, 38, was killed in Basra in September 2005.

"Khalid was part of a large, sometimes unsung, community of Iraqi news-gatherers, translators, and support staff, who take enormous risks every day to help us comprehend their country's struggle and torment," Bill Keller, executive editor of the *Times*, said in a statement.

Mustafa Gaimayani
Kirkuk al-Yawm and *Hawal*
Majeed Mohammed
Kirkuk al-Yawm and *Hawal*
July 16, 2007, Kirkuk

A triple bomb attack in the northern Iraqi city of Kirkuk killed at least 85 people, including editor Gaimayani and reporter Mohammed, and wounded more than 180 others.

A suicide attacker driving a truck packed with explosives detonated the vehicle near one of the offices of Iraqi President Jalal Talabani's party, the Patriotic Union of Kurdistan, in central Kirkuk, according to international news reports.

The blast damaged several adjacent buildings, including the offices of the Kirkuk Cultural and Social Association, killing Gaimayani, an editor for *Kirkuk al-Yawm*, and Mohammed, a sports reporter for the paper, Hashwan Dawoudi, deputy head of the association, told CPJ.

The association, which is funded by the Kurdistan Regional Government, publishes the weekly newspaper *Kirkuk al-Yawm* and the quarterly *Kirkuk* magazine, Dawoudi said.

At the time of the blast Mohammed and Gaimayani were preparing the weekly for publication, Dawoudi said. Seven other editors, including the editors-in-chief of both *Kirkuk al-Yawm* and *Kirkuk* were wounded in the explosion, he added.

Mohammed was also a correspondent and Gaimayani a writer for the Kurdish-language weekly *Hawal*, Dawoudi told CPJ. Seven years ago, Dawoudi established the Hawal Media Foundation, which published four newspapers, including *Hawal* and the Arabic-language weekly *Al-Naba*.

Gaimayani, who was also known as Mustafa Darwish, was in his mid-40s. He was a dual national with Swedish citizenship who moved with his family to Sweden in 1981 and returned to northern Iraq about four months earlier to work for the Hawal Media Foundation, Dawoudi told CPJ. Mohammed was in his mid-30s.

Adnan al-Safi, Al-Anwar
July 27, 2007, Baghdad

An unidentified gunman shot al-Safi, a correspondent for the Kuwait-based Al-Anwar satellite channel, outside the channel's offices in Baghdad's north-central neighborhood of Al-Etifiyah, according to Bassem al-Safi, a member of the reporter's extended family and a fellow journalist.

Adnan Al-Safi had just finished work and was waiting for a public van to take him home when the shooting occurred at 3 p.m. on July 25, the relative said. Al-Safi, shot in the head, was taken to a Baghdad hospital, where he died 48 hours later.

Bassem al-Safi told CPJ that the journalist appeared to be targeted; bystanders were uninjured. He told the Journalistic Freedoms Observatory, an Iraqi press freedom organization, that an armed group had been seen in the station's neighborhood. Al-Anwar is a moderate Shiite satellite channel focusing on Islamic culture and issues.

Adnan al-Safi founded and headed the Islamic Press Union in 2005, which held workshops and lectures on television, radio, and print journalism, said the relative, a fellow member of the union. The victim, who was in his late 30s, also worked for radio station Sawt al-Iraq and served as an adviser in the Iraqi Journalists Syndicate, according to the Journalistic Freedoms Observatory. He was survived by a wife and three children.

Amer Malallah al-Rashidi
Al-Mosuliya
September 3, 2007, Mosul

Al-Rashidi, 42, a camera operator for the private satellite channel Al-Mosuliya, left a relative's house in Mosul's eastern Al-Jazair neighborhood in the evening to catch a taxi when gunmen in a car opened fire, a source at the station told CPJ. The source said that after al-Rashidi fell to the ground, one of the gunmen got out of the car and shot him at close range.

The source, who asked not to be identified, believed that al-Rashidi was targeted because he was a journalist. Al-Rashidi was a well-known camera operator in Mosul, a place where armed groups have frequently targeted journalists. Al-Rashidi did not report receiving death threats prior to the shooting, the source told CPJ.

Before joining Al-Mosuliya, al-Rashidi worked for the state-run Al-Iraqiya channel, according to the source at the station. Al-Mosuliya was established about a year earlier to cover news in Nineveh province.

Muhannad Ghanem Ahmad al-Obaidi
Dar al-Salam
September 20, 2007, Mosul

Gunmen believed to be affiliated with al-Qaeda in Iraq killed al-Obaidi, 25, a presenter and producer for the Iraqi Islamic Party-owned radio Dar al-Salam, according to a source at the station. Al-Obaidi was heading home when a car intercepted him and a gunman emerged, the source said.

Police Brig. Abdul Karim al-Jubouri told the independent news agency Aswat al-Iraq that "the gunmen opened fire on the journalist, near Thiyab al-Iraqi Mosque in al-Moharibeen area." The Journalistic Freedoms Observatory, a local press freedom organization, reported that al-Obaidi resisted the gunmen when they attempted to abduct him, which led to his killing.

Al-Obaidi worked on social programs for Dar al-Salam, al-Jubouri said, adding that he was also a preacher at Mosul's Bazwayah Mosque, Aswat al-Iraq reported.

The source told CPJ that Dar al-Salam had received prior threats. Dar al-Salam and Baghdad TV, both owned by the Iraqi Islamic Party, a large Sunni political group, have been regularly targeted by insurgents. In April, a suicide attacker driving a garbage truck packed with explosives blew up the front of the building that houses Baghdad TV and Dar al-Salam in Baghdad.

Salih Saif Aldin
The Washington Post
October 14, 2007, Baghdad

Saif Aldin, 32, was killed at close range by a single gunshot to the head while photographing fire-damaged houses on a street in Baghdad's southern neighbor-hood of Al-Saydiya, the *Post* reported. Saif Aldin was on assignment interviewing residents about sectarian violence raging between Shiite militias and Sunni insurgents in the neighborhood, long a center of violence, the newspaper said. The *Post* reported that a man used Saif Aldin's cell phone to inform an employee at the paper that the journalist was killed.

Post Baghdad Bureau Chief Sudarsan Raghavan told CPJ that it was murky as to who shot Saif Aldin and why. Some residents suspected that the Iraqi Army, some of whose members were loyal to the Mahdi Army, a militia led by radical Shiite cleric Muqtada al-Sadr, was responsible for the slaying, the *Post* reported. Iraqi police said they suspected Sunni gunmen from the Awakening Council, a group consisting of Sunni tribes working alongside U.S. forces, the *Post* said.

Saif Aldin, who wrote under the pseudonym Salih Dehema for security purposes, began his journalism career as a reporter for the weekly *Al-Iraq al-Yawm* in Tikrit, and joined the *Post* in January 2004 as a stringer, the newspaper said. Saif Aldin had been arrested, beaten, and threatened while carrying out his assignments.

Leonard Downie Jr., executive editor of the *Post*, called Saif Aldin a "brave and valuable reporter who contributed much to our coverage of Iraq." Saif Aldin was known for his tenacity and his willingness to take assignments that put him in harm's way, the *Post* reported.

Shehab Mohammad al-Hiti
Baghdad al-Youm
October 28, 2007, Baghdad

Al-Hiti, 27, an editor for the fledgling weekly *Baghdad al-Youm*, was last seen leaving his home in Baghdad's western neighborhood of Al-Jamia to go to the paper's offices around midday, a source at the paper told CPJ. Iraqi security forces found the journalist's body later that afternoon in Baghdad's northeastern Ur neighborhood and transported it to Baghdad's Al-Tib al-Adli Hospital morgue, the source said.

A local journalist told CPJ that Ur neighborhood is adjacent to Baghdad's Sadr City, controlled by the Mahdi Army, led by radical Shiite cleric Muqtada al-Sadr. The CPJ source said that he was not aware of any prior death threats against the journalist. *Baghdad al-Youm* had been publishing for only three weeks.

KYRGYZSTAN: 1

Alisher Saipov, *Siyosat*
October 24, 2007, Osh

Saipov, editor of the independent Uzbek-language weekly *Siyosat* (Politics) and contributor to several regional news outlets, was shot three times at close range at around 7 p.m. in downtown Osh, a city bordering Uzbekistan, by an unknown gunman using a silencer, according to news reports and CPJ sources. He died at the scene.

Saipov, 26, covered Uzbekistan's political and social landscape for Radio Free Europe/Radio Liberty, Voice of America, and the Central Asia news Web site *Ferghana*. He had interviewed members of the banned Islamic groups Hizb-ut Tahrir and the Islamic Movement of Uzbekistan, according to local CPJ sources. Exiled opposition activist Shakhida Yakub, who was close to Saipov, told The Associated Press that the journalist had recently become politically involved with Uzbek opposition groups.

An ethnic Uzbek, Saipov lived in and reported from the southern Kyrgyz city of Osh, just across the border from the Uzbek city of Andijan. Saipov covered the aftermath of mass killings in Andijan in May 2005, when government troops shot at crowds of civilians protesting President Islam Karimov's regime. He reported on Uzbek refugees who fled and resettled in Kyrgyzstan. The Uzbek government put the Andijan death toll at 187; human rights groups say more than 700 were killed.

Prior to his murder, Saipov had received anonymous threats warning him to stop his press and political activities, a local source close to the journalist told CPJ. A state television channel in the Uzbek city of Namangan had recently aired a program smearing Saipov as a provocateur who tried to destabilize Uzbekistan with his reporting. Several state publications ran similar articles, the same source told CPJ.

Following the Andijan killings, Uzbekistan moved aggressively to expel, drive into exile, imprison, and harass independent journalists, human rights defenders, opposition activists, representatives of international nongovernmental groups, and witnesses. Many found refuge in neighboring Kyrgyzstan, but Uzbek security services infiltrated the area and continued harassing them there, according to human rights groups. Local press reports said that Uzbek security agents had been spotted in the heavily ethnic-Uzbek city of Osh.

Saipov had helped scores of Uzbek refugees in southern Kyryzstan, assisting them with lodging and linking them with resettlement agencies, AP said. He had also reported on the fate of Uzbek refugees in Iran for *Ferghana*, the news site said.

NEPAL: 1

Birendra Shah, Nepal FM, *Dristi Weekly*, and Avenues TV
October 4, 2007, Bara district

Shah was kidnapped on October 4 by members of the Communist Party of Nepal (Maoist) in central Nepal's Bara district. Maoist leaders issued a statement on November 5, saying that Shah had been murdered by members of their party on the day of the kidnapping, according to Guna Raj Luitel, news editor of *Kantipur Daily*.

Maoist leaders sought to distance themselves from the slaying, which they called an anarchic act by a district committee member, Lal Bahadur Chaud-

hary, and two associates.

Shah, local correspondent for Nepal FM, *Dristi Weekly*, and Avenues TV, had been critical of local Maoists in his reports.

His body was recovered by police in a forested area 100 miles (160 kilometers) south of Kathmandu on November 8, according to The Associated Press. A funeral held the next day attracted more than 3,000 mourners. Some of the crowd attempted to set fire to the house of one of the accused killers, the Voice of America reported.

OCCUPIED PALESTINIAN TERRITORY: 1

Suleiman Abdul-Rahim al-Ashi
Palestine
May 13, 2007, Gaza City

Gunmen wearing Presidential Guard uniforms stopped a taxi carrying al-Ashi, 25, an economics editor for the Hamas-affiliated daily *Palestine*, and Mohammad Matar Abdo, 25, a manager responsible for distribution and civic relations, Editor-in-Chief Mustafa al-Sawaf told CPJ. The taxi was stopped at 2:30 p.m. in a high-security area southwest of Gaza City that was controlled by Fatah, al-Sawaf and other journalists told CPJ.

Al-Sawaf said the two men were beaten before being shot on a public street. Al-Ashi died at the scene, while Abdo was taken to Al-Shifa Hospital in Gaza City, where he died at 3 a.m. on May 14, al-Sawaf and CPJ sources said. The description was based on interviews with eyewitnesses and an account that Abdo provided his brother before he died, al-Sawaf said.

The Palestinian Journalists Syndicate and the Palestinian Journalists Block both denounced the killings. Mohamed Edwan, a spokesman for President Mahmoud Abbas, said Fatah had nothing to do with the killings and that presidential guards were instructed to shoot only in self-defense. He said Fatah condemned the killings and urged that the perpetrators be punished.

Al-Ashi and Abdo were scheduled to meet with economic and tourism organizations in Gaza that afternoon, al-Sawaf told CPJ. The fledgling *Palestine* newspaper was launched in May. The murders came amid clashes in the coastal strip between the Fatah and Hamas factions.

PAKISTAN: 5

Mehboob Khan, freelance
April 28, 2007, Charsadda

Photographer Khan was killed in a suicide bomb attack aimed at Interior Minister Aftab Sherpao. The minister escaped with minor injuries, but 28 people died in the attack at a political rally in the small town of Charsadda in Pakistan's North-West Frontier Province.

Three other journalists were injured: ATV cameraman Arif Yousafzai; Siddiqullah, a reporter for the Urdu-language paper *Subah*; and reporter Ayaz Muhammad of the Associated Press of Pakistan.

Khan, a 22-year-old who had recently begun his journalism career, had contributed photos to local and national publications. He was believed to be working at the time.

Follow-up reports said the bomber was believed to have been a teenage male, and that security at the event may have been lax. The federal and provincial governments were investigating the attack, the *Daily Times* Web site reported.

Noor Hakim Khan, Daily Pakistan
June 2, 2007, Bajaur

Khan, a correspondent for the *Daily Pakistan* and a vice president of the Tribal Union of Journalists, was one of five people killed by a roadside bomb in the Bajaur region of the North-West Frontier Province, near Pakistan's border with Afghanistan.

Behroz Khan, the Peshawar-based reporter for *The News*, confirmed news reports that the victim was returning from covering a jirga, a traditional court. He had been invited to witness the demolition of a house belonging to the perpetrator of a February car bombing that had killed a local physician. The demolition was part of the disposition of the court case. Khan was traveling with a local official and a tribal chief who had taken a role in the case, according to news reports. Their car was third in a convoy returning from the area, reports said, and it might have been specifically targeted.

Javed Khan
Markaz and DM Digital TV
July 3, 2007, Islamabad

Khan, a photographer for the Islamabad-based daily *Markaz* and a cameraman for U.K.-based DM Digital TV, was shot in the chest and neck while caught in crossfire between government forces and the students of Lal Masjid (Red Mosque) in Islamabad, according to media reports. Four other journalists were wounded in the clashes.

News reports said gunfire came from both sides in the standoff. The source of the fatal shots was not immediately clear. Pakistani security forces had surrounded the mosque in an effort to end a months-long standoff. The mosque, generally seen as pro-Taliban, had been the center of efforts to remove what leaders saw as undesirable activity such as massage parlors and music shops.

Muhammad Arif
ARY One World TV
October 19, 2007, Karachi

Arif was among more than 130 people killed in an October 19 bombing in Karachi, which took place during a political rally held to celebrate former Prime Minister Benazir Bhutto's homecoming. The cameraman, who was on assignment, was survived by his wife and six children.

Zubair Ahmed Mujahid, *Jang*
November 23, 2007, Mirpur Khas

Mujahid, correspondent for the national Urdu-language daily *Jang*, was shot dead while traveling on a motorcycle with another journalist in the city of Mirpur Khas in the southern province of Sindh, according to local news reports. He was targeted by unidentified gunmen, also traveling by motorcycle.

Local journalists believed their colleague was slain because of his investigative reporting, according to Owais Aslam Ali, secretary-general of the local media group Pakistan Press Foundation. Mujahid was known for his critical writing on a variety of issues—including alleged mistreatment of the poor by local landlords and police—in his *Jang* weekly column, "Crime and Punishment." His coverage of alleged police brutality had led to arrests and suspensions of police officers, Ali told CPJ.

Mujahid was survived by a wife and four sons. No arrests were immediately reported.

PARAGUAY: 1

Tito Alberto Palma, Radio Mayor Otaño and Radio Chaco Boreal
August 22, 2007, Mayor Otaño

Palma, a reporter for the local radio station Radio Mayor Otaño and correspondent for the Asunción-based Radio Chaco Boreal, was having dinner at his girlfriend's home when two armed individuals in camouflage broke in at 10:40 p.m., according to press reports and CPJ interviews. Without saying a word, the two assailants began to fire their weapons, the owner of the house, Aparicio Martínez, told local reporters. Palma was shot in the head, neck, arms, and legs, Vicente Paéz, secretary-general of the Paraguayan Journalists Union, told CPJ. Palma's companion, Wilma Martínez, was wounded in the leg, according to local press reports.

Palma, 48, a Chilean national, often denounced organized crime, illegal smuggling of gas, and local government corruption in the southeastern province of Itapúa, a colleague at Radio Chaco Boreal, Erico González, told CPJ. Palma had also reported recently on the existence of illegal radio stations in Mayor Otaño, a small city on Paraguay's border with Argentina, 285 miles (460 kilometers) from Asunción.

The reporter had received death threats for years, González told CPJ, with the anonymous calls intensifying in the month before the slaying. According to a September report from the Inter American Press Association, one of the last text messages Palma received on his cell phone said: "I've been hired to kill you, to make you travel, we'll see each other soon."

A week prior to his death, Palma announced on the air that he was returning to Chile because of the threats, Paéz told CPJ. Palma had lived in Paraguay since 1991. The reporter also declared he was planning to take information on the mafia that operates in Mayor Otaño to the national television station Telefuturo before he left the country, the Asunción-based daily *ABC Color* reported.

Colleagues told CPJ they believed Palma was killed in retaliation for his work. Nelson Ramos, the local prosecutor in charge of the case, said he believed it was a revenge killing based on his reporting.

PERU: 1

Miguel Pérez Julca, Radio Éxitos
March 17, 2007, Jaén

Two hooded gunmen shot and killed the popular Peruvian radio commentator in front of his wife and children, according to news reports. Eyewitnesses quoted by the Lima daily *La República* said the attackers opened fire as the journalist and his family were nearing the front door of their home in northwestern Peru, then sped away on a motorcycle. Pérez's wife, Nelly Guevara, was wounded in the attack.

Pérez was host of the radio program "El Informativo del Pueblo" ("Bulletin of the People") on the Jaén-based station Radio Éxitos. Pérez, 38, had covered local crime and allegations of government corruption.

Guevara told local reporters that her husband had received death threats on his cell phone in the weeks prior to his death. She said that an unknown vehicle had followed Pérez on the afternoon of March 16.

In the days following the murder, Guevara said she received telephone calls at home from unidentified people who threatened to kill her and her three children, according to Peruvian news reports. Correspondents Juan Vásquez of América Televisión and Walter Altamirano of Radio Acajú told local reporters that they had also been threatened after covering news of the murder.

Four people were detained in connection with Pérez's murder, although three were released without charge, according to the press freedom group Instituto Prensa y Sociedad. One suspect, José Hurtado Vásquez, remained in custody. Jaén police accused Hurtado of hiring two local gunmen to kill the journalist. Investigators say Hurtado was angered by on-air criticism of his girlfriend, the director of a local nonprofit organization, according to Peruvian press reports. Hurtado denied the accusation, the Lima-based daily El Comercio reported.

Local colleagues and Lima-based journalists who spoke to CPJ said they were skeptical of the police investigation. According to La República, Pérez promised during his last show that he would reveal the names of "Jaén police officers who are in cahoots with drug traffickers and protect gangs of criminals." A few hours before the murder, several witnesses saw Pérez and Police Commander Jorge Velezmoro Ruiz at a local restaurant, La República reported. Velezmoro denied having seen Pérez that day, the newspaper said.

The slaying was the first involving a Peruvian journalist since the 2004 murders of two radio commentators, Alberto Rivera in Pucallpa and Antonio de la Torre Echeandía in Yungay.

RUSSIA: 1

Ivan Safronov, *Kommersant*
March 2, 2007, Moscow

Safronov, 51, a former Russian Space Force colonel and a respected military correspondent who covered defense, army, and space issues for the independent business daily *Kommersant*, fell more than four stories from a staircase window in his apartment building. The following narrative is drawn from CPJ interviews with Safronov's *Kommersant* colleagues and military experts, and from press reports.

On the day he died, Safronov talked to colleagues and family by phone and made plans with them for later in the day and for the following week. He visited a Moscow doctor for treatment of an ulcer, symptoms of which had recently abated. Safronov then went grocery shopping and took a trolley back home. Around 4 p.m., two university students living in a nearby apartment building heard a thud and saw Safronov on the ground and an open window in the building above. Safronov's groceries were on the landing between the fourth and the fifth floor of his apartment building. He died before help arrived.

The Taganka prosecutor's office in Moscow initially said the death was a suicide. Several days later, prosecutors opened an investigation into what they called "incitement to suicide," a provision of the Russian penal code that is defined as someone provoking a suicide through threats or abusive treatment. In September, prosecutors returned to their initial theory and declared the killing a suicide.

CPJ research shows Safronov had worked on a number of sensitive issues:

• In late February, Safronov had returned from Abu Dhabi, United Arab Emirates, where he had covered the annual International Defense Exhibition and Conference, a gathering of defense manufacturers. Colleagues said Safronov had called the newsroom from Abu Dhabi with information about a purported Russian sale of fighter jets and anti-aircraft missiles to Syria and Iran. The sale was said to be channeled through Belarus to conceal the origin. Safronov had planned to finish the story when he returned.

• Three days before his death, Safronov privately told colleagues at a news conference that he had information about an alleged Russian sale to Syria of the surface-to-air missile system Pantsir-S1, the fighter aircraft MiG-29, and the tactical missile Iskandar-E. He said he had been cautioned not to publish the information because of its international implications, but he did not say who had issued the warning.

• Safronov had been interrogated many times by state security agents for allegedly disclosing state secrets in his articles. He was never formally charged because he was able to demonstrate that he had relied solely on

public sources. In December 2006, Safronov angered authorities when he wrote about the third consecutive launch failure of the Bulava intercontinental ballistic missile.

Relatives, friends, and colleagues said Safronov had no reason to commit suicide. He had no personal enemies, no debts, and no life-threatening disease. He had been married for many years, had two adult children, and was expecting his first grandchild. He did not leave a suicide note.

SOMALIA: 7

Mohammed Abdullahi Khalif
Voice of Peace
May 5, 2007, Galkayo

Khalif, a contributor to the private radio station Voice of Peace in the semi-autonomous region of Puntland, was killed by crossfire while covering an army raid on an illegal gun market.

Khalif died from a bullet to the chest as soldiers were raiding the dealership to recover an assault rifle allegedly stolen from the army, according to the National Union of Somali Journalists and local journalists. One other person died and several others were wounded in the raid.

Khalif, believed to be about 25, had contributed news reports to the station on a voluntary basis since 2006, Director Mohamed Ali Ahmad told CPJ. He had worked as a station technician for several months before that, Ahmad said.

Abshir Ali Gabre, Radio Jowhar
Ahmed Hassan Mahad, Radio Jowhar
May 16, 2007, Jowhar

News editor Gabre and reporter Mahad of Radio Jowhar, a private station in Jowhar, 55 miles (90 kilometers) north of the capital, Mogadishu, were gunned down when a provincial governor's motorcade was ambushed by gunmen from a rival sub-clan.

Gabre and Mahad were riding in the first vehicle of the official convoy, a white pickup truck carrying officials and armed security guards, according to Station Director Saeed Ali Afrah. Gabre sustained gunshot wounds to his neck and left hand, while Mahad was shot in the head and chest, he said. The official was unharmed, but at least six people were killed and several injured in the ensuing gun battle, according to the independent station Radio Shabelle.

Gabre, 35 and the father of one, was also the head of the Middle Shabelle branch of the National Union of Somali Journalists and a stringer for the private Somali Broadcasting Corp., according to Afrah.

Mahad, 24, had been reporting for Radio Jowhar since its inception in October 2002. He was survived by a wife and three children.

Mahad Ahmed Elmi, Capital Voice
Ali Sharmarke, HornAfrik
August 11, 2007, Mogadishu

Prominent journalists Sharmarke and Elmi were killed in Mogadishu in two separate attacks on the same day. Unknown gunmen shot Elmi, director of Capital Voice radio, a private station run by HornAfrik Media, four times in the head at close range as he neared the door of his office early that morning, according to news reports and local journalists. He bled to death after being rushed to the hospital.

Elmi, 30, hosted a popular daily morning talk show in which Mogadishu residents phoned in reports about neighborhood issues such as crime and government security operations.

Sharmarke, founder and co-owner of HornAfrik Media, was killed just hours later after attending Elmi's funeral. The black Land Cruiser in which he was riding was struck by a remotely detonated landmine, according to the local news reports. None of the more than 20 other vehicles in the funeral procession was hit.

Sharmarke, 50, who had dual Canadian and Somali citizenship, was survived by two wives and two children, HornAfrik co-manager Mohamed Mohamud Elmi told CPJ. Elmi was survived by a wife and two children, according to news reports.

Abdulkadir Mahad Moallim Kaskey
Radio Banadir
August 24, 2007, Bardera

Kaskey, a correspondent for private Radio Banadir, was shot in the southwestern city of Bardera while returning from a journalism training workshop in Mogadishu, according to the National

Union of Somali Journalists and local journalist Mohamed Gaarane.

Kaskey died of a single bullet to the chest when local clan gunmen opened fired on a Toyota truck carrying 15 people, Gaarane said. At least two passengers were wounded in the incident, which occurred just after midnight.

Gaarane reported that officials of the local Geledle sub-clan, to which the gunmen allegedly belonged, announced they would hand over the perpetrators to provincial authorities.

Kaskey, 20, was an active reporter respected by his colleagues, according to Radio Banadir producer Ali Moalim. A day before his death, he had visited the offices of the press union in Mogadishu to discuss the working conditions of journalists in southwestern Somalia. He was also a correspondent for Radio Maandeeq in Gedo and Radio Daljir in the northeastern semi-autonomous region of Puntland, according to local media reports.

Bashiir Noor Gedi, Radio Shabelle
October 19, 2007, Mogadishu

Gedi, acting manager of the independent station Radio Shabelle, was assassinated outside his home in Mogadishu by unknown gunmen, according to station employees and local journalists. Gedi was attempting to return to his home in the Hamar Jadid neighborhood after he and other Radio Shabelle employees had been holed up in the station for roughly a week because of a series of threats, according to journalists who spoke with his family.

Radio Shabelle, considered one of the leading stations in Somalia, had been harassed, threatened, and attacked by both government security forces and insurgents because of its critical reporting of the ongoing violence in Mogadishu. The station was forced to close for 15 days before resuming broadcasts on October 3.

Radio Shabelle halted its normal programming after the slaying, which occurred around 7 p.m., and started airing verses from the Quran, the National Union of Somali Journalists reported.

SRI LANKA: 5

Subash Chandraboas, *Nilam*
April 16, 2007, near Vavuniya

Chandraboas, 32, editor of a small Tamil-language monthly magazine, *Nilam* (The Ground), was shot to death at around 7:30 p.m. near his home in the government-controlled town of Thoanikkal, near Vavuniya in ethnically Tamil Sri Lanka. His 8-year-old daughter told CPJ that the assassins spoke in Tamil and Sinhalese.

"His only work was journalism," said Sunanda Deshapriya of the Sri Lankan media rights group Free Media Movement. "There was no other reason to kill him."

A strong individualist who owned his own printing press, Chandraboas produced *Nilam* almost single-handedly and was recognized for his passion for literature as well as journalism. He had also contributed to the London-based magazine *Tamil World* and the Colombo-based magazine *Aravali* on a freelance basis.

Selvarajah Rajeewarnam, *Uthayan*
April 29, 2007, Jaffna

Rajeewarnam, a reporter for the Tamil-language daily *Uthayan*, was aboard a bicycle on assignment in Jaffna when he was shot by unidentified motorcycle-riding gunmen about 600 feet (180 meters) from a military checkpoint, according to *Uthayan* staffers.

Rajeewarnam, a Tamil, had worked for another Tamil paper, *Namadu Eelanadu*, which closed soon after its managing editor, Sinnathamby Sivamaharajah, was killed outside his home in Jaffna in August 2006. Rajeewarnam had worked at *Uthayan* for about four months.

Uthayan has often been under attack. In September 2006, CPJ called on Sri Lankan authorities to fulfill their duty to protect *Uthayan*'s staff after receiving a telephone plea from E. Saravanapavan, the paper's managing director, to publicize the numerous threats against his staff.

Isaivizhi Chempiyan, Voice of Tigers
Suresh Linbiyo, Voice of Tigers
T. Tharmalingam, Voice of Tigers
November 27, 2007, Kilinochchi

Three journalists for the Voice of Tigers radio station in Kilinochchi—announcer Chempiyan and technicians Linbiyo and Tharmalingam—were killed in a Sri Lankan Air Force air strike.

Fighter jets dropped a dozen bombs on the station shortly before Velupillai Prabhakaran, leader of the separatist Liberation Tigers of Tamil Eelam (LTTE), was due to broadcast a statement. At least five other people were killed in the strike against the LTTE-run station, according to local media reports.

TURKEY: 1

Hrant Dink, *Agos*
January 19, 2007, Istanbul

Dink, 52, managing editor of the bilingual Turkish-Armenian weekly *Agos*, was shot outside his newspaper's offices in Istanbul. Dink had received numerous death threats from nationalist Turks who viewed his iconoclastic journalism, particularly on the mass killings of Armenians in the early 20th century, as an act of treachery. In a January 10 article in *Agos*, Dink said he had passed along a particularly threatening letter to Istanbul's Sisli district prosecutor, but no action had been taken.

Prime Minister Recep Tayyip Erdogan condemned Dink's murder as an attack against Turkey's unity and promised to catch those responsible, according to international news reports. A day later, police arrested the alleged trigger-man, 17-year-old Ogün Samast, who reportedly confessed to the crime. Erhan Tuncel and Yasin Hayal, described as ultranationalist Turks opposed to

Dink's political views, were accused of conspiring with Samast to carry out the murder. In all, 19 people went on trial beginning in July.

In the last 15 years, 18 other Turkish journalists have been killed for their work, many of them murdered, making it the eighth-deadliest country in the world for journalists, CPJ research shows. The last killing was in 1999. More recently, journalists, academics, and others have been subjected to pervasive legal harassment for statements that allegedly insult the Turkish identity, CPJ research shows.

Dink, a Turkish citizen of Armenian descent, had been prosecuted several times in recent years—for writing about the mass killings of Armenians by Turks at the beginning of the 20th century, for criticizing lines in the Turkish national anthem that he considered discriminatory, and even for commenting publicly on the court cases against him. His office had also been the target of protests.

In July 2006, Turkey's High Court of Appeals upheld a six-month suspended prison sentence against Dink for violating Article 301 of the penal code in a case sparked by complaints from nationalist activists. His prosecution stemmed from a series of articles in early 2004 dealing with the collective memory of the Armenian massacres of 1915-17 under the Ottoman Empire. Armenians call the killings the first genocide of the 20th century, a term that Turkey rejects.

Ironically, the pieces for which Dink was convicted had urged diaspora Armenians to let go of their anger against the Turks. The prosecution was sharply criticized by the European Union, which Turkey has sought to join. Dink said he would take the case to the European Court of Human Rights in Strasbourg, France, to clear his name.

Dink edited *Agos* for all of the newspaper's 11-year existence. *Agos*, the only Armenian newspaper in Turkey, had a circulation of just 6,000, but its political influence was vast. Dink regularly appeared on television to express his views.

In a February 2006 interview with CPJ, Dink said that he hoped his critical reporting would pave the way for peace between the two peoples. "I want to write and ask how we can change this historical conflict into peace," he said.

In the interview, Dink said he did not think the tide had yet turned in favor of critical writers—"the situation in Turkey is tense"—but he believed that it ultimately would. "I believe in democracy and press freedom. I am determined to pursue the struggle."

UNITED STATES: 1

Chauncey Bailey, *Oakland Post*
August 2, 2007, Oakland

A masked gunman dressed in black clothes approached Bailey, editor-in-chief of the *Oakland Post* and four other weeklies, on a street in downtown Oakland, Calif., as the journalist was on his way to work about 7:30 a.m. The assailant shot Bailey multiple times at close range before fleeing on foot, Oakland police spokesman Roland Holmgren told CPJ. Bailey was pronounced dead at the scene.

Devaughndre Broussard, a handyman and occasional cook at Your Black Muslim Bakery, reportedly confessed to local authorities the next day. According to local press reports, Broussard said he was angered by Bailey's coverage of the bakery and its staff; his attorney later maintained the purported confession was made under duress.

Your Black Muslim Bakery was a one-time hub of Oakland community activism whose surviving owners and staff had been tied to various criminal activities—including charges filed after the murder that involved the alleged kidnapping and torture of two women in May 2007.

Bailey, 58, a veteran television and print journalist in California's Bay Area, covered a variety of issues including city politics, crime, and African-American issues. He had been named editor-in-chief in June.

ZIMBABWE: 1

Edward Chikomba, Zimbabwe Broadcasting Corporation (former)
March 31, 2007, Darwendale

Chikomba, a veteran cameraman formerly with the state-run Zimbabwe Broadcasting Corporation (ZBC), was abducted on March 29 near his home in the capital, Harare, by a group of armed men in a four-wheel drive vehicle, according to the Media Institute of South Africa, local journalists, and news reports. He was found dead two days later near the industrial farming area of Darwendale, 50 miles (80 kilometers) west of Harare, according to the same sources. Chikomba was beaten to death, sources close to his family told CPJ.

Several news reports said Chikomba's killing might be linked to his alleged leaking to foreign media of footage of badly beaten opposition leader Morgan Tsvangirai after the politician's release from police custody in February. Footage of Tsvangirai leaving a Harare courthouse with a suspected fractured skull, and then lying in a hospital bed, sparked international condemnation of President Robert Mugabe's regime. The footage aired on many foreign television stations, but not on ZBC, the country's sole television network, local journalists told CPJ.

Police spokesperson Assistant Commissioner Wayne Bvudzijena did not respond to CPJ's messages seeking comment. Chikomba was one of several senior ZBC journalists forced to step down in 2002 during a harsh media crackdown led by then-Information Minister Jonathan Moyo, according to local journalists.

23 JOURNALISTS KILLED: MOTIVE UNCONFIRMED

BRAZIL: 1

Luiz Carlos Barbon Filho
Jornal do Porto, JC Regional,
Rádio Porto FM
May 5, 2007, Porto Ferreira

Barbon, 37, was shot to death by un-identified individuals while sitting on a bar terrace in the southern city of Porto Ferreira, 140 miles (230 kilometers) from São Paulo. He was known for investigative reporting that exposed political corruption.

At 9 p.m., two hooded individuals on a motorcycle approached Barbon, a columnist for the local dailies *Jornal do Porto* and *JC Regional*, and contributor to the local station Rádio Porto FM, according to Brazilian press reports. Witnesses quoted in the local media said that one of the masked assailants stepped off the motorcycle and shot Barbon twice at close range, with one shot hitting the journalist in the upper abdomen and the other in his right leg. According to press reports, Barbon was taken to a local hospital, where he died at 11 p.m.

Police Chief Eduardo Henrique Campos told reporters that investigators were looking into Barbon's journalism as a motive. Campos added that Barbon was generally critical of local politicians in his commentary, making it difficult to pinpoint a specific story or area of coverage. Media reports said that at the time of his death, Barbon was investigating the embezzlement of government funds during the purchase of a garbage truck.

Barbon had worked as a journalist for 10 years, according to local press reports. In 2003, he drew wide attention with a report on a local child prostitution ring, published in the daily *Realidade*, which he owned. The report resulted in the convictions of four businessmen, five local politicians, and one other person, a waiter, the national newspaper *O Globo* reported. Only the waiter was still in jail, and one of the councilmen was later re-elected, according to local press reports. Due to financial difficulties, Barbon shut down *Realidade* in 2004. He ran unsuccessfully for city council the same year.

In his last radio interview, on April 19, Barbon accused 19 people connected with the local government of corruption. He warned that they should be held accountable if anything were to happen to him, the Brazilian news Web site *Comunique* reported.

After Barbon's death, local politicians quoted in the Brazilian press accused the journalist of extortion. They said he would threaten to publicly ridicule politicians if they did not pay him. No formal complaints supporting the allegations were immediately identified, however. A close friend was quoted as saying that Barbon was a man of principle who would never accept bribes.

Cátia Rosa Camargo, the journalist's wife, said that her husband had received a constant stream of threatening letters and telephone calls, according to international and Brazilian press reports. Local media reported that police advised Camargo and her two children to leave their home after receiving additional threats.

CHINA: 1

Lan Chengzhang
Zhongguo Maoyi Bao
January 10, 2007, Huiyuan

Unidentified men at an illegal coal mine in Huiyuan County, Shanxi province, severely beat reporter Lan on January 9, leading to his death the following day, according to news reports. Lan had been working for the Shanxi bureau of the Beijing-based newspaper *Zhongguo Maoyi Bao* (China Trade News) for less than a month, his colleagues told international and domestic reporters.

The death was first reported by an anonymous poster to an online forum, *Tianya*. Domestic and international news organizations picked up the report, quoting *Zhongguo Maoyi Bao* journalists for additional details. *Zhongguo Maoyi Bao* did not immediately report on the case itself. "He was beaten to death by a group of mining thugs," Wang Jianfeng, head of the paper's news department, told Agence France-Presse, adding that a newspaper team was sent to Shanxi to investigate and file complaints with local authorities.

Lan and a colleague had arrived at the coal mine when they were surrounded and attacked by unidentified men, according to an online account cited by the Guangzhou newspaper *Nanfang Ribao*. Lan was beaten severely while the unnamed colleague was restrained and assaulted, according to that account. The two men drove to a hospital in nearby Datong, where Lan died at 9 a.m. the next day.

Local officials claimed Lan did not have official certification so he was not a legitimate journalist, according to *Nanfang Ribao*. Police also accused Lan, a former miner, of seeking money from the mine's proprietors in exchange for keeping news of the illegal operation out of the newspaper. CPJ has documented a number of instances of blackmail journalism in China, undertaken by both accredited journalists and people purporting to be journalists. Lan's journalistic status and his intentions were widely debated by Chinese journalists.

COLOMBIA: 1

Javier Darío Arroyave, Ondas del Valle, September 5, 2007, Cartago

Arroyave, 41, news director for the Cartago-based radio station Ondas del Valle and host of the news program "¿Cómo les parece?," was stabbed early in the morning inside his home in Cartago, Col. Armando Burbano, a spokesman for Cartago police, told CPJ. Although the journalist's laptop computer was missing, there were no signs of forced entry, Col. Ricardo Restrepo, head of the Valle del Cauca police, told local reporters.

Colleagues at Ondas del Valle, which is affiliated with the national Caracol Radio, said Arroyave presented general political and social news that was not particularly critical of the government. The journalist also worked for the state environmental organization Corporación Autónoma Regional del Valle del Cauca, according to colleagues. He had worked as a Cartago correspondent for the national daily *El Tiempo* until 2005, and was recently a freelance contributor for the paper, a source at *El Tiempo* said.

In May 2005, Arroyave canceled his news program temporarily after continuous pressure from Luis Alberto Castro, then the Cartago mayor, whom the journalist accused of corruption, said Carlos Cortés, executive director of the local press freedom group Fundación para la Libertad de Prensa. Arroyave had not mentioned receiving threats in recent months, colleagues told CPJ.

Burbano told CPJ that investigators believe the murder was a crime of passion, but colleagues said they have not discounted Arroyave's journalism as a possible motive.

DEMOCRATIC REPUBLIC OF CONGO: 1

Patrick Kikuku Wilungula, freelance
August 9, 2007, Goma

Wilungula, 39, was gunned down near his home in Goma, North Kivu province, while returning home from a local conference on environmental protection, local journalists told CPJ. Wilungula was covering the conference as a freelance photojournalist. Eyewitnesses said the gunmen were wearing military uniforms and fled the scene with the journalist's digital camera, leaving behind 13,000 Congolese francs (US$30) and a mobile phone.

Local press freedom groups Journaliste en Danger, the Congolese Press Union, and Goma's association of photographers said they were investigating possible motives.

Wilungula had distinguished himself from other, mostly commercial, photographers in Goma, with his focus on photojournalism, contributing to several local publications, said César Balume, the president of Goma's association of photographers. He had been the official photographer of former North Kivu governor Eugene Serufuli.

EL SALVADOR: 1

Salvador Sánchez Roque, freelance
September 20, 2007, Florencia

Sánchez, a freelance radio reporter, was shot while on his way to buy milk at a nearby shop, according to press reports and CPJ interviews.

Sánchez, 38, covered social movements and protests in Florencia, a town four miles (seven kilometers) from the capital, San Salvador, said David Rivas, director of local Radio Mi Gente, for which Sánchez often reported. Protesters had told Sánchez to be careful about his coverage, Rivas told CPJ.

Weeks prior to his death, Sánchez told Rivas that he had received repeated death threats from the local arm of the Salvadoran gang Mara Salvatrucha. Sánchez did not cover gang-related news, colleagues told CPJ. Rivas said the callers did not specify why they were threatening Sánchez.

Salvadoran police arrested José Alfredo Hernández, a member of Mara Salvatrucha, on October 11. During a press conference that day, Héctor Mendoza, deputy director of police investigations, said Hernández had confessed to killing the journalist, whom he believed to be a police informant. Police were looking for two other suspects, the Salvadoran press reported.

and CPJ interviews.

Arnulfo Agustín Guzmán, director of Radio Sonora, told CPJ that López was shot in the head, back, and chest. According to his wife, Blanca Castellano, nothing was stolen from his car or wallet. López was taken to Roosevelt Hospital where he died moments after arrival, according to Guatemalan press reports.

López was one of the founders of Radio Sonora and worked there as a producer for 14 years, Agustín said. His program, "Cosas y Casos de la Vida Nacional," was critical of Guatemalan politics, Agustín added.

According to the journalist's colleagues and family, he had not received threats. However, Agustín told CPJ that the radio station had been repeatedly threatened over the phone. Local authorities were investigating but did not disclose a possible motive.

GUATEMALA: 1

Mario Rolando López Sánchez
Radio Sonora
May 3, 2007, Guatemala City

Veteran radio producer López was gunned down outside his home in Guatemala City. López, producer of the political debate program "Cosas y Casos de la Vida Nacional" and various social programs on national privately owned Radio Sonora, was shot at 7 p.m. as he was walking from his car to his home in a northern neighborhood in Guatemala City, according to local press reports

HAITI: 1

Alix Joseph, Radio-Télé Provinciale
May 16, 2007, Gonaïves

Joseph, station manager and host of a cultural show on local Radio-Télé Provinciale, was gunned down outside his wife's house in Gonaïves, 105 miles (170 kilometers) north of Port-au-Prince, according to press reports and CPJ interviews.

At 9:30 p.m., two unidentified men approached Joseph as he was sitting in a car in front of his wife's house, the radio station's director, Frantz Justin Altidor, told CPJ. Joseph's wife ran for help when she saw the two men draw their weapons, Altidor said. Moments later, neighbors found the journalist's body outside his car, shot at least 11 times, according to Haitian and international press reports. Local authorities were investigating, Altidor told CPJ.

Joseph hosted a popular Sunday morning program that featured music and news about cultural activities in Gonaïves, local journalists told CPJ. According to Altidor, Joseph managed the daily work of the radio station and often filled in as host of the station's daily news program. Also a high school philosophy teacher, Joseph was active in local cultural organizations, Altidor said.

In March, Altidor said, he received an anonymous call from a man who warned him that he did not like Radio-Télé Provinciale's stand on the disarmament of local gangs. Joseph informed Altidor that he had received similar phone calls at the radio station but did not pay attention to them. According to Altidor, Joseph had been recently threatened by an individual with whom he had a financial dispute unrelated to journalism.

IRAQ: 7

Hussein al-Jabouri, As-Saffir
March 16, 2007, Baghdad

Al-Jabouri, editor-in-chief of As-Saffir, was shot when he failed to stop his car at an Iraqi security checkpoint in Bagh-

dad's Al-Dora neighborhood on March 7, according to the Journalistic Freedoms Observatory, a local press freedom group. The group, citing his family, said al-Jabouri was driving home when Iraqi security officers opened fire.

A CPJ source said that the security officers transferred al-Jabouri to a hospital immediately afterward. His treatment continued in Amman, Jordan, but he died later that month, the source said.

Ali Khalil, Azzaman
May 20, 2007, Baghdad

Gunmen abducted and killed Khalil, 22, an editor for the Iraqi daily Azzaman, in Baghdad's southern Shurta Raba neighborhood, according to the paper and CPJ sources.

Around midday, Khalil left his in-laws' home with his wife, their newborn baby, and her father when gunmen in two vehicles stopped the journalist's car, according to the Journalistic Freedoms Observatory, an Iraqi press freedom organization. The gunmen ordered the passengers out, seized the car, and kidnapped Khalil. Iraqi police discovered his body three hours after the abduction in the same neighborhood, according to Azzaman and CPJ sources.

Khalil was shot multiple times in the head and back, and he appeared to have been beaten, the Journalistic Freedoms Observatory said. CPJ was unable to determine if he was killed because of his journalism.

Khalil's last news item focused on a call by some parliamentarians for the government-sanctioned assassination of militants, the Journalistic Freedoms Observatory reported. *Azzaman* is operated by the Azzaman Group, which is owned by Iraqi media tycoon Saad al-Bazzaz, head of radio and television under Saddam Hussein until 1992. The paper was critical of the Iraqi government.

Abdul Rahman al-Issawi
National Iraqi News Agency
May 28, 2007, Amiriyat al-Fallujah

Gunmen raided the home of al-Issawi, a reporter for the online National Iraqi News Agency, in Amiriyat al-Fallujah, near the Iraqi city of Fallujah in Anbar province, a CPJ source said. The assailants took the journalist, his brother, and his father to a nearby location and killed them. An editor at the news agency told CPJ that members of al-Issawi's family heard the shooting and engaged the gunmen. Five other members of the family were killed in the clash, he said.

The source told CPJ that al-Issawi worked for the National Iraqi News Agency for more than a year and had freelanced for several Iraqi publications.

Mahmoud Hassib al-Qassab
Al-Hawadith, May 28, 2007, Kirkuk

Al-Qassab, editor-in-chief of the defunct bilingual weekly *Al-Hawadith*, was gunned down near his home in the center of Kirkuk, local journalists told CPJ. Al-Qassab, who also headed the Turkmen Salvation Movement, was returning from his political party's office

when he was shot.

CPJ sources said they believed his murder was related to his political work rather than his journalism.

Saif Fakhry
Associated Press Television News
May 31, 2007, Baghdad

Associated Press Television News cameraman Fakhry, 26, was shot as he was heading to a mosque near his home in Baghdad's western neighborhood of Al-Aamariyah, The Associated Press reported. He had taken the day off to spend time with his pregnant wife, the news agency said.

Al-Aamariyah had been the site of intense fighting between al-Qaeda gunmen and Sunni extremist militants. It was unclear whether Fakhry was killed in crossfire or if he was targeted, according to the AP.

Jawad al-Daami, Al-Baghdadia
September 23, 2007, Baghdad

Several gunmen in a car shot al-Daami, 40, a producer for the independent Cairo-based satellite channel Al-Baghdadia, in Baghdad's southwestern neighborhood of Al-Qadissiya at around 4 p.m., a source at the channel told CPJ. The source said that al-Daami was heading home southwest of Baghdad. He added that al-Daami, a well-known poet, had gone to Baghdad to attend a cultural conference on his day off from work.

The motive for the killing was unclear, but the crime scene was in a neighborhood occupied by several militia groups known to target journalists, according to local reporters.

The Journalistic Freedoms Observatory, an Iraqi press freedom organization, quoted Al-Baghdadia sources as saying that al-Daami met with several colleagues earlier that day in Baghdad's Al-Mansour neighborhood to plan a young people's cultural forum. Al-Daami worked on cultural and social programs for Al-Baghdadia, writing and researching in his role as a line producer.

Ali Shafeya al-Moussawi
Alive in Baghdad
December 15, 2007, Baghdad

Al-Moussawi, a correspondent for the video-based news Web site *Alive in Baghdad*, was found shot to death in his home in the Al-Habibiya neighborhood of Baghdad, the Web site reported. Al-Moussawi was shot 31 times, the Web site said, citing a coroner's report.

Alive in Baghdad reported that al-Moussawi's body was found hours after Iraqi National Guard forces had raided the street where the reporter resides. The Web site said witnesses heard gunfire and that a relative was unable to reach al-Moussawi by phone during the raid.

Brian Conley, *Alive in Baghdad's* founder and director, said the circumstances and motive for al-Moussawi's murder were unclear. He said *Alive in Baghdad* was looking into a threat al-Moussawi received the previous week. The reporter had been working on a report about an Iraqi militia group.

MEXICO: 3

Amado Ramírez Dillanes
Televisa and Radiorama
April 6, 2007, Acapulco

Ramírez, 50, Acapulco-based correspondent for the broadcast station Televisa and host of the daily news program "Al Tanto" on local Radiorama, was shot to death near the city's main square.

After concluding his daily news show, Ramírez left Radiorama's offices at 7:30 p.m. and walked to his car, which was parked close by, said a colleague who asked not to be identified. Ramírez had just stepped into his car when an unidentified assailant shot him twice from outside the driver's window, the colleague said. Wounded in his left leg and chest, the journalist ran into the lobby of a nearby hotel. The attacker followed Ramírez and shot him in the back, the local press reported.

Ramírez reported general news for Televisa and "Al Tanto," the colleague said. In March, however, he aired a special investigation into the murders of local police officers. The Televisa report linked the crimes to local drug traffickers.

According to Misael Habana de los Santos, Ramírez' co-host at Radiorama, the journalist had received several death threats on his cell phone prior to the murder. Habana wrote in the national daily *La Jornada* that Ramírez had not paid attention to the threats, and that he refused to inform local police. State investigators did not speculate on the possible motive.

Saúl Noé Martínez Ortega
Interdiario
April 23, 2007, Nuevo Casas Grandes

Martínez, a crime reporter for *Interdiario*, a family-owned newspaper in Agua Prieta that comes out three times a week, was found dead in the northern state of Chihuahua on April 23, a week after he was abducted by armed individuals in neighboring Sonora state.

Martínez, 36, was seized on the night of April 16 outside a municipal police station in Agua Prieta, a city in the state of Sonora, on the Arizona border. Press reports said that after a high-speed chase, Martínez stopped his SUV at the entrance to the station and called for help. But heavily armed gunmen forced the reporter into their vehicle and drove away from the city center.

On the morning of April 23, a passerby discovered a body wrapped in a blanket on a road outside the town of Nuevo Casas Grandes, near the border between Chihuahua and Sonora, according to press reports and CPJ interviews.

The body was identified as that of Martínez, said the journalist's brother, Erick Martínez Ortega.

The reporter had been dead for approximately six days, said José Larrinaga Talamantes, a spokesman for the state attorney general's office in Hermosillo. He had been beaten and apparently died of a blow to the head, Erick Martínez told CPJ.

Martínez covered crime during night shifts for *Interdiario*, the journalist's father, Lorenzo, told CPJ. Investigators were looking into several possible motives, including alleged links between the reporter and local drug traffickers, a spokesman for the state attorney general's office said.

Gerardo Israel García Pimentel
La Opinion de Michoacán
December 8, 2007, Uruapan

Unidentified individuals followed reporter García through the streets of Uruapan, according to local press reports. As García entered the Hotel Ruán, where he lived, two gunmen shot him at least 20 times at close range, police told local reporters.

Police said some 50 shell casings, nearly all from AR-15 semiautomatic rifles, were found at the scene. Michoacán state police did not immediately announce possible motives for the murder. García, 28, covered agriculture full-time and crime part-time for *La Opinion de Michoacán*, colleagues told CPJ. Reporters at other newspapers told CPJ that García was considered a low-key reporter.

Michoacán's violent death toll for the year was at 339 at the time of García's murder, according to a tally compiled by the national daily *La Jornada*.

Michoacán is a key state for Mexico's powerful Gulf and Sinaloa drug cartels, which routinely battle over drug shipment routes from South America to the United States.

NEPAL: 1

Shankar Panthi, *Naya Satta*
September 15, 2007, Sunwal

Panthi, a correspondent for the pro-Maoist newspaper *Naya Satta*, was found fatally injured at around 1:30 a.m. alongside the Mahendra Highway in Sunwal village, in the southern district of Nawalparasi, according to local news reports.

Local residents said his bruised body was found in front of a petrol pump and that he appeared to have suffered head injuries, according to the *Kantipur Online* news site. Police said that Panthi's bicycle was hit by another vehicle in a road accident and that the journalist died while being taken to the hospital, according to reports.

Local residents staged demonstrations blocking a stretch of the busy highway for two days, demanding action against those responsible for Panthi's death and compensation for his family members.

Panthi was reporting on the destruction of a Young Communist League office on the night he was killed, according to Keshav Parajuli, president of the Nawalparasi chapter of the Federation of Nepalese Journalists. Panthi was also an "active Maoist cadre," according to *Kantipur Online*.

PHILIPPINES: 2

Hernani Pastolero
Lightning Courier Weekly
February 20, 2007, Sultan Kudarat

Pastolero, 64, editor-in-chief of the community newspaper *Lightning Courier Weekly*, was shot in front of his home in Sultan Kudarat township, on the southern Philippine island of Mindanao.

Pastolero was shot twice in the head by an unidentified assassin who escaped on foot, according to local media reports. Police Superintendent Joel Goltiao told local reporters that investigators had compiled a list of suspects. He declined to speculate about a possible motive. GMANews said the National Bureau of Investigation was looking into Pastolero's connection to a conflict between residential lot owners and a large private landholder.

President Gloria Macapagal Arroyo ordered the Philippine National Police to investigate, and presidential spokesman Ignacio Bunyes condemned the killing.

Ferdinand Lintuan, DXGO and *Sun Star*
December 24, 2007, Davao City

Lintuan, 51, the father of four children, was shot by two motorcycle-riding assailants as he was driving in downtown Davao City, according to local media reports and the Center for Media Freedom and Responsibility, a press freedom advocacy group. Lintuan had just left DXGO, an AM station owned by the Manila Broadcasting Company, with two colleagues who were uninjured in the attack. The colleagues said the attackers wore helmets with visors that hid their faces.

No one claimed responsibility for the attack. Lintuan was well known for his criticism of local politicians in Davao, a major city on the southern island of Mindanao. Lintuan, a veteran journalist, had been on the air at DXGO for about three months, leasing airtime under a practice known as "block timing."

Lintuan was also a columnist for the regional English-language daily *Sun Star*. He had recently alleged corruption in a local development project and had criticized illegal logging activities, the *Sun Star* and other papers reported.

The National Bureau of Investigation sent a team to Davao to assist local police. The government and opposition politicians offered more than 1 million pesos (US$24,000) for information leading to an arrest. The *Sun Star* said that Lintuan had survived an August 1987 attack inside DXRA radio in Davao. Three others died in the attack.

RUSSIA: 1

Vyacheslav Ifanov
Novoye Televideniye Aleiska
April 5, 2007, Aleisk

Ifanov, a 29-year-old cameraman for the independent television station Novoye Televideniye Aleiska (NTA) in the Siberian city of Aleisk, was found dead in his garage with his car running. On August 4, the Aleisk prosecutor's office ruled that there was no evidence of foul play. An autopsy found that he died from self-induced carbon monoxide poisoning.

The night before he died, Ifanov was featured on the syndicated television news program "Nashi Novosti." He described a January attack against him by unidentified members of a local military reconnaissance unit. In the April 4 broadcast, Ifanov said he hoped to identify his attackers soon with the help of police, the Moscow-based daily *Izvestiya* reported.

Local press reports quoted Ifanov describing the January 21 attack. Ifanov said he was filming what he thought was a suspicious gathering of men in camouflage gear in the center of Aleisk. The men, seeing Ifanov filming them, assaulted the journalist and broke his camera, he said. During the attack, Ifanov said, the men told him, "We warned you that military reconnaissance works here, but you didn't listen." The journalist sustained a concussion in the attack and spent several days in the hospital, according to local press reports.

Ifanov was found dead on April 5 by a neighbor, who heard the journalist's car running with the garage doors shut. Neighbor Viktor Langolf said Ifanov's body was slumped between his car and one of the garage walls, the Moscow-based news agency Regnum reported. Langolf said the garage doors were locked from the inside, according to local press reports. Police said there were no signs of violence, press reports said.

Sergei Plotnikov, a journalist who investigated the case for the Moscow-based press freedom group Center for Journalism in Extreme Situations, said he examined photos of the scene, and they did not reflect signs of a struggle.

Relatives, friends, and colleagues were skeptical Ifanov took his own life, according to local press reports. The autopsy report contained omissions and conflicting information, *Izvestiya* reported. For example, *Izvestiya* said, the report placed the body in two different locations in the garage.

On April 4, Ifanov worked until 7 p.m. and then spent the rest of the evening with a friend, Aleksandr Udin, who said the journalist had been in a good mood, according to local press reports. Udin said that the journalist mentioned there was some progress in the January attack but did not elaborate, *Izvestiya* reported. Ifanov left Udin's house at around 2 a.m. The autopsy said the journalist died about two hours later, *Regnum* reported.

Local press reports said that Ifanov had received threats prior to his death and was told to withdraw his criminal complaint in the January attack. NTA Director Yevgeny Filippov told CPJ he was unaware of threats against Ifanov.

SOMALIA: 1

Ali Mohammed Omar, Radio Warsan
February 16, 2007, Baidoa

Omar, a 25-year-old radio journalist and technician, was gunned down by three unknown assailants as he walked home in the southern town of Baidoa, local journalists and the National Union of Somali Journalists reported.

The assailants told Omar to stop, but he refused and attempted to run away, according to witnesses who spoke with local journalists. Witnesses said the gunmen shot Omar in the head and took his mobile phone, according to local journalists. The slaying was reported at around 8:30 p.m.

Omar worked for independent Radio Warsan and was a member of the southern chapter of the National Union of Somali Journalists. Radio Warsan, which had been closed by the government in January, had resumed broadcasting just days before the killing.

SRI LANKA: 1

Sahadevan Nilakshan, *Chaalaram*
August 1, 2007, Jaffna

Nilakshan, a 22-year-old journalism student and editor of the student-run *Chaalaram* magazine, was shot by unidentified gunmen at his home on the outskirts of Jaffna. The 4 a.m. shooting occurred during curfew hours in an area heavily guarded by the Sri Lankan military, according to the Colombo-based Free Media Movement. The gunmen arrived at Nilakshan's home in Kokuvil village by motorcycle.

The journalist died within hours of being taken to the Jaffna General Hospital for treatment of his injuries.

Nilakshan studied journalism at the Media Resource Training Centre at Jaffna University. He was killed just days after returning to the northern city of Jaffna from the capital, Colombo, where he had participated in an internship program along with other journalism students.

20 MEDIA SUPPORT WORKERS KILLED

AFGHANISTAN: 1

Sayed Agha, freelance
March 15, 2007, Helmand province

Agha, a driver, was kidnapped on March 5 by Taliban in Helmand province. He was seized along with *La Republicca* reporter Daniele Mastrogiacomo and freelance journalist Ajmal Naqshbandi.

According to Mastrogiacomo, Agha was beheaded several days after the group was grabbed. The Taliban accused him of being a spy. Mastrogiacomo was released on March 19; Naqshbandi was beheaded by his captors on April 8.

INDIA: 3

G. Gopinath, *Dinakaran*
M. Vinod Kumar, *Dinakaran*
K. Muthuranalingam, *Dinakaran*
May 9, 2007, Tamil Nadu

Three employees of the Tamil-language daily *Dinakaran* were killed in an attack on the newspaper's offices in the eastern Indian state of Tamil Nadu. The victims were identified as computer engineers Kumar and Gopinath and security guard Muthuranalingam, according to the news Web site *New Kerala*.

The employees died of asphyxiation after demonstrators threw firebombs into offices housing *Dinakaran*, Sun TV, and other media outlets, according to The Associated Press. The protesters were angry with an opinion poll published by *Dinakaran* that indicated public support for M.K. Stalin's bid for election as chief minister of Tamil Nadu, a post then held by Stalin's father, M. Karunanidhi. Stalin's chief political rival was his elder brother, M.K. Azhagiri.

Twelve people were arrested in connection with the attack, according to news reports.

IRAQ: 12

Nabras Mohammed Hadi
Iraq Media Network
Azhar Abdullah al-Maliki
Iraq Media Network
Sabah Salman, Iraq Media Network
February 7, 2007, Baghdad

Three guards working for the state-run Iraq Media Network were killed by guards employed by Blackwater Worldwide, a U.S. private security firm, *The Washington Post* reported.

Blackwater guards escorting an American diplomat to the Iraqi Justice Ministry took positions on the roof of the building, according to the *Post*. The Iraq Media Network compound, guarded by an Iraqi security team, was adjacent to the ministry at a distance of about 450 feet. An argument ensued between the Iraqi guards and some civilians who wanted to park a car between the ministry and the media compound, the *Post* said. When Hadi, 23, a guard stationed on a balcony in the compound, stood up with his weapon and shouted at the people on the ground, he was shot by a Blackwater sniper, the paper reported.

When colleagues tried to retrieve Hadi from the balcony, the sniper shot another guard, al-Maliki, 31, in the neck, forcing the others to retreat, the paper reported. An Iraqi army unit in charge of the area responded to the scene and withdrew the bodies of both guards. Hadi died at the scene, while al-Maliki succumbed to his wounds a few hours later at a nearby hospital. Guards discovered Salman, 40, charged with maintaining small arms, lying dead on the same balcony more than an hour after the sniper had fired his first shot, the *Post* said.

Guards from both the Iraq Media Network and the Justice Ministry, along with the Iraqi army commander and several network officials, said the slain guards did not fire their weapons or provoke the shooting. The Justice Ministry, the Interior Ministry, Iraqi police, and the Iraq Media Network found Blackwater responsible for the incident, the paper reported.

The security firm denied initiating the shooting, saying its employees returned fire after coming under threat.

Hussein Nizar, Baghdad TV
April 6, 2007, Baghdad

A garbage truck packed with explosives detonated near the main entrance of Baghdad TV's offices on April 5, killing Deputy Director Thaer Ahmad Jaber. Nizar, a guard, died from his injuries the following day. Eleven other employees were injured in the attack, according to CPJ sources.

The Journalistic Freedoms Observatory, an Iraqi press freedom organization, reported that the attackers fired at the station's guards, clearing the way for the truck. The front of the building, which houses the Sunni Iraqi Islamic Party-owned Baghdad TV and Radio Dar al-Salam, was destroyed along with several station and employee cars, according to news reports. The station's main transmission equipment was damaged, briefly interrupting its broadcast.

Adel al-Badri, Radio Dijla
May 3, 2007, Baghdad

Dozens of heavily armed gunmen stormed the independent Radio Dijla station in Baghdad's Al-Jamia district, killing guard al-Badri and injuring two other guards, Karim Yousef, acting director-general, told CPJ.

Around 2:30 p.m., dozens of masked gunmen attacked Radio Dijla with missiles and heavy machine guns, destroying equipment, and knocking the station off the air, Yousef said. The gunmen seized the first floor of the two-story building, causing Radio Dijla's 25 employees to flee to the second floor and fight off the attack, he said.

The assailants set off an explosive on the first floor, destroying the station's broadcast equipment, Yousef said. The gunmen fled shortly before Iraqi security forces arrived. Yousef told CPJ he called the security forces 10 minutes into the attack; his staff, he said, fought the gunmen for more than 30 minutes before they were rescued. The damage, Yousef said, was so extensive that the station could not immediately return to the air.

Radio Dijla is considered an independent news outlet. "We don't belong to ... any political or sectarian sides and we accept all Iraqi voices," Yousef said. "We asked the government several times to protect the road, to protect the station, but unfortunately to no avail."

Imad Abdul-Razzaq al-Obaid
Al-Raad
May 9, 2007, outside Kirkuk

Gunmen riding in an Opel without a license plate intercepted a vehicle carrying Raad Mutashar, 43, owner and director of a media company, and driver al-Obaid on a road southwest of Kirkuk at around 2 p.m., a company source told CPJ. The source said the gunmen killed Mutashar and al-Obaid, along with passengers Nibras Abdul-Razzaq al-Obaid and Aqil Abdul-Qadir.

Mutashar's company, Al-Raad, published a weekly newspaper, *Al-Iraq Ghadan*, and a related institute operated a news agency and a media educational center. A CPJ source said Mutashar was a prominent writer, poet, and journalist who started the company four years earlier. Imad Abdul-Razzaq al-Obaid and Nibras Abdul-Razzaq al-Obaid were Mutashar's brothers-in-law.

Ali Watan Rozouk al-Hassani
Al-Samawah
July 6, 2007, Al-Samawah

Gunmen shot al-Hassani, an administrative assistant and security guard for the local television station Al-Samawah, during violent clashes in Al-Samawah, capital of southern Al-Muthanna province, according to the Journalistic Freedoms Observatory, a local press freedom organization. Al-Hassani was driving to work when he was shot in the head.

Al-Samawah's building had been subjected to heavy shelling that had interrupted its broadcasts, station chief Saeed al-Badri told the observatory. Al-Hassani had cut a vacation short to help the station get back on the air, al-Badri said. A police spokesman told the observatory that the shooting took place about 330 feet (100 meters) from the television station.

Saeed Chmagh, Reuters
July 12, 2007, Baghdad

Driver and camera assistant Chmagh was killed along with photographer Namir Noor-Eldeen in eastern Baghdad during what witnesses described as a U.S. helicopter attack. The strike claimed the lives of 10 other Iraqis in the Al-Amin al-Thaniyah neighborhood, Reuters reported, citing a preliminary Iraqi police report.

Witnesses told Reuters that Noor-Eldeen and Chmagh arrived in the neighborhood about the time a U.S. helicop-

JOURNALISTS KILLED IN 2007

ter fired on a minivan. Video footage showed that the minivan was destroyed, Reuters reported. Initial reports suggested that the air strike took place during clashes between U.S. forces and insurgents, but witnesses later said there were no clashes, according to Reuters.

The Multi-National Force-Iraq press desk in Baghdad did not respond to CPJ's telephone and e-mail inquiries seeking comment.

Ziad Tarek al-Dibo, *Al-Watan*
Jassem Mohammad Nofan, *Al-Watan*
Khaled Mohammad Nofan, *Al-Watan*
October 14, 2007, southwest of Kirkuk

Gunmen ambushed five guards for the Tikrit-based weekly *Al-Watan* on the road between Kirkuk and Al-Riyadh in Iraq's northern At-Tamim province on the evening of October 14, according to CPJ sources and news reports. A local journalist identified the three slain guards as Ziad Tarek al-Dibo, Jassem Mohammad Nofan, and Khaled Mohammad Nofan, and the two injured as Alal al-Ghariri and Mohammad Shaker al-Samraee.

Al-Watan's deputy chief editor, Waqas al-Dowaini, told the Journalistic Freedoms Observatory, a local press freedom organization, that the guards were returning to Tikrit, northwest of Baghdad, after escorting the paper's chairman, Hatem Mawloud Mokhles, to Arbil. The gunmen attacked near Houd 18 village, southwest of Kirkuk. Al-Dowaini told the observatory that the victims were employed as guards for the paper and as personal guards for Mokhles, secretary-general of the Iraqi National Movement political party.

Abdullah [full name unavailable]
freelance
October 22, 2007, Baghdad

Unidentified kidnappers killed the driver for Radio Free Iraq correspondent Jumana al-Obaidi when they seized the reporter on her way to a scheduled assignment at the Iraqi Environment Ministry. The radio service, which said the driver was hired directly by the reporter, identified the victim only as Abdullah.

Al-Obaidi worked for Radio Free Iraq, the Arabic language service of Radio Free Europe/Radio Liberty, which broadcasts to Iraq from RFE/RL headquarters in Prague, Czech Republic.

The radio service said Iraqi police found the driver's body in Baghdad's Al-Shaab neighborhood shortly after the abduction. The radio service said he was in his late 20s and was survived by a wife.

RFE/RL reported that the journalist was freed on November 4. It did not reveal details about her release or the identity of her captors.

MEXICO: 3

Mateo Cortés Martínez
El Imparcial del Istmo
Agustín López Nolasco
El Imparcial del Istmo

Flor Vásquez López
El Imparcial del Istmo
October 8, 2007, Tehuantepec

On the afternoon of October 8, an Equinox SUV with tinted windows chased and then blocked a truck marked with the logo of the Oaxaca-based daily *El Imparcial del Istmo* along a highway connecting the cities of Salina Cruz and Tehuantepec, in southern Oaxaca state, according to Mexican press reports. According to *El Imparcial del Istmo*, unidentified individuals got out of the car and shot Cortés, the van's driver, and López and Vásquez, two delivery workers, at close range.

Luis David Quintana, *El Imparcial del Istmo*'s deputy director, told local reporters that the newspaper had received several threatening e-mail messages and letters in the last month warning that the paper should tone down its coverage of local drug-trafficking gangs.

OCCUPIED PALESTINIAN TERRITORY: 1

Mohammad Matar Abdo
Palestine
May 14, 2007, Gaza City

Gunmen wearing Presidential Guard uniforms stopped a taxi carrying Abdo, 25, a manager responsible for distribution and civic relations for the Hamas-affiliated daily, and Suleiman Abdul-Rahim al-Ashi, 25, an economics editor for the paper, Editor-in-Chief Mustafa al-Sawaf told CPJ. The taxi was stopped on May 13 at 2:30 p.m. in a high-security area southwest of Gaza City that was controlled by Fatah, al-Sawaf and other journalists told CPJ.

Al-Sawaf said the two men were beaten before being shot on a public street. Al-Ashi died at the scene, while Abdo was taken to Al-Shifa Hospital in Gaza City, where he died at 3 a.m. the next day, al-Sawaf and CPJ sources said. The description was based on interviews with eyewitnesses and an account that Abdo provided his brother before he died, al-Sawaf said.

The Palestinian Journalists Syndicate and the Palestinian Journalists Block both denounced the killings. Mohamed Edwan, a spokesman for President Mahmoud Abbas, said Fatah had nothing to do with the killings and that presidential guards were instructed to shoot only in self-defense. He said Fatah condemned the killings and urged that the perpetrators be punished.

Al-Ashi and Abdo were scheduled to meet with economic and tourism organizations in Gaza that afternoon, al-Sawaf told CPJ. The fledgling *Palestine* newspaper was launched in May. The murders came amid clashes in the coastal strip between the Fatah and Hamas factions.

ONE IN SIX JAILED JOURNALISTS
HELD WITHOUT CHARGE

N early 17 percent of journalists jailed worldwide in 2007 were held without any publicly disclosed charge, many for months or years at a time and some in secret locations, CPJ found in its annual worldwide census.

CPJ found 127 journalists behind bars on December 1, a decrease of seven from the 2006 tally. The drop was due in large part to the release in 2007 of 15 Ethiopian journalists who were either acquitted or pardoned of antistate charges stemming from a broad government crackdown on the press. CPJ and others had waged an intensive advocacy campaign on their behalf.

China, which has failed to meet its promises to improve press freedom before the 2008 Olympics, continued to be the world's leading jailer of journalists, a dishonor it has held for nine consecutive years. Cuba, Eritrea, Iran, and Azerbaijan rounded out the top five jailers among the 24 nations that imprisoned journalists.

Antistate allegations such as subversion, divulging state secrets, and acting against national interests remained the most common charge used to imprison journalists worldwide, CPJ found. About 57 percent of journalists in the census were jailed under these charges, many of them by the Chinese and Cuban governments.

The proportion of journalists held without any charge at all increased for the third consecutive year. Eritrea and Iran accounted for many of these cases, but the United States used this tactic as well. U.S. authorities did not file charges or present evidence against Al-Jazeera cameraman Sami al-Haj, held for more than five years at Guantánamo Bay, or Associated Press photographer Bilal Hussein, held in Iraq for more than 19 months. The U.S. military said Hussein's case would be referred to Iraqi courts for prosecution but continued to withhold details explaining the basis for the detention.

The practice of holding journalists without charge has eroded basic standards of fairness and accountability, CPJ found. Iranian authorities, for example, jailed Mohammad Seddigh Kaboudvand in July, but did not file formal charges or bring the editor before a judge. Kaboudvand's lawyer was not allowed to see him or review the government's case. Eritrean authorities would not even confirm whether the journalists in its custody were alive or dead. At least 19 journalists worldwide were being held in secret locations, CPJ found, with Eritrea the worst offender in this regard.

Continuing a decade-long trend, Internet journalists made up an increasing proportion of CPJ's census. Bloggers, online editors, and Web-based reporters constituted about 39 percent of journalists jailed worldwide. Print journalists made up the largest professional category, accounting for about half of those in jail.

The rise of Internet journalism and its risks were evident in China, where 18 of the 29 jailed journalists worked online. China's list includes Shi Tao, an award-winning journalist serving a 10-year sentence for e-mailing details of a government propaganda directive to an overseas Web site. The Internet giant Yahoo supplied account information to Chinese authorities that led to Shi's 2004 arrest and triggered an ongoing debate over corporate responsibility.

China continued to rely heavily on the use of vague antistate charges, imprisoning 22 journalists on accusations such as "inciting subversion of state power." Despite China's 2001 promises to the International Olympic Committee that it would ensure "complete media freedom," its leaders continued to jail reporters and operate a vast system of censorship. CPJ urged the IOC and the Games' corporate sponsors to hold Beijing accountable to its word.

Fidel Castro's absence from day-to-day power did not lead to media reform in Cuba, the world's second-leading jailer. Twenty-four Cuban journalists were imprisoned, CPJ found, most of them swept up in a March 2003 crackdown on the independent press. Eritrea ranked third, with 14 jailed journalists, all held in undisclosed prisons.

Two countries—Iran and Azerbaijan—were new to the list of leading jailers. Facing domestic dissent and economic troubles, Iranian authorities meted out harsher penalties to journalists. Twelve languished in Iranian jails. One of them, Adnan Hassanpour, editor of the now-banned weekly *Aso*, was sentenced to death after being convicted in January of endangering national security and engaging in propaganda against the state.

Imprisonments also spiked in Azerbaijan, where nine journalists were in jail.

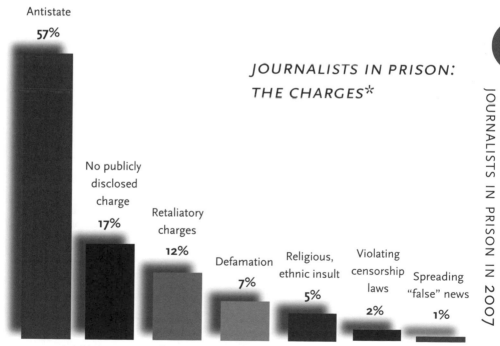

JOURNALISTS IN PRISON: THE CHARGES*

Antistate **57%**

No publicly disclosed charge **17%**

Retaliatory charges **12%**

Defamation **7%**

Religious, ethnic insult **5%**

Violating censorship laws **2%**

Spreading "false" news **1%**

* Adds up to more than 100% because multiple charges were filed in some cases.

The imprisoned ranks included editor Eynulla Fatullayev, whose April arrest came shortly after he published an in-depth report alleging an official cover-up in the 2005 slaying of fellow Azerbaijani editor Elmar Huseynov.

CPJ research shows that journalist imprisonments rose significantly after governments worldwide imposed sweeping national security laws in the wake of the 2001 terrorist attacks on the United States. Imprisonments stood at 81 in 2000 but have since averaged 129 in CPJ's annual surveys.

Here are other trends and details that emerged in CPJ's analysis:

- In about 12 percent of cases, governments used a variety of charges unrelated to journalism to retaliate against critical writers, editors, and photojournalists. Such charges range from regulatory violations to drug possession. In the cases included in this census, CPJ has determined that the charges were most likely lodged in reprisal for the journalist's work.

- Criminal defamation, the next most common charge, was lodged in about 7 percent of cases. Charges of ethnic or religious insult were filed in about 5 percent of cases, while violations of censorship rules account for another 2 percent.

- Print and Internet journalists made up the bulk of the census. Television journalists composed the next largest professional category, accounting for 6 percent of cases. Radio journalists accounted for 4 percent, documentary filmmakers 2 percent.

- The longest-serving journalists in CPJ's census were Chen Renjie and Lin Youping, who were jailed in China in July 1983 for publishing a pamphlet titled *Ziyou Bao* (Freedom Report). Codefendant Chen Biling was later executed.

CPJ believes that journalists should not be imprisoned for doing their jobs. The organization sent letters expressing its serious concerns to each country that imprisoned a journalist. In addition, CPJ sent requests during the year to Eritrean and U.S. officials seeking details in cases in which journalists were held without publicly disclosed charges.

CPJ's list is a snapshot of those incarcerated at midnight on December 1, 2007. It does not include the many journalists imprisoned and released throughout the year; accounts of those cases can be found at www.cpj.org. Journalists remain on CPJ's list until the organization determines with reasonable certainty that they have been released or have died in custody.

Journalists who either disappeared or were abducted by nonstate entities, including criminal gangs, rebels, or militant groups, are not included on the imprisoned list. Their cases are classified as "missing" or "abducted." Details of these cases are also available on CPJ's Web site.

127 JOURNALISTS IMPRISONED AS OF 12/1/2007

ALGERIA: 2

Djamel Eddine Fahassi
Alger Chaïne III
IMPRISONED: May 6, 1995

Fahassi was last seen on May 6, 1995, near his home in the Al-Harrache suburb of Algiers. On the day of his disappearance, Fahassi had left a neighborhood restaurant where he had been with friends at about 2:30 p.m. Eyewitnesses told his wife, Safia, that four well-dressed men with walkie-talkies accosted the journalist. They said the men called out Fahassi's name and then pushed him into a waiting car. He has not been seen since, and Algerian authorities have denied any knowledge of his arrest.

Fahassi was a reporter for the government-run French-language radio station Alger Chaîne III and a contributor to several Algerian newspapers, including the weekly *La Nation*, and the Islamic Salvation Front-affiliated weekly *Al-Forqane*, which was banned.

Prior to his "disappearance," Fahassi was targeted by Algerian authorities on at least two occasions in response to his published critiques of the government. In late 1991, he was arrested following the publication of an article in *Al-Forqane* that likened a raid by security forces on an Algiers neighborhood to a pogrom. He was convicted on January 1, 1992, by the Blida Military Court

of disseminating false information, attacking a state institution, and disseminating information that could harm national unity. He received a one-year suspended sentence and was released, having served five months in custody.

A few months later, on February 17, 1992, he was arrested for allegedly attacking state institutions and spreading false information and transferred to the Ain Salah Detention Center in southern Algeria. The facility detained hundreds of Islamist suspects in the months following the cancellation of the January 1992 elections. Fahassi was released on March 29 after a vocal campaign in the press, Safia Fahassi said.

In late January 2002, Algerian Ambassador to the United States Idriss Jazairy responded to a CPJ query, saying a government investigation had not found those responsible for Fahassi's abduction. The ambassador added that there was no evidence of state involvement.

Aziz Bouabdallah, *Al-Alam al-Siyassi*
IMPRISONED: April 12, 1997

Three armed men abducted Bouabdallah, a reporter for the Arabic-language daily *Al-Alam al-Siyassi*, from his home in the Chevalier section of the capital, Algiers, late on April 12, 1997. According to Bouabdallah's family, the men stormed into their home, and after they confirmed that the young man's name was Aziz, they grabbed him, put his hands behind his back, and pushed him out the door and into a waiting car. Bouabdallah was 22 at the time.

An article published in the daily *El-Watan* a few days after the abduction reported that Bouabdallah was in police custody, according to police sources, and that his release was imminent. The Bouabdallahs said police have not disputed the story.

In July 1997, CPJ received credible information that Bouabdallah was being held in Algiers at the Châteauneuf detention facility, where he had reportedly been tortured. Bouabdallah's whereabouts were unknown in 2007, and authorities have denied any knowledge.

Both family and colleagues expressed bewilderment about the motive behind Bouabdallah's disappearance. They say that he was not politically active. His mother, Shafia, said that he had been studying law for three years at the Faculty of Law in Ben Aknoun. "He wanted to become a judge," she said.

In late January 2002, Algerian Ambassador to the United States Idriss Jazairy responded to a CPJ query, saying a government investigation had not found those responsible for Bouabdallah's abduction and said there was no evidence of state involvement.

ARMENIA: 1

Arman Babadzhanian
Zhamanak Yerevan
IMPRISONED: June 26, 2006

The Yerevan prosecutor general summoned Babadzhanian, editor-in-chief of *Zhamanak Yerevan*, purportedly for questioning as a witness in a criminal case. Instead, authorities charged him with forging documents to evade military service in 2002 and took him into custody, according to international press reports.

At his trial, Babadzhanian pleaded guilty to draft evasion but said the charge was in retaliation for the paper's critical reporting. Days before his arrest, *Zhamanak Yerevan* published an article questioning the independence of the prosecutor general's office, according to the London-based Institute for War and Peace Reporting.

On September 8, 2006, a district court in Yerevan sentenced Babadzhanian to four years in prison on charges of forgery and draft evasion, according to the Armenian service of Radio Free Europe/Radio Liberty. An appeals court later reduced the penalty by six months.

On July 19, an independent Armenian committee that oversees requests for early release of convicts rejected Babadzhanian's appeal, according to local press reports.

AZERBAIJAN: 9

Sakit Zakhidov, *Azadlyg*
IMPRISONED: June 23, 2006

On October 4, 2006, a court in Baku convicted Zakhidov on a drug-possession charge and sentenced him to three years in prison. He was placed in the Bailovsk Prison in Baku.

Police arrested Zakhidov, a prominent reporter and satirist for the Baku-based opposition daily *Azadlyg*, and charged him with possession of heroin with intent to sell. Zakhidov denied the charge and said a police officer placed the drugs, about a third of an ounce, in his pocket during his arrest, according to local and international news reports.

His arrest came three days after Executive Secretary Ali Akhmedov of the ruling Yeni Azerbaijan party publicly urged authorities to silence Zakhidov. At a June 20, 2006, panel on media freedom, Akhmedov said: "No government official or member of parliament has avoided his slanders. Someone should put an end to it," the news Web site *EurasiaNet* reported.

Samir Sadagatoglu, *Senet*
Rafiq Tagi, *Senet*
IMPRISONED: November 15, 2006

Editor-in-Chief Sadagatoglu and reporter Tagi of the independent newspaper *Senet* were convicted of inciting religious hatred. Sadagatoglu was sentenced to four years in prison; Tagi to three. The convictions were linked to a November 2006 article headlined "Europe and Us." Tagi, the author, suggested that Islamic values were blocking development in the oil-rich Caspian Sea nation, according to international media reports. The article referred to Islam as a cause of infighting.

Tagi and Sadagatoglu received death threats from Islamic hard-liners in Azerbaijan and neighboring Iran. Grand Ayatollah Mohammed Fazel Lankarani, one of Iran's most senior clerics, issued a fatwa in November 2006 and attended the journalists' trial in April 2007.

Sadagatoglu and Tagi were among 114 political prisoners pardoned by presidential decree on December 28. Local press freedom advocates expected the two would be released by early 2008.

Faramaz Novruzoglu, *Nota Bene*
IMPRISONED: January 30, 2007

Reporter Novruzoglu of the weekly independent newspaper *Nota Bene* was sentenced to two years in prison for criminal defamation, according to local press reports. Novruzoglu was tried without a lawyer in proceedings that took place earlier than announced, Ilham Tumas, founder of *Nota Bene*, told the news Web site *Mediaforum.*

Interior Minister Ramil Usubov filed suit after *Nota Bene* published a series of articles critical of him and other senior government officials in December 2006, according to the independent Turan news agency. The articles focused on friction and corruption in the Interior Ministry.

Local journalists and human rights activists told CPJ that the lawsuits were an attempt to stifle critical coverage of the Interior Ministry in the aftermath of a former ministry official's trial on murder and kidnapping charges.

The journalist's wife, Tahira Allahverdiyeva, told the Baku-based Institute for Reporters' Freedom and Safety that

JOURNALISTS IN PRISON IN 2007

Novruzoglu's health had deteriorated in prison and that he suffered from a chronic intestinal ailment.

Novruzoglu was among 114 political prisoners pardoned by presidential decree on December 28. Local press freedom advocates expected that he would be freed by early 2008.

Eynulla Fatullayev, *Realny Azerbaijan*
and *Gündalik Azarbaycan*
IMPRISONED: April 20, 2007

Authorities targeted Fatullayev, editor of the independent Russian-language weekly *Realny Azerbaijan* and the Azeri-language daily *Gündalik Azarbaycan*, in a series of politically motivated criminal prosecutions. The persecution began shortly after Fatullayev published an in-depth report alleging an official cover-up in the 2005 slaying of fellow Azerbaijani editor Elmar Huseynov.

In April, a Yasamal District Court judge found Fatullayev guilty of libeling and insulting Azerbaijanis in an Internet posting that the journalist said was falsely attributed to him. The posting, published on several Web sites, said Azerbaijanis bore some responsibility for the 1992 killings of residents of the restive Nagorno-Karabakh region, according to local press reports. Fatullayev, ordered to serve 30 months, was jailed immediately after the proceedings, according to the independent news agency Turan.

With Fatullayev jailed, authorities evicted *Realny Azerbaijan* and *Gündalik Azarbaycan* from their Baku offices, citing purported fire safety and building code violations. Both later stopped publishing.

More charges against Fatullayev followed. A judge in the Azerbaijani Court of Serious Crimes found Fatullayev guilty of terrorism, incitement to ethnic hatred, and tax evasion on October 30. The journalist was sentenced to eight years and six months in prison, to be served concurrent to the 30-month term.

The terrorist and incitement charges stemmed from a *Realny Azerbaijan* commentary headlined "The Aliyevs go to war," which sharply criticized President Ilham Aliyev's foreign policy regarding Iran. The tax evasion charge alleged that Fatullayev had concealed income from the two publications.

Realny Azerbaijan was successor to the opposition weekly *Monitor*, which closed after the March 2005 assassination of Huseynov. Like its predecessor, *Realny Azerbaijan* was known for its critical reporting.

Yashar Agazadeh, *Muhalifet*
Rovshan Kebirli, *Muhalifet*
IMPRISONED: May 16, 2007

A Yasamal District Court judge found Editor-in-Chief Kebirli and reporter Agazadeh of the Baku-based opposition daily guilty of defaming President Ilham Aliyev's uncle, Jalal Aliyev, and sentenced each to 30 months in prison, according to local and international press reports. Jalal Aliyev is also a member of Azerbaijan's parliament.

Jalal Aliyev filed a libel complaint

against the journalists after a February article in *Muhalifet* criticized his business activities and those of his family, according to local and international press reports. The story, which relied partly on a Turkish news report, said the Aliyevs' import-export business profited from the family's political connections.

Kebirli and Agazadeh were among 114 political prisoners pardoned by presidential decree on December 28. Local press freedom advocates expected the two would be released by early 2008.

Nazim Guliyev, *Ideal*
IMPRISONED: November 6, 2007

Guliyev, editor-in-chief of the pro-government daily *Ideal*, was sentenced to two and a half years in prison on criminal defamation and insult charges.

Ramiz Zeynalov, head of the Interior Ministry Traffic Police Department, filed a complaint against Guliyev after *Ideal* published two articles describing alleged corruption in the department in May and August, according to local press reports. An appeals court freed Guliyev in December after the journalist reached "reconciliation" with Zeynalov, according to news reports.

Genimet Zakhidov, *Azadlyg*
IMPRISONED: November 10, 2007

A Yasamal District Court judge placed Zakhidov, editor of the opposition daily, in pretrial detention in Baku, a day after the journalist's arrest. Police arrested Zakhidov after nine hours of interroga-

tion and charged him with "hooliganism" and inflicting "minor bodily harm." The arrest stemmed from a confrontation in which the journalist appeared to have been set up by authorities.

On November 7, Zakhidov said, a young man and woman assailed him on a street in Baku. Zakhidov told reporters that the woman started screaming as if he had insulted her; a moment later, the man tried to attack him. With the help of passersby, Zakhidov said, he was able to fend them off. But the man and woman later filed complaints with police, and Zakhidov was summoned for questioning three days later.

Zakhidov was targeted in two other instances of official harassment. In September, Minister of Economic Development Geidar Babayev filed a defamation lawsuit over an *Azadlyg* article alleging misuse of ministry funds. In October, a state traffic police official filed a similar complaint over an article describing alleged corruption. Zakhidov's brother, prominent reporter and satirist Sakit Zakhidov, was also serving a prison term on a bogus charge of drug possession.

BANGLADESH: 3

Atiqullah Khan Masud, *Janakantha*
IMPRISONED: March 7, 2007

Masud, owner and publisher of the Bengali-language daily *Janakantha*, was escorted from his office by members of the Rapid Action Battalion during a raid in March. He was detained on several corruption charges, denied bail, and sent to Dhaka Central Jail under the Special Powers Act.

Masud was heavily involved in his newspaper, which was one of the few local publications openly discussing the state of emergency declared in Bangladesh in January. *Janakantha* had been warned by the government not to be so outspoken, according to local press freedom groups. The government denied that the detention had any connection to the newspaper.

Arifur Rahman, *Prothom Alo*
IMPRISONED: September 17, 2007

Rahman, a 20-year-old cartoonist, was taken into custody following a religious controversy sparked by a cartoon published in the satirical supplement of the daily *Prothom Alo* on September 17. Rahman was charged under the provisions of Section 54 of Bangladesh's Criminal Procedure Code, which gives police broad power to make arrests without a warrant.

The cartoon featured a boy calling his pet "Muhammad Cat" because of the Muslim custom of putting Muhammad before a male given name. The paper apologized and the supplement's deputy editor was fired when the joke was deemed offensive by Muslim groups, but hundreds gathered on September 21 to demonstrate against the newspaper. The demonstration was staged despite a ban on protests during the country's state of emergency.

Rahman had been awarded a government prize in August for an anti-corruption cartoon.

Zahirul Haque Titu
Inqilab, The New Nation
IMPRISONED: October 2, 2007

Titu, local correspondent for the dailies *Inqilab* and *The New Nation*, was detained on October 2 in his hometown of Pirojpur in southwestern Bangladesh, about 100 miles (160 kilometers) from Dhaka. The arrest was made under emergency ordinances put in place by the military-backed interim government in January. No reason was given for his apprehension, and there was no immediate move to bring him to trial, according to local press freedom advocates.

Titu, a former general secretary of the Pirojpur Press Club, wrote on a variety of topics. Titu and his elder brother, Shafiul Haque Mithu, Pirojpur reporter for the *Dainik Janakantha*, had been targeted for their reporting in the past by activists with the Bangladesh National Party and their fundamentalist allies in the Jamaat-e-Islami Party. Titu was hospitalized after a December 2006 attack, according to the Bangladesh Federal Union of Journalists.

BURMA: 7

U Win Tin, freelance
IMPRISONED: July 4, 1989

U Win Tin, former editor-in-chief of the daily *Hanthawati* and chairman of Burma's Writers Club, was arrested and sentenced to three years hard labor in 1989 on the spurious charge of arranging a "forced abortion" for an opposition politician. While in prison, his sentence was extended twice, building to 20 years. U Win Tin suffered at least two heart attacks in prison and has been shuttled between the notorious Insein Prison and Rangoon Hospital's prisoner wing.

U Win Tin helped establish various pro-democracy publications during the 1988 uprisings that the ruling military junta violently crushed. As a former joint secretary to the main opposition National League for Democracy (NLD) political party, U Win Tin was considered a close adviser to NLD party leader and Nobel Laureate Daw Aung San Suu Kyi.

In 1992, his initial term drawing to an end, U Win Tin saw his sentence extended on charges of "writing and publishing pamphlets to incite treason against the state" and "giving seditious talks" during the 1988 uprisings. In 1996, military authorities extended his term yet again on charges that he secretly published "antigovernment propaganda" from prison, including notes drawn up for a U.N. special rapporteur detailing human rights abuses at Insein.

In 1996, U Win Tin was held for five months in crude solitary confinement in kennels designed for the prison's guard dogs. Such deprivations contributed to the 77-year-old journalist's declining health, including a degenerative spine condition, heart disease, inflamed knee joints, dental problems, and a prostate gland disorder, according to the Assistance Association for Political Prisoners in Burma, a prisoner assistance group based in Thailand.

A senior Burmese military official offered to release U Win Tin in 2003 in exchange for the journalist signing a document promising to cease political activities, according to a report in *Le Monde*. U Win Tin refused.

Two years later, U Win Tin was subjected to a cruel manipulation, according to news reports. The Associated Press reported that the journalist was told he would be among the political prisoners released on July 6, 2005. In all, nearly 250 such prisoners were freed at the time.

But after gathering his belongings and attending a briefing on the conditions of release, U Win Tin was instead directed to a nearby office, according to a freed prisoner quoted in a Radio Free Asia dispatch. For unknown reasons, U Win Tin was not freed.

Maung Maung Lay Ngwe
Pe-Tin-Than
IMPRISONED: September 1990

Maung Maung Lay Ngwe was arrested and charged in 1990 with writing and distributing undisclosed publications that the authorities deemed to "make people lose respect for the government." The publications were collectively titled *Pe-Tin-Than*, which translates loosely as "Echoes." CPJ has been unable to confirm his current whereabouts, legal status, or records of his original sentencing 17 years ago.

Aung Htun, freelance
IMPRISONED: February 17, 1998

Aung Htun, a writer and activist, was imprisoned in February 1998 for writing and publishing a seven-volume book that documented the history of the student movement that led the pro-democracy uprisings of 1988. He was sentenced to a total of 17 years in prison, according to information compiled by the Assistance Association for Political Prisoners in Burma (AAPPB), a prisoner assistance group based in Thailand.

He was sentenced separately to three years for violating the 1962 Printers and Publishers Registration Act, the military government's main legal instrument of official censorship; seven years under the 1950 Emergency Provisions Act, which is used broadly to suppress any dissent against the regime; and another seven years under the 1908 Unlawful Associations Act, a draconian holdover from Burma's colonial era under British rule, according to the AAPPB.

The writer's health deteriorated during his detention. In 2002, Amnesty International issued an urgent appeal requesting that Aung Htun be granted access to medical treatment for complications related to growths on his feet, which had apparently inhibited his ability to walk, as well as a severe asthma condition. His health has deteriorated further in subsequent years, according to the Burma Media Association, an exiled press freedom advocacy group. Amnesty International issued another appeal in July 2007 for his immediate release on humanitarian grounds.

Aung Htun's book was finally released by the All Burma Federation of Student Unions on May 16, 2007.

Ne Min (Win Shwe), freelance
IMPRISONED: February 2004

Ne Min, a lawyer and former stringer for the BBC, was sentenced to 15 years in prison on May 7, 2004, on charges that he illegally passed information to "antigovernment" organizations operating in border areas, according to the Assistance Association for Political Prisoners in Burma, a prisoner assistance group based in Thailand.

It was the second time Burma's military government had imprisoned the well-known journalist, also known as Win Shwe, on charges related to disseminating information to news sources outside of Burma. In 1989, a military tribunal sentenced Ne Min to 14 years hard labor for "spreading false news and rumors to the BBC to fan further disturbances in the country" and the "possession of documents including antigovernment literature, which he planned to send to the BBC," according to official radio reports. He served nine years at Rangoon's Insein Prison before being released in 1998. His second arrest was in February 2004.

Exiled Burmese journalists who spoke with CPJ said that Ne Min sent news and information to political groups and exile-run news publications after his release from prison.

Thaung Sein (Thar Cho), freelance
Kyaw Thwin (Moe Tun), *Dhamah Yate*
IMPRISONED: March 27, 2006

Thaung Sein, a freelance photojournalist, and Kyaw Thwin, a columnist at the Burmese-language magazine *Dhamah Yate*, were arrested on March 27, 2006, and sentenced the following day to three years in prison for photographing and videotaping while riding on a public bus near the capital city, Pyinmana.

The two journalists were charged under the 1996 Television and Video Act, which bars the distribution of film without official approval. Under the law, every videotape in Burma must receive a certificate, which may be revoked at any time, from the government's censorship board.

Burmese security officials were under strict orders to stop and detain anyone found taking photographs near the capital. Thaung Sein, also known as Thar Cho, and Kyaw Thwin, more widely known by his pen name Moe Tun, were placed at Yemethin Prison in central Burma, according to the Assistance Association for Political Prisoners in Burma, a prisoner assistance group based in Thailand.

Both journalists appealed the decision on the argument that they had not taken film or video footage of restricted areas. On June 21, an appeals court based in the central town of Yemethin upheld the lower court's verdict without allowing defense witnesses to testify, according to information from their lawyer that was received by the Burma Media Association, an exile-run press freedom advocacy group.

Burma's secretive military government abruptly moved the national capital in November 2005 to Pyinmana, a newly built administrative center located 250 miles (400 kilometers) north of Rangoon. Regional news reports, citing official government documents, said the junta's decision to move the capital was motivated by fears of supposed military strikes.

Win Saing, freelance
IMPRISONED: August 28, 2007

Win Saing, a photographer, was arrested while documenting activists making offerings to monks during massive pro-democracy demonstrations. The protesters were marching against increased fuel prices that were announced on August 15. Local monks supported the demonstrations against the military government and became increasingly influential in their escalation as they continued into September.

More than 2,000 people were arrested during the severe crackdown that followed. Several journalists were detained and later released, but Win Saing remained in custody. No formal charges were immediately disclosed.

CAMBODIA: 1

Hem Choun, *Samrek Yutethor*
IMPRISONED: June 7, 2006

Hem Choun, a reporter with the Khmer-language newspaper *Samrek Yutethor*, was arrested by military police while reporting on the forced eviction of land squatters by military police from Sambok Chap village on the outskirts of the capital, Phnom Penh.

He was arrested along with three other villagers for their alleged role in leading a violent protest on May 31 against a private security company that had been hired to secure the land. That day, protestors dismantled metal fences erected around the village and burned down the village chief's empty house.

Choun's lawyer said that he covered the riot as a reporter and did not participate in the melee. The Cambodian Center for Human Rights (CCHR), a rights advocacy group that has provided legal counsel to the jailed journalist, told CPJ that police arrested Choun without a proper warrant and that they had refused to recognize him as a practicing journalist.

On June 8, Phnom Penh Municipal Court Investigation Judge Ke Sokhan charged Choun under Article 52 of the U.N. Transitional Authority in Cambodia criminal law, which relates to wrongful damage of property. He was convicted on November 30, 2006, and sentenced to two years in prison.

Choun was being held in crowded conditions at Phnom Penh's notorious Prey Sar Prison. According to CCHR, Choun developed respiratory complications during his detention, and prison authorities on at least one occasion denied him outside medical treatment.

CHINA: 29

Chen Renjie, *Ziyou Bao*
Lin Youping, *Ziyou Bao*
IMPRISONED: July 1983

Twenty-four years after their imprisonment in the early days of China's economic reform, Chen and Lin are the longest-serving journalists in CPJ's worldwide census. The two men, along with Chen Biling, wrote and published a pamphlet titled *Ziyou Bao* (Freedom Report). They distributed 300 copies of the pamphlet in the southern Chinese city of Fuzhou, Fujian province, in September 1982.

The following July, they were arrested and accused of making contact with Taiwanese spy groups and publishing a counterrevolutionary pamphlet. According to official government records of the case, the men used "propaganda and incitement to encourage the overthrow of the people's democratic dictatorship and the socialist system."

In August 1983, Chen was sentenced to life in prison, and Lin was sentenced to death with reprieve. Chen Biling was sentenced to death and later executed.

Fan Yingshang, *Remen Huati*
CHARGED: October 16, 1995

In 1994, Fan and Yang Jianguo printed more than 60,000 copies of the magazine *Remen Huati* (Popular Topics). The men had allegedly purchased fake printing authorizations from an editor of the *Journal of European Research* at the Chinese Academy of Social Sciences, according to official Chinese news sources. Printing authorizations are a prior restraint used to curtail independent publishing in China.

CPJ was unable to determine the date of Fan's arrest, but on October 16, 1995, he was indicted on charges of profiteering. On January 31, 1996, the Chang'an District Court in Shijiazhuang City sentenced him to 13 years in prison, with three years' subsequent deprivation of political rights, for publishing and distributing illegal "reactionary" publications. Yang escaped arrest and was not sentenced.

Fan's appeal was rejected on April 11, 1996, according to the Chinese government's response to a query by the San Francisco-based prisoners' advocacy group Dui Hua Foundation.

Hua Di, freelance
IMPRISONED: January 5, 1998

The imprisonment of Hua, a Stanford University scientist and permanent resident of the United States, raised objections from former U.S. President Bill Clinton, his colleagues at Stanford University, and others. But nine years later, he remained in jail.

Hua was arrested while visiting China and accused of revealing state secrets, a charge used frequently against journalists who write about controversial matters. Charges are believed to stem from articles that Hua had written in academic journals about China's missile defense system.

On November 25, 1999, the Beijing No. 1 Intermediate People's Court held a closed trial and sentenced Hua to 15 years in prison, according to the Hong Kong-based Information Center for Human Rights and Democracy. In March 2000, the Beijing High People's Court overturned Hua's conviction and ordered that the case be retried. This judicial reversal was extraordinary, and it appeared to be a response to international pressure. But the decision did not mean that he was freed.

Instead, after a retrial, the Beijing No. 1 Intermediate People's Court issued a modified verdict, sentencing Hua to 10 years in prison in November 2000. News of Hua's sentencing did not break until three months later, when a relative gave the information to foreign correspondents based in Beijing.

Requests for medical parole have been rejected. Hua suffers from a rare form of male breast cancer.

Yue Tianxiang
Zhongguo Gongren Guancha
IMPRISONED: January 1999

Along with his colleagues Wang Fengshan and Guo Xinmin, Yue started a journal campaigning for workers' rights after they were unable to get compensation from the Tianshui City Transport

Agency following their dismissal from the company in 1995. The first issue of *Zhongguo Gongren Guancha* (China Labor Watch) exposed extensive corruption among officials at the company, according to international media reports. Only two issues were ever published.

On July 5, 1999, the Tianshui People's Intermediate Court in Gansu province sentenced Yue to 10 years in prison on charges of "subverting state authority," according to the Hong Kong-based Information Center for Human Rights and Democracy. His colleagues Wang and Guo were sentenced to two years in prison and have since been released. All three men reportedly belonged to the outlawed China Democracy Party, a dissident group, and were forming an organization to protect the rights of laid-off workers.

In 2006, the U.S.-based prisoner advocacy group Dui Hua Foundation reported that Yue's sentence was reduced to nine years in March 2005. He turned 51 in Lanzhou Prison in December 2007.

Xu Zerong, freelance
IMPRISONED: June 24, 2000

Xu is serving a 13-year prison term on charges of "leaking state secrets" through his academic work on military history and of "economic crimes" related to unauthorized publishing on foreign policy issues. Some observers believe that his jailing may have been related to an article he wrote for the Hong Kong-based *Yazhou Zhoukan* (Asia Weekly) magazine revealing clandestine Chinese Communist Party support for a Malaysian insurgency in the 1950s and 1960s.

Xu, a permanent resident of Hong Kong, was arrested in Guangzhou and held incommunicado for 18 months until his trial. He was tried by Shenzhen Intermediate Court in December 2001, and his appeal to Guangzhou Higher People's Court was rejected in 2002.

According to court documents, the "state secrets" charges against Xu stemmed from his use of historical documents for academic research. Xu, also known as David Tsui, was an associate research professor at the Institute of Southeast Asian Studies at Zhongshan University in Guangzhou. In 1992, he photocopied four books published in the 1950s about China's role in the Korean War, which he then sent to a colleague in South Korea. The verdict stated that the Security Committee of the People's Liberation Army of Guangzhou later determined that the books had not been declassified 40 years after being labeled "top secret." After his arrest, St. Antony's College at Oxford University, where Xu earned his doctorate and wrote his dissertation on the Korean War, was active in researching his case and calling for his release.

Xu was also the co-founder of a Hong Kong-based academic journal, *Zhongguo Shehui Kexue Jikan* (China Social Sciences Quarterly). The "economic crimes" charges were related to the "illegal publication" of more than 60,000 copies of 25 books and periodicals, including several books about Chinese politics and Beijing's relations with Taiwan.

He was arrested just days after an article appeared in the June 26, 2000, issue of *Yazhou Zhoukan* in which he accused the Chinese Communist Party of hypocrisy by condemning other countries for interfering in its internal affairs by criticizing its human rights record.

Xu began his sentence in Dongguan Prison, outside of Guangzhou, but was later transferred to Guangzhou Prison, where it was easier for his family to visit him. He has been spared from hard labor and has been allowed to read, research, and teach English in prison, according to the U.S.-based prisoner advocacy group Dui Hua Foundation. He has suffered from high blood pressure and diabetes.

In 2006, Xu's family members were informed that he had received a nine-month reduction in his sentence, according to Dui Hua. Based on that, he would be scheduled for release in 2012.

Jin Haike, freelance
Xu Wei, *Xiaofei Ribao*
Yang Zili, *Yangzi de Sixiang Jiayuan*
Zhang Honghai, freelance
IMPRISONED: March 13, 2001

The four members of an informal discussion group called Xin Qingnian Xuehui (New Youth Study Group) were detained and accused of "subverting state authority." Prosecutors cited online articles and essays on political and social reform as proof of their intent to overthrow the Chinese Communist Party leadership.

Yang, Xu, Jin, and Zhang were charged with subversion on April 20, 2001. More than two years later, on May 29, 2003, the Beijing No. 1 Intermediate People's Court sentenced Xu and Jin to 10 years in prison each, while Yang and Zhang each received sentences of eight years. Each of the sentences was to be followed by two years' deprivation of political rights.

The four young men were students and recent university graduates who gathered occasionally to discuss politics and reform with four others, including an informant for the Ministry of State Security. The most prominent in the group, Yang, posted his own thoughts and reports by the others on topics such as rural poverty and village elections, along with essays advocating democratic reform, on a popular Web site, *Yangzi de Sixiang Jiayuan* (Yangzi's Garden of Ideas). Xu was a reporter at *Xiaofei Ribao* (Consumer's Daily). Public security agents pressured the newspaper to fire him before his arrest, a friend, Wang Ying, reported online.

The court cited a handful of articles, including Jin's "Be a New Citizen, Reform China" and Yang's "Choose Liberalism," in the 2003 verdict against them. Beijing Higher People's Court rejected their appeal without hearing defense witnesses. Three of the witnesses who testified against the four men were fellow members of the group who later tried to retract their testimonies.

Yang, Xu, and Jin were imprisoned at Beijing's No. 2 Prison. Yang's wife, Lu

Kun, who was also initially detained and questioned, was unable to visit him for four years after his imprisonment, she told reporters in 2005. Zhang, who initially suffered from ill health in detention, was jailed at Lishui Prison in Zhejiang province, where he made sweaters, his brother told CPJ.

Tao Haidong, freelance
IMPRISONED: July 9, 2002

Tao, an Internet essayist and pro-democracy activist, was arrested in Urumqi, the capital of the Xinjiang Uighur Autonomous Region (XUAR), and charged with "incitement to subvert state power." According to the *Minzhu Luntan* (Democracy Forum) Web site, which had published Tao's recent writing, his articles focused on political and legal reform. In one essay, titled "Strategies for China's Social Reforms," Tao wrote that "the Chinese Communist Party and democracy activists throughout society should unite to push forward China's freedom and democratic development or else stand condemned through the ages."

Previously, in 1999, Tao was sentenced to three years of "re-education through labor" in Xi'an, Shaanxi province, according to the New York-based advocacy group Human Rights in China, because of his essays and his work on a book titled *Xin Renlei Shexiang* (Imaginings of a New Human Race). After his early release in 2001, Tao began writing articles and publishing them on various domestic and overseas Web sites.

In early January 2003, the Urumqi Intermediate Court sentenced Tao to seven years in prison. His appeal to the XUAR Higher Court later in 2003 was rejected.

Zhang Wei
Shishi Zixun and *Redian Jiyao*
IMPRISONED: July 19, 2002

Zhang was arrested and charged with illegal publishing after producing and selling two underground newspapers in Chongqing, in central China. According to an account published on the Web site of the Chongqing Press and Publishing Administration, a provincial government body that governs all local publications, beginning in April 2001, Zhang edited two newspapers, *Shishi Zixun* (Current Events) and *Redian Jiyao* (Summary of the Main Points), which included articles and graphics he had downloaded from the Internet.

Two of Zhang's business associates, Zuo Shangwen and Ou Yan, were also arrested on July 19, 2002, and indicted for their involvement with the publications. Zuo printed the publications in neighboring Sichuan province, while Ou managed the publications' finances. At the time of their arrests, police confiscated 9,700 copies of *Shishi Zixun*.

The official account of their arrests stated that the two publications had "flooded" Chongqing's publishing market. The government declared that "the political rumors, shocking 'military reports,' and other articles in these illegal publications misled the public, poisoned the youth, negatively influenced society, and sparked public indignation." Zhang, Zuo, and Ou printed more than 1.5 million copies of the publications and sold them in Chongqing, Chengdu, and other cities.

On December 25, 2002, the Yuzhong District Court in Chongqing sentenced Zhang to six years in prison and fined him 100,000 yuan (US$12,000), the amount that police said he had earned in profits from the publications. Zuo was sentenced to five years and fined 50,000 yuan (US$6,000), while Ou was sentenced to two years in prison.

Abdulghani Memetemin
East Turkistan Information Center
IMPRISONED: July 26, 2002

Memetemin, a writer, teacher, and translator who had actively advocated for the Uighur ethnic group in the northwestern Xinjiang Uighur Autonomous Region, was detained in Kashgar, a city in Xinjiang, on charges of "leaking state secrets."

In June 2003, Kashgar Intermediate People's Court sentenced him to nine years in prison, plus a three-year suspension of political rights. Radio Free Asia provided CPJ with court documents listing 18 specific counts against Memetemin, including translating state news articles into Chinese from Uighur; forwarding official speeches to the Germany-based East Turkistan Information Center (ETIC), a news outlet that advocates for an independent state for the Uighur ethnic group; and conducting original reporting for ETIC. The court

also accused him of recruiting additional reporters for ETIC, which is banned in China.

Memetemin did not have legal representation at his trial.

Huang Jinqiu, *Boxun News*
IMPRISONED: September 13, 2003

Huang, a columnist for the U.S.-based Web site *Boxun News*, was arrested in Jiangsu province. Huang's family was not officially notified of his arrest for more than three months. On September 27, 2004, Changzhou Intermediate People's Court sentenced him to 12 years in prison on charges of "subversion of state authority," plus four years' deprivation of political rights. The sentence was unusually harsh and appeared linked to his intention to form an opposition party.

Huang worked as a writer and editor in his native Shandong province, as well as in Guangdong province, before leaving China in 2000 to study journalism at the Central Academy of Art in Malaysia. While he was overseas, Huang began writing political commentary for *Boxun News* under the pen name Qing Shuijun. He also wrote articles on arts and entertainment under the name Huang Jin. Huang's writings reportedly caught the attention of the government in 2001. Huang told a friend that authorities had contacted his family to warn them about his writing, according to *Boxun News*.

In January 2003, Huang wrote in his online column that he intended to form a new opposition party, the China Patriot Democracy Party. When he returned to China in August 2003, he eluded public security agents just long enough to visit his family in Shandong province. In the last article he posted on *Boxun News*, titled "Me and My Public Security Friends," Huang described being followed and harassed by security agents.

Huang's appeal was rejected in December 2004.

Huang's lawyer told CPJ in early 2005 that the journalist had been mistreated in prison and was in poor health. In February 2007, his family told *Boxun News* that his health conditions and treatment had improved. Huang was serving his sentence in Pukou prison, near Nanjing.

Kong Youping, freelance
IMPRISONED: December 13, 2003

Kong, an essayist and poet, was arrested in Anshan, Liaoning province. A former trade union official, he had written articles online that supported democratic reforms, appealed for the release of then-imprisoned Internet writer Liu Di, and called for a reversal of the government's "counterrevolutionary" ruling on the pro-democracy demonstrations of 1989.

Kong's essays included an appeal to democracy activists in China that stated, "In order to work well for democracy, we need a well-organized, strong, powerful, and effective organization. Otherwise, a mainland democracy movement will accomplish nothing." Several of his articles and poems were posted on the *Minzhu Luntan* (Democracy Forum) Web site.

In 1998, Kong served time in prison after he became a member of the Liaoning province branch of the China Democracy Party (CDP), an opposition party. In 2004, he was tried on subversion charges along with codefendant Ning Xianhua, who was accused of being the vice chairman of the CDP branch in Liaoning, according to the U.S.-based advocacy organization Human Rights in China and court documents obtained by the San Francisco-based Dui Hua Foundation. On September 16, 2004, the Shenyang Intermediate People's Court sentenced Kong to 15 years in prison, plus four years' deprivation of political rights. Ning received a 12-year sentence.

Kong suffered from hypertension and was imprisoned in the city of Lingyuan far from his family, making visits difficult. In a letter written to his family from prison, Kong said that he had received a sentence reduction to 10 years in his appeal, but that information could not be confirmed.

Yu Huafeng, *Nanfang Dushi Bao*
IMPRISONED: January 2004

Yu, deputy editor-in-chief and general manager of *Nanfang Dushi Bao* (Southern Metropolis News), was detained along with former editor Li Minying less than a month after the newspaper reported a suspected SARS case in Guangzhou, the first case since the epidemic died out in July 2003. Their imprisonment was followed in March 2004 by the jailing of *Nanfang Dushi Bao* former editor-in-chief Cheng Yizhong, who was held for five months.

The arrests appeared to be a part of a crackdown on the newspaper, which became popular for its aggressive investigative reporting on social issues and wrongdoing by local officials. The paper broke news that a young graphic designer, Sun Zhigang, was beaten to death in March 2003 while in police custody in Guangzhou. Public outcry over Sun's death led to the arrest of several local government and police officials, along with a change in national laws on detention.

On March 19, 2004, Dongshan District Court in Guangzhou, Guangdong province, sentenced Yu to 12 years in prison on corruption charges. Li, who also served on the Communist Party Committee of the newspaper's parent group, Nanfang Daily Group, was sentenced to 11 years on bribery charges. In an appellate trial held in June 2004, Li's sentence was reduced to six years in prison, while Yu's sentence was reduced to eight years.

According to the official Xinhua News Agency, Yu was convicted of embezzling 580,000 yuan (US$70,000) and distributing the money to members of the paper's editorial committee. The court also accused Yu of paying Li a total of 800,000 yuan (US$97,000) in bribes while Li was editor of *Nanfang Dushi Bao*. Li was accused of accepting bribes totaling 970,000 yuan (US$117,000).

Both men maintained that the money was acquired legally and was distributed in routine bonus payments to the staff. Chinese journalists familiar with the case have told CPJ that evidence presented in court did not support the corruption charges.

In 2005, Cheng Yizhong was named the recipient of the 2005 UNESCO/Guillermo Cano World Press Freedom Prize. He was not permitted to attend the award ceremony, but in his acceptance statement he asked to share the honor with Li and Yu: "Your suffering is the shame of China," he said. Later that year, more than 2,000 journalists in China signed an open letter to the Guangdong High People's Court appealing for the release of Yu and Li. Observers could remember no precedent to this show of support.

Li was released for good behavior in February 2007 after serving half of his sentence. Yu's sentence was reduced by one year. Yu's wife told CPJ that she travels monthly to Beijing to petition for the release of her husband.

Shi Tao, freelance
IMPRISONED: November 24, 2004

Shi, the former editorial director at the Changsha-based newspaper *Dangdai Shang Bao*, was detained near his home in Taiyuan, Shanxi province.

He was formally arrested and charged with "providing state secrets to foreigners" by sending an e-mail on his Yahoo account to the U.S.-based editor of the Web site *Minzhu Luntan* (Democracy

Forum). In the anonymous e-mail sent several months before his arrest, Shi transcribed his notes from local propaganda department instructions to his newspaper, which included directives on coverage of the Falun Gong and the upcoming 15th anniversary of the military crackdown on demonstrators at Tiananmen Square. The official Xinhua News Agency reported that the National Administration for the Protection of State Secrets later certified the contents of the e-mail as classified.

On April 27, 2005, the Changsha Intermediate People's Court found Shi guilty and sentenced him to a 10-year prison term. In June, Hunan Province High People's Court rejected his appeal without granting a hearing.

Court documents in the case revealed that Yahoo had supplied information to Chinese authorities that helped them identify Shi as the sender of the e-mail. Yahoo's participation in the identification of Shi and other jailed Internet writers and dissidents in China raised questions about the role that international Internet companies are playing in the repression of online speech in China and elsewhere.

In November 2005, CPJ honored Shi in absentia with its annual International Press Freedom Award for his courage in defending the ideals of free expression. During a visit to CPJ's offices in New York in June 2007, Shi's mother, Gao Qinsheng, highlighted the 2008 Beijing Olympics as an opportunity for the international community to renew calls for her son's release. In November,

members of the U.S. House Foreign Affairs Committee rebuked Yahoo executives for their role in the case and for wrongly testifying in earlier hearings that the company did not know the Chinese government's intentions when it sought Shi's account information.

Zheng Yichun, freelance
IMPRISONED: December 3, 2004

Zheng, a former professor, was a regular contributor to overseas online news sites, including the U.S.-based *Epoch Times*, which is affiliated with the banned religious movement Falun Gong. Zheng wrote a series of editorials that directly criticized the Communist Party and its control of the media.

Because of police warnings, Zheng's family remained silent about his detention in Yingkou, Liaoning province, until state media reported that he had been arrested on suspicion of inciting subversion. Zheng was initially tried by Yingkou Intermediate People's Court on April 26, 2005. No verdict was announced, and on July 21 he was tried again on the same charges. As in the April 26 trial, proceedings lasted just three hours. Though officially "open" to the public, the courtroom was closed to all observers except close family members and government officials. Zheng's supporters and a journalist were prevented from entering, according to a local source.

Prosecutors cited dozens of articles written by the journalist, and listed the titles of several essays in which he called for political reform, increased capitalism in China, and an end to the practice of imprisoning writers. On September 20, the court sentenced Zheng to seven years in prison, to be followed by three years' deprivation of political rights.

Sources familiar with the case believe that Zheng's harsh sentence may be linked to Chinese leaders' objections to the *Epoch Times* series "Nine Commentaries on the Communist Party," which called the Chinese Communist Party an "evil cult" with a "history of killings" and predicted its demise.

Zheng is diabetic, and his health suffered a decline after his imprisonment. After his first appeal was rejected, he intended to pursue an appeal in a higher court, but his defense lawyer, Gao Zhisheng, was himself imprisoned in August 2006. Zheng's family has been unable to find another lawyer willing to take the case.

Zhang Lin, freelance
IMPRISONED: January 29, 2005

Zhang, a freelance writer and political essayist who made a living by writing for banned overseas Web sites, was convicted of "inciting subversion of state power" and misrepresenting national authorities in his articles and in a radio interview.

Zhang, who spent years in jail in the 1990s for his pro-democracy activism and for organizing a labor union, was detained at a train station near his home in Bengbu, in central China's Anhui province. Police apprehended him

as he was returning from Beijing, where he had traveled to mourn the death of ousted Communist Party leader Zhao Ziyang. He was initially accused of "disturbing public order," but police formally arrested him on charges of inciting subversion after confiscating the computer he was using.

Bengbu Intermediate People's Court tried him on June 21, 2005, in proceedings that lasted five hours, his lawyer, Mo Shaoping, told CPJ. The defense argued that the six articles and one interview cited by the prosecution were protected free expression.

Zhang's wife told reporters that his imprisonment was connected to essays he wrote about protests by unemployed workers and official scandals. On July 28, 2005, the court convicted Zhang and sentenced him to five years in prison.

For 28 days in September 2005, Zhang waged a hunger strike to protest his unjust sentence and the harsh conditions at Bengbu No. 1 Detention Center. Officials there subjected him to long hours of forced labor making Christmas ornaments and refused to allow him to read newspapers or other material, according to his lawyer. During his hunger strike, he was fed through his nose. He was hospitalized briefly before returning to the detention center.

Zhang's appeals were rejected without a hearing, and he was moved to a prison in Anhui province. Zhang's wife told CPJ that his health has suffered during his imprisonment. They have a young daughter.

JOURNALISTS IN PRISON IN 2007

Li Changqing, *Fuzhou Ribao*
IMPRISONED: February 2005

Li, deputy news director of *Fuzhou Ribao* (Fuzhou Daily), was arrested in southern China's Fujian province in connection with an investigation of whistleblower Huang Jingao, a Communist Party official in Fujian province who wrote an open letter to the state-run *People's Daily* in 2004 denouncing corruption among local officials.

Huang won public support after describing death threats that he said forced him to wear a bulletproof vest. But in November 2005 he was convicted of accepting bribes and was sentenced to life in prison. Supporters said that the charges against Huang were politically motivated.

Li was initially accused of inciting subversion. He told his lawyer that he was tortured in detention and interrogated repeatedly about his defense of Huang in newspaper and online articles.

The unexplained subversion charge was later dropped and authorities filed a charge of "deliberately fabricating and spreading alarmist information." The new charge was related to an October 13, 2004, report in the U.S.-based Chinese-language Web site *Boxun News* reporting an outbreak of dengue fever, a viral mosquito-borne disease, in Fuzhou.

The author, identified by his lawyer as Li, anonymously reported more than 20 cases, according to *Boxun News*. In seeking to confirm the information, the Web site did its own research and updated the story to reflect 100 cases.

Li was tried in Fuzhou on January 19, 2006. Five days later, Gulou district court convicted Li and sentenced him to three years in prison. His appeal was rejected.

On November 20, the World Association of Newspapers awarded Li its Golden Pen of Freedom Award.

Ching Cheong, *The Straits Times*
IMPRISONED: April 22, 2005

Ching, a veteran Hong Kong reporter who was the China correspondent for the Singapore daily *The Straits Times*, was detained in Guangzhou while attempting to meet with a source to obtain transcripts of interviews with the late ousted leader Zhao Ziyang. Ching was held under house arrest in Beijing without access to a lawyer or his family until a formal arrest order was issued in August 2005 on espionage charges.

Official Xinhua News Agency reports in 2005 accused Ching of collecting millions of Hong Kong dollars to spy for Taiwan. Specific charges against him were not made clear until after his trial in a closed hearing in Beijing on August 15, 2006. On August 31, 2006, the Beijing No. 2 Intermediate People's Court convicted Ching of espionage and sentenced him to five years in prison, plus an additional year's deprivation of political rights.

The verdict in the case later appeared online and was published by several Hong Kong newspapers. The document accused Ching of accepting around 300,000 Hong Kong dollars (not millions as first reported by Xinhua) in fees to submit classified reports on political affairs, economics, and international relations for a Taiwan-based organization called the Foundation of International and Cross-Strait Studies, which authorities said was a cover for a Taiwan intelligence organization. Prosecutors said that Ching had met two representatives from the organization at a current events conference, and had done research for them, including sending them reporting that he and others had done for *The Straits Times*.

In his defense, Ching argued that he had no knowledge that the organization was a front for Taiwan intelligence—a charge the foundation itself strongly denied—and that he had provided no state secrets. Ching's appeal was rejected in November 2006.

Yang Tongyan (Yang Tianshui)
freelance
IMPRISONED: December 23, 2005

Yang, commonly known by his pen name Yang Tianshui, was detained along with a friend in Nanjing, eastern China. He was tried on charges of "subverting state authority," and on May 17, 2006, the Zhenjiang Intermediate People's Court sentenced him to 12 years in prison.

Yang was a well-known writer and a member of the Independent Chinese PEN Center. He was a frequent contributor to U.S.-based Web sites banned in China, including *Boxun News* and *Epoch Times*. He often wrote critically about the ruling Communist Party, and

he advocated the release of Internet writers Zheng Yichun and Zhang Lin.

According to the verdict in Yang's case, which was translated into English by the San Francisco-based Dui Hua Foundation, the harsh sentence against him was related to a fictitious online election, established by overseas Chinese citizens, for a "democratic Chinese transitional government." Yang's colleagues say that without his prior knowledge, he was elected "secretariat" of the fictional government. Yang later wrote an article in *Epoch Times* in support of the model.

Prosecutors also accused Yang of transferring money from overseas to Wang Wenjiang, who had been convicted of endangering state security. Yang's defense lawyer argued that this money was humanitarian assistance to the family of a jailed dissident and should not have constituted a criminal act.

Believing that the proceedings were fundamentally unjust, Yang did not appeal. Yang had already spent 10 years in prison for his opposition to the military crackdown on demonstrators at Tiananmen Square in 1989.

In June, Shandong provincial authorities refused to renew the law license of Yang's lawyer, press freedom advocate Li Jianqiang, who also represented imprisoned journalists Zhang Jianhong and Guo Qizhen.

Guo Qizhen, freelance
IMPRISONED: May 12, 2006

Guo was detained as he prepared to join a rolling hunger strike by the lawyer

Gao Zhisheng, who was later jailed. He was later formally arrested on charges related to his prolific writing for U.S.-based Chinese-language Web sites *Minzhu Luntan* (Democracy Forum) and *Epoch Times*.

The Cangzhou Intermediate People's Court tried Guo on charges of "inciting subversion of state authority" on September 12, 2006. He was convicted and sentenced to four years in prison, plus an additional two years' deprivation of political rights.

In the case presented to the prosecutor on June 16, 2006, the Cangzhou Public Security Bureau cited several online essays as proof of Guo's crimes, including one titled "Letting some of the people first get rich while others cannot make a living," in which he accused the Communist Party government of using its policies to support an "autocratic" and "despotic" regime. Guo was critical of corruption and widespread poverty in the country.

In his defense, Guo argued that his criticism of the Communist Party was protected by the Chinese constitution.

Guo is married and has a teenage son. In August 2007, Guo's wife Zhao Changqing told CPJ she had been barred from seeing her husband since June, when he was bruised from beatings sustained while in custody and had complained of deteriorating health, including high blood pressure and chest pains.

In June, Shandong provincial authorities refused to renew the law license of Guo's lawyer, press freedom advocate Li Jianqiang, who also represented impris-

oned journalists Zhang Jianhong and Yang Tongyan.

Zhang Jianhong, freelance
IMPRISONED: September 6, 2006

The founder and editor of the popular news and literary Web site *Aiqinhai* (Aegean Sea) was taken from his home in Ningbo, in eastern China's Zhejiang province. In October 2006, he was formally arrested on charges of "inciting subversion." He was sentenced to six years in prison by Ningbo Intermediate People's Court in March 2007, followed by one year's deprivation of political rights.

Authorities did not clarify their allegations against Zhang, but supporters believed they were linked to online articles critical of government actions. An editorial he wrote two days before his detention called attention to international organizations' criticism of the government's human rights record, and in particular, the poor treatment of journalists and their sources two years before the start of the Olympics. Zhang referred to the situation as "Olympicgate."

Zhang was an author, screenwriter, and reporter who served a year and a half of "re-education through labor" in 1989 on counterrevolutionary charges for his writing in support of protesters. He was dismissed from a position on the local writers association and began working as a freelance writer.

His Web site *Aiqinhai* was closed in March 2006 for unauthorized posting of international and domestic news. He had also been a contributor to several U.S.-based Chinese-language Web sites, including *Boxun News*, the pro-democracy forum *Minzhu Luntan*, and *Epoch Times*.

In September 2007, Zhang was transferred from the Ningbo Detention Center to Qiaosi Prison in Zhejiang province, despite continued appeals for his release on medical grounds. He suffered from a rare nerve disorder. His wife had not been allowed to contact him since June.

That month, Shandong provincial authorities refused to renew the law license of Zhang's lawyer, press freedom advocate Li Jianqiang, who also represented imprisoned journalists Guo Qizhen and Yang Tongyan.

Sun Lin, *Boxun News*
IMPRISONED: May 30, 2007

Nanjing-based reporter Sun was arrested along with his wife, He Fang, on May 30, according to the U.S.-based Web site *Boxun News*. Sun had previously documented harassment by authorities as a result of his audio, video, and print reports for the banned Chinese-language news site.

Sun was accused in the arrest warrant of possessing an illegal weapon, and a police statement issued on June 1 said he was the leader of a criminal gang. Lawyers met with Sun and He in June but the couple were later denied visits by counsel or family members, according to a *Boxun* report. A trial was postponed twice for lack of evidence.

Ma Shiping, freelance
IMPRISONED: June 16, 2007
Qi Chonghuai, *Fazhi Zaobao*
IMPRISONED: June 25, 2007

Police in Tengzhou detained Ma on June 16 on charges of carrying a false press card. Nine days later, police took Qi into custody on the same charge, although he was formally charged with extortion on August 2.

Two days before his detention, Ma posted photographs on the Xinhua News Agency Web site showing a new government office building in Tengzhou, a city in the eastern coastal province of Shandong. The posting, which attracted online comments, highlighted possible waste of local funds at a time when government spending was under scrutiny. Qi later defended the posting of the photos.

A journalist for 13 years, Qi was known for writing articles critical of the local administration. Some of his stories were published by the Falun Gong-affiliated *Epoch Times*. Ma, a freelance photographer, had local media affiliations but no official accreditation.

Qi's wife and lawyer told CPJ that the journalist was beaten by police during questioning on August 13. Qi and Ma were awaiting trial in late year.

Zi Beijia, Beijing TV
IMPRISONED: July 18, 2007

Police arrested Zi after he allegedly fabricated a July 8 story about the sale of steamed buns stuffed with cardboard.

Ten days after the report aired, Beijing TV apologized for the story and said that it was an invention. The Xinhua News Agency said Zi confessed, although a number of local journalists told CPJ that they believed the report to be factual and Zi to be innocent.

On August 12, the Beijing No. 2 Intermediate Court sentenced Zi to a year in prison for the unusual crime of "infringing on the reputation of a commodity." Zi's arrest came amid widespread international reports about food and product safety defects in China. After the arrest, CPJ research found that domestic news reports about consumer safety were noticeably tamer.

Lü Gengsong, freelance
IMPRISONED: August 24, 2007

The Hangzhou Public Security Bureau charged Lü with "inciting subversion of state power," according to human rights groups and news reports. Officials also searched his home and confiscated his computer hard drive and files.

The detention appeared to be connected to Lü's recent articles on corruption, land expropriation, organized crime, and human rights abuses, which were published on overseas Web sites. The day before his arrest, Lü reported on the trial and two-year sentence of housing rights activist Yang Yunbiao. Lü, a member of the banned China Democracy Party, was the author of the 2000 book, *Corruption in the Communist Party of China*, which was published in Hong Kong.

CUBA: 24

Pedro Argüelles Morán
Cooperativa Avileña de Periodistas Independientes
IMPRISONED: March 18, 2003

Argüelles Morán, director of the independent news agency Cooperativa Avileña de Periodistas Independientes in the central province of Ciego de Ávila, was detained during the first day of a massive March 2003 crackdown on dissidents and independent journalists. In April 2003, he was tried under Law 88 for the Protection of Cuba's National Independence and Economy and sentenced to 20 years in prison.

The 59-year-old journalist has been held at the Canaleta Prison in his home province since November 2005. He had been transferred from prison to prison several times before, according to CPJ research.

His wife, Yolanda Vera Nerey, told CPJ that her husband developed several ailments throughout his imprisonment and that other conditions worsened. An existing eye problem deteriorated to the point where Argüelles Morán became nearly blind. The journalist's arthritis grew progressively worse as well, she said.

Víctor Rolando Arroyo Carmona
Unión de Periodistas y Escritores de Cuba Independientes
IMPRISONED: March 18, 2003

A journalist for the independent news agency Unión de Periodistas y Escritores de Cuba Indpendientes in the western province of Pinar del Río, Arroyo Carmona was handed a 26-year prison sentence under Article 91 of the penal code for acting "against the independence or the territorial integrity of the state."

In 2005, Arroyo Carmona was sent to the Holguín Provincial Prison in eastern Cuba. He staged a two-week hunger strike in September 2005 to protest his imprisonment.

His sister, Blanca Arroyo Carmona, told CPJ that the 54-year-old journalist shared a barracks with numerous hardened prisoners. Arroyo Carmona has been diagnosed with diabetes, hypertension, and a case of pulmonary emphysema that has worsened because of inmates' cigarette smoke and the prison's lack of ventilation, his sister said.

Miguel Galván Gutiérrez
Havana Press
IMPRISONED: March 18, 2003

Galván Gutiérrez, a journalist with the independent news agency Havana Press, was tried under Article 91 of the penal code for acting against "the independence or the territorial integrity of the state." Galván Gutiérrez was handed a 26-year prison sentence.

In August 2007, the journalist was transferred from the maximum security Agüica Prison in Matanzas to the Guanajay Prison in his home province of Havana. His sister, Teresa Galván Gutiérrez, said conditions were better at the new prison, where Galván Gutiérrez shared a cell with only one other man.

Galván Gutiérrez was in generally good health, his sister told CPJ.

Julio César Gálvez Rodríguez
freelance
IMPRISONED: March 18, 2003

Gálvez Rodríguez, a freelance reporter based in Havana, was tried in April 2003 under Law 88 for the Protection of Cuba's National Independence and Economy. He was sentenced to 15 years in prison for "aiming at subverting the internal order of the nation and destroying its political, economic, and social system."

After a year and a half at La Pendiente Prison in the central Villa Clara province, Gálvez Rodríguez was transferred to Havana's Combinado del Este Prison. His family was allowed one visit per month.

Gálvez Rodríguez, 63, suffered from high cholesterol, hypertension, and respiratory problems, stepson Lionel Pérez Pedroso told CPJ. Throughout four years in prison, he was admitted to local hospitals multiple times. In early 2007, the reporter spent several months in the Combinado del Este Prison hospital for problems linked to his hypertension, according to Pérez Pedroso.

José Luis García Paneque, Libertad
IMPRISONED: March 18, 2003

García Paneque, director of the independent news agency Libertad in eastern Las Tunas, was tried and convicted in April 2003 under Article 91 of the

Cuban Penal Code for acting "against the independence or the territorial integrity of the state." He was handed a 24-year prison sentence.

Following a number of prison transfers, García Paneque was sent to Las Mangas Prison in the eastern Granma province in November 2005, said his wife, Yamilé Llánez Labrada. The reporter, who shared a cell with numerous hardened prisoners, was taken to the prison's infirmary after being assaulted by another inmate in August 2007, according to his wife.

Llánez Labrada told CPJ that her husband's health had deteriorated significantly since he was first imprisoned. García Paneque, 41, has been diagnosed with internal bleeding and malnutrition, and suffers from chronic pneumonia, according to Llánez Labrada. In June, the reporter was taken to a local hospital, where doctors told him he also had a kidney tumor. Llánez Labrada said her husband has received only infrequent medical attention.

Ricardo González Alfonso, freelance
IMPRISONED: March 18, 2003

González Alfonso, a Havana-based freelance journalist and correspondent for the Paris-based press freedom group Reporters Without Borders, was detained during the March 2003 crackdown and sentenced to 20 years in prison. He was tried under Article 91 of the Cuban penal code for acting against "the independence or the territorial integrity of the state."

The journalist was jailed initially in Camagüey's Kilo 8 Prison, where, according to his sister Graciela González-Degard, he was harassed and punished after a December 2003 hunger strike. In January 2005, he was transferred to the Havana Combinado del Este Prison, according to his wife, Alida de Jesús Viso Bello.

González Alfonso was being held in a small, hot, and poorly ventilated cell, Viso Bello told CPJ. The 57-year-old reporter has been diagnosed with hypertension, arthritis, allergies, and several digestive and circulatory ailments. During his time in jail, he has suffered from hepatitis and has had four different surgeries for problems linked to his digestive tract, his wife said.

Léster Luis González Pentón
freelance
IMPRISONED: March 18, 2003

González Pentón, an independent journalist in the central province of Villa Clara, was sentenced to 20 years in prison in April 2003, after being tried under Article 91 of the penal code for acting against "the independence or the territorial integrity of the state."

According to CPJ research, González Pentón was transferred several times among different prisons before being sent to the Villa Clara Provincial Prison, according to his mother, Mireya de la Caridad Pentón.

A cellmate assaulted González Pentón

in 2007, but the journalist was in generally good health, wife Yanet Ocaña told CPJ.

Alejandro González Raga, freelance
IMPRISONED: March 18, 2003

An independent freelance reporter in the central Camagüey province, González Raga was tried and sentenced to 14 years in prison in April 2003 under Article 91 of the Cuban penal code, which punishes those who act against "the independence or the territorial integrity of the state."

In 2004, González Raga was transferred to the Kilo 7 Prison in Central Camagüey, according to his wife, Berta María Bueno Fuentes. In February 2006, González Raga sent an open letter to overseas Web sites pleading for his freedom. In the letter, he said his health was deteriorating under poor prison conditions.

His wife, who said she saw the reporter for two hours every 45 days, said González Raga shared a barracks with more than 100 common prisoners. According to Bueno Fuentes, prison authorities imposed tougher restrictions on Gonsáles Raga than on other inmates. Bueno Fuentes told CPJ that her husband was suffering from a series of mental health ailments, including depression. He has also been diagnosed with hypertension and cardiovascular problems.

Iván Hernández Carrillo, Patria
IMPRISONED: March 18, 2003

Hernández Carrillo, a reporter for the independent news agency Patria, was sentenced to 25 years in prison following a summary trial under Law 88 for the Protection of Cuba's National Independence and Economy.

In 2003 and 2004, the reporter waged hunger strikes to protest the conditions of his imprisonment. He was subsequently transferred among several prisons. In 2005, Hernández Carrillo was placed at the Pre Prison in central Villa Clara, close to his home province of Matanzas. According to press reports, the 26-year-old journalist was permitted family visits only once every two months.

Alfredo Pulido López, El Mayor
IMPRISONED: March 18, 2003

In April 2003, Pulido López, director of the independent news agency El Mayor in Camagüey, was sentenced to 14 years in prison. He had been tried under Article 91 of the penal code for acting "against the independence or the territorial integrity of the state."

The journalist was first jailed at Combinado del Este Prison in Havana, where he was held for a year in solitary confinement, according to his wife, Rebeca Rodríguez Soto. He was transferred in August 2004 to the Kilo 7 Prison in Camagüey, where he was still being held in 2007.

Berta María Bueno Fuentes, wife of fellow imprisoned journalist Alejandro González Raga, told CPJ that Pulido López shared a cell with seven hardened prisoners. He had lost a significant amount of weight and had complained to his wife of depression, Bueno Fuentes said. Pulido López has been diagnosed with chronic bronchitis, high blood pressure, hypoglycemia, osteoporosis, and loss of eyesight, Rodríguez Soto told the Havana-based human rights group Consejo de Relatores de Derechos Humanos en Cuba.

José Gabriel Ramón Castillo
Instituto Cultura
y Democracia Press
IMPRISONED: March 18, 2003

Ramón Castillo worked as the director of the independent news agency Instituto Cultura y Democracia Press in the eastern province of Santiago de Cuba. He was tried in April 2003 under Article 91 of the penal code for acting against "the independence or the territorial integrity of the state" and was given a prison sentence of 20 years.

Ramón Castillo was being held at the Boniato Prison in Havana, where he shared a barracks with at least 100 inmates, according to his wife, Blanca Rosa Echavarría. In 2006, prison authorities harassed the journalist's family and progressively reduced the amount of food, medicine, and personal hygiene items the family was allowed to bring him, Echavarría told CPJ.

The journalist has been diagnosed with cirrhosis, diabetes, hypertension, and stomach ulcers, Echavarría said. He recently developed circulation problems in his legs and numerous growths on the face and body. Echavarría said her husband received treatment for diabetes but was seldom given medication for his other ailments.

Omar Rodríguez Saludes
Nueva Prensa Cubana
IMPRISONED: March 18, 2003

Rodríguez Saludes, a photojournalist, worked as director of the Havana-based independent news agency Nueva Prensa Cubana. In April 2003, he was tried under Article 91 of the penal code for "acting against the independence or territorial integrity of the state" and was handed a 27-year prison sentence.

The journalist was being held at the Toledo Prison in Havana, where his wife, Ileana Marrero Joa, said he shares a cell with several other inmates. Rodríguez Saludes was in good health, although he was diagnosed with gastrointestinal ailments and hypertension, said Marrero Joa.

Mijaíl Barzaga Lugo
Agencia Noticiosa Cubana
IMPRISONED: March 19, 2003

Barzaga Lugo, a reporter for the independent news agency Agencia Noticiosa Cubana, was tried and convicted under Law 88 for the Protection of Cuba's National Independence and Economy. He was given a 15-year prison sentence.

The reporter has been held at the maximum security Agüica Prison since 2005, his sister, Elquis Barzaga Lugo, told CPJ. Barzaga Lugo was allowed family visits every month and a half. His sister said authorities allowed the family to give him medicine but not always food during the visits. Barzaga Lugo, 36, shared a cell with 16 inmates.

Adolfo Fernández Saínz, Patria
IMPRISONED: March 19, 2003

Fernández Saínz, Havana correspondent for the news agency Patria, was tried and convicted under Law 88, which punishes anyone who commits acts "aiming at subverting the internal order of the nation and destroying its political, economic, and social system." In April 2003, he was handed a 15-year prison sentence.

Fernández Saínz, 58, was transferred among several Cuban prisons before being sent to Canaleta Prison in central Ciego de Ávila province, approximately 186 miles (300 kilometers) from his home in Havana. According to his wife, Julia Núñez Pacheco, the reporter shared a large cell with at least 27 common prisoners. Fernández Saínz was permitted family visits every two months, Núñez Pacheco told CPJ.

The reporter waged a number of hunger strikes to protest his imprisonment, CPJ research shows. He suffered from chronic hypertension, emphysema, osteoporosis, and a kidney cyst. Núñez Pacheco said her husband had received scant medical attention, with his family providing most of his medications during their visits. Núñez Pacheco has written several letters to Cuban authorities requesting that her husband be transferred to a prison closer to home, but she has received no response.

Alfredo Felipe Fuentes, freelance
IMPRISONED: March 19, 2003

An independent journalist in the western Havana province, Fuentes was tried under Article 91 of the Cuban penal code for acting against "the independence or the territorial integrity of the state." He was handed a 26-year prison sentence in April 2003.

Fuentes, 58, was jailed at the Kilo 5½ Prison in western Pinar del Río, his wife Loyda Valdés González, told CPJ. He shared a cramped barracks-style cell with at least 80 other prisoners, said Valdés González. The journalist lost a significant amount of weight since his imprisonment and suffered from chronic back problems, according to his wife.

Normando Hernández González
Colegio de Periodistas
Independientes de Camagüey
IMPRISONED: March 19, 2003

Hernández González, director of the news agency Colegio de Periodistas Independientes de Camagüey, was sentenced in April 2003 to 25 years in prison under Article 91 of the penal code, which punishes those who act against "the independence or the territorial integrity of the state."

In 2003 and 2004, the journalist waged several hunger strikes to protest the conditions of his imprisonment. According to CPJ research, he was transferred several times to prisons across the island. In September 2006, Hernández González was sent to the maximum security Kilo 7 Prison in his home province of Camagüey, said his wife, Yaraí Reyes Marín.

Hernández González has been diagnosed with intestinal ailments that have made it difficult to eat and have caused a significant loss of weight. In 2007, Hernández González suffered a bout of pneumonia; prison doctors also told him he tested positive for tuberculosis but had not developed the disease. The journalist was treated during the year at the Dr. Carlos J. Finlay Central Military Hospital in Havana, Reyes Marín told CPJ.

Reyes Marín requested medical parole for her husband in July 2006, according to news reports, but Cuban authorities did not respond.

Juan Carlos Herrera Acosta
Agencia Prensa Libre Oriental
IMPRISONED: March 19, 2003

Herrera Acosta worked as a Guantánamo-based reporter for the independent news agency Agencia de Prensa Libre Oriental. In April 2003, he was handed a prison sentence of 20 years under Law 88 for the Protection of Cuba's National Independence and Economy.

Herrera Acosta has consistently protested his imprisonment and the conditions in which he has been held, CPJ research shows. He has used hunger strikes, self-inflicted wounds, and anti-Castro slogans as part of his protest.

Prison authorities have, in turn, retaliated by mistreating the journalist and subjecting him to arbitrary prison transfers, according to press reports. Herrera Acosta has lost weight and has suffered from a variety of ailments since he was imprisoned, his wife, Ileana Danger Hardy, told CPJ.

José Ubaldo Izquierdo Hernández
Grupo de Trabajo Decoro
IMPRISONED: March 19, 2003

Izquierdo Hernández, a reporter in the western Havana province for the independent news agency Grupo de Trabajo Decoro, was sentenced to 16 years in prison following an April 2003 trial on charges of acting "against the independence or the territorial integrity of the state" under Article 91 of the penal code.

Izquierdo Hernández was jailed at the Guanajay Prison in his home province, where news reports said he had received inadequate medical treatment. The reporter has been diagnosed with a series of digestive ailments, as well as emphysema and asthma, according to CPJ research. In 2007, prison doctors also diagnosed a hernia and circulatory problems, the Miami-based Web site *Payolibre* reported. Izquierdo Hernández has been hospitalized several times during his imprisonment, including twice in 2007, according to press reports.

Héctor Maseda Gutiérrez
Grupo de Trabajo Decoro
IMPRISONED: March 19, 2003

Maseda Gutiérrez, a journalist with the independent news agency Grupo de Trabajo Decoro, was tried in April 2003 under Article 91 of the Cuban penal code for acting "against the independence or the territorial integrity of the state," and Law 88 for the Protection of Cuba's National Independence and Economy. He was convicted and sentenced to 20 years in prison.

In December 2005, Maseda Gutiérrez was transferred to the maximum-security Agüica Prison in the western Matanzas province. According to his wife, Laura Pollán Toledo, the journalist was held in a barracks with at least 70 hardened prisoners. Maseda Gutiérrez suffered from high blood pressure, his wife said.

Pollán Toledo told CPJ she sought amnesty for her husband in 2004, but the Cuban government did not respond.

Pablo Pacheco Ávila, Cooperativa Avileña de Periodistas Independientes
IMPRISONED: March 19, 2003

Pacheco Ávila, a reporter for the independent news agency Cooperativa Avileña de Periodistas Independientes, was tried under Law 88 for the Protection of Cuba's National Independence and Economy and sentenced to 20 years in prison.

Pacheco Ávila was being held at the Morón Prison in his home province, where he shared a small cell with 10 other prisoners, said his wife, Oleyvis García Echemendía. The journalist, 37, developed inflammation and joint problems in both knees and underwent surgery in May, García Echemendía told CPJ. Pachecho Ávila has also been diagnosed with high blood pressure, severe headaches, acute gastritis, and kidney problems, his wife said. He was receiving irregular medical treatment.

Fabio Prieto Llorente, freelance
IMPRISONED: March 19, 2003

Prieto Llorente, a freelance reporter in the western Isla de la Juventud, was tried in April 2003 under Law 88 for the Protection of Cuba's National Independence and Economy, and sentenced to 20 years in prison.

His sister, Clara Lourdes Prieto Llorente, said the reporter was being held in solitary confinement at El Guayabo Prison in his home province. The cell, which measured 5 by 9 feet, was poorly ventilated, said the sister. Prison authorities allowed monthly family visits.

Prieto Llorente, 44, has been diagnosed with emphysema and high blood pressure. Clara Lourdes Prieto Llorente told CPJ that her brother had been taken to a local hospital in June for a medical checkup and had a severe allergic reaction to penicillin. In September, he had an acute ear infection that was not treated, his sister said.

The reporter has suffered from depression as well, according to his sister. In 2006, she said, other inmates beat him when he protested on the anniversary of his imprisonment, and prison authorities punished him with solitary confinement after he expressed support for political change in the wake of President Fidel Castro's illness.

Omar Ruiz Hernández
Grupo de Trabajo Decoro
IMPRISONED: March 19, 2003

A reporter for the independent news agency Grupo de Trabajo Decoro in the central province of Villa Clara, Ruiz Hernández was sentenced to 18 years in prison in April 2003. He was tried under Article 91 of the penal code for acting "against the independence or the territorial integrity of the state."

In November 2005, Ruiz Hernández was sent to the Nieves Morejón Prison in central Sancti Spíritus. He had been transferred twice before, his wife, Bárbara Maritza Rojo Arias, told CPJ. At Nieves Morejón, the reporter shared a small cell with 12 hardened prisoners, who harassed and attacked him, Rojo Arias said.

Ruiz Hernández, 60, has been diagnosed with high blood pressure and other circulatory problems. Doctors told the reporter in 2007 that one of his retinas had become detached, but they did not immediately provide treatment, according to Rojo Arias.

Guillermo Espinosa Rodríguez
Agencia de Prensa Libre Oriental
IMPRISONED: October 26, 2006

A reporter for the independent news agency Agencia de Prensa Libre Oriental, Espinosa Rodríguez was tried on November 6, 2006, on the vaguely worded charge of "social dangerousness" contained in Article 72 of the penal code. After a 45-minute trial, the journalist was sentenced to two years of home confinement.

According to his cousin Diosmel Rodríguez, the reporter is permitted to leave his home only to go to work. As part of his sentence, Espinosa Rodríguez was forbidden from leaving his home province of Santiago de Cuba and from practicing journalism.

Espinosa Rodríguez was charged in connection with his coverage of a local dengue fever outbreak, which the official Cuban press ignored, according to CPJ research. Espinosa Rodríguez said the journalist would be forced to serve his term in prison if he did not comply with the terms of his sentence.

Oscar Sánchez Madan, freelance
IMPRISONED: April 13, 2007

Sánchez Madan, a freelance reporter in the western Matanzas province, was handed a four-year prison sentence following a one-day trial on the vaguely worded charge of "social dangerousness" contained in Article 72 of the penal code.

The journalist had covered a local corruption scandal, along with social problems in Matanzas. Authorities had detained him twice before and warned him to stop working as an independent journalist, Matanzas-based journalist Hugo Araña told CPJ.

Sánchez Madan was being held at the maximum security Combinado del Sur

Prison, outside the provincial capital of Matanzas, said Juan Francisco Sigler Amaya, a family friend and local human rights activist. The journalist shared a 19-by-10-foot cell with at least 17 other prisoners, Sigler Amaya told CPJ.

Sigler Amaya said prison authorities encouraged inmates to threaten and intimidate the reporter. Authorities denied Sánchez Madan access to a priest and to religious literature, and they routinely confiscated his mail, Sigler Amaya said.

EGYPT: 1

Abdel Karim Suleiman (Karim Amer)
freelance
IMPRISONED: November 7, 2006

The general prosecutor's office in the northern city of Alexandria ordered the arrest of blogger Abdel Karim Suleiman, known online as Karim Amer, on November 7, 2006, because of his online criticisms.

On February 22, a criminal court in the northern city of Alexandria convicted Suleiman, then 22, of insulting Islam and Egyptian President Hosni Mubarak. He received a four-year jail term, marking the first time an Egyptian blogger stood trial and was sentenced for his work.

Suleiman had been a student at Cairo's Al-Azhar University, the pre-eminent higher learning institution in Sunni Islam. He was expelled in 2006 because he frequently criticized the state-run religious university, which he accused of promoting extremist ideas, and Mubarak, whom he referred to as a dictator.

ERITREA: 14

Zemenfes Haile, Tsigenay
IMPRISONED: January 1999

Haile, founder and manager of the private weekly Tsigenay, was arrested for allegedly failing to complete his national service. CPJ sources said he was released from prison in 2002 but was assigned to extended military service. The sources said Haile's continued deprivation of liberty was part of the government's general crackdown on the press, which began in September 2001.

Ghebrehiwet Keleta, Tsigenay
IMPRISONED: July 2000

Keleta, a reporter for the private weekly Tsigenay, was seized by security agents on his way to work sometime in July 2000 and has not been seen since. CPJ sources said his continued detention was connected to the government's overall crackdown on the press.

Said Abdelkader, Admas
Yusuf Mohamed Ali, Tsigenay
Amanuel Asrat, Zemen
Temesken Ghebreyesus, Keste Debena
Mattewos Habteab, Meqaleh
Dawit Habtemichael, Meqaleh
Medhanie Haile, Keste Debena

Dawit Isaac, *Setit*
Seyoum Tsehaye, freelance
IMPRISONED: September 2001

Eritrean security forces jailed 10 local journalists without trial in the days following September 18, 2001. The arrests came less than a week after authorities abruptly closed the country's fledgling private press, purportedly to safeguard national unity in the face of growing political turmoil. Unconfirmed reports circulated in 2006 saying that three journalists had died in prison. CPJ was unable to confirm those reports, but credible sources did confirm the death of one prominent imprisoned journalist, Fesshaye "Joshua" Yohannes, in early 2007.

Authorities accused the journalists of avoiding the country's compulsory military service, threatening national security, and failing to observe licensing requirements. CPJ research indicates that the crackdown was part of a government drive to crush political dissent ahead of elections scheduled for December 2001, which were subsequently cancelled. The private press had covered a split between reformers and conservatives within the ruling elite, providing a forum for debate on the increasingly authoritarian regime of President Isaias Afewerki. An open letter in the leading independent weekly *Setit* published on September 9, 2001, for example, told the government that "people can tolerate hunger and other problems for a long time, but they can't tolerate the absence of good administration and justice."

In a 2006 CPJ interview, presidential spokesman Yemane Gebremeskel denied that the journalists were imprisoned because of what they wrote, saying only that they "were involved in acts against the national interest of the state." He said "the substance of the case is clear to everybody" but declined to detail any supporting evidence.

The journalists were initially held incommunicado at a police station in the capital, where they began a hunger strike on March 31, 2002. In a message smuggled from their jail, the journalists said they would refuse food until they were released or charged and given due process. Instead, they were transferred to secret locations, and no official information has been available since. The government has refused to divulge their whereabouts, their health, or even whether they are still alive.

"This is an Eritrean issue; leave it to us," Information Minister Ali Abdu told CPJ in June 2007 when he was asked to confirm reports of the death in prison of Yohannes, the award-winning co-owner of *Setit*. Several sources in the Eritrean diaspora disclosed to CPJ in February that Yohannes, 47, died on January 11, 2007, after a long illness in an undisclosed prison outside Asmara. One source said the journalist may have died much earlier in a prison in Embatkala, 21 miles (35 kilometers) northeast of Asmara. Yohannes received a CPJ International Press Freedom Award in 2002.

The government's monopoly on domestic media, the fear of reprisal among prisoners' families, and restrictions on the movements of all foreigners have made it extremely difficult to verify unofficial information.

An unbylined report, circulated on several Web sites in August 2006 and deemed by CPJ sources to be generally credible, claimed that journalists and opposition leaders arrested in the crackdown were moved in 2003 to a secretly built desert prison. CPJ sources, however, could not verify the report's claim that at least three journalists had died in custody. The report named the three as "Mr. Yusuf," believed by CPJ sources to refer to Yusuf Mohamed Ali of *Tsigenay*; "Mr. Medhane Tewelde," believed to refer to Medhanie Haile of *Keste Debena*; and "Mr. Said," believed to refer to Said Abdelkader of *Admas*. Eritrean officials did not respond to a November 2007 letter hand-delivered to the embassy in Washington and inquiring about the three journalists. Information Minister Ali Abdu told CPJ the same month that he had no information.

The case of *Setit* co-owner Isaac, an Eritrean with Swedish citizenship, has drawn national attention in Sweden, where diplomats, journalists, and grassroots activists have campaigned for his release. Isaac was released for a medical checkup on November 19, 2005, and allowed to phone his family and a friend in Sweden. Despite hopes that he would be freed, Isaac was returned to jail two days later with no ex-

planation, according to CPJ sources. In March 2007, Sweden's National Press Club awarded Isaac its Freedom of Expression and Press Prize, according to news reports.

Selamyinghes Beyene, *Meqaleh*
IMPRISONED: Fall 2001

Beyene, a reporter for the independent weekly *Meqaleh*, was arrested in fall 2001. CPJ sources believed that his detention was part of the government's general crackdown on the press, which began in September 2001. He was conscripted into the military in 2002 and assigned extended service, according to CPJ sources.

Saleh Aljezeeri, Eritrean State Radio
Hamid Mohammed Said
Eritrean State Television
IMPRISONED: February 15, 2002

During a July 2002 fact-finding mission to the capital, Asmara, CPJ delegates confirmed that on or around February 15, Eritrean authorities arrested Said, a journalist for the state-run Eritrean State Television (ETV); Aljezeeri, a journalist for Eritrean State Radio; and Saadia Ahmed, a journalist with the Arabic-language service of ETV. Ahmed was released in early 2005, according to CPJ sources.

The reasons for the arrests were unclear, but CPJ sources said they believed the detentions were related to the government's general crackdown on the press, which began in September 2001.

ETHIOPIA: 2

Saleh Idris Gama, Eri-TV
Tesfalidet Kidane Tesfazghi, Eri-TV
IMPRISONED: December 2006

Kenyan authorities arrested Eritrean state television journalists Gama and Tesfazghi at the Somali border in the aftermath of Ethiopia's military intervention in Somalia in late 2006. The detentions were disclosed in April through official statements and an anti-Eritrean propaganda videotape posted on the Ethiopian government Web site *Waltainfo*.

The video suggested the journalists were involved in military activities in Somalia. While Eritrean journalists are often conscripted into military service, the video did not present any evidence linking the journalists to military activity.

Tesfazghi, a producer, and Gama, a cameraman, were held for three weeks by Kenyan authorities and handed over to the Ethiopian-backed Somali transitional government in January 2007, according to the Eritrean Foreign Ministry. In April, the Ethiopian government acknowledged that it had detained 41 people who were "captured" in Somalia on suspicion of "terrorism," according to news reports. The government said detainees would be tried "before the competent military court" but did not identify them by name. Ethiopian Foreign Ministry spokesman Wahid Belay told CPJ that authorities would not provide information about the journalists. Their whereabouts, legal status, and health were unknown in late year.

THE GAMBIA: 1

"Chief" Ebrima Manneh
Daily Observer
IMPRISONED: July 7, 2006

Manneh, a journalist for the state-controlled *Daily Observer*, was arrested after he tried to republish a BBC report critical of President Yahya Jammeh. Manneh's colleagues witnessed his arrest by two plainclothes officers of the National Intelligence Agency at the premises of the *Daily Observer*. Gambian security agencies and police have refused to provide information on his whereabouts, health, and legal status.

Local journalists said Manneh was seen in July at the Royal Victorian Teaching Hospital in Banjul and again in September in the far eastern Fatoto Prison. The Media Foundation for West Africa filed legal action in the Community Court of the Economic Community of West African States in 2007, seeking a court order compelling the government to release Manneh. The court, based in Abuja, Nigeria, held hearings in July, September, and November, but Gambian officials failed to attend and gave no explanation. Additional hearings were scheduled for 2008.

IRAN: 12

Mohammad Hassan Fallahiyazadeh
Al-Alam
IMPRISONED: November 1, 2006

Authorities arrested Fallahiyazadeh, 32, on November 1, 2006, and transferred him to Tehran's Evin prison, according to the Iran-based human rights group Human Rights Activists in Iran. His detention stems from his reporting about the government's harsh treatment of Iranian-Arab protestors in the Khuzestan provincial capital, Ahwaz, the group said.

A Revolutionary Court handed him a three-year prison sentence in late April for propaganda against the Islamic regime and for communicating with opposition groups abroad, according to Human Rights Activists in Iran and Amnesty International. Fallahiyazadeh, who belongs to Iran's Arab minority, was denied access to a lawyer, the human rights group said.

Fallahiyazadeh was a reporter for the state-run Arabic language satellite channel Al-Alam and for several Arab media outlets, such as Lebanon's Future TV, according to Amnesty International and Human Rights Activists in Iran. He once worked as managing editor of the now-defunct student publication *Aqlam al-Talaba* at the Shahid Chamran University of Ahvaz.

Adnan Hassanpour, *Aso*
IMPRISONED: January 25, 2007

Security agents seized Hassanpour, a journalist and former editor for the now-defunct Kurdish-Persian weekly *Aso*, in his hometown of Marivan, in Kurdistan province, according to news reports. A Revolutionary Court convicted him in July of endangering national security and engaging in propaganda against the state, one of his attorneys, Sirvan Hosmandi, told CPJ. Hassanpour was sentenced to death.

Iranian judiciary spokesman Ali Reza Jamshidi was quoted by the official Islamic Republic News Agency confirming that Hassanpour was "sentenced to execution on the charge of moharebeh," The Associated Press reported. Moharebeh, or fighting with God, has been used by the Iranian authorities against people who allegedly take up arms to violently overthrow the regime. Hosmandi told CPJ that the journalist was being held in Kurdistan province's capital, Sanandaj.

Saleh Nikbakht, another attorney representing the journalist, told the Iran Student News Agency that Iran's National Supreme Court upheld the death sentence on October 22. He said Hassanpour was convicted of spying, providing information about military bases, assisting suspected criminals in crossing Iran's borders, and having contacts with an official at the U.S. State Department.

Hosmandi told CPJ that the charges against Hassanpour were not proved in court and were supported with merely a report from security officials. The courts have not publicly disclosed the basis for their rulings. Hassanpour's sister, Lily, told CPJ that the accusations made against her brother were false and that she believed his critical writings were behind the charges.

Aso was banned in August 2005 following its coverage of violent protests in Kurdistan province that summer.

Ahmad Ghassaban, *Sahar*
IMPRISONED: May 3, 2007
Majid Tavakoli, *Khat-e Sefer*
IMPRISONED: May 9, 2007
Ehsan Mansouri, freelance
IMPRISONED: May 22, 2007

Tehran authorities arrested these three Amirkabir University of Technology students following distribution of newsletters carrying articles deemed insulting to Islam, according to news reports. The students said they had no involvement in the publications. They said a hard-line conservative student group fraudulently used the names and logos of legitimate student publications as a dirty trick, news reports said.

In October, a Tehran Revolutionary Court found all three students guilty of propaganda against the regime and insulting the supreme leader, according to *AUTNews*, the Web site of the Islamic Student Association at Amirkabir University. Defense lawyer Mohammad Ali Dadkhah told *AUTNews* that the court sentenced Ghassaban, managing editor of the student newspaper *Sahar*, to 30 months in prison; Tavakoli, managing editor of the student paper *Khat-e Sefer*, to three years; and Mansouri, a cartoonist accused of drawing insulting caricatures, to two years.

All three appealed the verdict. Dadkhah said they still faced charges in criminal court of insulting the Prophet Muhammad and Islamic principles, *AUTNews* reported. The students were subjected to torture during interrogations, according to news reports quoting

their families.

The students—all members of the reformist Islamic Student Association—said the fraudulent publications were designed to disrupt the group's annual campus election. They claimed that student members of the Basij—a militia affiliated with Iran's Revolutionary Guard, an elite unit under the supreme leader's control—were behind the bogus newsletters, according to *AUTNews*. Immediately following distribution of the newsletters, the Basij attacked the publications and their activist leaders, according to online sources.

Saeed Metinpour, *Yarpagh*
IMPRISONED: May 25, 2007

The Committee to Defend Azerbaijan's Political Prisoners (ASMEK) reported that authorities seized Metinpour, 32, an editor for the Azeri-language weekly *Yarpagh*, and his wife, Atiyeh Taheri, in the northwestern city of Zanjan. They jailed Metinpour, transported his wife home, and searched the couple's property. The officers confiscated Metinpour's personal computer, books, and other personal belongings. They cut the telephone lines and warned Taheri not to tell anyone about the incident.

The charges against Metinpour remained undisclosed. Defense attorney Mahmoud Faghihi was denied access to his client beginning in October.

Metinpour, who contributed to the daily *Mardom-e No* and other local papers, frequently criticized Iran's social and political system and the regime's harsh treatment of Azerbaijani activists. In his last piece before his arrest, he described Iranian police carrying out missions for the Security and Intelligence Ministry. Local journalists who spoke with CPJ said they believed his articles were behind his imprisonment.

Authorities transferred Metinpour among several jails, including Tehran's Evin prison, ASMEK reported. Taheri was able to speak with him a few times by phone for short periods, ASMEK reported. The journalist's mother was allowed to visit him once.

Metinpour was previously arrested on February 21 along with other Azerbaijani journalists during a protest in Zanjan on International Mother Language Day. They had been demonstrating against government restrictions that prohibited them from writing and publishing Azeri-language material. Metinpour was released on bail after 10 days in solitary confinement,

Jelil Ghanilou, freelance
IMPRISONED: June 27, 2007

Security officials seized Ghanilou, 30, from his home in Zanjan, the capital of northwestern Zanjan province, on June 27, his brother, Tavakol Ghanilou, told CPJ. They held Ghanilou for nearly four months at the Ministry of Intelligence and Security jail in Zanjan before transferring him on October 21 to another prison, Tavakol Ghanilou said.

Ghanilou had not been tried when CPJ conducted its December 1 census, and the charges against him had not been disclosed. Tavakol Ghanilou told CPJ that he believed Ghanilou's articles about the civil and cultural rights of Iran's ethnic Azerbaijani minority were behind his current detention.

Authorities had arrested Ghanilou earlier in the year as well. On February 21, he was seized while attending a protest in Zanjan organized by Azeri journalists and cultural activists for International Mother Language Day. They were demonstrating against government restrictions prohibiting them from writing and publishing material in their native language. He was released on bail after spending 26 days in solitary confinement. Tavakol Ghanilou told *Advar News*, which is affiliated with the Office for Fostering Unity, a pro-reform student organization, that Ghanilou was subjected to physical and psychological torture during that detention. That case remained pending in late year, Tavakol Ghanilou told CPJ.

Ghanilou worked as a freelancer for several local newspapers, including the daily *Mardom-e No*, the weekly *Farday-e Roushan*, the now-defunct weekly *Omid-e Zanjan*, and the monthly magazine *Payk-e Azerbaijan*, according to Alireza Javanbakht, spokesman for the Committee to Defend Azerbaijan's Political Prisoners.

Mohammad Seddigh Kaboudvand
Payam-e Mardom
IMPRISONED: July 1, 2007

Plainclothes security officials arrested

journalist and human rights activist Kaboudvand, 45, at his Tehran accounting offices, according to Amnesty International and CPJ sources. He was being held at Evin prison in Tehran.

Authorities accused Kaboudvand, head of the Human Rights Organization of Kurdistan and managing editor of the weekly *Payam-e Mardom*, with acting against national security and engaging in propaganda against the state among other things, according to his organization's Web site. They had been pressuring him to close the organization and disavow its mission, the group reported. He had not been officially charged with any crime or brought before a judge, according to CPJ sources. His lawyer had not been allowed to see him or review his file, the sources said.

Payam-e Mardom was suspended on June 27, 2004, after 13 issues, according to news reports. The term of the ban ended on July 1, 2007, the day Kaboudvand was jailed. Kaboudvand had published articles about torture in Iranian jails and advocated a federal system of government for the Islamic republic.

Ejlal Ghavami, *Payam-e Mardom*
IMPRISONED: July 9, 2007

Authorities arrested Ghavami, an editor at the weekly *Payam-e Mardom*, in Kurdistan's provincial capital, Sanandaj, on July 9, according to news reports and CPJ sources.

A Revolutionary Court in Sanandaj sentenced Ghavami to three years in prison for covering banned protests held before the governor's office in Kurdistan province in 2005, according to Reuters, which cited the Iranian Students News Agency. The journalist's lawyer, Nemat Ahmadi, told the Iranian Students News Agency that an appeals court upheld the verdict, the news Web site *Rooz* reported.

Ahmadi said the court convicted Ghavami of "activities against state security by participating in illegal gatherings, propaganda against the state and in support of opposition groups and for insulting official authorities," *Rooz* reported. He said his client attended the protest solely as a reporter.

Payam-e Mardom was suspended on June 27, 2004, after 13 issues, according to news reports. The term of the ban ended on July 1, 2007.

Ako Kurdnasab, *Karafto*
IMPRISONED: July 21, 2007

Security officials arrested Kurdnasab, 23, a journalist for the weekly *Karafto*, on July 21 at the newspaper's offices in the Kurdistan provincial capital, Sanandaj, journalists at the weekly told CPJ. On September 21, a Revolutionary Court in Sanandaj convicted him of spying against the regime and sentenced him to three years in prison, his lawyer, Kourosh Fattahi, told CPJ. In November, a Kurdistan appeals court changed the charge to propaganda against the regime and reduced his sentence to six months.

Fattahi told CPJ that there was no specific evidence to support either of the charges. In Kurdnasab's interrogation file, he was accused of reporting on protests and strikes, but authorities did not provide a basis for the accusations, his lawyer said.

Authorities held and interrogated Kurdnasab for nearly two months without granting him access to a lawyer before referring him to court on September 10, according to online news reports.

Maryam Hosseinkhah
Change for Equality, Zanestan
IMPRISONED: November 18, 2007

A Revolutionary Court summoned and arrested online journalist Hosseinkhah in Tehran on November 18, according to the Iran-based Web site *Change for Equality*. The judge charged her with disturbing public opinion, engaging in propaganda against the regime, and spreading false news, *Change for Equality* reported. Bail was set at one billion rials (US$107,000). Authorities transferred her to Tehran's notorious Evin prison because she was unable to pay the amount, *Change for Equality* reported.

Hosseinkhah's lawyer, Nobel Peace Prize laureate Shirin Ebadi, told *Change for Equality* that her client was jailed because she wrote articles on women's rights for online sites and newspapers.

Hosseinkhah worked as an editor for the Women's Cultural Center-affiliated Web site *Zanestan* and the *Change for Equality* Web site. *Change for Equality* seeks to amass one million signatures urging reform of Iranian laws discriminating against women. In November 2007, the Ministry of Culture and Islamic Guidance ordered the closure of *Zanestan*, according to *Change for Equality*.

Reza Valizadeh, *Baznegar*
IMPRISONED: November 27, 2007

Security officers arrested Valizadeh, a blogger and editor of the Web site *Baznegar*, in Tehran, according to news reports. He was detained after President Mahmoud Ahmadinejad's office complained about an online article describing the presidential security team's purchase of four bomb-detecting dogs from Germany, according to news reports. Other media had covered the story as well, including *The Guardian* of London.

Valizadeh was being held at Tehran's Evin prison. Charges were not immediately disclosed, according to news reports.

IRAQ: 2

Bilal Hussein
The Associated Press
IMPRISONED: April 12, 2006

Hussein, an Iraqi photographer for The Associated Press, was taken into custody by U.S. forces in Ramadi, capital of Iraq's Anbar province, for "imperative reasons of security" on April 12, 2006, and held without charge or the disclosure of evidence of a crime.

The U.S. military alleged that Hussein had ties to insurgents. "He has close relationships with persons known to be responsible for kidnappings, smuggling, improvised explosive attacks, and other attacks on coalition forces," according to a May 7, 2006, e-mail from Maj. Gen. John Gardner to AP International Editor John Daniszewski.

The military claimed Hussein's photographs showed he had prior knowledge of insurgent attacks, allowing him to arrive at scenes of violence before they occurred. Kathleen Carroll, executive editor of the AP, said the news organization reviewed 900 images taken by Hussein and found no evidence that he arrived before attacks took place.

According to the AP, the most specific allegation cited by U.S. officials—that Hussein was involved in the Iraqi insurgent kidnapping of two Arab journalists in Ramadi—was discredited after the AP investigated the claim. The two abducted journalists had not implicated Hussein in the kidnapping; they had instead praised him for his assistance when they were released. The military's only evidence supporting its claim appeared to be images of the released journalists that were found in Hussein's camera, the AP said. Hussein's attorney, Paul Gardephe, said the military later acknowledged that it did not possess evidence supporting the allegation, the AP reported.

In December 2007, the U.S. military referred the case to the Iraqi justice system for possible prosecution. The military cited alleged links between Hussein

and Iraqi insurgents but continued to disclose no evidence to support the accusation.

Hussein shared a 2005 Pulitzer Prize with other AP photographers for their work in Iraq.

Faisal Abbas Elias (Faisal Ghazaleh)
Kurdsat
IMPRISONED: November 18, 2007

Kurdish security forces raided the home of Elias, a cameraman for the Patriotic Union of Kurdistan-affiliated satellite channel Kurdsat, in the Nineveh provincial town of Bashika, according to the Journalistic Freedoms Observatory, a local press freedom group.

Colleagues of Elias, also known as Faisal Ghazaleh, told the observatory that he was arrested and transferred to the security directorate in Dohuk, the capital city of Dohuk province, in Iraq's Kurdistan region. Officials at Kurdsat and at the Kurdistan Journalists Syndicate told CPJ that authorities provided no details about the arrest other than stating that the cameraman was being held for "security" reasons.

ISRAEL and the OCCUPIED PALESTINIAN TERRITORY: 2

Walid Khalid Hassan Ali, *Palestine*
IMPRISONED: May 18, 2007

Israeli forces detained West Bank Bureau Chief Ali of the Hamas-affiliated daily *Palestine* at his home near the

West Bank city of Salfeit on May 18, the journalist's wife told CPJ.

Ali's attorney, Tamar Pelleg, told CPJ that on June 12, an Israeli military judge approved the six-month administrative detention order issued by an Israeli military commander against the reporter. Pelleg appealed the decision, but it was upheld by a military appellate judge on July 16. In November, Pelleg said, a judge extended the detention for another six months.

According to court documents obtained by CPJ, the appellate judge ruled that "in light of the appellant's recent propensity for military activity, I came to the conclusion that the security of the area and the public obligate the detention."

Despite that assertion, Pelleg said she believed Ali's work at *Palestine* played a role in the detention. Israeli authorities did not detail the factual basis for the detention, and the evidence remained secret.

Ali has been transferred among several prisons and kept in solitary confinement since early September, his wife told CPJ. Mustafa al-Sawaf, the paper's editor, said he believed Ali was arrested because of his work for the paper.

Pelleg told CPJ that Ali was accused of being a prominent leader in Hamas, although her client had not been charged with any offense and the evidence used to hold him remained secret. She added that Ali did not deny knowing Hamas members but said that his ties to them were purely social. Ali previously served more than four years in administrative detention without charge. He was released in August 2006.

**Atta Farhat, *Al-Watan, Golan Times,*
and Syrian TV**
IMPRISONED: July 30, 2007

A special unit of the Israeli police force raided the home of Syrian journalist Farhat, 35, in the northern Golan Heights village of Baqaata in the early morning of July 30, the Syrian Center for Media and Freedom of Expression, a local nongovernmental organization, and its partner, the Paris-based International Federation of Human Rights, said in a joint statement. Police searched the property, seized the reporter's personal computer and cell phone, and arrested him, according to the groups.

Pursuant to a court order, Farhat was held in Al-Jamala Prison, about nine miles (14 kilometers) southeast of Haifa. He appeared before an Israeli judge several times but was not charged, the organizations reported. They said his requests for "temporary release" pending further court proceedings were denied.

The groups said in their joint statement that Israeli authorities had not disclosed the reasons for Farhat's detention, but that he may be accused of "collaborating with an enemy state." The center said it suspects the allegation is directly related to his journalistic activities for Syrian media. Farhat is editor-in-chief of the daily news Web site *Golan Times* and a correspondent for the Syrian daily *Al-Watan* and state-run Syrian TV. Farhat published articles in the Syrian press describing the living conditions of Syrians under Israeli rule in the contested territory.

MALDIVES: 1

Abdullah Saeed (Fahala)
Minivan Daily
IMPRISONED: March 26, 2006

Saeed, known as Fahala, was among several journalists employed by the opposition Minivan News Group who were targeted with legal action in 2006. Saeed, a reporter for the newspaper *Minivan Daily*, was initially sentenced to a two-month term for refusing to take a urine test after he was first detained in October 2005. In April 2006, he was sentenced to life imprisonment on charges that he intended to sell drugs. His colleagues believe the charges were fabricated and that he was targeted to silence coverage that was critical of the government.

In the trial against Saeed, his lawyer argued that police planted drugs in the journalist's clothing after calling him to the station for unspecified reasons. The lawyer said that police found no drugs during an initial search of the journalist's pockets—while the lawyer was present—only to discover 1.1 grams of heroin after isolating Saeed and removing his clothes from view.

Minivan Daily, affiliated with the Maldivian Democracy Party, was established in July 2005 as the first daily newspaper not aligned with the government of Maldivian President Maumoon Gayoom, who has ruled since 1978. Minivan means "independence" in Dhivehi. Saeed was being held at high-security Maafushi Prison.

NIGER: 2

Moussa Kaka
Radio France Internationale
and Radio Saraounya
IMPRISONED: September 20, 2007

Kaka, a veteran radio journalist distinguished for his exclusive coverage of several armed rebellions of nomadic Tuaregs in northern Niger since the 1990s, was arrested on charges of "complicity in a conspiracy endangering the authority of the state," over alleged links with an armed Tuareg uprising since February.

Calling Kaka a "bandit" (the government's term for the rebels) under the guise of a journalist, government spokesman Ben Omar Mohamed told CPJ in September that the charges were not linked to journalism.

The charges, based on recordings of telephone conversations between the journalist and rebel leader Agali Alambo, included allegations that Kaka had negotiated payment with Alambo for footage and photos, according to defense lawyer Moussa Coulibaly and local journalists. Kaka had done exclusive interviews with rebel leaders and taken photos that were reprinted in several newspapers in the capital, Niamey, in July.

In November, a Niamey court dismissed the recordings on the grounds that they were illegally obtained, but Kaka remained behind bars pending a government appeal, according to Coulibaly and local journalists.

Ibrahim Manzo Diallo, *Aïr Info*
IMPRISONED: October 9, 2007

Diallo, director of the bimonthly *Aïr Info* in the northern town of Agadez, was arrested by plainclothes police at the airport in Niamey as he prepared to board a flight to Paris for a professional seminar.

Diallo was held without charge in Niamey and transferred two days later to a police station in Agadez, where authorities had imposed a three-month state of alert in August that gave security forces blanket powers of arrest and detention, according to local journalists. In November, a court in Agadez charged Diallo with criminal conspiracy over his alleged involvement in an antigovernment demonstration in Agadez in August, according to local journalists and Diallo's lawyer, Moussa Coulibaly. Diallo is also an activist with the civil society organization Alternative Espaces Citoyens.

Local journalists believed the arrest stemmed from a September 26 *Aïr Info* report that listed 20 people arrested in the Agadez region on suspicion of rebel links, according to Agence France-Presse.

CPJ research indicates that Diallo's imprisonment was part of a pattern of government harassment designed to stifle critical coverage in his newspaper, the only publication in the rebel hotbed of Agadez. In July, authorities suspended the paper for three months and stripped its annual government subsidy of 1.4 million CFA francs (US$3,000) over articles allegedly "undermining the morale of troops," according to local journalists and news reports.

PHILIPPINES: 1

Alex Adonis, DXMF Radio
IMPRISONED: February 19, 2007

Radio commentator Adonis was sentenced to four and a half years in prison on January 31 on a criminal libel complaint lodged by a congressman in Davao del Norte province, according to local media and press freedom groups.

The complaint, originally filed in October 2001 by Davao First District Representative Prospero Nograles, related to an alleged tryst involving the congressman. Nograles said the report was untrue.

News reports said Adonis was unable to afford legal representation or attend court proceedings because of the distance from his home. The verdict was announced in his absence, and the period in which Adonis could lodge an appeal lapsed. Adonis, 43, has a wife and two daughters.

RUSSIA: 3

Boris Stomakhin
Radikalnaya Politika
IMPRISONED: March 22, 2006

Stomakhin, editor of the monthly newspaper *Radikalnaya Politika* (Radical Politics), was jailed on March 22, 2006, on charges of inciting ethnic hatred and making public appeals for extremist activity. The Butyrsky District Court in Moscow sentenced him to five years in prison in November 2006. He and his family said authorities were punishing him for his harsh criticism of Kremlin policy in Chechnya.

In his ruling, Judge Lyubov Ishmuratova said Stomakhin's articles "approved Chechen terrorists' criminal actions aimed at annihilation of Russian people as an ethnicity." The ruling quoted Stomakhin as writing: "Let tens of new Chechen snipers take their positions in the mountain ridges and the city ruins and let hundreds, thousands of aggressors fall under righteous bullets! No mercy! Death to the Russian occupiers! ... The Chechens have the full moral right to bomb everything they want in Russia."

Stomakhin, who had pleaded not guilty, said he was "tried for his views and not for any real crime. ... In the articles, I expressed my opinion, with which people were free to agree or disagree," the news agency RIA-Novosti reported. He said an opinion was not a "call to action."

Police arrested Stomakhin in March 2006, a day after he fell from the window of his fourth-floor Moscow apartment while trying to elude police, according to local press reports. Stomakhin suffered leg and back injuries.

In May 2007 the Moscow City Court reviewed Stomakhin's appeal for early release but left the verdict unchanged, the independent news agency Kavkazky

Uzel reported. On June 25, 2007, Stomakhin was transferred from a Moscow prison to a prison in the city of Nizhny Novgorod. Officials did not tell Stomakhin, his family, or defense counsel what prompted the transfer or how long it would last, local press reports said.

Anatoly Sardayev
Mordoviya Segodnya
IMPRISONED: June 29, 2007

On June 29, 2007, the Lenin District Court in Saransk found Sardayev, editor of the independent weekly *Mordoviya Segodnya*, guilty of embezzling money and misusing funds as head of the Mordoviya postal service in 2004. He was sentenced to five and a half years in prison and fined 105,000 rubles (US$4,100). Sardayev was taken into custody immediately after the court hearing.

Sardayev's colleagues believe he was targeted because of *Mordoviya Segodnya*'s continuing criticism of local governor Nikolai Merkushkin. The Moscow-based Center for Journalism in Extreme Situations (CJES) detailed conflict between Sardayev and Merkushkin dating to 2004.

Sardayev, a member of the Mordoviya parliament at the time, irritated local authorities that year by making repeated inquires into the legal basis for tax breaks given to Mordoviya energy companies. The same year, the Lenin District Prosecutor's Office in Saransk opened a criminal case against Sardayev on what they said was his abuse of authority, forgery, appropriation, and squandering of funds. About six months later, Saransk prosecutors imprisoned Sardayev for a week for allegedly failing to appear in court. The detention came just as Sardayev was working on a *Mordoviya Segodnya* edition that detailed a list of businesses owned by Merkushkin and his family, according to local press reports.

In the 2007 case, Mordoviya postal employees testified that Sardayev had used postal service money to build a public tennis court and to restore an old post office building in Saransk, CJES correspondent Igor Telin reported.

Nikolai Andrushchenko
Novy Peterburg
IMPRISONED: November 23, 2007

Police in St. Petersburg arrested Andrushchenko, co-founder and editor of the weekly *Novy Peterburg*, on suspicion of defamation. The next day, a local court placed him in pretrial detention on charges of defamation and obstruction of justice. The combined charges carried up to six years in prison.

Authorities claimed the charges stemmed from Andrushchenko's 2006 coverage of a murder investigation in St. Petersburg. However, colleagues said they believe Andrushchenko's imprisonment was the result of *Novy Peterburg's* critical coverage of local authorities and its pro-opposition articles.

Local authorities had repeatedly harassed the 64-year-old Andrushchenko, the paper's co-founder, Alevtina

Ageyeva, told CPJ. Andrushchenko was beaten by unknown assailants on his way home on November 9. Copies of the November 15 edition of *Novy Peterburg*, which carried an article about a dissenters' march and a critical story about St. Petersburg's police chief, were bought out wholesale; the company in charge of distributing the paper refused to supply newsstands with more.

A week later, the newspaper's printing house refused to print the next edition, which carried a front-page article by opposition leader Garry Kasparov.

On November 23, St. Petersburg police officers raided the *Novy Peterburg* newsroom and copied computer files, saying that Andrushchenko was suspected of defaming officials. The same day, officers of the St. Petersburg's Directorate for Combating Organized Crime raided Andrushchenko's house and placed him under arrest, according to local press reports.

RWANDA: 1

Agnès Nkusi-Uwimana, *Umurabyo*
IMPRISONED: January 12, 2007

Nkusi-Uwimana, director of the bimonthly journal *Umurabyo*, was arrested on charges of divisionism, sectarianism, and libel in connection with the publication of an anonymous letter critical of the government.

In April, a court in the capital, Kigali, sentenced Nkusi-Uwimana to a year in prison and ordered her to pay damages of 400,000 Rwandan francs (US$760) after she pleaded guilty in exchange for a reduction in sentence, according to local journalists.

The unsigned letter compared ethnic killings during President Paul Kagame's Tutsi-dominated administration to those of the previous Hutu regime.

TUNISIA: 1

Slim Boukhdhir
freelance, *Al-Quds al-Arabi*
IMPRISONED: November 26, 2007

Police in Sfax detained Boukhdhir, a well-known blogger and contributor to the London-based *Al-Quds al-Arabi*. He was charged with "aggression against a public employee" and "violation of public morality standards," according to the journalist's lawyer.

Boukhdhir was also charged under a 1993 national identity card law with "refusal to show his identification card to a public security agent." On December 4, a court in the suburban city of Sakiet Ezzeit sentenced Boukhdhir to one year in prison.

Boukhdhir has staged several hunger strikes in recent years to protest government harassment and authorities' refusal to grant him a passport. He was assaulted as he left an Internet café in Tunis in May, shortly after writing an online story critical of the first lady's brother. Human rights groups condemned the arrest as politically motivated.

U.S. NAVAL BASE GUANTÁNAMO BAY: 1

Sami Muhyideen al-Haj, Al-Jazeera
IMPRISONED: December 15, 2001

Al-Haj, a Sudanese national and assistant cameraman for Al-Jazeera, was detained by Pakistani forces after he and an Al-Jazeera reporter attempted to re-enter southern Afghanistan at the Chaman border crossing in Pakistan. About a month later, he was handed over to U.S. forces and eventually sent to the U.S. Naval Base at Guantánamo Bay, Cuba, in June 2002.

According to declassified U.S. military documents, al-Haj was accused of being a financial courier for Chechen rebels and assisting al-Qaeda and extremist figures. But al-Haj has not been convicted or charged with a crime, and the military has not publicly disclosed any evidence against him.

Al-Haj's London-based lawyer, Clive Stafford Smith, maintained that his client's continued detention was political. He said U.S. interrogators have not focused on al-Haj's alleged activities but instead on obtaining intelligence on Al-Jazeera and its staff. U.S. military interrogators allegedly told al-Haj that he would be released if he agreed to inform U.S. intelligence authorities about the satellite news network's activities, Stafford Smith said. Al-Haj refused.

During an Administrative Review Board hearing in September 2007, U.S. military authorities cited the cameraman's Al-Jazeera training as evidence of terrorist involvement, according to Stafford Smith. The lawyer, who is barred from attending such proceedings, based his comments on a review of the hearing transcript. The military hearings determine whether a prisoner should continue to be held.

UZBEKISTAN: 5

Muhammad Bekjanov, *Erk*
Yusuf Ruzimuradov, *Erk*
IMPRISONED: March 15, 1999

A court in the capital, Tashkent, sentenced Bekjanov, editor of the opposition newspaper *Erk*, to 14 years in prison and Ruzimuradov, an employee of the paper, to 15 years. They were convicted of publishing and distributing a banned newspaper that criticized President Islam Karimov, participating in a banned political protest, and attempting to overthrow the regime.

Both men were tortured during their pretrial detention in Tashkent City Prison, which left them with serious injuries, Tashkent-based human rights activists told CPJ. On November 15, 1999, Bekjanov was transferred to "strict regime" Penal Colony 64/46 in the city of Navoi. Ruzimuradov was transferred to "strict regime" Penal Colony 64/33 in the village of Shakhali near the southern city of Karshi.

The wives and children of both men fled to the United States in 1999 after their arrests, Erk Party Secretary-General Aranazar Arifov told CPJ.

In 2003, reporters with the London-based Institute for War and Peace Reporting and The Associated Press interviewed Bekjanov in the Tashkent Prison Hospital while he was being treated for tuberculosis contracted in prison. In the interview, Bekjanov described torture and beatings that resulted in a broken leg and hearing loss in his right ear, IWPR reported.

In 2007, Bekjanov was jailed in the southwestern city of Kasan, according to the independent news Web site *Uznews*. His wife, Nina Bekjanova, who was allowed to visit him in October 2006, said he told her that he was still subjected to beatings and torture that, among other things, caused him to lose most of his teeth, *Uznews* reported.

Exiled journalists, human rights workers, and other CPJ sources said they did not know of Ruzimuradov's whereabouts or his health.

Gayrat Mehliboyev, freelance
IMPRISONED: July 24, 2002

Police arrested Mehliboyev at a bazaar in Tashkent for allegedly participating in a rally in support of the banned Islamist opposition party Hizb ut-Tahrir. Following the arrest, police searched his bed in a local hostel and claimed they found banned religious literature that prosecutors later characterized as extremist in nature, according to international press reports.

Prior to his February 2003 trial, Mehliboyev was held in pretrial detention for more than six months. As evidence for his alleged participation in a religious extremist group, prosecutors presented political commentary Mehliboyev had written for the April 11, 2001, edition of the state-run weekly newspaper *Hurriyat*. Arguing that religion was the true path to achieving social justice, the article questioned whether Western democracy should be implemented in Uzbekistan. Prosecutors claimed the article contained ideas from Hizb ut-Tahrir.

At the proceedings, Mehliboyev openly stated several times he was beaten in custody but the court ignored his comments, a Tashkent-based representative of Human Rights Watch told CPJ.

On February 18, 2003, the Shaikhantaur District Court in Tashkent sentenced Mehliboyev to seven years in prison, convicting him of anticonstitutional activities, participating in extremist religious organizations, and inciting religious hatred, according to local and international press reports. The sentence was later reduced on appeal to six and a half years in prison.

Ortikali Namazov
Pop Tongi and *Kishlok Khayoti*
IMPRISONED: August 11, 2004

Namangan regional authorities in eastern Uzbekistan charged Namazov, editor of the state newspaper *Pop Tongi* and correspondent for the state newspaper *Kishlok Khayoti*, with embezzlement after he wrote a series of articles about alleged abuses in local tax inspections and collective-farm management.

His trial began on August 4, 2004, and lasted two weeks. On August 11, 2004, before the verdict was reached, authorities took him into custody. Five days later, the Turakurgan District Criminal Court in Namangan region convicted Namazov and sentenced him to five and a half years in prison. Namazov complained the judge was biased and did not allow him to defend himself.

Prior to her own imprisonment in 2005, local human rights activist Mutabar Tadjibaeva monitored Namazov's trial. She told CPJ that local authorities harassed Namazov's family during the trial, cutting his home telephone line, and firing his daughter from her job as a school doctor. Namazov was serving his sentence at a prison in eastern Namangan.

Dzhamshid Karimov, freelance
IMPRISONED: September 12, 2006

Karimov, nephew of President Islam Karimov, disappeared in his native city of Jizzakh only to be discovered in a psychiatric hospital in Samarkand, where he had been involuntarily placed by Uzbek authorities. Government officials did not release any information about court proceedings that led to the committal, and they did not permit independent experts to examine Karimov, according to press reports.

Karimov had worked for the London-based Institute for War and Peace Reporting and later contributed to a number of independent newspapers and online publications, including the Almaty-based news Web site *Liter*. According to CPJ research, Karimov criticized both local and federal authorities in his coverage of Uzbek social and economic problems.

Prior to his arrest, local authorities closely monitored his activities. After his mother petitioned authorities to remove all listening devices from her house, law enforcement agents set up surveillance equipment in a neighboring building in August 2006, the Moscow-based news Web site *Ferghana* reported. The same month, Karimov's passport was seized by authorities in Jizzakh after he applied for an exit visa to attend a journalism seminar in neighboring Kyrgyzstan.

VIETNAM: 2

Tran Khai Thanh Thuy, *To Quoc*
IMPRISONED: April 21, 2007

Writer and journalist Thuy was detained at her home in Hanoi, where she had been under house arrest since November 2006, according to news reports. She was charged with violating Article 88 of Vietnam's criminal code, which prohibits dissemination of information that authorities deem harmful to the state, the reports said.

Thuy had posted several pro-democracy essays online, according to people familiar with her writings. She was also accused of being a member of the pro-democracy group Bloc 8406, illegally organizing a trade union, and supporting a dissident human rights group, according to news reports. Thuy was a 2007 recipient of a Hellman-Hammett Grant administered by Human Rights Watch.

Nguyen Thi Thanh Van
Viet Nam Dan Chu
IMPRISONED: November 17, 2007

Thanh Van, a French citizen and journalist for Vietnamese exile media, was arrested along with a group of four political activists associated with the pro-democracy Viet Tan party.

Thanh Van is an editorial member of the overseas-based Vietnamese monthly *Viet Nam Dan Chu* and contributes to the radio program "Chan Troi Moi," which is regularly broadcast to Vietnam from Japan and the United States. She and the others were arrested by security officials during a meeting with local democracy activists at a private residence in Ho Chi Minh City, according to a source associated with the Viet Tan party. The government did not immediately disclose charges.

Thanh Van was released on December 12 with three of the activists. No formal charges were brought.

CPJ INTERNATIONAL PRESS FREEDOM AWARDS

Since 1991, CPJ has honored several journalists from around the world with its annual International Press Freedom Awards. Recipients have shown extraordinary courage in the face of great risks, standing up to tyrants and documenting events in dark corners of the world. Here are the 2007 awardees:

Mazhar Abbas, PAKISTAN

Abbas is a well-known champion of press freedom who has endured repeated threats during his 27-year career as a journalist. He is deputy director of ARY One World Television, an Urdu- and Hindi-language 24-hour news channel, and secretary-general of the Pakistan Federal Union of Journalists.

In May 2007, Abbas was one of three journalists who found envelopes with bullets attached to their cars as they emerged from a Karachi Press Club meeting. He was on the hit list of the Mohajir Rabita Council, an ethnic political group in Pakistan's southern province of Sindh, which is allied with President Pervez Musharraf. At the journalists union, Abbas led resistance to the Musharraf administration's attempt to silence press criticism. He was arrested after protesting the closure of three independent TV channels for reporting on anti-Musharraf demonstrations.

CPJ

A former correspondent for Agence France-Presse, Abbas covered the kidnapping and murder of *Wall Street Journal* South Asia Bureau Chief Daniel Pearl in 2002, along with the ensuing investigation.

Gao Qinrong, CHINA

Gao, who worked as a reporter for China's official Xinhua News Agency in the northern province of Shanxi, spent eight years in prison for his work. In 1998, after a lengthy investigation, he exposed a scam irrigation project in the drought-stricken

CPJ

province. Xinhua didn't publish the report, but it was circulated in the internal edition of *People's Daily*, which is distributed to Communist Party leaders.

When the story was leaked and went on to attract national attention, local officials blamed Gao. He was arrested on a laundry list of bogus charges, including embezzlement, fraud, and even pimping. He was sentenced to a 12-year jail term after a closed-door, one-day trial.

During his incarceration, Gao ran a prison newspaper and wrote several articles about reforming the prison educational system. His sentence was reduced for good behavior and he was freed in 2006. After his release, Gao gave lengthy interviews to Chinese and international news organizations, asserting his innocence and seeking reinstatement to his job with Xinhua. Coverage of his case drew new attention to the issue of press freedom in China and the arbitrary nature of journalist imprisonments. With at least 29 journalists in prison, China is the world's leading jailer of journalists.

Dmitry Muratov, RUSSIA

Muratov is editor-in-chief of *Novaya Gazeta*, one of the few critical news outlets with national reach in Russia today. He founded the paper in 1993 and is still its driving force.

In 1993, after leaving the popular daily *Komsomolskaya Pravda*, Muratov and colleagues started *Novaya Gazeta* with the goal of creating "an honest, independent, and rich" publication that would influence national policy. It was a lofty goal considering they began with two computers, one printer, two rooms, and no money for salaries. An initial boost came from former Soviet President

Novaya Gazeta

Mikhail Gorbachev, who donated part of his 1990 Nobel Peace Prize award to pay for computers and salaries.

Now with a staff of 60, *Novaya Gazeta* is known for its in-depth investigations into sensitive topics such as high-level corruption, human rights violations, and abuse of power. It has paid a heavy price for this pioneering work, with three of its reporters killed in seven years. The most recent was investigative journalist Anna Politkovskaya, who gained international recognition for her independent coverage of Chechnya and the North Caucasus.

Despite the Kremlin's success in marginalizing independent reporting, *Novaya Gazeta* continues to wield considerable influence with its uncompromising editorial stance.

Adela Navarro Bello, MEXICO

Zeta

Navarro is general director of the newsweekly *Zeta* in the border city of Tijuana. Created in 1980, *Zeta* is one of the only publications to regularly publish investigations into organized crime, drug trafficking, and corruption in Mexico's northern states. The cost of *Zeta's* coverage has been high: Héctor Félix Miranda, the publication's co-founder, was murdered in 1988, and Francisco Ortiz Franco, a co-editor, was slain six years later.

In 1997, after an assassination attempt against J. Jesús Blancornelas, co-founder and then director of *Zeta*, Mexican authorities provided Navarro with a bulletproof vest and two bodyguards. Blancornelas, who won CPJ's International Press Freedom Award in 1996, died in 2006 of natural causes.

Before becoming general director, Navarro worked as a writer, columnist, and member of *Zeta's* editorial board. In 1994, she covered the Chiapas conflict for the newsweekly. Since then, she has interviewed presidents, ministers, governors, and leaders of Mexican political parties. Today she writes the column "Sortilegioz."

Under Navarro's direction, *Zeta* has pursued its mission of lifting the lid off drug trafficking in Tijuana, and it has pushed for exhaustive investigations into the murders of its two editors.

INTERNATIONAL PRESS FREEDOM AWARD RECIPIENTS 1991-2006

1991

Byron Barrera, *La Época*, Guatemala
Bill Foley and Cary Vaughan, United States
Tatyana Mitkova, TSN, former Soviet Union
Pius Njawe, *Le Messager*, Cameroon
IMPRISONED: Wang Juntao and Chen Ziming, *Economics Weekly*, China

1992

Muhammad al-Saqr, *Al-Qabas*, Kuwait
Sony Esteus, Radio Tropic FM, Haiti
David Kaplan, ABC News, United States
Gwendolyn Lister, *The Namibian*, Namibia
Thepchai Yong, *The Nation*, Thailand

1993

Omar Belhouchet, *El Watan*, Algeria
Nosa Igiebor, *Tell*, Nigeria
Veran Matic, Radio B92, Yugoslavia
Ricardo Uceda, *Sí*, Peru
IMPRISONED: Doan Viet Hoat, *Freedom Forum*, Vietnam

1994

Iqbal Athas, *The Sunday Leader*, Sri Lanka
Daisy Li Yuet-wah, Hong Kong Journalists Association, Hong Kong
Aziz Nesin, *Aydinlik*, Turkey
In memory of staff journalists, *Navidi Vakhsh*, Tajikistan
IMPRISONED: Yndamiro Restano, freelance, Cuba

1995

Veronica Guerin, *Sunday Independent*, Ireland
Yevgeny Kiselyov, NTV, Russia
Fred M'membe, *The Post*, Zambia
José Rubén Zamora Marroquín, *Siglo Veintiuno*, Guatemala
IMPRISONED: Ahmad Taufik, Alliance of Independent Journalists, Indonesia

1996

J. Jesús Blancornelas, *Zeta*, Mexico
Yusuf Jameel, *Asian Age*, India
Daoud Kuttab, Internews Middle East, Palestinian Authority Territories
IMPRISONED: Ocak Isik Yurtcu, *Ozgur Gundem*, Turkey

1997

Ying Chan, *Yazhou Zhoukan*, United States
Shieh Chung-liang, *Yazhou Zhoukan*, Taiwan
Victor Ivancic, *Feral Tribune*, Croatia
Yelena Masyuk, NTV, Russia
Freedom Neruda, *La Voie*, Ivory Coast
IMPRISONED: Christine Anyanwu, *The Sunday Magazine*, Nigeria

1998
Grémah Boucar, Radio Anfani, Niger
Gustavo Gorriti, *La Prensa*, Panama
Goenawan Mohamad, *Tempo*, Indonesia
Pavel Sheremet, ORT, *Belorusskaya Delovaya Gazeta*, Belarus
IMPRISONED: Ruth Simon, Agence France-Presse, Eritrea

1999
María Cristina Caballero, *Semana*, Colombia
Baton Haxhiu, *Koha Ditore*, Kosovo
Jugnu Mohsin and Najam Sethi, *The Friday Times*, Pakistan
IMPRISONED: Jesús Joel Diáz Hernández, Cooperativa Avileña de Periodistas Independientes, Cuba

2000
Steven Gan, *Malaysiakini*, Malaysia
Zeljko Kopanja, *Nezavine Novine*, Bosnia-Herzegovina
Modeste Mutinga, *Le Potentiel*, Democratic Republic of Congo
IMPRISONED: Mashallah Shamsolvaezin, *Asr-e-Azadegan* and *Neshat*, Iran

2001
Mazen Dana, Reuters, West Bank
Geoff Nyarota, *The Daily News*, Zimbabwe
Horacio Verbitsky, freelance, Argentina
IMPRISONED: Jiang Weiping, *Qianshao*, China

2002
Ignacio Gómez, "Noticias Uno," Colombia
Irina Petrushova, *Respublika*, Kazakhstan
Tipu Sultan, freelance, Bangladesh
IMPRISONED: Fesshaye Yohannes, *Setit*, Eritrea

2003
Abdul Samay Hamed, Afghanistan
Aboubakr Jamaï, *Le Journal Hebdomadaire* and *Assahifa al-Ousbouiya*, Morocco
Musa Muradov, *Groznensky Rabochy*, Russia
IMPRISONED: Manuel Vázquez Portal, Grupo de Trabajo Decoro, Cuba

2004
Alexis Sinduhije, Radio Publique Africaine, Burundi
Svetlana Kalinkina, *Belorusskaya Delovaya Gazeta*, Belarus
In memory of Paul Klebnikov, *Forbes Russia*, Russia
IMPRISONED: Aung Pwint and Thaung Tun, freelance, Burma

2005
Galima Bukharbaeva, Institute for War and Peace Reporting, Uzbekistan
Beatrice Mtetwa, media and human rights lawyer, Zimbabwe
Lúcio Flávio Pinto, *Jornal Pessoal*, Brazil
IMPRISONED: Shi Tao, freelance, China

2006
Jamal Amer, *Al-Wasat*, Yemen
Atwar Bahjat, Al-Arabiya, Iraq
Madi Ceesay, *The Independent*, Gambia
Jesús Abad Colorado, freelance, Colombia

CPJ BURTON BENJAMIN MEMORIAL AWARD

S ince 1991, CPJ has given the Burton Benjamin Memorial Award to an individual in recognition of a lifetime of distinguished achievement in service of press freedom. The award honors Burton Benjamin, the CBS News senior producer and former CPJ chairman who died in 1988. In 2007, CPJ honored Tom Brokaw.

2007
Tom Brokaw
NBC News

Tom Brokaw was anchor and managing editor of "NBC Nightly News" for 24 years, stepping down in December 2004. He continues to work for NBC News, reporting and producing documentaries and providing expertise during breaking news events. He is a longtime CPJ supporter, joining the Board of Directors in 1993.

Brokaw's career has been filled with honors and exclusives. He has covered every presidential election since 1968 and was NBC's White House correspondent during the Watergate scandal. On March 19, 2003, he was the first American news anchor to report that the war with Iraq had begun. Brokaw secured the first exclusive U.S. one-on-one interview with Soviet President Mikhail Gorbachev, earning him an Alfred I. duPont-Columbia University Award. And he was the only anchor to report from the scene on the night the Berlin Wall fell. Brokaw's documentary reporting has earned numerous honors, including two Peabody Awards and an Emmy.

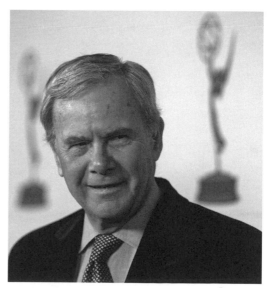

In 1998, Brokaw became a best-selling author with the publication of *The Greatest Generation*. His fourth best-selling book, *A Long Way from Home*, a look at growing up in the American heartland, was released in 2002. Brokaw's latest book, *Boom! Voices of the Sixties*, examines a turbulent era in American history.

Reuters

BURTON BENJAMIN MEMORIAL AWARD RECIPIENTS 1991-2006

1991
Walter Cronkite
CBS News

1992
Katharine Graham
The Washington Post Company

1993
Ted Turner
CNN

1994
George Soros
Open Society Institute

1995
Benjamin C. Bradlee
The Washington Post

1996
Arthur Ochs Sulzberger
The New York Times

1997
Ted Koppel
ABC News

1998
Brian Lamb
C-SPAN

1999
Don Hewitt
CBS News

2000
Otis Chandler
Times Mirror Company

2001
Joseph Lelyveld
The New York Times

2002
Daniel Pearl
The Wall Street Journal

2003
John F. Burns
The New York Times

2004
John S. Carroll
Los Angeles Times

2005
Peter Jennings
ABC News

2006
Hodding Carter III

CONTRIBUTORS

The Committee to Protect Journalists is extremely grateful to the foundations, corporations, and individuals whose generosity made our press freedom work possible in 2007:

Advance Publications, Inc.
Agence France-Presse
Robert E. Albertson
Andy Alexander
Ronald Allen and Adaora Udoji
Marcia and Franz Allina
ALM Media, Inc
Altria Group Inc.
Christiane Amanpour
The American Ethical Union
American Express Company
Andrews McMeel Universal Foundation
Argus Media Inc. / Petroleum Argus
Carol Ash and Josh Friedman
Ashbridge Corporation
The Associated Press
Australian Associated Press
Dean Baquet
Harriet S. Barlow
Barbara Becker and David Bolotsky
Alex Belida and Pat Reber
The Belo Foundation
Lucy W. Benson
Tom Bettag
Robin Bierstedt
Mary Billard and Barry Cooper
The Morton K. & Jane Blaustein Foundation
Susan Blaustein and Alan Berlow
Michael R. Bloomberg
Bloomberg
Michele Braithwaite
Brands2Life
Meredith and Tom Brokaw
Jeffrey Brown
Brunswick Group LLC
Business Week/McGraw-Hill
Byron Calame
Carnegie Corporation of New York
Virginia Carter
CBS News
Chicago Tribune Foundation
Hope Childs
Cisco Systems
Citi

CNBC/Fast Money
CNBC
CNN
Steve Coll
Columbia University Graduate School of
 Journalism
Ronald C. Columbus
Community Counseling Service Co.
Condé Nast Portfolio
Condé Nast Publications
Continental Airlines
Ann K. Cooper
Sheila Coronel
David Corvo
Cox Newspapers
Crowell & Moring LLP
Kenneth Cukier
Ann Curry
Dan Klores Communications, Inc.
Debevoise & Plimpton LLP
Deloitte & Touche
Elisabeth DeMarse
Detroit Press Club Foundation
Deutsche Bank
George Dillehay
Disney-ABC Television Group
Dow Jones Company
Dow Jones Foundation
Drue Heinz Trust
E.M.P. Inc
The Economist Group
Daniel J. Edelman
Renee Edelman
Anthony Effinger
Stanley Eisenberg
Richard and Gail Elden
Ernst & Young LLP
David Evans
Joni Evans
Elizabeth F. Farnsworth
Serkalem Fasil
Jeremy Feigelson
La Fetra Foundation
Lawton Wehle Fitt

M. L. Flynn
Forbes Media
The Ford Foundation
Ford Motor Company
Fox News Channel
Thomas L. Frank
Freedom Forum & Newseum, Inc.
Soraya Gage
Gannett Foundation
Anne Garrels
GE Commercial Finance
GE Foundation
Stephen J. Geimann
General Electric
Bob and Nancy Giles
The Glickenhaus Foundation
James C. and Toni K. Goodale
Cheryl A. Gould
Jeff Green
Jeff Greenfield
Bill and Caryl Grueskin
The Iara Lee & George Gund III Foundation
The Marc Haas Foundation
Sharon Held and Ian Hague
HBO
Ian Haig
Hearst Newspapers
Cherie Henderson
The Herb Block Foundation
Don and Marilyn Berger Hewitt
Peter Heydon
Sidney Hillman Foundation
Ambassador and Mrs. John L. Hirsch
James F. Hoge
Hugh M. Hefner Foundation
Kathleen E. Hunt and Bernard Estrade
Charlayne Hunter-Gault
Gwen Ifill
The Inner Circle
Barbara and Steven Isenberg
R. Larry Jinks
Judd Kahn
Kahn Charitable Foundation
Thelma and Myron Kandel
Kei Advisors LLC
Gay and Don Kimelman
Kevin Klose
John S. & James L. Knight Foundation
Ronald S. Konecky
Ted Koppel
Jane Kramer
Matt Lauer

Esther and David Laventhol
Isaac Lee
Joanne Leedon-Ackerman
Bokara Legendre
Lehman Brothers
Cindi Leive
Robert Lenzner
The Leon Levy Foundation
Anthony Lewis
George Lewis
John Lindburg
Steve Lipin
Los Angeles Times
Susan Lyne
Jim Maceda
Robert MacNeil
Charles Madigan
The Malayala Manorama Co. Ltd.
Joan Malkin
Maria Mann
Amy and Dave Marash
Andres Martinez
Kati Marton
Sir Deryck Maughan
John H. McArthur
The McClatchy Company
McCormick Tribune Foundation
Mike McCurry
McKinsey & Company
MediaNews Group Inc.
Merrill Lynch & Co. Inc.
Geraldine Fabrikant Metz and Robert T. Metz
Andrea Mitchell and Alan Greenspan
The Mosaic Foundation
MSNBC.com
N.S. Bienstock Inc.
National Press Foundation
Anne and Victor Navasky
NBC News
NBC Universal
New Hampshire College and University
  Council
News Corporation
The New York Times Company
The New York Times Company Foundation
The New Yorker
Samuel I. Newhouse Foundation Inc.
Newmark & Co. Real Estate Inc.
Newsday
Newsweek
Edward N. Ney
The Nieman Foundation for Journalism

NY Daily News/U.S. News & World Report
Oak Foundation
Open Society Institute
William A. Orme and Deborah Sontag
Burl Osborne
Peter and Susan Osnos
James H. Ottaway Jr.
The Nicholas B. Ottaway Foundation
The Overbrook Foundation
Charles L. Overby
Clarence Page
Pakistan Post
Mark Palermo
William C. Paley
PARADE Publications
Jan L. Paschal
Norman Pearlstine
Gladys and Raymond Pearlstine Charitable
  Remainder Trust
Barry R. Petersen
Peter G. Peterson
Jane C. Pfeiffer
Philip L. Graham Fund
Philip Morris USA
Debra and Stone Phillips
Erwin R. Potts
Prudential Financial, Inc.
Joyce Purnick and Max Frankel
Sir William Purves
Radio Free Asia
Dan Rather
Resort Quality Controls Inc.
Reuters
Susan and Gene Roberts
Michael Rosenbaum
Sandra Mims Rowe
The Rudin Foundation
Tim Russert
Paul Salopek
Albert and Marjorie Scardino
David Schlesinger
Seymour Schwartz
Stephen A. Schwarzman
Scripps Howard Foundation
Joan Shapiro & James Shapiro Foundation
Joel Simon
Harry Smith
Sony Corporation of America
St. Petersburg Times
Paul E. Steiger
Ian Strachan
Jeanne Straus and Richard Tofel

Sir Howard Stringer
Jose Luis Gutierrez Suarez
Pierre Taillefer
Paul C. Tash
Zephyr Teachout
Anne Thompson
The Thomson Corporation
TIBCO Software Inc.
Time Inc.
TIME Magazine
Elizabeth J. Tisel
Audrey and Seymour Topping
Samantha Topping
Torstar Corporation
Laurel Touby
Jeffrey Trimble
Garry Trudeau and Jane Pauley
UBS
Verizon Communications
Viacom
The Svetlana and Herbert M. Wachtell
  Foundation
Wachtell, Lipton, Rosen & Katz
Edward C. Wallace and Dr. Pamela Falk
Mike Wallace
Thomas J. Wallace
The Wall Street Journal
The Washington Post Company
Washingtonpost.Newsweek Interactive
Weil, Gotshal & Manges LLP
John D. Weis
Jann S. Wenner
Bill Wheatley
Mark Whitaker
Shelby White
Pete Williams
Scott Williams
Williams F1 Team
Chris Winans
Judy Woodruff
David Young
William D. Zabel, Esq.
Jocelyn and Bill Zuckerman
Anonymous (7)

We also extend our gratitude to the many contributors who supported the Committee to Protect Journalists with gifts under $500, not listed here due to space limitations.

MEMORIAL AND HONORARY CONTRIBUTIONS

The Committee to Protect Journalists is grateful to the friends and family of the following people, in whose name generous contributions were made:

In honor of Sasha Aslanian: Elizabeth J. Tisel

In honor of Tom Brokaw: Ron Allen and Adaora Udoji, Phil Alongi, Robert Bazell, Steve Capus, Christine Colvin, David Corvo, Subrata De, Robert Dembo, Bob Epstein, Dianne Festa, M.L. Flynn, Andrew K. Franklin, Dawn Fratangelo, Soraya Gage, Cheryl Gould, Brett and Susan Holey, Suzette Knittl, Marc Kusnetz, Susan LaSalla, Matt Lauer, George Lewis, Jim Maceda, Andrea Mitchell and Alan Greenspan, Frieda Morris, Lisa Myers, Danny Noa, Michele Neubert, Beth O'Connell, Bonnie Optekman, Gia Pace, Tim Russert, Anne Thompson, Bill Wheatley, and Robert and Patti Windrem

In honor of Sherry Ricchiardi and Frank Folwell: J.M. Brown

In honor of Paul E. Steiger: Alyssa Brill, Dow Jones

In honor of Mary Lynn Young and Kirk LaPointe: Peter Klein

In memory of Jack N. Anderson: Patricia Olsen

In memory of Mark Fineman: Susan Blaustein and Alan Berlow

In memory of Lars Erik Nelson: Nathan Buchwald, Brian P. Moss, Mary L. Santarcangelo

In memory of Anna Politkovskaya: Charles Madigan

In memory of Bernard Shapiro: Gloria J. Ellis, Donald L. and Susan L. Pyne, Robert F. Scholl, and Beverly G. Toomey

IN-KIND CONTRIBUTIONS

Some of the vital resources that help make our work possible are in-kind services and contributions. CPJ thanks the following for their support in 2007:

Agence France-Presse, The Associated Press, Debevoise & Plimpton LLP, Factiva, Fox News Channel, and Reuters Group PLC.

Continental Airlines Continental Airlines is the preferred carrier of the Committee to Protect Journalists.

CPJ AT A GLANCE

How did CPJ get started? A group of U.S. foreign correspondents created CPJ in response to the often brutal treatment of their foreign colleagues by authoritarian governments and other enemies of independent journalism.

Who runs CPJ? CPJ has a staff of 24 at its New York headquarters, including area specialists for each major world region. CPJ has a Washington representative and consultants stationed around the world. A board of prominent journalists directs CPJ's activities.

How is CPJ funded? CPJ is funded solely by contributions from individuals, corporations, and foundations. CPJ does not accept government funding.

Why is press freedom important? Without a free press, few other human rights are attainable. A strong press freedom environment encourages the growth of a robust society, which leads to stable, sustainable democracies and healthy social, political, and economic development. CPJ works in more than 120 countries, many of which suffer under repressive regimes, debilitating civil war, or other problems that harm press freedom and democracy.

How does CPJ protect journalists? By publicly revealing abuses against the press and by acting on behalf of imprisoned and threatened journalists, CPJ effectively warns journalists and news organizations where attacks on press freedom are occurring. CPJ organizes vigorous public protests and works through diplomatic channels to effect change. CPJ publishes articles and news releases; special reports; a magazine, *Dangerous Assignments*; and *Attacks on the Press*, the most comprehensive annual survey of press freedom around the world.

Where does CPJ get its information? CPJ has full-time program coordinators monitoring the press in Africa, the Americas, Asia, Europe and Central Asia, and the Middle East and North Africa. They track developments through their own independent research, fact-finding missions, and firsthand contacts in the field, including reports from other journalists. CPJ shares information on breaking cases with other press freedom organizations through the International Freedom of Expression Exchange, a global e-mail network.

When would a journalist call upon CPJ? *In an emergency.* Using local and foreign contacts, CPJ intervenes whenever local and foreign correspondents are in trouble. CPJ notifies news organizations, government officials, and human rights organizations immediately of press freedom violations. *When traveling on assignment.* CPJ advises journalists covering dangerous assignments. *When covering the news.* Attacks against the press are news, and they often serve as the first signal of a crackdown on all freedoms. CPJ is uniquely situated to provide journalists with information and insight into press conditions around the world.

HOW TO REPORT AN ATTACK ON THE PRESS

CPJ needs accurate, detailed information in order to document abuses of press freedom and help journalists in trouble. CPJ corroborates the information and takes action on behalf of the journalists and news organizations involved. Anyone with information about an attack on the press should contact CPJ. Call collect if necessary. Our number is (212) 465-1004. Sources may also e-mail to the addresses below, or send a fax to (212) 465-9568.

What to report:

Journalists:
- Arrested
- Censored
- Harassed
- Killed
- Threatened
- Wrongfully expelled

- Assaulted
- Denied credentials
- Kidnapped
- Missing
- Wounded
- Wrongfully sued for libel or defamation

News organizations:
- Attacked, raided, or illegally searched
- Closed by force
- Materials confiscated or damaged

- Censored
- Transmissions jammed
- Wrongfully sued for libel or defamation

CPJ needs accurate, detailed information that includes:
- Background, including the journalists and news organizations involved.
- Date and circumstances.

Contact information for regional programs:

Africa: (212) 465-9344, x112 E-mail: africa@cpj.org
Americas: (212) 465-9344, x120 E-mail: americas@cpj.org
Asia: (212) 465-9344, x140 E-mail: asia@cpj.org
Europe and Central Asia: (212) 465-9344, x101 E-mail: europe@cpj.org
Middle East and North Africa: (212) 465-9344, x104 E-mail: mideast@cpj.org

What happens next:

Depending on the case, CPJ will:
- Investigate and confirm the report, sending a fact-finding mission if necessary.
- Pressure authorities to respond.
- Notify human rights groups and press organizations around the world, including IFEX, Article 19, Amnesty International, Reporters Sans Frontières, PEN, International Federation of Journalists, and Human Rights Watch.
- Increase public awareness through the press.
- Publish advisories to warn other journalists about potential dangers.

CPJ STAFF

Executive Director Joel Simon
Deputy Director Robert Mahoney
Editorial Director Bill Sweeney
Director of Development and Outreach John Weis
Director of Finance and Administration Lade Kadejo
Communications Director Abi Wright
Journalist Assistance, Impunity Campaign Coordinator Elisabeth Witchel
Washington Representative Frank Smyth
Deputy Editor Lauren Wolfe
Webmaster and Systems Administrator Mick Stern
Journalist Assistance Associate Karen Phillips
Communications Assistant Andrew Levinson
Assistant Director of Development Denise Abatemarco
Executive Assistant and Board Liaison Sebastian Dettman
Receptionist and Office Manager Janet Mason

REGIONAL PROGRAMS

AFRICA
Program Coordinator Tom Rhodes
Research Associate Mohamed Hassim Keita
Program Consultant Tidiane Sy

THE AMERICAS
Senior Program Coordinator Carlos Lauría
Research Associate María Salazar
Program Consultants Monica Campbell and Marcelo Soares

ASIA
Program Coordinator Bob Dietz
Research Associate Madeline Earp
Program Consultant Shawn W. Crispin

EUROPE AND CENTRAL ASIA
Program Coordinator Nina Ognianova
Research Associate Muzaffar Suleymanov

MIDDLE EAST AND NORTH AFRICA
Senior Program Coordinator Joel Campagna
Research Associate Ivan Karakashian
Program Consultant Kamel Eddine Labidi

INDEX BY COUNTRY

DATE DUE	RETURNED	
NOV 0 4 2016	OCT 2 8 2016	

CI

JOURNALISTS
York, NY 10001
info@cpj.org
n: www.cpj.org